AUGUSTINE AND MODERNITY

Augustine and Modernity is a fresh and challenging addition to current debates about the Augustinian origins of modern subjectivity and the Christian genesis of Western nihilism. It firmly rejects the dominant modern view that the modern Cartesian subject, as an archetype of Western nihilism, originates in Augustine's thought. Arguing that most contemporary interpretations misrepresent the complex philosophical relationship between Augustine and modern philosophy, particularly with regard to the work of Descartes, the book examines the much overlooked contribution of Stoicism to the genealogy of modernity, producing a scathing riposte to commonly-held versions of the "continuity thesis."

Michael Hanby identifies the modern concept of will that emerges in Descartes' work as the product of a notion of self more proper to Stoic theories of immanence than to Augustine's own rigorous understandings of the Trinity, creation, self and will. Though Augustine's encounter with Stoicism ultimately resulted in much of his teaching being transferred to Descartes and other modern thinkers in an adulterated form, Hanby draws critical attention to Augustine's own disillusionment with Stoicism and his interrogation of Stoic philosophy in the name of Christ and the Trinity. Representing a new school of theology willing to engage critically with other disciplines and to challenge their authority, *Augustine and Modernity* offers a comprehensive new interpretation of *De Trinitate* and of Augustinian concepts of will and soul. Revealing how much of what is now thought of as "Augustinian" in fact has its genealogy in Stoic asceticism, it interprets the modern nihilistic Cartesian subject not as a logical consequence of a true Christian Trinitarian theology, but rather as the consequence of its perversion and abandonment.

Michael Hanby is Arthur J. Ennis Fellow in Core Humanities at Villanova University. An original contributor to *Radical Orthodoxy: A New Theology* (Routledge, 1999), he has a special interest in Augustine and his influence on modern philosophy.

AUGUSTINE AND MODERNITY

Michael Hanby

 Routledge
Taylor & Francis Group

LONDON AND NEW YORK

First published 2003
by Routledge
11 New Fetter Lane, London EC4P 4EE

Simultaneously published in the USA and Canada
by Routledge
29 West 35th Street, New York, NY 10001

Routledge is an imprint of the Taylor & Francis Group

© 2003 Michael Hanby

Typeset in Baskerville by
BOOK NOW Ltd
Printed and bound in Great Britain by
MPG Books Ltd, Bodmin

British Library Cataloguing in Publication Data
A catalogue record for this book is available from the British Library

Library of Congress Cataloging in Publication Data
Hanby, Michael, 1966–
Augustine and modernity / Michael Hanby.
p. cm. – (Radical orthodoxy series)
Includes bibliographical references and index.
1. Augustine, Saint, Bishop of Hippo. 2. Self–Religious aspects–Christianity–History
of doctrines–Early church, 30–600. 3. Philosophy, Modern. 4. Self
(Philosophy)–History. 5. Religion and philosophy–History. I. Title, II. Series.

BT713.H36 2003
189.2–dc21   2002031937

ISBN 0-415-28468-6 (hbk)
ISBN 0-415-28469-4 (pbk)

This trinity of the mind is not the image of God because it remembers, understands, and loves itself, but because it can remember, understand, and love Him by whom it was made.

Augustine, De Trinitate XIV.12.15

It is only the will, or freedom of choice, which I experience within me to be so great that the idea of a greater faculty is beyond my grasp; so much so that it is above all in virtue of the will that I understand myself to bear in some way the image and likeness of God.

Descartes, Meditations IV

I am obliged to you for drawing my attention to the passage of St. Augustine relevant to my [*I think, therefore I am*]. I went today to the library to read it, and I find that he really does use it to prove the certainty of our existence. He goes on to show that there is a certain likeness of the Trinity in us, in that we exist, we know that we exist, and we love the existence and knowledge we have. I, on the other hand, use the argument to show that this I which is thinking is an immaterial substance with no bodily element. These two are very different things.

Descartes, To Colvius

CONTENTS

ACKNOWLEDGMENTS

I would like to thank those without whose help this book would not have been possible: chiefly, my mentor, John Milbank, from whom I have learned more than I can say; Stanley Hauerwas, whose generous advice and encouragement have provided constant guidance; and Robert Wilken, Eugene Rogers and Charles Matthewes, who graciously welcomed me to Virginia in midstream and who have offered valuable advice and support. James Wetzel read an earlier version of the manuscript, and I appreciate both his generosity and his commentary. I would also like to thank Clare Johnson at Routledge for her helpfulness throughout and Alissa Hinckley who did wonderful work proofreading and correcting the text. This book would be much poorer, if not impossible, without her efforts.

My debts to other friends and mentors are too numerous to mention fully. Still, I would like to thank Geoffrey Wainwright, whose name barely appears here but whose influnce is imprinted on virtually every page; as well as Graham Ward, Catherine Pickstock, Simon Oliver, John Montag, SJ, Connor Cunningham, Phillip Blond, and Peter Candler. In addition, I owe much to my friends and colleagues in the Department of Humanities and Augustinian Traditions at Villanova, especially Eugene McCarraher an exceedingly steadfast and generous soul who read and criticized the manuscript and D. C. Schindler, a profound human being in every sense, whose philosophical insights have vastly improved it.

I have been nurtured and sustained over the years by wonderful parish communities, Saint Joseph's in Durham, North Carolina, Little Saint Mary's in Cambridge, and now Saint Mark's Church in Philadelphia. I would especially like to thank Fr. Richard Alton of Saint Mark's for his unceasing prayer when it seemed that I was "in the weeds," and the Monk's crowd—Leslie Delauter, Nora Johnson and Jay Blossom—for both moral and editorial support.

Finally, I cannot express sufficient thanks to my parents, whose unfailing love, generosity and goodness made possible my improbable trek from our home in Berryville, Arkansas, and to my wife Stephanie, who has sacrificed much for me and for this book. Stephanie is not a scholar; most of what she knows of Augustine she has learned from me. But most of what this book is really about I have learned from her, and she understands it far better than I do. This is her book too.

Parts of this book have appeared previously in *Modern Theology* and reappear with their permission.

ABBREVIATIONS

Augustine:

Conf.	Confessiones	The Confessions
Cont. Duas Ep. Pel.	Contra Duas Epistulas Pelagianorum	Against Two Letters of the Pelagians
Cont. Jul.	Contra Julianum	Against Julian
De Beata Vita	De Beata Vita	The Happy Life
De Civ.	De Civitate Dei	The City of God
De Corrept.	De Correptione et Gratia	Admonition and Grace
De Div. Q. ad Simplic.	De Diversis Quaestionibus ad Simplicianum	To Simplician on Diverse Questions
De Div. Q. 83	De Diversis Quaestionibus Octoginta Tribus	On Eighty-Three Different Questions
De Doct.	De Doctrina Christiana	On Christian Doctrine
De Dono Pers.	De Dono Perseverantiae	On the Gift of Perseverance
De Fide et Sym.	De Fide et Symbolo	On Faith and the Creed
De Gen. ad Lit.	De Genesi ad Litteram	On the Literal Meaning of Genesis
De Gen. C. Manich	De Genesi contra Manichaeos	On Genesis, against the Manichees
De Gest. Pel.	De Gestis Pelagii	On the Deeds of Pelagius
De Grat. Christ.	De Gratia Christi	On the Grace of Christ
De Grat. Test.	De Gratia Novi Testamenti	On the Grace of the New Testament
De Lib.	De Libero Arbitrio	On the Free Choice of the Will
De Mag.	De Magistro	On the Teacher
De Mus.	De Musica	On Music
De Nat. Bon.	De Natura Boni	On the Nature of the Good
De Nat. et Grat.	De Natura et Gratia	On Nature and Grace
De Pecc. Mer. et Rem.	De Peccatorum Meritis et Remissione	On Merit and the Forgiveness of Sins

De Praed. Sanct.	*De Praedestinatione Sanctorum*	*On the Predestination of the Saints*
De Spir. et Lit.	*De Spiritu et Littera*	*On the Spirit and the Letter*
De Trin.	*De Trinitate*	*On the Trinity*
De Util. Cred.	*De Utilitate Credendi*	*On the Usefulness of Believing*
De Vera Relig.	*De Vera Religione*	*On True Religion*
En Psa.	*Ennarationes in Psalmos*	*Expositions on the Psalms*
Ep.	*Epistulae*	*Letters*
In Jo. Ep.	*In Johannis Epistulam ad Parthos Tractatus*	*Tractates on the First Letter of John*
Retr.	*Retractationes*	*Retractions*
Serm.	*Sermones*	*Sermons*
Solil.	*Soliloquia*	*Soliloquies*
Tract. in Jo.	*Tractatus in Evengelium Joannis*	*Tractates on the Gospel of John*

Aquinas:

ST	*Summa Theologiae*	

Cassian:

Conf.	*Collationes*	*The Conferences*

Plotinus:

Enn.	*Enneades*	*Enneads*

1

INTRODUCTION
Thinking with and about Augustine

This book is about a fall from grace. It charts the transition from a conception of self-hood rooted in the Body of Christ and the love of the Trinity to a notion of self as a graceless autonomy of the will. It begins to trace the collapse of the Augustinian theological vision which sustained Western Christianity for just over a millennium. All of which is to say that it is also a book about what we have become and the gods who have come to elicit our devotion.

Constructively, the book develops a "systematic Augustinianism" from a reading of Augustine's *De Trinitate* which should be situated among the current "revisionist" interpretations of his thought. Polemically, it counters two positions on the basis of this genealogy of decline. The first is a tendency, by no means universal but still well entrenched within the academic guilds, to treat the philosophical Augustine separately from the doctrinal Augustine. Undoubtedly this reflects the marginal role Christianity now occupies in our culture and its negligible effect in informing our vision and our conceptions of time, history and what "really" determines them. It also contributes to the second tendency, equally well entrenched, which sees the "modern self" instituted by René Descartes as the legitimate fruit of Augustine's seed and the logical outcome of something called the Western metaphysical tradition which has now collapsed under the weight of its internal contradictions, sweeping away Christianity in its train. It is a story whose end, as we imagine it, determines the criteria for what counts as the middle, and it typically excludes two prominent features of the argument put forth here: the characteristically "religious" aspects of Augustine's thought and the philosophical prominence of stoicism, both in the nascent Christian tradition and in early modernity.[1] This story is partly a story of the latter's "conquest" of the former, and inasmuch as one aspect of this thesis is correct—that questions about the relationship between Augustine and Descartes are really questions about the kind of event modernity is and the status of Christianity within it—one could speculate that this neglect of stoicism is

1

the result of our taking its immanentism as the normative screen against which invocations of transcendence will be evaluated.

The first chapter rehearses the more common story of Augustinian-Cartesian continuity and some of the charges against Augustine (and the Christian tradition) that emerge from it. While I call some attention to the deficiencies of these accounts, the Augustinianism of subsequent chapters is my response to them. In Chapter 2 I begin to develop an "integrated" Augustine, one for whom what is philosophically interesting—his theory of language, his anthropology, his treatment of *voluntas*—emerges as a function of what is doctrinally important: his trinitarian theology, his Christology, and the ecclesiology and doctrine of grace which follow upon them. Chapter 3 develops this understanding "microcosmically" at the level of "moral psychology," showing how Augustinian volition presupposes and requires a trinitarian economy and christological mediation. Augustinian "will" and "subjectivity" are a function of Augustine's trinitarianism and Christology. They are, in short, doxological. Situated within Christ's union of creature and creator, they seek and praise the divine beauty and invoke the love between the Father and the Son as a prior gift. This is grace; it is what makes action intelligible for Augustine. It is finally what makes human action human.

Augustine's understanding of the Holy Spirit as *donum*, which recalls creation through the unity of Christ into the beauty of divine love, is a milestone in trinitarian theology. And it undergirds two other significant achievements: Augustine's critique of pagan virtue in *De Civitate Dei*, understood in the best case as diverse variations upon stoic self-mastery; and his assaults on the Pelagians who are themselves dependent upon goals and presuppositions of a stoic morality whose intelligibility is derived from the monism and immanentism of stoic cosmology.

Chapter 3 begins to examine this encounter. While Augustine's attacks on these schools call the agent of this morality into question, his achievement against the stoics and Pelagians was not simply a matter of "grace's" triumph over "nature" or "will." Rather it was a cosmological triumph. Implicitly it vindicated and instituted nature as the gratuitous creation of a transcendent God against the machinations of the *pyr teknikon*, the self-crafting fire of stoicism, for which any interaction between human and divine must be a "tensional" interchange between immanent forces. And it instituted "free will" as free precisely as graced, precisely insofar as it attains to the good which is the aim and motive of our every act, a good explicated as the love between the Father and the Son. Augustine's trinitarian and christological achievements made it possible to convey Christianity's understanding of this transcendent gratuity and its non-competitive relationship to created effects more deeply into the economy, into the microcosm of the doxological soul. It is a vocative, ecstatic soul which is more itself the more God is in it and it is in God, just as Jesus is paradigmatically human for being hypostatically united to the ecstatic delight of divine love. This is Augustinian grace and Augustinian freedom. To fail to grasp it is to fail to grasp the profound implications of divine transcendence, of a gratuitous creator God. It is to fail to grasp the meaning of the *imago dei* fulfilled in Christ.

Yet it is not easily grasped. Chapter 4 will consider one such failure, that of the so-called Semi-Pelagians. The Semi-Pelagian controversy was a watershed for two reasons. First, it served as a vehicle for the transmission of Augustine's thought to the West in the years after his death. Second, it was an encounter between Augustine's doctrine of grace, grounded in his trinitarian and christological achievements, and a pre-Augustinian tradition, one indebted to stoic morality, which had not yet come under the scrutiny of Augustine's critique of pagan virtue. This version of "stoic" Christianity, having infiltrated the asceticism of the monastic orders, would continue and prosper as an independent tradition. Yet the encounter would also produce an Augustinianism transformed in conformity with the presuppositions of formally stoic virtue that Augustine had once opposed. Each would serve as host for latent presuppositions, derived from stoic immanentism, not easily reconcilable with the emerging orthodoxy. The full nihilistic implications of these presuppositions would not be unleashed until the Christian doxological context which contained and redirected them was eroded.

These implications emerge with Descartes, whose intent to master nature through a *mathesis universalis* already attests to this erosion, and with his conception of will which completes it. Chapter 5 will consider this outcome and the stoic debts which facilitate it. It is here that the polemic against the "continuity thesis" reaches its culmination. For I shall demonstrate that Descartes' *res cogitans*, thought to issue naturally from the seed of Augustine's thought, is a bastard offspring whose other parent is a stoic voluntarism that Augustine had once contested in the name of Christ and the Trinity.

There is something here to dissatisfy nearly everyone. Theologians will likely think this book too philosophical; philosophers will likely think the reverse. Historians may well complain that it is insufficiently historical, and all might find it insufficiently exegetical. Allow me, then, a short discourse on method, and let me acknowledge at the outset that this book is at once an essay on the theology of Augustine *and* a constructive Augustinian theology, with the two tasks separated by an often unclear line of demarcation. For instance, I synthesize the *De Trinitate* and then allow that synthesis to interpret other Augustinian texts, including those written prior to *De Trinitate*. This is rather heterodox when compared with conventional ways of appropriating Augustine, but it is intentional and not without justification.

As the initial chapter suggests, any appropriation of a historical figure is always, if only implicitly, for the sake of present circumstances, and presuppositions about the nature of those circumstances—even basic ontological assumptions about the linear nature of time and history that authorize a strictly genetic, historical approach—inevitably help organize the material in question. Such presuppositions are just as operative for those accounts which I contest as it is for this one—they too have their "canon within the canon." And this canon is informed by judgments and ontological presuppositions extrinsic to the canon itself. In this case, however, the criteria informing my organization of the Augustinian canon are theological. They belong to the larger tradition of which Augustine himself was a part and to whose authority he would submit, even as he helped to alter and articulate that tradition. And inasmuch as they are analogous to Augustine's own exegetical criteria put forth in *De Doctrina Christiana*, they arguably lay greater claim to being Augustinian than an approach which simply claims to offer a "historical Augustine."

A certain measure of "anachronism" is thus unavoidable. Yet for a perspective as deeply committed as Augustinianism to tradition as an ontological modality, this is not a defect. For this is the modality of creation. There is always something intrinsically formal, intrinsically analogous about it; it is always and simultaneously ancient *and* new. From within this position, the real question concerns the ends funding the appropriation, and here, I hope, Augustine is my ally.

Despite the license I am claiming for this "method," I nevertheless think that this constructive appropriation is not only more Augustinian but also a superior critical approach to Augustine. There are several reasons for this, not the least of which is that I think Augustine's own ontological commitments, which I have tried to emulate, are more adequate to the reality of what happens when meaning is transacted than that allowed by unreflective "exegesis" or "history." First, I think it is more adequate than a genetic approach both to the fecundity and nature of meaning, which always floats free of the circumstances of its composition and escapes the possession of its author. It is also arguably more adequate to the complexities of a textual inheritance like Augustine's. Writing a long diachronic corpus is never simply a matter of slow accretions. It can take a lifetime to "catch up" to the import of one's own best insights, and the relationship between any two insights along the diachronic continuum is a matter of judgment on the basis of formal criteria which transcend the continuum itself. Secondly, this approach allows me to incorporate into my account aspects of Augustine's thought which are typically excluded in both the standard philosophical and theological treatments. Finally, however, Augustine's texts present a real question about whether a linear, genetic approach is adequate to the depths of his own ontology and practice. In contrast, this appropriation comports, albeit analogously, with Augustine's own exegetical practices, his own theory of language, and his own understanding of the way truth reveals itself in time. By Augustine's own lights, the best literal reading of Augustine's theology would be a new Augustinian theology. Indeed the best literal reading of Augustine would be a figurative reading of Augustine.

The present book does not and could not go far enough in this direction. This would require, among other things, that we internalize typology as the very mode of time's passage, and this is a habit unsupported by any modern discipline, be it academic or not. Yet perhaps the book does go just far enough to help us see what was lost in the collapse of Augustinianism, and to see in Descartes, and in ourselves inasmuch as we are his children, another more ominous figure, a type as it were, which Augustine had long ago diagnosed.

1

A GRIM PATERNITY?

The alleged sins of the Father

Saint Augustine occupies a vexed place in modernity's vexed self-understanding. At the root of this understanding, and the cultural economic and political institutions that embody and sustain it, is something called the "modern self." This self is an abstraction, to be sure, one that glosses over both the philosophical difference in detail between its Cartesian, Lockean and Kantian versions and the sociological difference between Catholics, Muslims and liberals. But inasmuch as this abstraction is the counterpart to the equally abstract power that manages and regulates it, it remains analytically useful. This self, simultaneously mastering the universe and draining it of any intrinsic meaning, is understood by many who employ it, though by no means all, to be at the root of the banality and brutality that has so infected modern culture and rendered the modern soul empty.

According to a common story that we shall soon consider, Augustine is instrumental in giving birth to this self, notably in the *res cogitans* of René Descartes. Yet the stakes in this conclusion extend well beyond the historic importance of the Bishop of Hippo Regius. It has been suggested that Augustine, along with Saint Paul, *invented* Western Christianity.[1] The statement is a hyperbolic acknowledgment of Augustine's obviously profound influence, but it does suggest something of what is at stake in this contemporary reappraisal. In its theological guise, the reassessment of Augustine is part and parcel of contemporary Christianity's on-going self-assessment in the West (some would say its penance), and, to a certain extent, its crisis of confidence. In its philosophical and political guise, it is part of modern culture's ongoing reassessment of Christianity, an extension perhaps of modernity's constitutive counter-identification with Christianity and its perennial urge to police the Church. For many in the first camp, this endeavor offers Christianity the opportunity to liberate itself from a great litany of sins frequently traced back to Augustine—the instrumentalization of "nature," a stifled sexuality, hatred of matter and the body, a soulless individualism, the oppression of women and even the

Holocaust. Yet for others in this camp this reassessment also offers Western Christianity the opportunity to become the West that never was, to liberate itself from itself, either for a romanticized Christianity of the East or, more typically, for a less particularist version befitting the liberal "consensus" of secular democracies. For those in the latter camp, particularly those of Nietzschean persuasion, the fact that "the Augustinian ideas that largely shaped the intellectual countenance of Western (Latin) Europe for centuries were transformed in the hands of Descartes into forces that led to its destruction" exemplifies the transvaluation of values, and thus provides exquisite evidence for Christianity's intrinsic nihilism.[2] Questions about Augustine and Descartes, or about the relationship between Augustinian and modern selves, are therefore questions about what kind of event modernity is, what, if anything, can be done about it, and whether Christianity has any place in it.[3]

Despite the common plotline in the story of the proto-Cartesian Augustine (and despite real material differences among its proponents), the Augustines produced by this narrative tend to obey the contemporary divisions between the academic guilds, though this obedience is neither universal nor perfect.[4] There are undoubtedly deep reasons for this conformity. Some are historical, and some, for historical reasons, are built into the structures of these disciplines themselves, which are not apt to recognize certain events—the decline of the Church or changes in sacramental practice, for instance—as ontological problems.[5] The current principles organizing what counts as ontology exclude those for practical reasons which are traceable to the schism between the guilds. In this same vein, the Reformation, which both foreshadowed and was embroiled in the fracturing of the disciplines, produced an Augustinianism fearful of Augustine's "Platonism," an anxiety carried forward into several of the contemporary theological critiques of Augustine.[6] The ironic result was to make possible for subsequent study by disciplines unhinged from theology an Augustine who would be *nothing but* a Platonist. So, on the one hand, it is typical to find an "Augustine of philosophical interest," usually the Augustine of the Cassiciacum dialogues, the *Confessiones* (especially book VII), and *De Trinitate*, inasmuch as the purpose of the latter is to establish the mind's self-relatedness. For this Augustine the ecclesial concerns of *De Civitate Dei*, or the Christology of *De Trin.* XIII, are relegated to a merely practical realm if they appear at all, and he is a far cry from the *doctor caritatis* of the later Pelagian disputes. On the other hand, there remains "the Augustine of doctrinal interest," the *doctor caritatis*, codifier of predestination, inventor of the two cities, an Augustine long held at arms length by theologians embarrassed over this legacy, now of interest primarily to historians.

I want to reconstruct an Augustinianism more inclusive of these diverse aspects of Augustine's thought. Given what the "Augustinian question" has come to mean, doing so will necessarily mean restating the meaning of the

7

modern. But, before we can do that, we must first consider both the grand story of modern origins in which Augustine plays such a crucial role and the various cases against him.

The grand architect and the builders

"On the way from Plato to Descartes stands Augustine."[7] Charles Taylor's remark is more than a historical observation. Rather it denotes Augustine's crucial status as a lynchpin connecting the ancient to the modern, within a history which moves almost ineluctably toward a modern *telos* that casts a retrospective shadow over all that preceded it. This, in fact, is one of Taylor's weaknesses.

Augustine is important to Taylor's story because of his contribution to the "moral sources" constitutive of modern identity and because this contribution anticipates Descartes. Foremost among these contributions is radical reflexivity or a profound sense of "inwardness." This reflexive self will later combine a Protestant affirmation of everyday life with deistic and romantic conceptions of nature to produce a self that grounds both a liberal agreement on moral standards and a general agnosticism over the sources of those standards. Taylor cites a famous passage in support of this inwardness. "Do not go outward; return within yourself. In the inward man dwells truth."[8] Yet beneath this general rubric are a number of more specific contributions that specifically foreshadow Descartes' *cogito*. The first and most obvious of these are the proto-cogitarian arguments that appear variously throughout the Augustinian corpus, but the contributions do not end there.[9] Taylor adduces a strong dualism between the bodily and the non-bodily underlying "inwardness" in both thinkers. Augustine's proof of God's existence in *De Lib*. II anticipates Descartes' third *Meditation*, a point that Stephen Menn will later develop more thoroughly.[10] And he follows Charles Kahn (who more or less concurs with Albrecht Dihle), in claiming that Augustine's concept of will, at least in one of its senses as the stoic "power to confer or withhold all-things-considered-assent," marks a crucial turning point in the history of philosophy and the self and antici- pates the later Cartesian notion.[11]

I intend the Augustinianism of subsequent chapters to stand as my material response to this interpretation; in this chapter I intend only to raise questions about the structure of Taylor's narrative, the "sources" it omits, and the questions it neglects to ask. It should be noted from the outset that Taylor is eminently fair to Augustine if not adequate to him. In fact his account of the relationship between Augustinian and Cartesian thought notes many significant differences between them which I will later use to call this general story into question, differences neglected by others who further develop the case for continuity. Taylor rightly notes that Augustinian interiority, constituted in a relationship to a God more intimately related to the self than itself, is in a sense radically *exterior*. "In an important sense, the truth is not in me. I see truth 'in' God. Where the meeting takes place, there is a reversal."[12] He notes another sense of "will," as "a basic disposition of our being," which, whether an adequate characterization, differs markedly from Descartes' stoic version.[13] Taylor notes Descartes' dependence upon stoicism and the neostoic revival both for his ethics and physics, a dependence which signals a further departure from Augustine. The result in Descartes is not only a new, mechanistic cosmology and a more radical dualism of body and soul but a new conception of "self-mastery," evident in his novel account of the passions, in which "the hegemony of reason is a matter of instrumental control."[14] This instrumentalist self will soon merge with liberal capitalist conceptions of selfhood rooted in proprietorship.

Postmodern critics like Eric Alliez will allege that this instrumentalism is endemic to Augustine's understanding of will, his distinction between enjoyment and use, and even the division between the celestial and terrestrial cities, but Taylor seems to recognize an almost anti-Augustinian novelty here—certainly in the realm of ontology.[15] Yet if this is true, why does this observation not complicate the argument for continuity? Would different ontologies not constitute different "language games"—to put it in Wittgensteinian terms—that govern the sense of the terms, the "pieces" in the "game"? Can we say that Augustinian inwardness and Cartesian inwardness are the same? What criterion of identity determines the meaning of "same" here? This problem haunts not only Taylor's treatment of Augustine and Descartes but also his notion of modern identity as well. In the words of one set of critics, "he does not entertain the question whether a standard like dignity is actually a different standard depending upon whether the source to which you appeal is Reason or God."[16]

The thinness in the modern identity that binds the narrative into a unity results in a thin account of the thinkers who compose this unity. Absent from the relationship between the soul and God in Taylor's Augustine is anything either particularly theological or, indeed, particularly Christian. His one mention of the triunity of *memoria, intelligentia* and *voluntas* makes the trinitarian context of its elaboration appear incidental, and it certainly *is* incidental to Taylor.[17] This is particularly odd given his insistence on the necessity and inevitability of "frameworks" for even initiating a quest for the good life and Augustine's insistence in *De Trinitate* that the one Christ himself, God and human, is the context or "framework" of the quest.[18] Surely this remark is cause for wondering if perhaps Taylor is understating the difference between the Augustinian and Cartesian selves. And if the primary utility of this trinitarian similitude is its analogy with the filiation of the Son and procession of the Spirit (to take the conventional but problematic interpretation), this would seem to call for some analysis of how the Augustinian self is constituted in relation to the sites where this trinitarian economy manifests itself, namely, Christ and the Church. This is especially true since both the soul and the city "answer" to each other by obeying the same dynamnic of sin, dissolution and conversion, just one of many macrocosmic/microcosmic isomorphisms that complicate the meaning of Augustinian interiority, as we shall see in subsequent chapters.[19] Indeed for Augustine, the self is only finally realized in the heavenly city.[20] This is not merely the lesson of *De Civitate Dei*, but of the final books of the *Confessiones*, and it is exhibited throughout the latter work in Augustine's typological self-understanding.[21] As the self undergoes its *conversio*, its interiority comes to be constituted, not simply in relation to the God who transcends the distinction between inner and outer, but by the "exterior" politics of the heavenly city that mediate this relationship as the body to the headship of Christ.[22] This is where the criticisms of Hauerwas and Matzko strike their sharpest blow. Taylor "does not see that Augustine's politics is a counter-interpretation of his account of the modern self."[23] A more adequate reading of Augustine, one which accounted for the interpretive role of the heavenly city and Christ's ecclesial body, might have made Taylor less sanguine about Augustine's role as a bridge, and it might have altered his characterization of the modern. Inasmuch as questions about the continuity between Augustine and Descartes are questions about what kind of event modernity is, omissions which call this continuity into question also call into question both Taylor's characterization of the present and its relationship to the past.

Any historical narrative (the present one included) presupposes a plot structure, and, consequently, a priori standards and subsequent historical events which implicitly organize the narrative. Taylor takes great care to avoid anachronism (especially with the question of Cartesian deism or atheism), and yet these glossed difficulties lead one to wonder whether the task of reading "Augustine after Descartes," to borrow James Wetzel's phrase, hasn't led him to invest Augustine with a kind of "retrospective Cartesianism," at least by way of anticipation.[24] Retrospective anticipation is dangerous, however, for it leads one to prize certain features of a thinker's work over others (or to prize the history of ideas over institutions), on the basis of how they are supposed to have contributed to some later event.[25] There is inevitably a price to be paid in this, and in this case it is the standard omission of those specifically Christian aspects of Augustine's thought that might radically redefine, or criticize, the modern self. But this says more about us and the way that we have come to understand philosophy, and ourselves, than it says about Augustine.

The thinness of Taylor's Augustine is undoubtedly due to the latter's limited, albeit crucial, role in the much larger narrative of modern identity. The account does not claim to be an exhaustive interpretation of Descartes' Augustinian debts, and that is not its strength. Rather, Taylor's significance is as a master architect giving structure to a story whose basic features are

[margin handwritten note: "Retrospective universalism"]

held in common by thinkers who otherwise scarcely speak the same philosophical and theological language. Of course this does not mean that all are relying upon Charles Taylor, though some may be, and all, including Taylor, have Gilson's depiction of Augustine's "Christian Philosophy" and its proto-Cartesian elements in their background.[26] Instead, it means that for whatever creative contributions Taylor has made in giving a plot structure to the story of the modern self, it is a plot that already reflects some deeply held assumptions and convictions about the shape and meaning of that history.

Others who perhaps lack Taylor's grand vision have taken this broad sketch and developed it in much more detail. Stephen Menn is perhaps the most meticulous proponent of continuity. He argues not simply for Descartes' indebtedness to the features of Augustine's thought noted by Gilson and Taylor but for a common "discipline for approaching wisdom" that results in a shared series of "intellectual intuitions."[27] Many of these comport, albeit in greater specificity, with those listed by Taylor, though Menn, perhaps signaling a deeper break from Gilson than Taylor, under-emphasizes the degree to which Descartes' stoic debts make him anti-Augustinian.[28] This will prove crucial, and I shall develop this point, along with a deeper critique of Menn's position, in the final chapter.

Though dissenting from both Taylor and Menn on the question of Augustine's continuity with Plotinus, Wayne Hankey otherwise concurs with this story. He has built a small cottage industry assaulting the contemporary theological retrieval of Augustine, which he finds ironically constituted within the philosophical space permitted by Heidegger and Derrida.[29] This space requires "a deconstruction of the Augustinian self, or better, a deconstruction of the Augustinian self such as it has been constructed for the sake of postmodern Christian philosophy."[30] This deconstruction, he thinks, forever defers union of the human and divine and requires Augustine's apologists either to suppress, occlude or omit key features from the thought of the "historical" Augustine, features stressed by Taylor, Menn, and even Derrida himself. In asserting his own position, he contends for a kind of Augustinian subjectivity with a series of claims that should be uncontroversial, taken in themselves.

> Knowledge is finally for Augustine what makes us happy. We seek union with the Good in contemplation. Vision is the realization of what love seeks; love is a steadfast perceiving. We are made happy by this contemplation because knowledge of ourselves, other persons, and indeed, all things in the Word is normative knowledge. Wisdom knows the thing and its good, and judges it by its good all at once. Fact and value cannot be separated here . . . The contemplation, or wisdom, which makes us happy is knowledge of all things in the Word.[31]

The problem is not with this assertion, but rather with what Hankey's own sins of omission cause him to neglect. The question he fails to pursue with sufficient rigor is what it means "to know" when both the act and object of knowledge are love. This failure should be correlated to the complete lack of a Christology or ecclesiology in Hankey's Augustine, which are themselves aspects of a more fundamental failure to contend with what is most revolutionary in Augustine's trinitarianism, his conception of the Spirit as *donum*.[32] Because he ignores this modification, Hankey cannot countenance that "self-possession" might be *constituted* precisely in giving. Hence Hankey is unable to see that the corporate charity insisted upon by Rowan Williams might be the form of our participation in *sapientia,* and he is unable to register the irreducible difference between intertrinitarian *sapientia* and our own as anything but a series of oppositions which would forever postpone union with God. Difference from God cannot be the ground of union. Either certainty of God and self is given a "truthful basis" in the certainty of the self and preserved in the stability of a comprehensive gaze or union can never occur.

These omissions are odd. For, like Alliez in his postmodern critique, Hankey wants to attribute Augustine's proto-Cartesian subjective self-unity to what is most Christian in his thought, a transformation of Plotinus' divine triad that carries "self-reflexivity all the way through" in a manner impossible for Plotinus since "there is no reflexive self-othering in the One."[33] This then foregrounds both the Augustinian and Cartesian *cogito*, Augustine's rejection of the sensible, and the aforementioned oppositions between the sensible and intelligible, time and eternity, and *sapientia* and *scientia.* These oppositions then determine the menu of Augustines that Hankey permits us to entertain. He would have us choose between an utter loss of subjectivity on the one hand and the loss of time and materiality on the other, between a substantial self locked in an ahistorical dialectic with a God mirrored in the reflexivity of its own mental functions, whose surety grounds the possibility of union with God, or a dissipating subjectivity whose union with God is forever deferred in the Heraclitan flux of time and history. With these options framing his dilemma, he asks us, "Can we decide between these two Augustines?"[34]

This essay poses a different question: *must* we decide between these two Augustines? For, as subsequent chapters will show, it is the work and achievement of Augustine's Christ to refuse these despairing, dualistic possibilities by joining them in hypostatic union, and this work will prove inseparable from the very *donum*, and the ecclesial *corpus*, that Hankey, Taylor, and Menn neglect.

They are not unique in this neglect, however, and before we can develop this alternative Augustine it is first necessary to consider another Augustine at home in the sort of grand drama told by Taylor. This is the Augustine of much of contemporary systematic theology.

The West that never was: the theological critique

Though the contemporary theological critique of Augustine is ironically *more* critical and more reductionist than Taylor's positive, philosophical and historical appropriation, it largely agrees with the overall structure of Taylor's story. Catherine LaCugna, for instance, writes that Augustine's innovations "were more than merely doctrinal. The changed metaphysical options for the theology of God changed politics, anthropology, and society as well."[35] Intrinsic to this change was a debased conception of personhood exhibiting the sort of "inwardness" described by Taylor. This spells the defeat of the doctrine of the Trinity, "with disastrous political results," as it supplants God's gratuitous self-communication with a subjective unity—and mastery—at the root of political, economic and patriarchal oppression.[36] In a similar vein, Colin Gunton lays the enormous burden for the West's current theological crisis, its agnosticism and confusion over the knowledge of God and the apparent irrelevance of trinitarian doctrine, almost foursquare on Augustine's shoulders.[37] In both accounts, Augustine's "individualism" is central to the problem.

While Taylor's account of Augustinian "inwardness" largely neglects Augustine's trinitarianism, for the theologians this inwardness takes its root from Augustine's neoplatonic perversion of Cappadocian trinitarian theology.[38] The effect of this perversion is to sever the integral relation between *theologia* and *oikonomia*, and thus to sacrifice a genuine historical economy of salvation for an "interior" interaction between the soul and a God who, for all practical purposes, mirrors the subject's self-enclosure. The cause goes to the heart of Augustine's trinitarian theology. He "begins," so it is alleged, by emphasizing the divine unity over the generation and procession of the Son and Spirit and by favoring the divine *natura* or *substantia* over the *personae*. He thus "separates" the substance and persons by making the former prior and separates the economic and immanent Trinities by making the trinitarian form of God, and ultimately the incarnation of Christ, incidental to the historical economy.[39] If one detects a spirit of rapprochement with the East here, it is because these critics appropriate wholesale the textbook Orthodox criticisms of Latin theology.[40] "The West, as the study of the trinitarian theology of Augustine and Thomas Aquinas witnesses . . . identified the being, the ontological principle of God with His substance rather than with the person of the Father."[41]

This sort of argument depends on three dubious, interrelated assumptions. The first is the presupposition of a "starting point" that radically distinguishes Augustine from the Eastern fathers. Such clear origins may be characteristic of systematic theology as it is currently constituted, but it is anachronistic when applied to Augustine, for whom our "starting point" is always a response to God's self-communication. For ontological reasons we shall consider in subsequent chapters, there can be, strictly speaking, no pure origin for Augustine. Augustinianism begins and ends in prayer, which is to say it never properly "begins" at all. This is an explicit problem in both the *Confessiones* and *De Trinitate*, and it is indeed the mediation of the one Christ, giving the Spirit with the Father, that "solves" it.[42] Lewis Ayres has further called this presupposition into question, but, allowing it to stand for "grammatical" purposes, he has shown that if there is any concern that is "fundamental" to Augustine's trinitarian theology, it is the concern to maintain the inseparability of operations, a point axiomatic to both Latin and Eastern theology.[43] Within this preoccupation, the crucial question concerns how the persons work inseparably given the fact that we do not say, for instance, that the Son descended in the form of a dove or the Father was crucified. Indeed, contrary to Gunton's charge, in *Serm.* 52 Augustine does not move from an assumed unity and then attempt to account for a genuine plurality. Rather he begins from the "sort of separated Trinity" (*quasi separabilem Trinitatem*) apparent in the baptism of Christ, the paradigm text for Augustine's alleged difficulty, and moves to demonstrate the paradoxical unity of the *personae* demanded by the Catholic axiom.[44] All the while he holds to the irreducibility of the three persons. This inveighs directly against the second assumption.

In treating of Augustine, LaCugna assumes that substance and relation are opposed, meaning that one must take priority over the other.[45] This causes her to assert an embarrassing contradiction between Augustine's ingenious use of relative predication to denote what is proper to the Father, Son and Spirit in Book V and his equation of person and substance in Book VII.[46] Yet, as we shall see in the subsequent chapter, Augustine rejects the use of *substantia*, on precisely the grounds that it implies a substrate prior to the differentiation of persons. Moreover, Augustine's attempt in *De Trinitate* to elaborate the divine essence as love, means that essence *requires* relation. Augustine, that is to say, defines essence itself in relational terms while deploying the distinction between substantive and relative predication as a "grammatical" device to protect divine simplicity, the inseparability of operations and the distinction between *personae*. LaCugna's need to impute contradiction derives in part from her failure to see the implications of equating the divine essence with love; yet one could even suggest something of a contradiction here. Despite her own constructive endeavor to think of *persona* as relational and ecstatic, it appears to be the residual, a priori presupposition of a substantial notion of personhood on her own part that causes her to impute the contradiction to Augustine.[47] Even more to the point, however, is this. LaCugna's failure to grasp the implications of equating divine essence with love causes her to fail to see precisely how Augustine's elaboration of the Trinity corresponds to the economy, or, rather, how the economy is unfolded within the interval of trinitarian love manifest in Christ. This is the third dubious move.

LaCugna simply follows Gunton when he asserts that "Augustine, by losing the mediatorship of the Word, at once distances God from the creation and flattens out the distinction between the persons of the Trinity."[48] So she neglects Augustine's christology altogether. Yet Gunton himself does not arrive at this conclusion by examining the crucial christological discussions of *De Trinitate* IV and XIII, where Augustine actually elaborates on what it means to say that *in Christ* "is our true peace and firm bond of union with our Creator, that we should be purified and reconciled through the Mediator of life."[49] Rather he situates the very possibility of an Augustinian Christology within Augustine's alleged hatred of matter and then asserts that this orientation to matter precludes a genuine Christology. This is how he interprets Augustine's contention in Book III that "it is through his creature, not in his own substance" that God appears under visible forms, and in Book IV that "the voices or the sensible forms and figures were produced before the incarnation of the Word . . . through the angels," a conclusion for which there is plenty of Scriptural witness. "The prefiguring of the Son in the Old Testament is not by means of the Word, but by angels; God is not *substantially* involved."[50]

But this is exactly the wrong conclusion. In asserting that "it is through the creature," and not "in his own substance" (*per suam substantiam*) that God creates sensible effects, Augustine is not denying that "it is by means of the Word" that the Word itself is prefigured.[51] These are not mutually exclusive alternatives, and no attentive reader of the *Confessiones* could arrive at that conclusion.[52] Instead, he is noting, first, a perfectly orthodox distinction between those theophanies which signal Christ's advent and the hypostatic union itself and, secondly, that the substance of God is never "visible" apart from the mediation of creatures, be they material or intellectual, the definitive instance of which is Jesus himself.[53] The conclusion *affirms* the need for the incarnation.[54]

Gunton's assertion that Augustine gives "inadequate hypostatic weight" to the Spirit by designating him, uniquely, as charity, should be correlated to his christological failure.[55] We will examine the interrelation of the Son and Spirit so understood in the next chapter. In Gunton's case, this problem leads to some rather astonishing conclusions. After accusing Augustine of an impoverished pneumatology, he writes that "it is the action of the Spirit in the economy not simply to relate the individual to God, but to realize in time the conditions of the age to come."[56] He then criticizes Augustine for not having a "conception of the Spirit as realizing the conditions of the age to come particularly through the creation of community."[57] The remark is odd enough given Augustine's figurative reading of Genesis as prefiguring the Church.[58] It is even more stunning given the thousand or so pages Augustine devotes to describing the elect city of God, especially since this city is defined as such by its love, which is *precisely* the work of the Spirit.[59] But it is significant for our purposes now because it indicates

15

Gunton's impoverished view of Augustine's Christology. For Augustine conceives of Christ as including the community of the faithful as his Body; he even goes so far as to call them one *person*. As we shall see in the next chapter, the Spirit plays an integral role in bringing this unity about, and charity is an apt description of it.

The neglect of this point says something about the hermeneutical standpoint of these theologians. The distinction used in moral philosophy between the first and third person perspectives might be instructive here. When LaCugna and Gunton talk about "the economy," they appear to be speaking from the third person perspective, the perspective of an *observer*, and generally mean the economy as portrayed in Scripture. Augustine, by contrast, views the economy from the first person perspective, which is to say, as a *participant*.[60] This should not be confused with the claims of Augustine's critics that he reduces the economy to the individual's relation to a functionally unitary God. To the contrary, we have seen intimations of a microcosmic/macrocosmic isomorphism between the soul and the city and intimations of the ecclesial economy as a temporal extension of the life of Christ at once temporal and eternal. However, this first person status does require something of Augustine that the observer's "positivist" orientation to sheer theological data does not: an account of how one's very capacity to recognize the economy *as economy* exemplifies one's location within it.[61] Not only does this need treat the economy more as an ongoing trinitarian work and less as an artifact but it is also crucial to understanding how Augustine's Christology "functions" in *De Trinitate*. We will consider this function in detail in subsequent chapters.

The anxiety over the state of Christianity in the West is well founded and insightful, as is the observation that the advent of this crisis is bound up with the de-trinitization of God. Yet the attempt by Augustine's theological critics to burden him with responsibility for it fails on historical as well as theological grounds. They take the tendency of scholastic manuals in general and Aquinas in particular to treat *De Deo Uno* and *De Deo Trino* in abstraction from the economy as evidence of the defeat inflicted on the doctrine at the outset by Augustine.[62] Yet if this is true, then the West was *never* really trinitarian. The current crisis in theology and the corresponding identity crisis of the subject cut loose from its theological moorings has been lying there, ticking like a time bomb, for nearly two millennia.

Recent scholarship has raised serious doubts about this interpretation of Aquinas.[63] Thomas' understanding of the divine unity as *activity*, and specifically, the immanent activities of knowing and loving, means, ultimately, that divine unity is to be understood in terms of the procession of the Son and Spirit from the Father.[64] The division of *de Deo Uno* and *de Deo Trino* is a false problem. Furthermore, Aquinas' "Aristotelian" cognition returns one to sense knowledge and thus *to* the economy, and ultimately to Christ, the self-communication of divine goodness.[65] And finally, the pedagogical structure of the *Summa*, in which the theological virtues, themselves gifts of the Spirit and acquired communally through the habit of *religio*, makes these gifts intrinsic to proper knowledge of God in beatitude—thus enfolding the very study of theology within the trinitarian life.[66] More pertinent to the purposes of this chapter, however, is the assumption that theological treatises are the surest sign of the West's trinitarian health.[67] By LaCugna's own lights, the unity of *oikonomia* and *theologia* places a primacy on doxological practice.[68] She therefore devotes a chapter to consideration of the creedal and liturgical forms of the pre-Nicene Church. It is odd, then, that she does not consider the crucially integral role that the Mass has played in constituting the Western social body, another result, perhaps, of the tendency to treat the economy as an observed artifact. Augustine's account of the eucharistic sacrifice sets the stage for this role.

> So then, the true sacrifices are acts of compassion, whether towards ourselves or towards our neighbors, when they are directed towards God. . . . This being so, it immediately follows that the whole redeemed community, that is to say, the congregation and fellowship of saints, is offered to God as a universal sacrifice, through the great high priest who offered himself in his suffering for us—so that we might be the body of so great a head—under the form of a servant. For it was this form he offered, and in this form he was offered, because it is under this form that he is Mediator, in this form he is the Priest, in this form he is the Sacrifice. Thus the apostle first exhorts us to offer our bodies as a living sacrifice . . . because we ourselves are that whole sacrifice. This is the sacrifice of Christians, who are "many, making up one body in Christ." This is the sacrifice which the Church continually celebrates in the sacrament of the altar, a sacrament well known to the faithful where it is shown to the Church that she herself is offered in the offering which she presents to God.[69]

We see reiterated here a number of themes that are integral to the *De Trinitate*. First, Augustine has made compassion, transposed into peace in Book XIX, intrinsic to the divine self offering in the Mass. Inasmuch as both offerings fall under the Spirit's designation as *donum*, this is tantamount to making the role of the Spirit within the godhead integral to Christ's sacrifice in the Mass and on the cross, as we shall see in the next chapter.[70] Furthermore, Augustine claims here that this sacrifice constitutes Christ's one body, an echo of *De Trinitate*'s assertion that the one Christ, head and ecclesial body, is one person.[71] It is hard to imagine a more intimate union of *oikonomia* and *theologia*.

In making the Mass constitutive of the social body, the Christian West attempted to enact this account, in part through the penitential machinery

17

that acknowledged the inevitable shortcomings in the attempt.[72] It would retain the Augustinian sense of the *corpus mysticum*, until about the twelfth century, when "mystical" would begin to acquire a connotation the opposite of "real."[73] The constitutive aspect of the rite, the role of the Spirit as *donum*, and the Augustinian emphasis on peace were each visible in the role that the West accorded to the *pax*. In the early centuries of the Church, the Holy Kiss was traditionally exchanged as a greeting at the offertory, no doubt in an attempt to follow the command of Matthew 5.22–3. Yet in the West, from about the early fifth century, it was moved to a position after the consecration and fraction, immediately before reception of the Eucharist, the clear implication being that it is Christ's sacrifice in and through the Mass, and thus the triune life itself, that constitutes communal peace.[74] Indeed it is not too strong to say that, in a time of infrequent communion, the *pax was* communion for the laity, and between the seventh and thirteenth centuries it received several additions, including the *agnus dei*, which elicited in turn much commentary conforming to Augustine's "descending order" of peace in *De Civitate Dei*.[75] Numerous extra-eucharistic factors conspired to support and embody this understanding. The practical and theoretical primacy accorded to the theological virtues and their contraries, a primacy visible to this day in the carvings of choir stalls, pews, and roods, ultimately correlated the moral life to the gift of grace and thus the work of the Spirit, before being supplanted first by an emphasis on the Ten Commandments, also reflected in wood, and finally by a formal and abstract power.[76] And the stellar career of the feast of Corpus Christi, which attempted, with mixed results, to harmonize the stratified community and make visible the peace effected by the eucharistic host, underscored the constitutive role of Christ's offering at the head of the social body.[77]

The contemporary attempt by theologians to saddle Augustine with responsibility for the woes of modern secularism thus suffers from two fundamental flaws. While the sense of crisis is genuine and profound, and while they are even correct in recognizing that the nature of this crisis has to do with our relationship to the Christian Trinity, they mischaracterize the Western theological inheritance and leave us with an Augustine who is woefully impoverished. It is an Augustine with little or no Christology, no ecclesiology, no real appreciation of history. Ironically, it will take one of Augustine's sharpest critics, one unsympathetic to Christianity, to recognize the importance of these features of his thought.

Love in the time of avarice: the postmodern critique

Perhaps the most remarkable criticism of Augustine comes from Eric Alliez, a former student of Gilles Deleuze. For, unlike Charles Taylor and

Augustine's theological critics, Alliez does not occlude the specifically Christian features of Augustine's thought for a broader continuity with neoplatonism. To the contrary, it is precisely these features, distinct from Plotinus and absent from our earlier commentators, which destine Augustine and the West for nihilism.[78] This negative conclusion and the sense of its predestination are stronger here than in anyone we have considered thus far. The Reformers' destructive blows, Descartes' mathematical mastery of nature and Weberian rational calculation all lie latent in the soul laid bare in the *Confessiones* and the City on pilgrimage toward God.[79] The only real question is why it took so long. This fated predicament is the logical outcome of Alliez's grand ambition: to uncover the metaphysical figure of capitalism.

Like a Gilson without a pristine past, Alliez seeks to recall the entire "metaphysical tradition" of the West, by which he really means Christianity, from its inception to its late scholastic collapse.[80] Unlike Gilson, he views and organizes this tradition through a Marxist definition of exchange value or Aristotelian *chrematistics*, "which empties the city of its presence to itself by freeing the (monetary) sign of any relation to its natural referent."[81] This problem is formally identical to the representation and willful manipulation of a spatialized present, proper only to the soul, by the Augustinian-Cartesian *cogito*. That is to say, it is identical to the subjective conquest of time. Yet since Marx's definition governs Alliez's metaphysical analysis, the "natural referent" which is the alternative to *chrematistic* value should be seen to stand in place of Marx's "use-value;" and, like Marx, Alliez's account (despite its historicism) suffers from a certain positivism about what constitutes "the natural" as he arbitrarily imposes upon Augustine an alien physics and metaphysics that are only thinkable in the wake of Augustinianism's defeat.[82]

Alliez wants to show that these developments are not accidental but essential to Christianity, which means he has to show how the Christian and particularly Augustinian conception of the relationship between Creator and creature actually produces its mirror opposite and subordinates the Creator, and everything else, to the creature. *Because* it *invents* genuine transcendence, "it is the nature of Christianity to be delivered up to this new immanence."[83] Alliez must therefore show, in contrast to the customary view that the secularizing development of capitalism occurs as a consequence of Reason's assertion of its own self-sufficiency, that

> the dynamics of transcendence . . . the divine economy henceforth implies a principle of dissociation, a specific break between what is beyond and what is here below, which, far from fulfilling itself in a negative logic with regard to the terrestrial city, in the end favors the autonomy of the temporal.[84]

The isomorphism between the soul and the city plays a fundamental, though negative, role here, as each exemplifies this "Niebuhrian" economy of separation, this dissociation between the eternal ideal and temporal reality that allegedly follows from the Augustinian soul's relation to the transcendent God. This economy is crucial for Alliez, because it is this that allows for "the break between the time of things and the converted time of the soul," which in turn enables "the primacy of the will over the order of nature" and thus, *chrematistics*.[85] In short, this negative economy makes room for the "*definition* of time as *distentio animi*," understood as a "psychological" turn, distinct from cosmic time, both toward and away from the motion of the world.[86] Again, the rupture effected by this turn is vital, because "the split is the only thing that can introduce us into a world dominated by intentionality."[87] Cartesian dominance is therefore built into the entire Christian view of sin and redemption from the outset. For the separation itself is a result of "avarice," of the soul's original desire for self-divination, a desire which destroys the pre-lapsarian *aevum* and institutes ontic time as we know it, now "the number of a 'violent' motion" which locates the soul on the nether side of an unbridgeable abyss.[88]

As evidence of the dual aspect of this economy, Alliez cites the earthly resignation of the heavenly city, through which Augustine renounces "the submission of the temporal order to the absolute order of eternal justice," thus paving the way for Luther, whom he cites.[89] He points to the Augustinian "solution to the problem of property rights"—*justa possessio*—and to Augustine's battles with (and suppression of) the Donatists and Pelagians. To admit them on their own terms within the Christian fold would be "to wish to reconnect the human and the divine in this world—and to repeat, in content, the Incarnation."[90]

The economy of the soul recapitulates this separation in parallel fashion, and is indeed dependent upon it. Since sin, in short, is the principle of time's individuation, "the historical time of change is not the cosmic time of creation."[91] Time of itself now insinuates its very difference from eternity and the very eternity it must therefore entail within itself in the form of self-presence. This paradoxically assures the surety of subjective time, which has now leaped "outside the cosmic rut of eternal equality that was subordinating earthly things to heavenly ones," to intend eternity in memory's voluntary extension into *expectatio*. This completes the definition of time as *distentio animi*. "So it is that the 'transcendental' deduction of an original time, organized by the eternity around which it gravitates, is succeeded by the phenomenological induction of a renovated time, reaching out toward the eternity to which it aspires."[92]

Alliez's critique is formidable and arguably more perceptive than many of those sympathetic with Augustine's Christianity.[93] Still, it is questionable on a number of fronts. The first problem is the economy of separation, both in its relation to the Trinity and in its instantiation in the city and the soul. On Augustinian terms, of course, this economy of separation is unintelligible. Even if one were to cede Alliez's account of the two cities, the damned, because of their privative relation to the beauty of their own form, still fulfill a contingent function within the Augustinian economy of beauty and thus exemplify the triumph of divine *iustitia*.[94] Subsequent chapters will show that the economy of beauty is integral to Augustine's trinitarianism, his Christology, his understanding of *natura*, and his account of volition; so Alliez's neglect of this economy implies a great void in his Augustine. This is apparent in his disregard for Augustine's trinitarianism. While he duly acknowledges that Augustine's trinitarianism implies a "partition without division, '*inseperabilis distinctio*,'" he makes nothing of it. He refuses to consider that this *distinctio* might *encompass* the difference between God and creation and thus eternity and time within the greater, paradoxical difference of trinitarian unity. Furthermore, he does not advert at all to the third *hypostasis*, and so it is not surprising that his accounts of Pelagianism, Donatism and Augustinian private property altogether miss the form of unity between God and the created economy. This is bound up with a christology and soteriology that are parodic at best, as Alliez reads onto Augustine a dialectical account of the crucifixion that Augustine himself explicitly rejects.[95]

Neglecting divine and created beauty, presupposing a propitiatory account of the atonement, and quarantining it from the inter-trinitarian economy, it then becomes possible for Alliez to register the prescriptions of *De Civitate Dei* in the negative terms of separation, as a concession that divine *justitia* is an otherworldly phenomenon. However, on a trinitarian reading of the atonement, one that correlates Jesus' self-gift and resurrection with the mutual gift and delight between the Father and the Son, this *iustitia* manifest in the incarnation appears precisely *as* mercy and as a pattern or *forma* whose beauty delights and moves those who encounter its embrace. Within this register, the Donatists and Pelagians are not heretical because they seek to violate Alliez's negative economy and "reconnect the human and divine in this world." Augustine's criticisms are virtually opposite these. These movements are heretical, first, because they imply a denial of the objective efficacy of the rites that constitute Christ's body, and secondly, because their commitment to an essentially pagan virtue precludes this unity and fails to see that "our justice . . . though genuine . . . is nevertheless only such to consist in the forgiveness of sins rather than in the perfection of virtues."[96]

In one sense Alliez is correct. Both the ontological difference and the fall institute, each in their distinct ways, a kind of distance which must be traversed by earnest.[97] Yet neither distance is an absolute "separation." Even the distance of a defective will is privative and thus dependent upon a prior analogy. The distance intrinsic to the ontological difference is the ground of our similitude to God, as subsequent chapters will show, and the

21

interval of the gift, in which our desire for the beauty of the Son may partake of the delight between the Father and the Son. This longing is *itself* a form of union "with the same God whose prophets foretold the events we now see happening" in the life of the Church.[98] These hardly seem the words of someone who has utterly disjoined cosmic and psychological time.

All of Alliez's evidence can be assimilated to this register. The idea of *iusta possessio*, for instance, serves two functions within it. On the one hand, this is a figure of the new *iustitia*, inasmuch as it permits the earthly city to be itself. On the other hand, it still destabilizes the absolute right to property by submitting the rights of legitimate ownership to criteria of the common good—a far cry from Lockean possession. So too with the Pelagians and Donatists. One might quarrel with Augustine's endorsement of civic coercion or the logic of his means/end reasoning, but he justifies it as mercy—as being for the correction and thus the good of those who have alienated themselves from their own commitments. Banal as it may seem and unsatisfying as it is, this is why it is permissible to beat the Donatists but not to torture them, kill them or deceive them.[99]

The economy of separation, manifest here in the political realm, underlies a double maneuver that Alliez imposes upon the Augustinian soul. First, this economy allows Alliez to posit an absolute break between the time of the soul and cosmological time, a move that makes "the unity of a sense which constitutes or gives" the ground of time and the forerunner to the transcendental unity of apperception.[100] This break, combined with the absolute difference between God and the creature, nevertheless still implies the soul's absolute dependence. The effect, and Alliez's second maneuver, is to lock the Augustinian soul into the prototypical oscillation of onto-theology, aided and abetted by the implicit equation of volition (in one sense at least) with assertion or projection. The subject established in a kind of self-grounding autonomy (with God localized in memory) nevertheless "induces a fictive voice from on high" as its own precondition in order to validate itself.[101] Subjective mastery is complete when Alliez invokes the authority of Deleuze to underwrite the spatialization of the present, diagnosing how Augustine's illicit subordination of the *graphe* to the voice "makes a transcendent object jump outside the chain," in order to aid in its mastery.[102] This criticism, it will turn out, entails a physics all its own, and it comes in spite of Augustine's refusal to grant "spatial" extent to the present and his insistence, in the co-articulation of time and space in *De Musica*, that a thing's "time spans precede its space spans."[103] Yet there already appears to be a curious circularity to Alliez's own reasoning, born perhaps of his neglect of the trinitarian and christological constitution of the subject. If indeed the Augustinian *mens* is as dependent as Alliez rightly claims, then on its own terms it could never be the "auto" that is the subject of autobiographical writing. This accounts for a feature of the *Confessiones* that Alliez ignores completely—its tendency to make its own subject typological and figurative.[104] Therefore in order to read the Augustinian soul as foregrounding ontotheological oscillation, the rupture between the two poles of that dialectic has to be taken as normative a priori. In other words, in order to account for Augustinian self-positing it is necessary not simply to find but to presuppose and *promote* the economy of separation that the narrative claims to discover. Alliez must take this separation and all that it entails for language and representation as normative in order to read onto Augustine's language anti-Augustinian functions which Augustine himself is alleged to have invented. Wittgenstein's observation is appropriate here. "We predicate of a thing what lies in the method of predication."[105]

It is crucial to Alliez that the *distentio animi* be received as a *definition* of time, severed from cosmological time. He therefore lays great stress on Augustine's refusal to equate time with celestial motion and his attention to the problem of time's measurement; for "the definition of time as distention of the soul cannot be produced before the problem of measurement has been resolved."[106] But this too is circular. Augustine allegedly "defines" time as distention because he severs temporality and cosmology. Why does he sever temporality and cosmology? Because he defines time as distention. Nevertheless, this circle helps to establish the great contrast between two modes of conceiving time, upon which depends Alliez's case for the subject who leaps "outside the cosmic rut of eternal equality that was subordinating things of the earth to heaven."[107]

There are at least two reasons why this is dubious, the first of which emerges from resituating Augustine's meditations on time within the broader genre and purposes of the *Confessiones*. Alliez ignores these purposes, despite his fixation on Augustinian "intentionality," and thus begs some crucial questions. He asserts Augustine's need to solve the problem of measurement; yet what, within the broader context of the *Confessiones*, *is* the problem of measurement? And why, as an independent topic, would it be of any interest?

One gets a sense of the answer locating these meditations within the question posed in Book IX and throughout: "Who am I and what am I?"[108] Situated within this concern and within the quest to recollect oneself under the form of divine justice, the question of time, and of how one in time determines the nature of time, might be restated: "How is the idea of a history (especially *my* history) intelligible at all? By what standards is my life a coherent, intelligible story?" It is this question of *standards* that renders the question of time's measurement paradoxical, for, as Wetzel notes, if measurement as such were really the issue, celestial motion would do just fine. Yet for this problem, Augustine "indicts the classical view for irrelevance, not for error."[109]

James McEvoy contends that we should not take the paradoxes of temporal passage "as flat, apodictic contradictions," but rather as aporetic moments in a dialectic that strains for an as yet unachieved wholeness, a warning that cautions against taking the *distentio animi* as a final definition.[110] The aporia of standards helps account for a word play that Augustine executes on the meaning of *distentio*, a pun barely noted by Alliez. In its first sense, when Augustine describes his command over times in measuring his impressions in the "present activity" of attention or his recitation of a psalm from memory, it conveys the sense of "his mind's encompassment of time."[111] Yet as soon as he concludes this point, he reverses it with a pun that makes distention into a sign of dissipation and dissolution.

> But since your mercy is better than lives, behold my life is a distention or distraction. But your right hand has upheld me in my Lord, the Son of man, mediator between you, the One, and us, the many, who are dissipated in many ways upon many things; so that by him "I may apprehend in whom I have been apprehended," and may be gathered together again from my former days . . .

> But now "my years are wasted in sighs," and you, O Lord, my comfort, my Father, are eternal. But I am distracted amid times, whose order I do not know, and my thoughts are torn asunder by tumult and change.[112]

This second sense of distention indicates a soul subject to conditions of temporal flow which it does not itself contain, subject, in other words, to the ravages of cosmological time, though commentators have tended to emphasize this negative aspect, neglecting that the passing away of finite things is also their becoming.[113] This emphasis is in fact underscored by the constitutive role of memory, a feature notably absent from the Cartesian *cogito* who only surely is in the moment of his self-assertion. The role of memory attests to the simultaneous importance and yet irreducibility of both an "external" temporal flow and "internal" perception.[114] But there is more. Far from locating the subject outside and over against the cosmic rut, the aporia reflected in the two senses of distention makes the *mens* intelligible, yet only finally and fully so in relation to the "totality" that contains Augustine even as he partly transcends it, a totality to which he is finally refused access.[115] As a consequence, the question of measurement is never finally solved and never can be, and doxological dispossession becomes the form of a self-knowledge always revisable under the new temporal instantiations of the form of eternal justice.[116] The only true measure of all terms in the equation—Augustine as measurer and measured—is beyond measure. Yet just this form of dispossession disturbs the one-sided equation of temporal flow with loss and challenges Alliez's contention that time as such is merely the time of avarice.

The real question is not whether cosmological time, the time of physical motion and the psychological perception of perdurance are discontinuous.

Rather the real question is whether this difference constitutes an absolute rupture that effaces "real" time, or whether it can be exhibited in some kind of analogy or harmony. This question, in other words, is over the ontology and cosmology that situate this articulation of time. Alliez criticizes Augustine for having abstracted "presence," and the subject who contains it, from temporal sequence. Yet at the very moment of this aporetic turn, in *Confessiones* XI.29, Augustine invokes the Son's mediation and insinuates that it does effect some sort of harmony, that the same cosmological time which is the vehicle for dissipation and loss can become the vehicle for restoration, for creation, for receiving oneself as gift.[117] As a consequence, it suggests further that Christ's advent is not merely a "punctual" event in time's linear flow, but rather somehow determinative of the relationship between time and eternity, and thus of the nature of time itself. As subsequent chapters will show, this too is a function of the economy of beauty that Alliez neglects.

The possibility of a christological understanding of time raises once again the Augustinian question of standards, and when this question is put to Alliez it brings us full circle to our original criticisms: that his organizing principle entails a certain positivism about "nature" that he then foists upon the text. Underlying this is a certain metaphysical positivism as well. We have already seen this in his transcendental invocation of an immanent Deluzian chain, the necessary precondition for an illicit "jump" by a "transcendent object." It is further evident when he invokes Aristotle.

> Thus, far from supposing the wholly Aristotelian extrinsic determination of knowing through the object—that something must be allowed to appear without doing it violence because the criterion of truth resides within it—the intentionality of cognition is detached from the philosophical realism of the formal (and not absolute-real) identity between subject and object such as it is in itself, and depends no longer on anything other than the intuition of God within Me; that is to say, on the primacy of the will over the order of nature.[118]

The assertion of the primacy of will goes hand in hand with his reduction of the soul to intentionality, both of which are intended to foreshadow the Cartesian *cogito*. However, Alliez never analyzes Augustinian volition. He does not consider the integral relationship, to be developed in subsequent chapters, between the will and the economy of beauty; so he pays no heed either to the vast chasm separating Augustinian and Cartesian volition or to the erotic relationship between the Augustinian will and Augustinian nature. Instead he smuggles in a physics of his own, with the a priori supposition of a "chain" of singularities each possessed of their immanent criterion of truth which are then effaced by the will's self-assertion.

25

There is an irony to this. While Alliez sets out to attribute the contingent rise of *chrematistics* to Augustine and the Christian tradition, it is in fact his own identitarian commitment to a purely singular and immanent criterion of truth which insures that any predication or qualification to substances, particularly qualifications answering to the transcendentals, will be *chrematistic* in character. It is little wonder, then, that *chrematistics* emerges, without contingency, as the pre-ordained destiny of the West. It is built into the linear, agonistic metaphysics intrinsic to Alliez's analysis. For a purely immanent criterion of truth, without relation, without analogy implying both self-transcendence and a measure that transcends the self, is destined for effacement by "extrinsic" denomination. Quite simply, in making truth purely immanent, in reducing the criterion of truth to the individual, Alliez ironically ensures a transcendental name as the real truth: violence. It is this that foregrounds the juxtaposition of subject and object, this that foregrounds an ontological disjunction of quality and quantity, and thus this that foregrounds the reduction of "the chain" to a Cartesian *res extensa*. Only Alliez is not in the foreground. In his neglect and suppression of the Trinity, the economy of beauty, and Augustinian volition, it is Alliez and not Augustine who is more truly the Cartesian.

We have now seen several contemporary Augustines, each in some senses so different that his respective promoters scarcely speak the same philosophical and theological languages. Yet each conforms in broad outline, for good or for ill, to the story of modern origins given such expression by Charles Taylor. As a consequence, this story of the event that Augustine is thought to have helped cause produces commonalities among these Augustines that transcend the diference between Taylor's humanistic optimism and Alliez's nihilism. Each is bound to the other by what it lacks, a *theological* understanding of this event, which means that none of these Augustines is organized according to theological criteria of the kind that Augustine would be bound by faith and by office to endorse. Therefore while the event of modernity, the event that shapes us, might help us to decipher the Augustine necessary to underwrite our contemporary self understanding, the emergent Augustine helps us very little to decipher, let alone criticize, modernity. He helps us little to come to terms with the depths of what we no longer believe.

For that, we need an alternative.

2

DE TRINITATE AND THE AESTHETICS OF SALVATION

The aesthetics of salvation

The Augustines of the previous chapter all depend upon the neglect or suppression of key features of his thought. This chapter intends to counter these inadequate portrayals by reconstructing a more comprehensive "Augustinianism," from the *De Trinitate* and other texts, wherein what is philosophically interesting—Augustine's theory of language, anthropology, moral psychology and treatment of *voluntas*—emerges as a function of what is doctrinally most important: his trinitarian theology, Christology, and the ecclesiology and doctrine of grace which flow from them.

The argument requires that Augustine himself be resituated within the ontological context from which he presumed to write, namely, the hypostatic unity of the one Christ, in which the creation unfolded within the love between the Father and the Son is recalled to union with its Creator.[1] The effect is to reconfigure cosmology as creation, creation as soteriology, soteriology as aesthetics and aesthetics as doxology. There are three stages to this demonstration, dispersed through the three sections of this chapter. The first is something of an overview that sketches in broad strokes the claim that Augustine's cosmology is an aesthetic soteriology. Within this aesthetic soteriology there is a dual concern for both the apprehension and the manifestation of the divine beauty. Both concerns invoke Augustine's Christology. The second section considers more specifically Augustine's explication of the generation and procession of the trinitarian *personae*, in order to demonstrate how this aesthetic soteriology is coextensive with Augustine's understanding of the Trinity as transcendent love. Within this analysis, a revised sense of the so-called psychological analogy will begin to take shape. This sense will come to fruition in the final section, as all of these strands converge in Augustine's Christology, which passes over into ecclesiology. In its unity of *sapientia* and *scientia*, *exemplum* and *sacramentum*, time and eternity, Augustine's Christology becomes the focal point for the manifestation of the eternal beauty of God in the temporal economy and the unfolding of the temporal economy within the eternal beauty of God.

27

And Christ becomes the mediator toward whom the Augustinian *mens* is ordered, by whom and in whom it acts and through whom the psychological analogy is rendered intelligible. Demonstrating this will suffice as a challenge to the charge that Augustine's trinitarianism somehow excludes the economy from the dialectical dance between the soul and God. It will also provide the basis from which to turn the tables on the charge of incipient nihilism, in the remaining chapters.

These are fundamentally theological claims, not historical or exegetical ones. Still, the historical occasion of *De Trinitate* testifies to this aesthetic concern and gives a clue to the sometimes elusive unity of the work.[2] In considering this occasion, Michel Rene Barnes has isolated a fundamental conflict between Augustine's trinitarian theology and that of the second generation Latin *Homoians*. The controversy orbits around the question of the material revelation of the Son, and, through him, the indivisible operation of the whole Trinity. Barnes succinctly summarizes the point of contention. "The Homoians claim 'If material not divine,' while Augustine wants to assert 'Material, in order to bring us to the divine.'"[3] This is "because only a material existence can perform the epistemological (or anthropological) function of leading us to the vision of God."[4]

Christ's "function" is one whereby he reincorporates an estranged creation into the trinitarian life of God.[5] As such, it will prove inseparable from the meaning of the incarnation and passion. Yet I will argue that this "function," even in the passion, is aesthetic, in two senses. The first is a concern for the manifestation of the divine beauty in creation, or rather, the restoration of creation as a manifestation of the beauty of the divine love. The second is a concern for our apprehension of it.[6] Both elements converge concretely in Augustine's Christology. Barnes's observations are crucial because they establish these aesthetic priorities at the beginning of *De Trinitate*.

Carol Harrison makes this "aesthetic priority" an organizing principle for understanding Augustine's entire corpus as a unified whole.[7] Its importance is attested throughout Augustine's career, for instance, in the harmonic "musical" ontology of *De Musica* and *De Libero Arbitrio*, themes that will recur with explicit christological and trinitarian overtones in *De Trinitate*. Augustine's ninth homily on the First Epistle of John succinctly states the relationship between this "aesthetic" preoccupation, with its dual facets, and Augustine's soteriology.

> "Let us love, because he first loved us." We did not yet love Him: by loving we are made beautiful . . . our soul, my brethren, is ugly because of sin: by loving God it becomes beautiful . . . He first loved us, Who is always beautiful; and what were we when He loved us, but foul and ugly? But not to leave us foul; but to change us, and from deformity make us beautiful. How shall we become beautiful?

> By loving Him who is always beautiful. Inasmuch as love grows in you, in so much beauty grows; for love is itself the beauty of the soul.[8]

This love, at once God and the gift of God, transforms our misshapen deformity into beauty by drawing us into the beauty beyond measure. This logic, stated with such simple brevity in the homily, is the central preoccupation of the *De Trinitate*, permeating it throughout, often in areas where one is unaccustomed to looking for it.

Beneath this simplicity, however, lie several features of Augustine's thought which will help to make the *De Trinitate* intelligible as a single work. The first is the identification of Christ with the *forma* or beauty of God, which Augustine variously characterizes as supreme measure without measure (*mensura sine mensura*), the measure of the soul, and supreme Truth, Unity, Form, and Number.[9] The identification of Christ as both beauty and form is an ontological identification; for Augustine equates *forma* or *species* with beauty, without remainder, from the Cassiciacum dialogues onwards.[10] This identification will prove crucial: to the integral role of beauty in the explication of the Trinity as triune love, to the aesthetic "function" of Augustine's Christ in both manifesting and drawing us into the divine love, and to the meaning of the passion as the supreme exemplification of that love.

The second feature is the role of the beautiful in inciting *our* love. I shall have much more to say about this in subsequent sections, but it is absolutely integral both to Augustine's trinitarian speculations and his "theological psychology." The third is the location of our desire for the beautiful within the anterior enticements of the beautiful itself, which is to say, within the grace of Christ. The remark also suggests, finally, that our participation in this beauty, our recovery of form, is itself the restoration of a kind of aesthetic order consonant with the ontological equation of beauty and form— such that to become deformed is *esse minus*, and to become beautiful through love is *esse magis*.[11] To become beautiful is to approach the One who is.[12]

Augustine's view has obvious affinities with the neoplatonism of Plotinus, and the theoretical exposition of beauty is a recurrent theme of the Cassiciacum dialogs. Interestingly, however, Harrison observes a *greater* emphasis upon the role of created beauty as Augustine's thought becomes more ecclesiastical. Harrison attributes this to a deepening appreciation of the consequences of the Fall and our need for beauty to draw us toward its transcendent source.[13] While this seems plausible, it is less than sufficient, and one can suggest two more reasons for this emphasis. First, this development also reflects the difference between the Christian Trinity and the neoplatonic hypostases and the central role which Augustine accords to delight, both in the movement of the human will and in the filiation of the

Son and spiration of the Spirit. Second, it reflects the importance of the incarnation of Christ as the visible manifestation of divine beauty, and of his passion in reforming creation to its ultimate beatification.

Harrison's thesis and Barnes's exegesis illuminate aspects of the *De Trinitate* which typically remain hidden from view. Yet if we situate the text against the backdrop of these broader, extraneous concerns, and if we keep Augustine's anti-homoian polemic before our eyes, the *De Trinitate* begins to unfold bracketed by two concerns. The first, announced at the close of Book I, is derived from an amalgam of biblical references.[14]

> That after this meaning, then, the Lord said, "Why askest thou me about the good? there is none good but One, that is, God," is probable upon these proofs which I have alleged, because that sight of God, whereby we shall contemplate the substance of God unchangeable and invisible to human eyes (which is promised to the saints alone; which the Apostle Paul speaks of as "face to face"; and of which the Apostle John says, "We shall be like Him, for we shall see him as he is;" and of which it is said, "One thing have I desired of the Lord, that I may behold the beauty of the Lord," of which the Lord Himself says, "I will both love him, and will manifest myself to him," and on account of which alone we cleanse our hearts by faith, that we may be those "pure in heart who are blessed for they shall see God": and whatever else is spoken of that sight: which whosoever turns the eye of love to seek it, may find it most copiously scattered through all the Scriptures), that sight alone, I say, is our chief good, for the attaining of which we are directed to do whatever we do aright.[15]

This announcement of the 'chief good' and this quest for transforming vision set the course for the remainder of the *De Trinitate*. This conclusion is supported by a second, complementary bookend, which further illustrates the unity of the treatise. It comes at the culmination of the work in Book XV. Having set as the goal in Book I the vision of God's beauty, Augustine asks in the final book— significantly—just before the elaboration of the Spirit as *dono*, "how or where does the Trinity manifest itself?"[16]

It is this crucial question, I submit, which the *De Trinitate* as a whole sets out to answer. The remainder of this section will consider this answer, dividing it into three complementary parts which converge in Augustine's Christology. This makes the interrelation of the various aspects of this tripartite answer as important as any single part on its own.

The first part concerns an Augustinian "semiotics" or "theology of language," and it impinges upon both aforementioned aspects of the general aesthetic concern: apprehension and manifestation.[17] *De Doctrina Christiana* (or perhaps *De Magistro*) is usually taken as the *locus classicus* of this topic.[18] However, since Augustine takes it up in a theological and ontological context in *De Trinitate*, I will argue as a theological point that Augustinian signification should be understood as a function of Augustine's trinitarian theology, a thesis which entails two crucial implications. This serves, first, to situate all signs within the Father's speaking of the Son and the Son's *responsio* to the Father. This will mean, secondly, that all creatures are most fully constituted in their creaturehood *as* signs within the delight intrinsic to this exchange.[19] This is important both for interpreting the theophanies of the early books and for situating them ontologically and providentially in reference to the Incarnation. The *signa* of the theophanies signify Christ not only in respect of their content (e.g., Moses' staff signi-fying Christ) but also because the form of theophany suggests a relation-ship between temporal flow and God's eternal gratuity that anticipates the christological consummation of the time/eternity union in Book XIII. Creation participates in this union doxologically, and properly becomes creation to the extent that it does so, manifesting at the same time the beauty of the Trinity in whom it participates.

The second part of the answer is implied by the first. If the Trinity is manifest in creatures made signs of the divine love, then the appearance of the Trinity is intrinsically bound to the most enduring of these signs: the Church, whose temporal unfolding likewise exhibits, in intensified form, the gift exchange and the ratio of time to eternity entailed in the christological union. Hence the church only exhibits this status as the Body of Christ, and thus at a distance at once erotic, temporal and ontological from its head. Thus the third and final facet of the answer is implied by the second. The other aspects point to it and depend upon participation in it for their consummation. This final facet is the unity of the one Christ— head of the body, who is both *exemplum* and *sacramentum*, *scientia* and *sapientia*, eternal and temporal, creature and creator. It is precisely in uniting these pairs, through the one Christ, that the indivisible Trinity manifests itself, and precisely through this union that fellow creatures, as members of Christ's Body, are able to manifest this indivisibility articulated as love. In sum, the Trinity is manifest in a creation constituted as an icon of the God who is love, and thus a creation whose very form is Church, whose highest expression is the crucified, resurrected and glorified Christ.[20]

Let us consider each facet of this answer in turn.

Creation and the signification of God

Augustine's treatment of the Old Testament theophanies in Books II and III of *De Trinitate* occurs within his broader concern to demonstrate that the material appearance of the Son does not compromise his equality with the Father, the indivisibility of their operations, or the transcendent immut-ability of the triune essence. It is these concerns that provoke his famous appropriation of the Pauline distinction between the *forma dei* and *forma servi* for adjudicating the various meanings of scriptural references to the Son. And it is these conditions that both necessitate the material revelation of the Son and align this issue with the question of the theophanies, though Augustine is careful to distinguish in kind between the theophanies and the Incarnation.[21] Still, the invisibility and immutability of the divine essence, along with this rule, lead Augustine to a conclusion about the theophanies that anticipates the Son's subordination to the Father under the aspect of the *forma servi*. He concludes that in all the visible and sensible manifestations of God "the creature [is] made subject in order to signify the invisible and intelligible God."[22]

Already in this brief remark Augustine mentions both of the afore-mentioned aspects of a "theology of language," a God whose act somehow constitutes the intelligible contents of creaturehood and a creature rendered a sign of this God. Later, in Book III, Augustine will pose the question of whether the creatures through whom the divine appearances were wrought were created specifically for that purpose. The question will lead him on several long digressions, where he discusses, in turn, the order of proximate causes descending from God's act as final cause, the hier-archical order of a creation which distends from this act through the pious spirits of the angels to the spirit subject to sin, to the bodies they govern and the seemingly exceptional nature of miracles.[23] The former parts seek to describe how all the lower parts of creation are dependent upon the higher, and ultimately upon God who "make[s] and administer[s] the creature from the innermost and highest-turning point of causation," the latter to locate miracles within the context of the prior divine government of the universe.[24]

The upshot of this is that the theophanies mark only an intensified form of what creation already is: an order whose form reflects the wisdom of God.[25] This is apparent in Augustine's discussion of "that country that is above and heavenly," where

> the will of God . . . diffuses itself through all things by certain most perfectly ordered movements of the creature; first spiritual, then corporeal; and uses all according to the unchangeable pleasure of its own purpose, whether incorporeal things or things corporeal, whether rational or irrational spirits, whether good by his grace or evil through their own will.[26]

It is ultimately this "aesthetic" order, both a reflection of and a partici-pation in the action of the one "with whom primarily rests the measure, number and weight of all things existing," that marks creation *as* creation. Hence the claim that all creatures are most fully constituted in their creaturehood precisely as signs that both manifest and participate in the divine beauty: "what wonder if also in the creature of heaven and earth, of sea and air, God works the sensible and visible things which He wills in order to signify and manifest [*significandum et demonstrandum*] himself in them?"[27]

This "*et*," which links *signa* to God's *demonstrandum*, is crucial to the meaning of Augustinian signification and to the theological and cosmological contexts in which it occurs. It dispels the charge that Augustine lays the groundwork for early modern conceptions of representation, in part by making the participation of the sign in the beauty it signifies more than adventitious.[28] This will be crucial both in that sign of all signs, the *sacramentum* of Christ, and in his Body the Church. Ultimately, this formula suggests something of the formal ratio of creature to creator restored and consummated in Christ.[29] We can see this by looking more closely at *De Doctrina Christiana*, where Augustine's semiotics forms a more central part of the discussion of biblical exegesis, and whose exegetical prescriptions Augustine seems to follow in these books of *De Trinitate*.

The charge of representation is based upon Augustine's distinction between *signa* and *res*. "All doctrine concerns either things or signs, but things are learned by signs . . . [E]very sign is also a thing, for that which is not a thing is nothing at all; but not every thing is also a sign."[30] The deleterious effects of this distinction, and the chasm it appears to institute between the subject and sign that signify and thus allegedly circumscribe their object, and that object itself become apparent when it is taken in tandem with Augustine's crucial distinction between enjoyment and use.[31] Together they seem to portend a kind of instrumentalism whereby signs are to be manipulated like capitalist exchange values at the arbitrary behest of a "sense which constitutes or gives."[32] The signified objects, circumscribed by the *signa*, are now thought to be subordinate to the caprice of the will.[33] At first glance, William Babcock's observation of Augustine's exegetical procedures appears to corroborate this view, though he does not make or endorse this charge. He elaborates upon Augustine's contention that "schemes of signification are socially constructed," a point which will eventually become crucial as we consider the ontological significance of the Church. And he notes that, for all of Augustine's attention to diverse significations, he nevertheless "stipulates in advance what the terminus of the scriptural signs is."[34] "[T]he *plenitudo* and *finis* of the Law and of all the sacred Scriptures is the love of a Being which is to be enjoyed and of a being that can share that enjoyment with us."[35]

As I suggested in the previous chapter, the problem with this line of criticism is that it is guilty of what it opposes. It predetermines the ontological status of the objects in question, and in so doing overlooks the implicit ontology of Augustine's formulations—made more explicit in the theophanies of *De Trinitate*. On this view things *are* "to be enjoyed or used." And God, being immutable, "does not enjoy use but uses us."[36] Thus the distinction between *signa*, which are always *res*, and *res*, which are not always *signa*, is inherently unstable—a fact already apparent from the way that both *modus, species* and *ordo* and the *mensura, numerus* and *pondus* of creatures signify and participate in the *mensura sine mensura* of God. [37]

This instability then throws into question what it means to be a *res*, for, at the most basic level, it appears that intelligibility and signification are "built in" to the meaning of creaturehood. Furthermore, despite Augustine's distinction between *signa naturalia* (for example, smoke signaling fire) and *signa data* ("smoke" used with the intent to signify something else), both the implicit ontology of *De Doctrina Christiana* and the theophanies of *De Trinitate* permit the transition of the *signa naturalia* into *signa data*, and within the latter the further "upward" transition from *signa propria* to *signa translata*.[38]

What is this implicit ontology? To say that the *plenitudo* and *finis* of the law and the end and principle of all the requisite significations are charity or *dilectio*, specifically "the love of a Being which is to be enjoyed and can share that enjoyment with us"[39] is to say that signification has its origin and end in the gift and delight between Father and Son.[40] Furthermore, to say that God uses us is to suggest that things are finally things precisely in the degree to which they participate in the doxological beauty of God, in short, in the degree to which they *become* "signs" signifying and manifesting this beauty—which also means that they "are" only in and as relations, both to God and other *signa*.[41] The role accorded to *modus, species*, and *ordo* or *mensura, numerus* and *pondus* testifies to this conclusion. The entailment of the intelligible in the material, which I shall discuss in the next chapter, will corroborate it further.

Two implications forestall the charge of representation or instrumentalism. First, though Babcock is right that Augustine stipulates in advance the terminus of the scriptural signs, this stipulation does not foreclose on identically repeatable "meaning" whose object the sign merely "represents."[42] Augustine's own exegesis is empirical evidence of this claim; his insistence in the *Confessiones* of a plenitude of true meanings for a single text suggests its theoretical justification.[43] The ontological warrant that underlies this insistence throughout the Augustinian corpus derives, in part, from the very nature of truth's oneness, which defies its circumscription or possession.[44] Moreover, we have already seen that the insistence upon a plenitude of charity as the terminus of scriptural signs is tantamount to the insistence that the end and principle of the said signs is the love between Father and Son. This, in turn, is tantamount to saying that it is the very nature of this plenitude to be *generative*. Hence the empirical example of Augustine's own multivalent exegesis should come as no surprise. It is precisely because *this* plenitude is the terminus of the signs that it is really no terminus at all, really no foreclosure upon meaning, but is instead ever generative of meaning, which is to say new forms of relation to the end, in non-identically repeatable circumstance. *Signa* are coextensive with temporality, which is to say coextensive with creation, the constant bringing forth of the new from nothing.

This brings us to the second reason why a grammar of representation is inadequate here. The intrinsic intelligibility of creatures and their "use" by God mean that signs do not merely "represent" the charity they "signify;" they participate in it and indeed are unfolded in it, all the while neither exhausting it nor being exhausted by it. Hence the importance of the *et* in *significandum et demonstrandum*. The sign, while neither exhausted in nor exhausting the signified, is not adventitious to it—a point that will be crucial to correlating Christ's status as *sacramentum* with the efficacy of his passion. The theophanies are significant, both in "signifying" God and in manifesting, and thus participating in, him, which makes the signs also significant *as* things (and vice versa). Of course this is supremely clear in the unity of Christ. Christ is his own doctrine and thus the most perfect coincidence of sign and thing, "the reality to be known and the language for its understanding," yet his visible human form and divine nature neither exhaust nor consume each other.[45] Neither is this human form, as sign, adventitious to the signified, or else Christ's incarnation and passion would serve merely an exemplary function, and not an ontologically efficacious one.

All of this is crucial for a preliminary grasp of the soteriology of *De Trinitate*, which will eventually break down or transfigure its own binaries—time/eternity, inner/outer. On the interpretation just offered, Augustine's "theology of language" appears as the counterpart to a doctrine of creation which is intrinsically "linguistic" and consummated in the Word made flesh. Moses' rod, as a historical *event*, can signify the beauty manifest through Christ's passion without losing its integrity as a historical singularity because it has that same beauty as a principle, because it is itself a participation in the activity of that form which manifests itself historically *as* the passion, and which gives it form as a singularity.[46] It is a sign because it participates in what it signifies, and in so doing it anticipates the efficacious sign par excellence, the *sacramentum* of Christ in Books IV and XIII, in whom sign and signified perfectly coincide.

It should be clear, then, that the typology of the theophanies is more than a mere linguistic or exegetical strategy. Entailed in this understanding is a unique, non-linear ratio of time to eternity which will be consummated in the particularity of the one Christ, head and body. The theophonies invest time itself with a typological and sacramental—even a eucharistic—structure which prefigures Christ's unification of temporal *scientia* and eternal *sapientia,* joining the universal to a concrete particular in analogically repeated ways.[47] Michel de Certeau recognized this structure in his analysis of the Eucharist itself.

The sacrament ("sumere Christum") and the Church ("sumi a Christo") were joined (the term "communio" was, moreover, common to both) as the contemporary performance of a distinct, unique "event," the kairos, designated by the "historical body" (Jesus). The caesura is therefore of the temporal sort, in conformity with Augustinian theology. It separates from the original event the manifestation of its effects in the mode of the Church-Eucharist pair, which is the "liturgical" combination of a visible community or people (laos) with a secret action (ergon) or "mystery." The fact is, the linear series extending from the apostolic origins (H) to the present Church (C) is sustained in its entirety by the sacrament (S), conceived as a unique and everywhere instituting operation (the "mystery"), linking the kairos to its progressive manifestation. Distinct times (H and C) are united by the same invisible "action." This is the paradigm of "the tradition."[48]

In this "invisible action," the relationship of temporal flow to eternity is transformed and redeemed, as Certeau's remark about "the paradigm of the tradition" suggests. This is crucial for understanding the "aesthetics of salvation" and for seeing how Augustine's ontology concludes in the particularity of Christ and the Church, in a particular "elect" time which organizes times both past and future. For first, this action links the manifestation of God to a particular series of signs, once again making *these* signs integral to that manifestation without negating the claim that the *modus*, *species* and *ordo* of all creatures exhibits the divine beauty. Secondly, this can be, more generally, because the visible manifestation of the action of God signals not an antithesis between the eternity of the Word and the series unfolded within and mediated by it but rather a kind of *convenientia* or *coaptatio* between them.[49] The terms recall the numerology of the *De Musica*, which is soon to make its reappearance in *De Trinitate's* account of Christ's mediation and passion. In the former work, Augustine gives time a kind of precedence over space, as the persistence of "vertical" numerical ratios in a note or chord and in a sequence of notes or chords becomes detached from the length or interval of its temporal, "horizontal" passing in a manner analogous to the way in which a polyphonic chant or a struck chord is able to form one *simultaneous* sound, whether in memory or actual performance, in virtue of its very passing.[50] "Terrestrial things are joined to celestial, and their time circuits join together in a harmonious succession for a poem of the universe."[51] The result is paradoxical, for, as Catherine Pickstock observes, "It is impossible, rationally, to resolve the aporias of time. Neither a pure flow nor pure present moments make any coherent sense. And yet in music we *hear* this impossible reconciliation."[52] Just as there is no antithesis (*pace* Wayne Hankey), though there remains a fundamental ontological difference, between the eternity of divine *sapientia* and the series unfolding within it, so there is no antithesis, though there remains the greatest difference, between the *successio saeculorum*, the *dispensatio similitudinum*, the *cognitio historica* and that "contemplation [which] is held forth to us as the end of all actions."[53] Indeed the relationship is complementary precisely in virtue of this difference. Basil Studer notes that in the anti-porphyrian argument of Book IV, Augustine challenges the Neoplatonists' competence to pronounce on the resurrection—an argument he will later extend, importantly, to make faith in the resurrection a *precondition* for true contemplation —on grounds that it belongs to the *successio saeculorum*, for which the philosophers lack the adequate *cognitio historica*.[54]

It is now becoming apparent how Augustine's ontology codetermines the universal with the particularity of the Head and Body of Christ. Just as the rhythmic interval can unfold *because* of the persistence of its ratio *heard* in the simultaneity of a polyphonic sounding, so too this temporal unfolding occurs horizontally *as a consequence* of its harmonic "vertical" mediation within the Father's speaking and the Son's "reply" in the Spirit. Hence the *cognitio historica*, preserved and transmitted in the witness of the apostles and martyrs and yet instantiated ever new in the singularity of contingent circumstance, is unfolded within and mediated by the form of this response, a form transcending to those concepts. This historical knowledge is now intrinsic to both the form and content of contemplation.[55]

The upshot of these observations is crucial, both as a segue to the second, ecclesial component of the answer to the question of *De Trinitate* XV and as an indication of the importance of these historical "particulars" in relation to Augustine's view of eternity. To locate the unfolding of time within the Son's response to the Father is in effect to instantiate a notion of mediation with respect to Christ and his Body which has two facets. On the one hand, Christ incorporates us into his *responsio* to and vision of the Father; on the other hand, the particular liturgical rites, practices, and narratives "mediate" Christ, making him "visible" in analogically repeated ways to our hope and intention. The result is a "concrete universal" which makes the historically particular integral to the manifestation of the transcendent and thus transfigures the time/eternity relationship in the direction of the christological union. Thus though it is correct to say that Israel and the Church may be called elect because they realize a certain *form* of doxological community, this is inadequate, because the formal and material aspects of this tradition are inextricably intertwined and are codetermined together. They can no more be disentangled than *sapientia* can be discretely disjoined from *scientia*. Instead we must say that this *historical* community, as the body of Christ, is intrinsic to the very manifestation of this "form."[56] Hence this *historical* community, in all its narrative and material specificity enters into the very definition and determination of doxology even as the formality of all forms informs this community.[57] In brief, precisely because Augustine's trinitarian ontology concludes in his Christology, it implies the doctrine of election.

Here Babcock's observation about the importance of social schemes of meaning returns at the ontological level, and we have to admit a measure of credence to Alliez's criticism. If truth designates not simply the relationship between the intellect and its objects, but the relationship of those objects to the mind and love of God, then there is no way around the fact that our perception of the truth will be dependent upon the quality of our intention, which is always mediated socially through language and habit. *De Trinitate* underscores this point through the mutual entailment of memory, intellect and will. The *City of God* is devoted to demonstrating the second part of it; the *Confessiones* is devoted, in part, to demonstrating it in the first person. All three are committed to its inverse corollary: that a perversion of love is also a perversion of vision.[58] This suggests that if "truth" is to mean more than logical coherence, truth claims are dependent upon the cultic context of their utterance, upon the Church as the historic form of a new creation. Yet it is this very same conception that prevents truth from doing violence to its objects, insofar as it is truth, for two reasons. First, the dependence of truth upon charity means that our perception of the truth of any object is contingent upon a proper regard for those objects and a referral of those objects to their ultimate end. The second is implied in a point we have already seen. The fact that their criterion of truth lies in their relation to the plenitude of divine love means that the truth of any object is itself infinite, and defies circumscription by a totalizing gaze. As we shall see, it calls forth another sort of response.

"How or where does the Trinity manifest itself?" We have taken this question as the animating question of *De Trinitate* as a whole and suggested a single answer with three facets. The first of these facets consisted in the way that creatures themselves are established in their creaturehood *as* signs manifesting the love which is their principle and end. And we have seen that this account entails a certain construal of the ratio of time to eternity which at once requires the integrity of a particular, "elect" history and the mediation of this series by its transcendent source and end.

This construal of creation as signs manifesting the beauty of divine love entails the second aspect of this answer. It consists, quite plainly, in the Body of Christ which is at once the temporal manifestation of the love between Father and Son and the form of a restored creation in the image and movement of that love. This conclusion is not in conflict with the stated goal of ascension to the vision of the divine glory if we keep in mind the consequences of this position: that it is only *in Christ*, and through rendering perfect in our own sight the visible *species* of our hope, that personhood and true being are finally possible for us.[59] The hope of "beatific vision" and the prescription of ecclesial life in time do not conflict (as Hankey implies) if one assumes that participation in the vision and delight between Father and Son is constitutive of what it means for *Jesus* to be human, and that incorporation into this delight through Christ is finally what it means for *us* to be human.[60] If participation in the divine beauty through the love between Father and Son is constitutive of our humanity and if indeed Jesus makes both this beauty and this humanity visible, then it follows that sight and manifestation are not two concerns at all.[61] Rather our participation in the Son's vision of the Father is inseparable from the manifestation of this beauty *in* us. When Augustine conceives of memory, intellect and will as mutually entailing each other, he will make vision inseparable from love, and love inseparable from a prior gift. The microcosm of the soul, in other words, will confirm and strengthen this macrocosmic conclusion.

Throughout his writings, Augustine does in fact link ecclesial life with the manifestation of God's beauty. And it is not a coincidence that the driving question in *De Trinitate* XV is posed just before Augustine launches into a discourse on the life of corporate charity.[62] More importantly, however, we can establish this link between charity and Augustine's "aesthetic concern" in the confluence of at least two features of the *De Trinitate*. We see the first in Book VIII, as Augustine asserts that the primary concern in knowing God as Trinity is to examine "what is true love, nay, rather what is love."[63] This understanding encompasses both the genuine love of God and neighbor, making them inseparable and reflecting again the codetermination of the universal and particular. Commenting on the fact that Scripture sometimes appears to commend the latter kind of love without the former, he remarks,

> [T]he Law and the prophets hangs on both precepts. But this, too, is because he who loves his neighbor must needs also love above all else love itself. But "God is love; and he that dwelleth in love, dwelleth in God . . . Wherefore they who seek God through those Powers which rule over the world, or parts of the world, are removed and cast away far from Him; not by intervals of space, but by difference of affections."[64]

It is here that we can first glimpse the Trinity as love partly because, as we shall eventually see, even this presupposes participation in the anterior gift of the Spirit. What is remarkable at this stage is that Augustine simply identifies our love with this anterior love of God.[65]

> Let no one say, I do not know what I love. Let him love his brother, and he will love the same love. For he knows the love with which he loves, more than the brother whom he loves. So now he can know God more than he knows his brother; clearly known more, because more present; known more, because more within him; known

more, because more certain. Embrace the love of God, and by love embrace God.[66]

A second passage, in Book XII, makes the link between corporate charity and divine beauty even more explicit. Following the book of Job, Augustine conflates *sapientia,* which he will later identify with the person of Christ, with worship. Crucially, he links this worship to the sight and appearance of God.

> I find it written in the Book of Job . . . "Behold piety, that is wisdom; but to depart from evil is knowledge." In thus distinguishing, it must be understood that wisdom belongs to contemplation, knowledge to action. For in this place he means by piety the worship of God, which in Greek is called θεοσέβεια . . . And what is the worship of Him except the love of Him, by which we now desire to see Him, and we believe and Hope that we shall see Him; and in proportion as we make progress, see now through a glass in an enigma, but then in clearness.[67]

When one considers the two passages in apposition, an aporia emerges which will prove crucial to Augustine's christological display of the trinitarian operations, to his account of our apprehension of them, and, more broadly, to what has been called Augustine's "metaphysics of conversion."[68] On one side, Augustine identifies our acts of love with the plenitudinous presence of God himself, more closely united to the agent than the object of her affections, united, indeed, more closely than the agent is united to herself. Love itself suggests an epiphany here. On the other side, however, this same love insinuates a distance and a deferral of vision, suggesting a kind of lack upon which *eros* depends.

However, the import of this aporia cannot become clear until we consider the third and final facet of the answer to the question posed at the conclusion of *De Trinitate,* the one toward which the others point. I suggested as the first facet that Augustine envisions the Trinity as manifest in creatures made to exemplify trinitarian charity. In the second, I suggested that the sign par excellence of this charity is the worship of the Church participating in the exchange of love between Father and Son such that this worship was itself actually the form of a restored creation. Augustine's Christ encompasses both notions. It is he who manifests this beauty. It is in him and his beauty that creatures are made *signa* of God, and through him, precisely in rendering creatures as *signa,* that a certain order is restored rendering creation once again creation.

We can see this convergence by attending to Augustine's development of the Pauline notion of the Body of Christ. In Book IV, Augustine all but conflates Christ and the Church into a single "organism" while maintaining the distinction between Head and Body.[69]

> He did not say, I and they are one thing; although, in that He is the head of the church, which is His Body, He might have said, I and they are, not one thing, but one person, because the head and body is one Christ . . . since they could not be so in themselves, separated as they are one from another by diverse pleasures and desires and uncleannesses of sin; whence they are cleansed through the Mediator, that they may be one in Him . . . through the same will most harmoniously conspiring to the same blessedness, and fused in some way by the fire of charity in one spirit.[70]

The mediation of Christ constitutes the Church as one body manifesting the love between Father and Son "by the fire of charity." If mediation conflates Christology and ecclesiology, *via* and *patria*, so, too, will it bring about a conflation of the concerns which made up the two sides of our aporia: manifestation, which seemed to do with presence, and vision, which seemed to do with lack. The apprehension of the beauty of God, in other words, will be coextensive with its appearance in the visage of the saints who apprehend. Notice furthermore that these two concerns correspond to the two ways in which we originally understood soteriology to be aesthetic for Augustine. The first sense is given in the stated objective of the *De Trinitate*: to help render its readers fit to "see" God. The second, now coextensive with the first, consists in the restoration of creation as a kind of order that manifests divine beauty. To see the convergence of these concerns is to see how salvation is aesthetic and aesthetics are doxological for Augustine.

It will take the remainder of the chapter and some of the next fully to display *how* Augustine's Christ effects the first of these aesthetic functions in the microcosm of the soul. In the remainder of this section I wish to demonstrate *that* salvation is aesthetic for Augustine, by demonstrating "macrocosmically" how Augustine's Christ effects the second of these aesthetic functions.

The aesthetics of the cross

The numerology of *De Trinitate* IV is reminiscent of both *De Musica* and *De Libero Arbitrio*, where Augustine contends for the convertibility of number and wisdom and concludes that wisdom "reaches from end to end mightily and disposes all things sweetly."[71] The aesthetic implications of this prooftext are not incidental, for in a subsequent portion of the argument (and later, in *De Lib.* III), Augustine conflates a thing's numbers with its form. We have already discussed Augustine's conflation of beauty and form; a further conflation of number and form is tantamount to a conflation of number and beauty. So it is here, as Augustine concludes that we judge the numbers of things external to the soul according to "certain laws of beauty" intrinsic to the soul. I shall elaborate on the significance of this in later sections. He then launches into a hymn to wisdom, praising wisdom because it "speak[s] to us in the beauty of every created thing."[72] As a material object is at rest, "its numbers remain in place." In motion, "its numbers vary through time."[73] In both cases these numbers are testifying to its beauty, to the numerical, "rhythmic" harmony of a created order and to the supreme beauty of the form of eternal wisdom.

De Trinitate extends this numerology further by elaborating upon the context of its ultimate unfolding: Christ's life, death and resurrection. This move corroborates our contention that salvation has an intrinsically aesthetic component. Augustine's subsequent argument corroborates it further. Noting the double death of body and soul in sin, Augustine suggests that Christ's single death and resurrection "agrees" with our double.[74] This relationship of agreement he names with the Greek *harmonia* and describes it as expressing a ratio of "the single to the double where there is the greatest consonance of coaptation."[75] Augustine then divines numerous cosmological meanings from this ratio. The ratio is contained within the ternary number, but the numbers added to reach it, one and two, when added to the ternary, make six, a number which is perfect because it is complete in its third, sixth, and half. From his estimation of the perfection of the number six, Augustine then proceeds to consider the many places in which Scripture and tradition commend this number and in which the ratio of single to double is apparent: the six days of creation, the six ages of man, the three days of the resurrection, the building up of the Church in the new temple of Christ's Body and various others.[76]

It is obvious that Augustine sets great store by the importance of this *convenientia* or *harmonia*. Yet its meaning is initially obscure. As Gerhart Ladner rightly notes, its symbolic content cannot be strictly correlative to the Trinity. For the Trinity is no more "three" in the ordinary sense than the specific "mental functions" of memory, intellect and will correspond each to a trinitarian person.[77] What, then, is the importance of these terms, and how do they relate to redemption?

The discussion in *De Trinitate* IV both includes and precedes Augustine's discussion of Christ's role as mediator, and it is this, I suggest, that provides part of the key to these passages. The christological discussions of Book XIII, where Augustine resumes this theme, further warrant this conclusion. This latter book begins much like Book XIX of *De Civitate Dei*, with an argument over the nature of beatitude and the universal will toward it. As in *De Civitate Dei*, Augustine argues that beatitude must include immortality, and that this immortality must, in turn, include the immortality of the whole person, soul and body. This conclusion then warrants both an argument for the necessity of faith, since this immortality is not yet present, and a succinct, and perfectly patristic, summation of the nature of redemption.

> "The Word was made flesh, and dwelt among us" men,—how much more credible is it that the sons of men by nature should be made the sons of God by the grace of God, and should dwell in God, in whom alone and from whom alone the blessed can be made partakers of that immortality; of which that we might be convinced, the Son of God was made partaker of our mortality?[78]

To be redeemed is to participate in the divine life. Augustine's task then becomes to display *how* the incarnate Son brings about this participation, and *why* the incarnation and passion are appropriate. Significantly, he conceives of this task not as the explanation of a necessity, of why there is no alternative to the incarnation, but in the aesthetic terms of why it is fitting. And he uses the same term from Book IV, *congruum*,[79] to describe this fittingness and a similar term, *concorditer*, to describe the indivisible work of the Son and Spirit in our redemption.[80] Indeed it is in these terms that he elaborates upon Christ's passion and defeat of the devil not simply as an act of power, but of justice: "He held back what was possible to Him, in order to do what was fitting."[81] It is crucial then to uncover the meaning of this *congruum*. Augustine's own remarks suggest that it is central to an understanding of the passion, so a closer look at the passion should illuminate the meaning of this term. And if we can discover the meaning of *this* "congruity," it will illuminate the harmony of Book IV.

In the first instance, Christ's incarnation is "suitable" because, in deigning to assume a mortal form and bear our evils, it is "demonstrated to us at how great a price God rated us, and how greatly he loved us."[82] The formulation recalls one side of our original aesthetic concern: manifestation. Yet Augustine immediately correlates this manifestation with the bestowal of gifts, which he assigns, crucially it turns out, to the mission of the Spirit in the *fides quae per dilectionem operatur*.[83] Thus Christ's descent also suggests the other side of the aesthetic concern: participation or restoration which, in a world colored by sin, entails reconciliation. This then prompts Augustine to a consideration of Romans 5 and the difficult question: "What is meant by 'justified in His blood'? What power is there in this blood? And what is meant by 'being reconciled by the death of his Son'?"[84] This reconciliation will be the key to the aesthetics of the Cross.

Immediately, Augustine rejects as incoherent the sort of propitiatory sacrifice that is often misattributed to Anselm, which would have Christ's death somehow appeasing the offended anger of the Father.[85] If the love of the Father were simply the consequence of Christ's passion, there would be no motive in the first place either for our creation or our re-creation. It must instead be the "motive" of the passion.[86] This love is the key to the aesthetics of the cross, in two ways.

The first involves the intrinsic relationship between divine descent and divine *iustitia*. The justice which defeats the devil is fitting, in part, because it is a reconciling contrary to the devil's own injustice which exhibits a kind of harmony in itself, a sort of *concordia discordis*, effected through a chiasm.[87] Whereas the devil "by the fault of his own perversity, was made a lover of power," Christ's love assumes the *forma servi*, even unto death on a cross, in humility.[88] *see note*

The second follows from the first. Christ's condescension is an extension of his good will which, as we learn from the earlier consideration of the universal will to beatitude, consists both in having what one wills and in willing well, or justly.[89] The *iustitia* of Christ must meet both conditions, and for both he must be human and divine.

The first condition is a question of capacity, the second of "form and content." Each requires the supposition of Christ's two natures. The devil's fall, which carries all creation in its train, so alienates creatures from the source of their being that the movement of their life terminates "justly" in death,[90] hence Augustine's language both of "the debt of death" and of loosing creatures from the devil's maw.[91] This requires the condescension of Christ, that he "go to the dead."[92] And for this he must be human. But he must also "illuminate" death, conquer it and restore creation to its source. And for this he must be God.

We can understand this movement more clearly as an extension of the "form and content" of Christ's good willing if we consider what it means, not just to will well, but simply to will. This is in part a question of the interrelation of *memoria*, *intellectus*, and *voluntas*. I shall take this issue up in the next section. However, by this point in *De Trinitate* Augustine has already taken up this question, in Book XI. And *voluntas* makes its appearance there under strict conditions: "[I]n all cases the will does not appear unless as the combiner of parent and offspring."[93]

When we apply this understanding of *voluntas* to the good will of the one Christ, we can see that this his good will has the same effect. His self-donation is a gift for the sake of his enemies primarily because his life is a gift of the Father, given back to the Father by the Son: "Father, into your hands I commend my spirit."[94] And yet, with the Spirit traversing the great distance of Holy Saturday, the Father returns this gift yet again, as glory, in the resurrection. Insofar as Jesus incorporates all of humanity within this exchange, Christ's good will completes the end of willing as such, uniting "parent and offspring" in God.[95] Thus Christ's good will, the origin of his *iustitia*, completes Augustine's soteriology. It shows how Christ restores creation to the love and delight between the Father and the Son. It is no accident that Augustine moves straight from a discussion of the passion to a discussion of election.[96]

A superficial reading might yield a couple of objections at this point. In fact, one might argue, Augustine has not shown how Christ saves us. His account is, by turns, mimetic and arbitrary, leaving the crucial ontological link obscure. Insofar as Christ's incarnation and passion serve a merely exemplary or hortatory function, insofar as its "purpose" is to inspire faith, there remains an ontological void between Jesus' death and ours. More negatively still, perhaps, Augustine's notion of a saving *iustitia* that somehow delivers us from a "debt" incurred by the devil seems arbitrary, and it appears to prefigure the worst ransom theories of the atonement.[97]

Both objections partake of a common error which in turn obscures other important features of Augustine's thought. They assume that one can finally draw a distinction between being and volition, or, more properly, *dilectio*, whereas it is one of Augustine's chief purposes in *De Trinitate* to show how the divine essence simply *is* love without remainder. It is this *dilectio*, which "is chiefly to be regarded in this inquiry which we make concerning the Trinity and knowing God."[98] Just as our participation in this love will finally constitute the *imago dei* for Augustine, so the ultimate convertibility of the *dilectio*, displayed in Christ's incarnation and passion, with the being of the divine essence is the positive counterpart to the negative identification of disobedience and death.[99] It is really to "death", and not the devil per se, that Augustine speaks of a debt that Christ pays, the devil serving—significantly—as the *mediator mortis*.[100] If we keep the convertibility of *dilectio* and the divine *esse* in view, the devil's mediation appears as the deathly mediation of a false love for that which, without proper referral, is nothing. It is, in effect, a mediation of death by death, a love of death under the illusion of life and a perverse mimesis of the Trinity which perverts the trinitarian image while residually retaining it.[101]

Moreover, if *dilectio* is ultimately convertible with the divine *esse*, and if everything finally *is* by participation in God, then there is no such thing as *sheer* mimesis, *mere imitatio*. Just as in our earlier discussion of signs, where things achieve their ultimate status as signs of the divine beauty by participation in it, so here a mimetic intention must already be a participation in that which we intend. And, as we shall see in subsequent sections, the dual status which Augustine attributes to Christ as *exemplum* and *sacramentum*, *scientia* and *sapientia* will bear the burden of demonstrating just this point. As the unity of eternal *sapientia* and temporal *scientia*, it will be precisely as an exemplar that Christ can mediate eternal *sapientia* to us and bind us into one ontological body. Though we have yet to see just *how* Augustine articulates this, the charity of the Spirit will be that bond, and the beauty of the exemplar will be crucial to the enticement of that charity.

> That you might know that Christ, Who is loved, is beautiful, the Prophet says, "Fairer in beauty than the children of men," His beauty surpasses [that of] all men. What is it we love in Christ—His

crucified limbs, His pierced side, or His love? When we hear that He suffered for us, what do we love? Love is loved. He loved us that we might in turn love Him; and that we might return His love He has give us His Spirit.[102]

Understanding Augustine's soteriology, and the congruity of the incarnation and passion, we can now see how this soteriology casts light on the meaning of congruity as the key to the mysterious numerology of *De Trinitate* IV and its portent of a macrocosmic, aesthetic harmony. The ratio of single to double, which Augustine so commends in the harmonious unfolding of creation, cannot chiefly refer to the relationship between the trinitarian persons themselves, who, as previously noted, are not "three" in any ordinary sense.[103] Rather the fittingness of Christ's just willing is twofold. First, it exhibits the supreme beauty of this love and the fact that Christ's entire life is thus "a manifestation of his eternal filiation."[104] Second, by manifesting this beauty, Christ incorporates us into it. The ratio of single to double and its fittingness refer to this incorporation in the "hypostatic unity" of Christ, who contains that ratio in himself in two ways: in his "three substances: God, soul, and flesh," and in the response of his single death and resurrection to our double death.[105] For this response is none other than the Son's response of love to the Father.

This manifestation and incorporation bind into indissoluble union the two sides of our aesthetic concern and make the manifestation of God inseparable from the restoration of a kind of cosmic harmony; for the apprehension of the divine beauty manifest as Christ is already a participation in the economy of that beauty.[106] As such the very manifestation and apprehension of the beauty of God in Christ is already a restoration of the harmony of creation, even if it takes the form of earnest, and is inseparable from a new order already participating in that beauty: the order of charity. Creatures of that order thus become signs of that beauty.

> "He had no form or comeliness that we should look at Him." The deformity of Christ forms you. For if He had not wished to be deformed you would not have received back the form that you lost. Therefore, He hung deformed upon the cross, but His deformity was our beauty.[107]

To say, in Augustinian terms, that manifestation already implies participation is to say that Augustinianism always presupposes a prior gift. This presupposition deprives it of an originary ground from which to begin, whether by deduction or induction. Rather it always starts *in media rei*. If this portion of my analysis has had to presuppose some of the conclusions which we have yet to reach, it is a reflection of this fact. For an account of Augustine which claims to be Augustinian will also begin *in media rei*, and will be as subject as Augustine's own thought to the aporetic truth that while the macrocosm helps to render its isomorphic microcosm more intelligible, it is equally true that the microcosm helps to illuminate the macrocosm.

This is true of the point currently in question, that the distinction between manifestation and apprehension within Augustine's aesthetic soteriology is an artificial one. The point is crucial for grasping Augustine's doxological cosmology for two reasons. First, it testifies to the transcendence of the trinitarian macrocosm by making what is at once most alterior and extrinsic interior to the microcosm of the created *mens*. Second, it makes the *mens* which attains to the status of *imago dei* a microcosm of a creation whose true form is that of the *civitas dei*. Indeed the status of the microcosmic image depends upon this civic macrocosm for its likeness.[108] The situation of the reformed creation within the unity of Christ's Body, which makes that creation an intelligible manifestation of the trinitarian *taxis*, helps to illuminate the point. Yet a full illustration of the point requires more. We must elucidate Christ's "hypostatic union" of *exemplum* and *sacramentum*, of *scientia* and *sapientia* and show how the microcosmic soul, unfolded within this union, participates in the embrace between Father and Son through the *fides quae per dilectionem operatur*. Only then will the claims of this section attain their full weight. Yet, the point remains; our restoration as icons of the divine beauty is inseparable from our vision of that beauty. Thus for Augustine salvation consists in this vision, a vision which itself manifests the beauty and love that the Trinity is. Precisely how this beauty is articulated as love, and precisely how it is manifested as Trinity to us and in us, however, are the questions to which we now turn.

Delight and the beauty of God

As we have already noted, Augustine's references both to the eternal Son and to the incarnate Christ as the *forma* or beauty of God are legion. Even though the full implications of this understanding will not be evident until the final section, we have nevertheless begun to see how Christ in his unity manifests this beauty to us and in us. It is in apprehending this beauty, which always presupposes the gift through which we apprehend, that we are incorporated more fully into the life of God.

This section is dedicated to the display of three other points, however. The first is how this beauty and its convertibility with goodness and truth are integral to the generation and procession of the second and third *personae* (the latter principally from the Father and yet from both Father and Son).[109] The second is how the convertibility of these transcendentals in God's simplicity renders that simplicity triune. The third and final point is perhaps the most important: that this convertibility is integral to the explication of God's triunity as love. This makes Christ as the *forma* or

beauty of God crucial not simply to the beauty of creation which participates in him but to the elaboration of his generation from the Father. And
it is because of the interdependence of these points and the multivalence of
the Son's beauty, that this "aesthetic" rendering of the Trinity passes over
into a doxological ontology.

Lewis Ayres has shown us how important the grammar of simplicity is to
Augustine's trinitarianism, how this grammar (along with the correlative
distinction between substantive and relative predication) serves the same
functions for Augustine that the "real distinction" does for Aquinas. It
helps to preserve the ontological difference between creature and creator,
the simultaneous difference and equality of the trinitarian *personae* and the
indivisibility of their operations, and it preserves trinitarian differentiation
by denying a substantial substrate conceptually or ontologically prior to the
distinction of persons.[110] However, this grammar does leave Augustine with
the aporetic difficulty of attempting to demonstrate how simplicity can be
triune. The so-called psychological analogy aids in this endeavor, since it
provides a triadic similitude for consideration which does not depend upon
the relation between a subject and an external object.[111] Yet Augustine
remarks that he first begins to make progress with this difficulty as he
begins to contemplate the implications of St. John's assertion that God is
love. Recognizing both that love can only be love in the act of loving and
that it must have an object, Augustine had discerned within St. John's
identification the now famous triad of lover, beloved, and love.[112]

Beauty, it turns out, is an integral part of the explication of this triad.
Augustine clarifies Hilary's designation of the *personae* as Eternity, Form
and Gift by insisting that the designation between form and eternity should
not be interpreted so as to imply the inequality of the Son, but rather the
opposite. The justification he gives for this contention, and its relationship
to the third term, is "aesthetic."

> For if an image perfectly fills the measure of that of which it is the
> image, then the image is made equal to that of which it is the image
> . . . And in respect to this image he has named form, I believe on
> account of the quality of beauty, where there is at once such great
> fitness, and prime equality, and prime likeness, differing in nothing,
> and unequal in no respect, and in no part unlike, but answering
> exactly to him whose image it is.[113]

The Son is the image of the Father because of his equality with the Father
from whom he is derived. This equality is constitutive of the Son's beauty, a
kind of self-exceeding splendor constituted as beauty precisely in a relation
of "erotic" love.[114] For insofar as the Son is a reflection of the Father who
speaks the Word, the Son's own beauty is constituted in the *activity* of a
response.[115] This means that the Son too is beautiful in being ecstatic, in

being a "surplus" to himself. After stating how all things are contained within the beauty of this form, Augustine continues

> Therefore that unspeakable conjunction of the Father and His Image is not without fruition, without love, without joy. Therefore that love, delight, felicity, or blessedness, if indeed it can worthily be expressed by any human word, is called by him, in short, Use; and is the Holy Spirit in the Trinity, not begotten, but the sweetness of the begetter and of the begotten, filling all creatures according to their capacity with abundant bountifulness and copiousness, that they may keep their proper order and rest satisfied in their proper place.[116]

The final remark recalls the aesthetic soteriology of the previous section. By introducing delight in conjunction with love, Augustine also raises a crucial new point: that the convertibility of goodness and beauty is integral to the explication of the Trinity as triune love and of love as trinitarian. To elaborate this point, it is necessary to propose, in addition to divine simplicity, two more "grammatical rules."

Both rules can be inferred from Augustine's consideration of the "*Meno*" aporia in Books VIII and IX, and terminate in a crucial Augustinian conclusion: "A word is knowledge together with love."[117] The first, and its inverse, emerges as Augustine considers the paradoxical question of how we can know and love a just man when we ourselves are not just. The rule is that one cannot love what one does not in some sense know, and that one's activity in knowing entails the love of some object for whose sake the known object moves us to attention.[118] The rule is doubly significant, for it suggests not only that every act of intellect is also an act of will and vice versa, but that the formal objects of each, the true in the former case and the good in the latter, must likewise be mutually entailed in, convertible with, each other. And of course the grammar of simplicity necessitates this anyway.

The second rule lies latent in that remark cited from *De Trinitate* VI. It is worth revisiting.

> That conjunction . . . is not without fruition, without love, without joy. Therefore that love, delight, felicity, or blessedness is called by him, in short; Use; and is the Holy Spirit in the Trinity.

One can easily see how this remark, when coupled with the grammar of simplicity, concludes in the recognition of a third *persona* bearing all the predicates attached to the other divine persons. More subtly buried in it, however, is the role that delight in the beautiful must play in explicating this conjunction of love, a point that will later prove crucial to an Augustinian account of volition. The point, and our rule, is this. The transcendental conjunction of the true and the good entailed in the first rule must have the character and splendor of the beautiful in order to account for the movement of our affection. That is, truth and goodness must *delight* us, and thus be convertible with the beautiful, in order to move our love. "For unless there were a grace and beauty in things, they could in nowise move us."[119] Thus immediately upon correlating the beauty of the Son with his response to the Father, Augustine remarks:

> For in that Trinity is the supreme source of all things, and the most perfect beauty, and the most blessed delight. Those three, therefore, both seem to be mutually determined to each other and are in themselves infinite . . . in that highest Trinity one is as much as three together, nor are two anything more than one. And they are infinite in themselves. So both each are in each, and all in each, and each in all, and all in all, and all are one.[120]

Though Augustine's chief analogue for explicating the Trinity is the lover, beloved, love triad, the grammar of simplicity requires that we transpose that triad into this one: source, beauty, and delight. Taking the two triads together helps to illuminate them both, by laying bare how this love is *both* erotic *and* productive and how the convertible good and beautiful are both principle, movement and end of the triad of lover, love, and beloved which God is. In this way, filiation and spiration pass over into aesthetics, but only because aesthetics itself passes over into doxology.

The grammar of simplicity is crucial here. Augustine insists, on the one hand, that whatever it might mean to call the Son wisdom or the Spirit love, it cannot mean that the Father begets his wisdom in such a way so as not to be his own wisdom, nor that the Spirit is Love in such a way that the Father is not his own love. Just as one alone is not less than three together, nor three together more than any one, so whatever is predicated substantially of each singly must also be predicated of each separately and each together, without any change in quantity or quality.[121] Likewise, as we have already noted in discussing the missions, to say that the Word was in the *principio* with the Father is to say that it is with the Word that the Son was sent, such that being sent is the work of both the Father and his Word.

When we consider the filiation of the Son from the side of the Father in light of the grammatical strictures we have set forth, we can see that the Father's knowledge and love of the Son cannot be the "consequence" of his being begotten. Rather the Son is in some sense already "given" in the Father's very giving of life to the Son. This is part of what it means to say that "both the Father is with the Son, and the Son with the Father, always and inseparably."[122] To say that the Son is always already given in and with the Father is not to say that he is his own origin. Yet as the end of the Father's intention and gift, the Son must in some sense already "provoke" or elicit that intention as a principle. This is due partly to the requirements of simplicity. The Father is never Father without the Son. However, another of our rules comes into play here as well. The Son must "provoke" the love of the Father because one cannot love what one does not know.

Hence though the Father in his productivity "intends" the Son, the Son's beauty is in some sense the principle of his own begottenness, eliciting the Father's intention just as, in Aquinas' subsequent treatment, the will is at once moved both by itself *and* by its object as end and principle.[123] The movement, considered under the first aspect, has "the good" as its "formal object." Considered under the second aspect, it has "the beautiful" as its "formal object." Simplicity dictates, however, that this division can only be a division according to the formal aspect under which we consider it—a division according to idea, not according to being. The "movement" is one; the "object" is one. The beautiful and good are therefore, once again, convertible.

Thus the Son's beauty turns out to be the key to explicating the Trinity as both *eternal* love and eternal *love*: first, because it is this beauty which elicits the *delectatio* and the *eros* of the Father; second, because the convertibility of this beauty with the good makes the Son himself the object of the Father's intention. Yet there is a still simpler way to put the matter. The Son is begotten out of the Father's *delight* in the beauty of the Son, but the Father's delight must presuppose that the Father is never Father without the Son.

We have seen how the assertion that "God is love" requires the transcendental convertibility of the good and the beautiful.[124] Let us now see how love renders this simplicity triune. We can see the role of the Spirit's spiration in the Son's filiation when we understand this filiation as a consequence of the Father's delight in the Son; for the Father's delight in the Son is intrinsic to the Son's being begotten. Moreover one can see, when viewed from the side of the Son, how this results in an economy of gift between Father and Son that exhibits the inseparability of operations and the procession of the Spirit *principaliter ex patre filioque*. One can even begin to see how this *theologia* is manifest in the life of Christ as a doxological sacrifice of the love, received as giving itself, from the Father, a giving *responsio* constitutive of the Son as the form and beauty of God. Creation truly becomes creation *in Christ*, by participating in this exchange, and in so doing becomes a "sign" of the love which is its origin and end.[125]

Augustine's account of the filiation and procession displays this logic. Developing a christological grammar appropriate to Christ's two natures, Augustine appropriates the Pauline distinction between the *forma dei* and the *forma servi*. This allows him to get a grip on difficult scriptural passages such as the assertion in John 14 that the Father is greater than the Son and Jesus' statement in John 5 that "The Son can do nothing of Himself but what he sees the Father do."[126]

The John 5 pericope is crucial. As a way of asserting both the filiation of the Son from the Father, the indivisibility of operations, and the substantial equality of each, Augustine takes this statement to mean that the Son is constituted precisely in "seeing the Father."

> It remains, therefore, that these texts are so expressed, because the life of the Son is unchangeable as that of the Father is, and yet He is of the Father; and the working of the Father and the Son is indivisible, and yet so to work is given him from the Father; and the Son so sees the Father that He is the Son in the very seeing of Him.[127]

Simplicity demands that there can be no division between the "form" of the Son's vision of the Father and the "content" of that vision, a fact reflected in Augustine's conclusion that it is love itself which is loved in the Trinity.[128] To say then that the Son is constituted as the Son in the seeing of the Father is to say that the "form" of his seeing must be the "same" as the "content" of what he sees. What, then, is the "content" of the Son's vision of the Father? "Work," that is to say, the Son's sight of the Father is the sight of his giving life to the Son out of delight in his beauty. Yet since simplicity demands that there be no distinction between form and content, and since the "content" of the Son's sight of the Father cannot be separated from the "form" of his seeing, the Son's very sight of the Father giving life to the Son must itself be a *giving*.

> For to be of the Father, that is, to be born of the Father, is to Him nothing else than to see the Father; and to see Him working is nothing else than to work with Him: but therefore not from Himself, because He is not from Himself.[129]

We can thus see how the Son is constituted, in his seeing of the Father, in giving. Yet again, simplicity requires us to understand that God gives nothing in himself which is not God; so the gift inherent in the Son's sight of the Father's giving, the fruit of their exchange, must have predicated of it all that is predicated of the Father and the Son. This gift is thus constituted as a third person, proceeding *principally* from the Father, but from the Father and the Son.[130] This gift of the Father "cannot be passive, an object to be passed on by the agency of Father and Son."[131] Rather the gift itself must be giving. "For he is given as a gift of God in such way that He Himself also gives Himself as being God."[132] Thus the Son's vision of the Father, in and with the Spirit, is inseparable from his own gift of love to the Father, a gift which is himself a gift of the Father. The Father gives giving to the Son who gives in return. Conversely, this gift to the Father or rather this giving constitutive of the Son's generation from the Father, is inseparable from and convertible with the Son's vision of the Father. And since this

52

giving is operative *both* in the Father's intention of, his love for the Son *and* in the Son's vision of the Father, he uniquely merits the name of love, being at once God and a divine person in his own right and the love of the Father and the Son.[133]

There are a couple of things to notice here that will prove important in subsequent chapters, at both the ontological and anthropological levels, since Augustine understands humanity to be created in the image and ordered toward the likeness of God.[134] To say that the Son is "constituted" in his vision of the Father and that this vision is itself convertible with a giving is to recognize two things. First, personhood is *constituted* not primarily as substance but precisely in the *act* of reciprocated giving.[135] It is constituted ontologically, to the extent that this adjective has application to God, *doxologically*. Consequently, "it is *God* who prays," as Herbert McCabe so beautifully put it.[136] Secondly, and despite the passive character of our terms for "begotten," we can see that there is no passivity in this generation.[137] The Son's very reception of himself is itself constituted in act, in the act of seeing the Father which is also a giving from delight in the recipient. Together these points will not only determine the meaning of *De Trinitate's* goal, what it is to gaze upon the divine beauty, but what it will mean truly "to see" at all.

We can illuminate this point by returning to the structure of intentionality. Though he insists on the great unlikeness between our minds and the Trinity, Augustine asks us to consider, near the end of Book XV, the mutual entailment of memory, love and knowledge in each other and the implication that we cannot love what we do not know and remember, cannot remember what we do not know and return to through love, and we cannot know what love does not seek and what we do not remember.[138] Hence while we can distinguish between these three, we can finally never discretely delineate them. Love, knowledge, and memory each seem to have the others entailed within them.

We may thus attribute to the Son's vision of the Father, the distance of a certain *studium*, an *eros*, a zealous seeking, so that we may say of the Spirit, as Rowan Williams does, that it is "love in search of an object."[139] For one only sees what claims one's attention, and it would have no claim if it could not be formulated as the object of a seeking or as at least proximately related to an object of desire. In either case, a certain construal of infinite distance is required.

However this "distance" must be disciplined by the imperatives entailed in our various grammatical rules. For to say that the Spirit is love in search of an object is already to invoke the object as principle of the seeking, since one cannot love what one does not know. Hence this infinite "distance" of extension and intention in the erotic spiration of the third *persona* is not the distance of *lack*. Rather it is the infinite distance of an infinite plenitude, of the infinite determination of love to itself, a distance which is filled with the "abundant bountifulness and copiousness" of "the most perfect beauty" and intended, extended and traversed by "the most blessed delight."[140]

Augustine's account also allows us to see Christ's passion manifesting these trinitarian relations in terms that he himself does not quite articulate, but which are consistent with his aim, as Christ's submission to death and his resurrection together display both God's triune love and the infinite distance intrinsic to that love.[141] From the foregoing account we can see that the Son assumes a position of infinite distance from the Father precisely *because* he is the perfect image of the Father's love. For as we have just seen, this image, as the image of a plenitudinous love, entails an infinite intention and extension in the Spirit who proceeds from the Father and the Son and "causes" each to abide in the unity of the other. To assert this distance as infinite is to assert at once both the unity, identity and equality between the Father and Son and a difference between the Father and the Son which is infinitely *greater* than that between God and creation, since God has no real relation to creation and since not even non-being is opposite to God.[142] This distance and difference can thus encompass creation to the point of the Son's union with a death which even exceeds creation's exile, transfiguring the very meaning of death. This soteriological point is reminiscent of one made by Balthasar: "that the Redeemer, in his solidarity with the dead, has spared them the integral experience of death."[143]

This elaboration of the divine life as love allows one to take Christ's passion seriously without destroying the Trinity or slipping into a patripassianism that collapses the relationship of Father to Son into a self-negating dialectic secretly celebrating sin and death. To the contrary, it is *only* if the distance between the Father and the Son is itself God, only, that is, if God is love and love is trinitarian, that the passion is intelligible as a divine act. The distance which encompasses our death must be a divine distance intrinsic to the Father's self-donation of love in the Son, the Son's active, giving reception of this gift from the Father and the procession of the Spirit from each. These active relations by which the Son and Spirit differentially go forth while remaining in the Father can then be transposed into the events of the economy: the incarnation, Christ's self-donation and the Father's delight in raising him to new life in the unity of the Spirit. Though given the prominence of the "*Meno*" aporia and the codetermination of the universal and particular, we must simultaneously affirm that it is the events of the biblical economy which reveal the Trinity as love. To see Christ's passion and resurrection as manifesting the active, reciprocal donation intrinsic to the divine life is to see once again that this passion is not passive. Rather this "passivity" is encompassed within the perfect actuality of his reception of active giving from the Father: hence the importance of those Gospel texts which insist on Jesus' power to lay down and take up his life.

Christ's work as savior in assuming our mortality is an expression of the life of divine love. As such this work is inseparable from the Son's status as the *forma* or beauty of the Father, in whom the Father delights, a feature of Augustine's thought integral to the articulation of that love. Consequently, Christ's work as savior is inseparable from his work as mediator in recalling us to the divine life, and his work as mediator is inseparable from his many "functions" as the *forma* or beauty of God. If it is the work of Augustine's Christ as the mediator between God and humanity to unfold us as creation and recall us as salvation within this movement of the divine life, and if this *creatio*, *formatio*, and, ultimately, this *conversio* occur within the unity of his enhypostasization, then our *conversio* will be a participation in the Father's delight in the beauty of the Son, a beauty constituted as a perfect reflection in the Son's responsive vision of the Father. This participation is itself a reception; this reception is itself a giving. Thus once again our apprehension of this vision will be inseparable from our becoming a manifestation, as charity and as doxology, of the very beauty which we seek. Which is to say, that the Son's mediation, and our participation in it as his Body, will entail the inseparable operation of the Spirit expressing the mutual delight between the Father and the Son. It is the task of the final section to disclose the vestige of this image in us by demonstrating the inseparability of this operation, its intimation in our every action and in all our knowledge, and its manifestation in the Body of Christ, mediated by its Head.

The Body of Christ and the eros of faith

In the two previous sections, we have seen first how Augustine conceives of salvation as a restoration of the "aesthetic" harmony of creation which is both visible *to* us in Christ and manifest *in* us "typologically" through participation in the unity of Christ's humanity and divinity. This unity is the archetype of the ratio of time to eternity and indeed the transcendent form in which time, as the *modus vivendi* of creation, unfolds and participates.[144] This disrupts a strictly linear conception of time, crossing the horizontal "line" with a vertical axis for a conjunction that is both present at and formally determinative of each point along the line. This is the ontological basis for the typology. Secondly, we have shown that this participatory harmony of creation, effected through Christ's Body, is itself understood as a participation through love in Christ the supreme beauty, who is constituted as such through the Father's delight in him and his responsive vision of the Father. In consequence both the "form" and "content" of our participation are doxological, and this marks at once *both* our participation in the Son's response to the Father and our reception of the gift of the Holy Spirit shared between the Father and the Son.

Salvation is aesthetic. It consists in the restoration of beauty from the beautiful itself, and it takes the form of the love of the beautiful—because the beautiful *is* love, and because apart from participation in this love there is finally nothing. Jesus' incarnation and passion unfolds and manifests the beauty of trinitarian love in time. Yet Christ does not merely manifest this beauty to us, but mediates our participation in it. The numerical harmonies, the "double mediation" of the Head and Body of Christ, and indeed the very aporetic structure of intentionality, each require the mediation of the beloved—both as first cause and principle of our love. So too does the temporal referral of end upon end.[145] For Augustine the unfolding of creation is also a *reformatio* situated within the interval of delight between the Father and the Son and manifesting that delight at each point of its unfolding.[146] It is for this that Augustine will be able to say "the whole nature of the universe proclaims that it has a most excellent creator."[147]

In this section, I intend to examine this mediation more closely and to demonstrate more clearly how all of the themes we have heretofore been considering converge in Augustine's Christology. I shall do this by considering three facets of that Christology. The first is the "hypostatic union" of Christ.[148] Christ's union of humanity and divinity is the union of creator with creature, *sapientia* with *scientia*, and time with eternity. Consequently, Christ himself becomes paradigmatic for the ratio of time to eternity and, furthermore, becomes the *context* for the *reformatio* by which creation is recalled to its God. One important result of this conclusion in subsequent chapters will be that it offsets the ways in which Augustine is typically understood as a dualist. The second facet of Augustine's Christology under consideration here is the aesthetic "function" of Augustine's Christ as he both manifests the divine beauty and mediates our participation in it. The last incorporates the other two. It consists in showing how Jesus, in manifesting this beauty and mediating it to us, simultaneously displays the indivisible operations of the trinitarian *personae* as the beauty of transcendent charity. This account should then be taken as a rebuttal to the line of criticism noted in Chapter 1, which accuses Augustine of slighting both the Trinity and the temporal economy for an atemporal dialectic between a unitary God and the soul. There is something both positivist and untheological about this criticism, as it inserts Christ's life into a linear conception of time and history defined independently of that life. By contrast, it must be asserted that the meaning of the temporal economy depends upon how Christ defines the relationship between time and eternity. When we understand this, it becomes clear that the economy and time itself manifest trinitarian love and that Augustine actually pushes this love more deeply into the economy than his critics. Both points intersect in our doxological love of God's beauty. This will change the sense of the so-called psychological analogy.

"Through him we travel to him": Christ as the
context of salvation

Central to the point that the "hypostatic union" of Augustine's Christ is the context for creation's *reformatio* is the claim, demonstrated persuasively by Lewis Ayres, that our "progress in faith and contemplation occurs *within* the two natured person."[149] Augustine signals the fundamental importance of this point at the very outset of *De Trinitate*. He quotes approvingly from Romans 11.36, "For of Him and through Him and in Him are all things."[150] And he soon invokes Colossians 3.3–4, "Your life is hid with Christ in God; when Christ, who is our life shall appear, then you shall also appear with Him in glory."[151] The first passage is important since it occurs at the outset of the work and signals one of its central themes, but the second is particularly telling. It is always significant when Augustine cobbles together disparate Scripture passages to make a theological point, and here he couples this latter pericope with an excerpt from 1 Corinthians 13.12: "We see now through a glass in an enigma, but then face to face."[152] By linking these texts, Augustine thus joins what it means to be "in Christ" to progress in our apprehension of the vision of God.

I have already intimated that three correlative pairs, *exemplum/sacramentum*, *tempus/aeternatis* and *scientia/sapientia*, are integral to this understanding.[153] A look at Book XIII confirms this. Analyzing the prologue to John's Gospel, Augustine allocates the first fourteen verses to a concern for the contemplation of things eternal. The remainder he takes to be concerned with *scientia* of temporal things. Having made this division, and having already situated the universal pursuit of beatitude within the ambit of the incarnation and passion, Augustine reaches a famous conclusion:

> Therefore Christ is our knowledge, and the same Christ is also our wisdom. He himself implants in us faith concerning temporal things. He himself shows forth the truth concerning eternal things. Through Him we reach on to Him: we stretch through knowledge to wisdom; yet we do not withdraw from one and the same Christ "in whom are hidden all the treasures of wisdom and knowledge."[154]

This remark is vital for establishing Christ's unity as the context of creation's salvific *reformatio*. If we are to understand the full implications of this assertion, we must come to grips with several important points which lie latent in it. First, the christological unity of *sapientia* and *scientia* undermines the opposition in Augustine's dualistic contrast of time and eternity without dialectically collapsing them into a "higher synthesis." Augustine remains adamant to preserve the ontological difference between God's transcendent immutable and mutable natures, just as the hypostatic union preserves the human and divine natures as distinct.[155] Yet, as we shall see further in the next chapter, it is *because* of this difference and not in spite of it that Augustine is able to arrive at a proto-Chalcedonian construal of Christ's unity. This will prove indispensable to his understanding of both grace and nature. Rather than an antithetical contrast between *scientia* and *sapientia*, contemplation and action, eternity and time, this unity suggests rather a complementary relationship. Eternal beauty, the object of contemplation, is manifest precisely *through* the unfolding of the temporal—much like the musical distinction between ratio and interval in the earlier section—in profound union with it. Indeed, as already suggested, the analogical unity of the temporal is itself mediated by the *ergon* and the *mysterium* which is triune charity.[156]

Secondly, this unity defies any attempt to erect a rigid border or an anti-thesis between the "inner" and "outer" man. Instead it suggests not only a mutual instruction between them, but also that "interiority" is constituted precisely through radical exteriority.[157] One reason lies in the theory of action implicit in the earlier trinitarian speculations: the alterior object of intention, formally the intelligible good, must function as the first cause and principle of the intention under the aspect of the beautiful. It follows then that a proper Augustinian response to the divine voice is not a flight from the temporal, but a proper referral of the temporal to its eternal origin and end. And by insisting upon the mutual entailment of appetibility and intelligibility, Augustine even pushes this sequence of referrals back into intelligibility itself, into the very derivation of intelligible species "one from the other, the second from the first, the third from the second, the fourth from the third,"[158] which are to be "referred to that final end by which we will blessedly" by "several wills that are bound together."[159]

These observations, thirdly, rebut the charge that Augustine sets the soul in atemporal apposition to a de-trinitized God at the expense of the temporal economy. In a manner perhaps reminiscent of the Platonic isomorphism between the soul and the City, Augustine has in fact made the soul a microcosm of the ecclesial macrocosm which is now the proper form of that economy. And since this "civic" macrocosm is now itself a microcosm of trinitarian *dilectio*, this makes the *civitas dei*, the ecclesial body with Christ at the head, once again the middle term between the soul and God, a fact apparent in the very ecclesial language Augustine employs to describe his interior life. This isomorphism is apparent throughout the Augustinian corpus, the most obvious example being the way in which the soul and the heavenly City are "reformed" and constituted in the doxological sacrifice of Christ, "thus becoming acceptable to God because of what [they have] received from his beauty."[160] Yet further examples abound, as when Augustine takes the seven ages of man as a recapitulation in microcosm of the days of creation with its metahistorical seventh day, which redounds, in turn, to the harmonies in Augustine's "numerical" or "musical" ontology.[161]

This relationship of microcosm to macrocosm isn't merely one of analogy or similarity. Augustine is adamant in denying that one can isolate any proper *proportio* between the soul and the Trinity.[162] Rather the relationship is one of the former's participation in the ecstatic gratuity of the latter, which again requires the mediation of the middle term: the Body of Christ.[163] For in order to make sense of a temporal sequence of referrals, one must presuppose a historical *civitas*, an *ordo amoris*, facilitating both the practicability and intelligibility of such a referral, a claim which both presupposed and confirms our earlier treatment of signs.[164]

Hence soul and city alike assume and enact a kind of latent political doxology in the service of some set of goods. And the relationship of *sapientia* to *scientia*, which confounds the borders between soul and city, implicitly raises the question of the Augustinian doctrine of election by situating both the soul and "the other city" within the unity of Christ's Body. From within its vantage one discerns that "if you regard them carefully, every kind of creature and every movement that can be considered . . . speaks to our instruction . . . like so many voices crying out to us, telling us to recognize their creator."[165] Such a regard, a modification of perspective and knowledge, is necessarily inseparable from a modification of desire.

These three points all attest to the first major facet of Augustine's Christology, that the hypostatic union of divinity and humanity, time and eternity, is the context of the *reformatio* of creation. The coincidence of time and eternity, creature and creator, *via* and *patria* in Christ disturbs the traditional ways of reading Augustine as a dualist. We "travel through" (*per ipsum pergimus ad ipsum*) Christ in time, which is in Christ, to reach Christ.[166]

This not only makes life in time the complementary means to eternity, but also transposes the question of the relation of the eternal creator to temporal creation onto a different plane. The former is now understood as transcendent love; the latter as Church which participates in and manifests the former. Hence the effect is to transpose the question of the relationship of eternity to time into a question of the relationship of Christ the Head to his Body, and thus ultimately, of the relationship of the Son to the Father. Within this construal, time and eternity are not mere antitheses. Rather time is again unfolded within and held in coherence by the interval of eternal delight and love between the Father and the Son—a delight which is *ubique totum*.[167] The temporal traverses—and in so doing, *manifests*—the Son's gift response to the gifting of the Father. Indeed just as Augustine says "the Trinity, which is inseparable in itself, is manifested separably by the appearance of the visible creature," so one could say that the Son's response to the Father is the very form of time's passing.[168] For the union between head and body is a dynamic one: the union is now *for the purpose* of a future fulfillment, the head drawing the body."[169] And the question of the relation of eternity to time is a question of this dynamic.

Exemplum et sacramentum: *Christ as mediator*

The preceding analysis suffices to establish *that* Augustine conceives of the one Christ as the form and "location," the ontological context both for his cosmology and the *exercitatio mentis* of the *De Trinitate*. And as we suggested earlier in the chapter, his role as the context of creation's *reformatio* is inseparable from his work as mediator and his manifestation of the indivisible work of the Trinity. The purpose of this subsection is to display the relationship between those two roles, to show how Jesus is mediator because he manifests the indivisible work of the Trinity, or—to put it differently—*how* the one Christ "functions" within the trinitarian ontology which Jesus himself manifests.

Like the "purpose"of the incarnation, the question of its "function" can be problematic, depending upon whether one appeals to criteria internal or external to the Christian narrative in posing it. Augustine, of course, fits the first description, and this is the question to which he has set himself. He states that the purpose of his christological speculations in Book IV is to show "why and how Christ was sent in the fullness of time by the Father," to the end that "our faith by seeing shall come to be truth."[170] It was partly in virtue of this purpose that Christ's incarnation is said to be "fitting," though I have tried to extend the implications of that term to Augustine's understanding of justice and to his understanding of our participation in the doxological beauty of God.[171] Yet more pertinent to our point here is that Augustine states that Christ is mediator incorporating our double to his single, and us into the concord between giver and given, precisely in virtue of this "purpose" and "function."[172]

Earlier we considered the strange numerology of Book IV and concluded that Christ's mediation restores creation to its participation in the delight between the Father and the Son, which restores, in turn, a kind of aesthetic harmony. The christological union of Creator and creature, which serves as the context of this *reformatio*, underscores this conception. A closer inspection of Book IV reveals that Christ's dual status as *exemplum* and *sacramentum*, which follows from his unity, is integral to this mediation and is thus the locus of this function. Commenting on Christ's harmonization of our double death by his single resurrection, Augustine writes,

> Therefore, on account of this double death of ours, our Saviour appointed his single death, and to cause both our resurrections, He appointed beforehand and set forth in sacrament and example his own resurrection. For He was not a sinner or impious, that, as though dead in spirit, He should need to be renewed in the inner man, and to be recalled as it were to the life of justice by repentance; but being clothed in mortal flesh, and in that alone dying, in that alone rising again, in that alone did He answer to

> both for us; since in it was wrought a sacrament as regards the
> inner man, and an example as regards the outer.[173]

There are several important points packed into this. First, stretched out
between our two deaths and resurrections is an interval of time coextensive
with a second interval, between the full union of the ecclesial Body with
Christ the Head, that is now the form of time itself.[174] A second implication
will become clearer as we proceed. In the unity of Christ as *exemplum* for the
outer man and *sacramentum* for the inner, there is both a certain "erotic"
distance between the inner and outer man and an erasure of the border
dividing one from the other. Third, the many senses of Christ as *exemplum*
suggest once again Christ as the *forma* or beauty of God, and this will have
important consequences when the agent's relationship to this exemplar is
situated within the ambit both of Christ's unity and the trinitarian gift.

Let us consider this now from two interrelated angles. The first concerns
the implications of construing Christ's exemplary function as the visible
manifestation of the beauty of God. The second concerns how the convertibility
of the exemplary and sacramental functions locates our every action
within the unity of Christ's person and how, subsequently, this impinges
upon his trinitarian psychology and the trinitarian similitude in us.

Equating Christ's exemplary status with his manifestation of the beauty
of the Father raises the question of how this beauty functions within the
purposes of Augustine's soteriology as outlined heretofore. We have
already seen this function in the trinitarian archetype considered from the
"erotic" angle. The Son's beauty was understood to provoke the intention
of the Father even as his goodness was the object of that intention. When we
consider further that this beauty is constituted precisely in the Son's
responsive vision, his reply of gratuity, to the giving of the Father, we can
anticipate Augustine's response. "[W]e *have to be persuaded* how much God
loved us, lest from despair we should not dare to look up to Him."[175]

Augustine here invests the beauty of the Word, that beauty which manifests
the Son to our sight, with the character and function of eloquence. As
beauty it has a certain splendor which delights us and thus moves us to the
love of love itself.[176] In so doing, it draws us into its ambit. In other words,
Christ's exemplary function is *rhetorical*; he is the sign of signs, the *plenitudo*
and *finis* of all signs, whose purpose is to delight and captivate our love.
"When I am lifted up from the earth, I will draw all people to myself."[177]
It is thus that he is able to "draw us towards the Father and overcome
our obsession with the material."[178] Already we have seen how Augustine
understands Christ's passion as a manifestation of the beauty of divine love
that restores the harmony between creature and Creator. This observation
only deepens that assessment. For Augustine even conceives of the cross in
"rhetorical" fashion, asserting in his commentary on Psalm 127 that what is
loved in our vision of the crucified Christ is love itself.[179] This is not because

Augustine minimizes the crucifixion, but because he understands the passion to manifest the eternal doxology. By the captivation of our love, we are drawn into this doxology and slowly cleansed to contemplate the truth which is this love itself. This contemplation is thus itself doxological.

There are numerous ways in which Augustine understands Christ to fulfill this exemplary function, to move us to contemplation precisely through action, through "things which were wrought in time with a view to produce faith."[180] Robert Dodaro sees this structure at work in Augustine's comments in *Epistula* 55 and in *De gratia testamenti noui* (*ep.* 140), where Augustine elaborates on Ephesians 3.16–19. "The 'breadth . . . length . . . and height' about which Paul spoke represents the exemplum: the justice of Christ as it is seen in the crucifixion. The image of the crucified Christ functions as a text."[181]

Augustine does not stop, however, at the level of exemplary symbolization. Instead he invests this cruciform *figura* with an open quality that draws us onward and more deeply into itself. This is entirely consonant with the "theology of language" in *De Doctrina Christiana*. In Christ who *is* his doctrine, there is no gap between sign and signified, form and content.[182] And since the divine *delectatio* which is intrinsically productive is itself the *plenitudo* and *finis* of the signs, neither the signified is exhausted in the sign, nor the sign exhausted in itself. Rather the sign is generative of a plenitude of meanings precisely as a consequence of the plenitude which informs it. This implies a level of action intrinsic to the exemplar but not identical to it.

> However the "depth" (*altitudo/profunditas*) mentioned in the Pauline text "refers" to the hidden character (*absconditas/occultum*) of *sacramentum* or *mysterium* symbolised in the extension of the cross beneath the surface. It is this invisible portion of the cross which "supports" the visible, "textual" *figura crucis*. Augustine referred to this "depth" as *sacramentum* and *mysterium* . . . Although we can not be conscious of it, it is by means of this mystery that we recognise and understand whatever we do of the *figura crucis*; it "presents" us the image of Christ's justice. We are able to interpret Christ's teaching on justice because the source of that teaching, and therefore its meaning, interpretation and proper practical application by the Christian, must be said to derive from the mystery which is *gratia Christi*.[183]

The interplay between Christ's exemplary and sacramental functions exhibits the same formal structure as the "*Meno* aporia" of *De Trinitate* VIII, a point which will later prove important. Of more immediate significance is the rhetorical nature of these dual functions and how it displays the formal relationship between *eros* and the beautiful. Interpreting Christ's very flesh as a veil of the glory of the Father, Augustine makes our relationship to the incarnate Christ erotic.[184] Dodaro concludes,

> in *De peccatorum meritis et remissione* Augustine suggested for the first time that the structure of the unity of natures in Christ (unum) accounts for the hiddenness of religious knowledge: *sapientiae atque scientiae thesauris in Christo absconditis*. This led him to assert that the moral ambivalence which Christians experience . . . is a phenomenon which can best be interpreted in the light of the incarnation. The incarnation is treated in this context as a divine rhetoric, the purpose of which is to teach and exhort (commendare) Christians.[185]

Is Augustine then a kind of closet Heideggerian, implying that God perpetuates a kind of transcendental deceit? Hardly. Augustine does not interpret the veil of Christ's flesh (and subsequently, the veil of scriptural signs) as a kind of cruel trick masking the vacuous wake of an *esse* revealed to be nothing.[186] Rather he interprets the veil as a "cloud of flesh" which at once tempers for our eyes the blinding brightness of the divine plenitude and reveals that plenitude as infinite love. [187] We will eventually see how the erotic "distance" insinuated here manifests the donative character of this plenitude. More immediately, however, we should note that it defies a totalizing gaze as surely as any *nihil*. For, as Catherine Pickstock puts it, it follows from the bountiful character of the divine infinity that it is always "more." Therefore one can "only experience it positively via the process of slipping away from it."[188] "In the process of uncovering what is essentially mystery we do not transform its content into a clear perception."[189] Augustine invests Christ's flesh with the structure of a secret, but its secrecy results from its unity with a plenitude of love, such that this "slipping away" is actually a "movement toward" which coextends with Christ the Head drawing the Body to himself. This movement will eventually manifest our participation in the indivisible operations of the Trinity, in the gift of the Spirit proceeding from the Father and the Son.

Christ's exemplary status therefore does not exhaust the plenitude it reveals. Rather the very structure of the *exemplum* reveals this plenitude to be inexhaustible, to be more than we can grasp. Thus our grasping must itself take the form of a letting go, a gift, which makes us partakers in the Son's response to the Father. This is built in to the very structure of Christ's rhetorical function, but it does not complete it. In order fully to glimpse that function and Christ's mediation in all its salvific depth, we must consider from a second angle the unity of Christ's exemplary and sacramental functions.[190]

Christ's exemplary and sacramental functions unveil an aporia which shows us once again to be situated within the christological unity. The designation of Christ as *exemplum* recalls our earlier discussion of signs, and this creates a problem of recognition which makes Christ the paradigm instance of the dilemma of *De Trinitate* VIII: the recognition and love of the just man when we are not what we love. This problem is compounded by another already familiar from our consideration of the trinitarian *personae*. To make Christ an *exemplum* which we seek is also to open up what appears to be an infinite distance between us and Christ as the object of our seeking, a distance which requires the mediation of that object as the principle of our seeking. It will require, in the terms of our earlier discussion, that Christ be both "the reality to be known and the language for its understanding."[191]

There are, in fact, several distances here, coinciding in "perpendicular" relation to one another. The *figura* of Christ is itself mediated to us through the unfolding of his Body in time, which is unfolded and mediated in turn within the Son's eternal relationship to the Father. So Christ's exemplary status evokes a kind of temporal distance.[192] Yet the distance insinuated between Christ the *exemplum* and his Body, while inclusive of the temporal distance, is no more reducible to it than the musical ratio is reducible to the interval of its passing.

There is a second distance built into Christ's exemplary status. The very presence of an exemplar which we intend and love implies an infinite distance between the intention and its fulfillment, a distance which from one point of view, appears as the distance of a *lack*. As Elizabeth Anscombe puts it, "The primitive sign of wanting is *trying to get*."[193] Plato understood this, as Jacobi would much later in contending against the sufficiency of Fichte's "absolute I."[194] Augustine's own argument against the sufficiency of pagan virtue in *De Civitate Dei* XIX, where the very presence of virtue testifies to the irascibility of our condition, puts the same fundamental point in different form.

That point is this. Insofar as any activity, including philosophical activity, is *purposive*, it confirms its own openness and insufficiency. "Trying to get" means "not yet having."[195] And yet insofar as our "trying to get" is only intelligible in virtue of its object, we affirm the very thing which we do not yet have. Since all activity—even thinking and knowing—entails desire on Augustinian terms, even the minutest human action exhibits this openness.[196] So in making Christ an exemplar who is the object of our love and intention, Augustine opens an infinite distance between the body and the head, between the exemplar and the less than exemplary.[197] This distance is the distance of *faith*.

Augustine is not as explicit in the *De Trinitate* as he is elsewhere in insisting that faith is an intrinsic and inescapable part of any human community.[198] Yet if we press this logic to its limit we can see that Augustine in fact goes beyond even this necessity, and this begins to illuminate the relationship between his Christology and the trinitarian similitude in us. In making desire intrinsic to all intelligibility Augustine invests knowledge with the distance of *eros*, a distance compounded by another when the temporal distance of memory is added. By doing so he essentially makes doxology the form of all human activity, and builds at least the *simulacra* of faith, hope and charity into the formal structure of all human knowing.[199] For knowledge entails *attention*, and attention entails the desire of wanting to know, of *seeking*, by which knowledge is able to "come into" its object.[200] Insofar as this seeking entails a return to memory in an act of attentive love, the relationship of knower to known is that of "trying to get," of "not having," and, as we shall soon see, of mediation.[201] And yet this relationship simultaneously entails a formal hope in, and is thus an affirmation of, the sought.[202] In Jacobi's version of the argument, the result is to make faith intrinsic to knowledge itself. For knowledge entails, formally, a kind of *fides qua* which traverses and fills the distance between the seer and the seen. The very fact that we attend, and that attention entails a desire to know, incorporates into the form of our knowledge itself "the conviction of things not seen."[203] "Faith, hope, and love *abide* . . ."[204]

Under the aspect of *exemplum*, a kind of erotic faith appears to view constituted by lack and distance between the agent and the object. However, this one-sided image is illusory, just as it was earlier when we considered the convertibility of the formal objects of *eros* and intention in the production of the second and third trinitarian *personae*. For this image is aporetically crossed and canceled out when we consider the unity of Christ's exemplary and sacramental functions. We cannot seek and love what we do not in some sense already know.[205] Hence if Christ as *exemplum* institutes a certain erotic distance between the lover and beloved, the seer and the seen, Christ as *sacramentum* mediates and fills that distance with the plenitude of the gift, just as the distance between the Father and the Son is itself God.

This conception is apparent in the conclusion to Book VIII, which reaches aporia at the precise point where Augustine invokes Christ's mediation in the *Confessiones*.[206] Augustine takes it as a commonplace that we love the justice which we are not, and his elaboration upon the Trinity as both the good and the love of the good and upon the mutual entailment of memory, intellect and will in the *vestiga trinitatis* warrant this presupposition. This entailment results from an axiom which we have already employed in our consideration of the trinitarian *personae*: that we cannot love what we do not know. This raises the aforementioned problem of recognition, a problem that Augustine "solves" by declaring that we gaze on the form of an indestructible truth which we are not. Of course this is no "solution" in any conventional sense, as we have already discussed. It provides no origin, no deductive principle from which to begin, no vantage from which to survey our relationship to that form. Instead it insists that we respond doxologically, that we relinquish such conceits. It follows from this, then, and from the mutual entailment of memory, intellect, and will, that our "gaze" upon this form is inseparable from our love of it. And it follows, further, that our love of this form could not be demarcated from the inexhaustible plenitude of the form itself. So it happens that:

> The man therefore who is believed to be just, is loved through that form and truth which he who loves and discerns and understands within himself; but this very form and truth itself cannot be loved from any other source than itself.[207]

Love of this form can only be from this form itself. And since this form is its own content, the love of this form turns out to be the love of loving itself, which has its source in the love loved.

Love must love something; it must have a desirable object which functions as the beautiful, eliciting our desire.[208] "For unless there were a grace and beauty in things, they could in nowise move us."[209] In order to love the *exemplum*, we have to know it, which already presupposes the movement of love. Love and knowledge therefore mutually entail each other, or, as Augustine puts it, "A word is knowledge together with love."[210] This means that our love of the *exemplum* as an end, though it presupposes and entails the distance between seer and seen, must nevertheless already entail some knowledge of that end. This knowledge must therefore already be mediated and moved by delight in that end as first cause and principle. The distance between knower and known in our relationship to the *exemplum* is thus collapsed into the distance between seer and seen, and thus the ratio of knower to known is intrinsically the plenitudinous distance between the Father and Son. This interval, this infinite distance, is for us also the interval of time, the distance between now and the time that the species of the seen is rendered perfect in the sight of the seer, and the measure of the image in us is equal to that from which it takes its measure. Which is to say that the distance between seer and seen is again collapsed into the distance between the Head and Body of Christ. The ratio, though not reducible to the temporal interval, mediates the unfolding of the temporal interval until such time as we "shall see him as he is."

This distance between seer and seen, traversed by faith, is not an empty distance; it is not the distance of the void, of "separation" in Alliez's sense. For the very traversal of this interval both affirms the end "formally" as a matter of faith and already "materially" presupposes delight in the beauty of the object which moves it. Hence this faith is a *fides quae per dilectionem operatur*.[211] But as the capacity to seek the end already presupposes the mediation of the end, it presupposes that the end is somehow already *given*, that the end is indeed a gift. Our love of and intention of the end as *exemplum* requires for its intelligibility the mediation and giving of that end as *sacramentum*. The very distance which makes possible this seeking is itself a plenitude, just as the infinite distance of the gift between the Father and Son is itself God. This is why Augustine will say that God gives himself in such a way that "He gives himself as being God."[212] It is why he will make the astonishing claim that "you see the Trinity if you see love."[213] For if our love is moved by God's anterior gift, then it will be impossible to delineate the *dilectio* with which we seek the end from the *dilectio* which gives the end as principle of our intention. Consequently it is this gift, this *dilectio*, "that makes us to abide in God, and Him in us."[214]

It is therefore the Spirit, the gift, who is the plenitudinous distance of our love. In this distance, the ratio of time to eternity, a relation named "creation," becomes once again the image and vehicle of an eternity understood as transcendent charity. "For the Spirit is a gift eternally, but a thing given in time."[215] If there is a void, a lack, a caesura between time and eternity, immanence and transcendence, it consists in a *dissimilitudo* of an altogether different kind. "For approach to God is not by intervals of place, but by likeness, and withdrawal from Him is by unlikeness."[216] Aquinas, in glossing this point, is perhaps even more direct. "We draw near to God by no corporeal steps, since He is everywhere, but by the affections of our soul, and by the actions of that same soul do we withdraw from him."[217]

There are several things to notice here. First, this "doxologizing" of human activity reiterates Augustine's view that all are members incorporate in the bodies of either of the two Adams, citizens of either of the two cities characterized by their respective objects of worship and subject to either of the two mediators.[218] It accords further with the insistence that sin is itself a perverse mimesis of the Trinity and a deformation of the trinitarian image that confirms the beauty of that image even while denying it.[219] The choice therefore is not "whether mediation" but between the mediator of life and the mediator of death. As in *De Civitate Dei*, the answer turns upon the objects of our love.

We noted that Augustine locates Christ's mediation at precisely the point where he considers Christ's dual status as *exemplum* and *sacramentum*. And we have discussed repeatedly how it is the function of this mediation to "harmonize" us into the concord between giver and given. Our earlier demonstration of the implications of Christ's *sapiential* and *sciential* unity gave us part of the picture of how this works. We are now in a position to see the other part. Christ as exemplar provokes in us and draws us on by the love which he himself gives sacramentally, and by which he draws us into the delight between the Father and the Son.

The doxologization of action and the inescapability of gift and mediation, though it displays how Christ incorporates us into the divine love, also does more than this. It displays how there is no "*outside*" to this love and thus confirms our contention that the Trinity is the "doxo-ontological" context for Augustine and his thought. The fact that we cannot "get behind" the aporia of Book VIII means that we can never get outside the ambit of the gift and of mediation. Hence, contrary to those who insist on reading Augustine as a proto-Cartesian and as a figure of metaphysics, we see that this aporia, the acceptance of this gift, leaves Augustine no vantage from which to draw the transcendental borders, no discrete origin from which to begin, no place from which to initiate a phenomenological reduction of the conditions of our reception,[220] for as soon as one initiates anything, one confirms, as Jacobi might say, the anteriority of what one intends and the mediation of a good which precludes such a reduction.

Instead of a point of origin, we find that we have always already been anticipated by God's gift, that we are constituted in and by the radical otherness of God. Therefore, as we shall see in the final chapter, there could be no Cartesian *epoche* in Augustinian terms, superficial similarities notwithstanding. For "there is nothing that can be said of the mind's relation to itself without the mediation of the revelation of God as its creator and lover."[221] Augustine therefore asserts that the mind is not the image of God because it can remember, understand, and love itself, but because it "can remember, understand, and love Him by whom it was made."[222] Indeed only by doing so can it finally be itself.[223] Emilie Zum Brunn understands this, but Gerhart Ladner perhaps puts it best: "Only the saint truly *is*."[224] But she only *is*, and is as an image of God, paradoxically, because of her very difference *from* God, because she can receive the gift whereby she most fully becomes herself in God's love of, delight in, and giving of himself. She can become herself by becoming God's.[225] "We see all these things, and we see that they are very good, because you see them in us, who have given to us your Spirit by whom we might see them and in them love you."[226]

Operae trinitatis indivisa sunt: *the work of the Trinity and the mediation of Christ*

This brings us to the final point, how the indivisible operations of the trinitarian *personae* are visible precisely *in* the unity of Christ. This should be fairly obvious by now. For Augustine, the minutest action invokes mediation because every action embodies desire and the intelligibility of the desired. Knowledge itself, which has the formal structure of the *fides quae per dilectionem operatur*, is determined "materially" by its object, just as the difference between *caritas* and *cupiditas* is determined not by a difference of operation but by their respective objects.[227]

Though the pairing occurs only once in the *De Trinitate*, it will become commonplace in the anti-Pelagian writings for Augustine to gloss Paul's "faith which works through love" with a further amendment from the Apostle: "love is diffused in our hearts through the Holy Ghost which is given to us."[228] In *De Spiritu et Littera* V.3 Augustine pairs this passage with 2 Corinthians 5.7, in which we walk "by faith not by sight." Already we have noticed the significance of Augustine's habitual prooftexts. What is the upshot of all this?

Earlier we saw how our very recognition of Christ as exemplar presupposed his status as sacramental gift. As exemplar, he both manifested and obscured the brilliance of the divine beauty, and this dual gesture served to draw us onward, through the *eros* of faith, into the plenitude of this beauty. The coupling of this cluster of texts is tantalizingly suggestive. For it insinuates that Christ manifests the divine *theologia* precisely in the unity of his exemplary and sacramental functions and manifests the divine beauty in us precisely in our relationship to these functions. Put differently, it suggests that the "erotic" character of our action both takes its form from and is situated and unfolded within the interval of gift and delight between the Father and the Son. And it suggests that this inter-trinitarian taxis is itself displayed in the unity of Christ.

We saw in the previous section how the Son's filiation from the Father entails the Father's delight in the Son, and that this delight implies a certain infinite distance between them. Yet this distance is also their unity, and is itself divine, such that we understand the Holy Spirit to be entailed in the very generation of the Son. Conversely we saw how the Son's vision of the Father, a vision constitutive of the Son, is coextensive with a giving of the giving given by the Father to the Son. Thus Augustine concludes that the spiration of the Third is principally from the Father but also from the Son, and that the Spirit, at once a divine hypostasis and the love of the Father and the Son, uniquely merits the name of love.[229] We can begin to see this manifest economically if we look yet again to the aporia from *De Trinitate* VIII, though this time with Christ's unity kept firmly in view.

Christ's exemplary status has the splendor of the beautiful. Conveyed through the historical unfolding of signs, it evokes from us an intention, a desire, a seeking of the beautiful. This seeking implies a certain distance, as we have already discussed. Yet even to recognize it, to seek it, we must turn to it in love, and to love it, it must already be somewhat known and *given* to us. So the very visibility of the *exemplum* implies at once the distance of intention, the mediation of the intentional object and the *gift* of that object as first cause and principle of our intention. It is finally impossible to draw a border here, to delineate the *dilectio* with which we seek the end from that with which it is given, an impossibility compounded by the fact that it is love which we love in loving the *exemplum*. To recognize this is to recognize that the distance in which we seek is not an empty distance, but rather the interval of the gift, just as the interval between the Father and the Son is itself divine. The distance of our seeking thus manifests and participates in the Son's eternal filiation from the Father *and* his giving of giving in the Holy Spirit in and with the Father. This donation is affirmed by the very form and preconditions of this *eros* which must already participate in that which it seeks in order to seek it.

Having asked "how or where does the Trinity manifest itself?" Augustine passes immediately into a discussion of the Spirit as love, as the gift between the Father and the Son, who constitutes the Body of Christ precisely in being given.[230] This is not a coincidence. For it is precisely in this drawing of the body to the Head, through the *fides quae per dilectionem operatur*, a *dilectio* diffused in our hearts by the Holy Spirit which is given to us, that God is revealed in creation and creation is revealed to be in God. It is within *this* body that the *exercitatio mentis* of *De Trinitate* occurs, to this union, to this love, that it aims. This is its point and purpose, but then this is the point and purpose, and the form and context, of the unfolding of creation itself within the love of the Trinity.

We noted in the previous chapter several lines of criticism which appeared to share little in common except a basic narrative for locating Augustine within the West's tendency toward modernity. Yet there is perhaps something which these criticisms share in common, whether the charge be that Augustine's trinitarian theology fails to admit the economies of creation and salvation within its ambit (LaCugna and Gunton), that the Augustinian *mens* prefigures Cartesian subjectivity (Taylor, Menn, Hankey, Alliez) or that Augustinian subjectivity effects an "economy of separation" and subsequent onto-theological oscillation between beings and Being that redounds to the power of a capricious will (Alliez).

All share a certain narrative of theological and philosophical history which sees Augustine at the root of some of modernity's most fundamental presuppositions about the self in relation to God. In its most extreme and militant version, this narrative views the Cartesian *cogito* and its methodical destruction and reconstruction of the world as the logical and nihilistic terminus of Augustine's thought and thus of Western Christianity. We have already begun to address that story, and I shall address the relationship between Augustine and Descartes specifically in the final chapter. The Augustine we have unveiled here further refutes this story, for the same reasons that he refutes the more congenial, theological criticisms. It is quite obvious that Augustine does not conceive of a unified divine substance either analytically or ontologically prior to the trinitarian *personae*; indeed he rejects such a conception altogether.[231] And contrary to the charge that Augustine somehow abandons the historical economy, we can now see that he at once pushes the trinitarian operation into the economy more deeply than we are inclined to think *and* pushes this economy more deeply into the trinitarian *taxis* by making its very form Church. Thus while Augustine champions the contemplation of an immaterial, eternal God, and a freeing of the mind from its captivity to corporeal images, he nevertheless makes a turn *toward* the economy and a proper regard *toward* created beauty integral to contemplation. This is a function of his understanding of incarnation. Perhaps our failure to understand this derives not from flaws inherent to Augustine but to the fact that we no longer think or live as if the

70

incarnation were true, that we have yet to come to terms with the depths of what we no longer believe.

To contemplate this is to recognize what both sets of criticisms share in common. Each of these criticisms is only possible, these thoughts only thinkable, within the space of a rupture of Augustine's doxological ontology. Where selfhood is constituted doxologically within the interval of love between Father and Son, there can be no autonomous subjectivity and no outside to these economies. Where creature is bound to creator in hypostatic union, the nihilation of creation cannot be the path to God, but only the refusal of God's gratuity. There can be no subject from which to extrapolate to the existence of an infinite *causa sui* set over against human thinking while remaining a mere representation within it. There can be no unmediated presence to self, no strictly linear chain to jump outside of. These criticisms, then, can be unraveled, these questions reversed. For these thoughts to be possible, Augustine must first be unthought. The remainder of the book will illustrate one component of that endeavor.

3

CHRISTOLOGY, COSMOLOGY AND THE MECHANICS OF GRACE

On the intelligibility of the Pelagian controversy

Despite many centuries of ecclesiastical condemnation and textbook commentary, it is not immediately clear just why the Pelagian controversy was originally controversial. Why it should continue to matter and how this ancient controversy is relevant to the story of modern origins is perhaps even less obvious. Numerous factors, both ancient and modern, conspire to complicate our understanding. For one thing, recent scholarship has made it increasingly obvious that each party to the original debate conceived of the stakes differently, raising a real question whether the debate revolved around a single subject matter at all. This tendency toward incommensurability would only intensify as the controversy passed into subsequent generations, and a different geographical region, with the so-called Semi-Pelagians. Moreover, both ancient and modern readers alike have tended to abstract Augustine's doctrine of grace from its intellectual and ontological context, to treat it merely as a function of the anti-Pelagian polemics. Little heed is paid to the *De Trinitate*, for instance, either in the original debate or in modern analyses of it, save insofar as it might yield some clue to the genetic development of Augustine's later doctrine.[1]

The failure of much of modern scholarship to avail itself of this text is indicative of its failure to come to grips with the ontological stakes of the question—a fact which suggests in turn a great ontological distance between most contemporary scholars and Augustine. This distance, aided by a kind of immanent naturalism and abetted by the Protestant fear of "works righteousness" and the imperial Church, is evident in how the Pelagian question has been framed for us: "*whether* grace or nature?"[2] As a consequence, Rebecca Harden Weaver is able to assert that "the *subordination* of the human will and action to grace calls into question the degree to which human actions are genuinely human."[3] Though not intended to compliment Augustine, the remark ironically repeats the ontological presuppositions of Augustine's seventeenth-century apologists.[4] Yet these presuppositions, both then and now, merely beg two theologically prior questions which better capture the stakes of the original debate: *"what kind of nature?"* and "what kind of self?"

The original controversy was not blind to these questions, particularly in its early stages. It had begun over the question of traducianism as the mode both for transmitting the contagion of sin and for incarnating new souls. It would conclude with Augustine's assertion, in *De Correptione et Gratia,* of humanity's collective fulfillment in the person of the one Christ, an echo of the *De Trinitate* which held that the whole Christ, the Head with its members, is to be thought of as one *person*.[5] Within this register, *natura* acquires a multivalent sense, referring both to our pre-lapsarian communion and to our future, eschatological state. Only provisionally and partially does it denote our condition under sin.[6]

The "Pelagian question," as we have inherited it, is therefore both historically and theologically inadequate and for the same reasons: because it imposes definitions upon the debate which have not come under the discipline of theological scrutiny. I shall counter this in the ensuing section by contending that Augustine's doctrine of grace flows from the doxological ontology articulated in the previous chapter, and that his objections to the Pelagians were thus fundamentally christological and ultimately trinitarian in nature.[7] At issue, in other words, is the Trinity itself and whether nature, the meaning of being human, and human agency are understood to occur within Christ's mediation of the love and delight shared as *donum* between the Father and the Son. Consequently, if James Wetzel is right and Pelagianism is incoherent as a moral psychology and a philosophy of action, it will have failed *precisely in virtue of its status as a christological problem*.[8] For it is Christ who determines for Augustine what it means to be human, the Trinity who determines what it means to be and Christ working inseparably with the other trinitarian *personae* who incorporates us fully and finally into our being. Apart from this there is only sin and death, and, as the *Confessiones* demonstrates, the wages of sin is incoherence.[9]

It is here that we can begin to see the relevance of the Pelagian controversy for our understanding of modern origins. Pelagianism institutes a rupture in this christological and trinitarian economy, and, insofar as it determines the direction of subsequent Christian thought, creates possibilities for human nature "outside" the Trinity and the mediation of Christ. This is due largely to an account of volition which the Pelagians import from stoicism, whose agents are situated within a very different ontological context. By transposing the stoic *hegemonikon* into a Christian ontological context, Pelagianism transposes into that context some of the fundamental consequences and fatal contradictions of the immanent monism which was its original home. In subsequent chapters I shall trace these possibilities, demonstrate how they insinuate themselves into the transmission of

Augustinianism, and show how Descartes both repeats them and is conceptually and historically dependent upon them; and I would suggest now that the attempt to saddle Augustine with the ultimate paternity of Descartes' *res cogitans* takes these ruptures as normative. In this chapter, however, my primary intent is to show how Pelagianism ruptures Augustine's trinitarian economy by supplanting his christological "anthropology."

I shall therefore proceed in four stages, developing two lines of thought in apposition before merging them into a unity in the third section. For the remainder of this section, I shall briefly recapitulate the conclusions of the previous chapter and then reconsider Augustine's response to the Pelagians, to the end of establishing his Christology and trinitarian theology as the context and substance of his objections. From this conclusion there will follow the need to set out the regulative grammar governing a conception of agency which occurs within the trinitarian act, both *in se* and *ad extra*. Thus in the next section I shall contend that the question of the relationship between human and divine agency is a subset of the problem of created participation in the act of the immutable Creator—though within Augustine's conflation of *esse* and *dilectio*, we could just as easily recognize creation as a subset of sanctification. This problematic of creation will both govern how we must think of the two terms in the relationship, the divine and human, and determine the grammar of causality within which the "doctrine of grace" should be understood to occur. The stage will then be set for the second strand of thought, in which the Augustinian *mens* appears to view as a doxological self constituted through its participation in the delight shared between the Father and the Son and in the unity of Christ's one body, human and divine. It is here, in the final section, that Augustine's moral psychology will fully emerge as a function of his Christology, and Pelagianism's incoherencies will be exposed and attributed to deficiencies in the same regard. Yet these deficiencies have consequences, and I shall begin to show how these Pelagian deficiencies, owing to stoic debts, entail and import into Christian thought and practice some of the fundamental contradictions, and fatal consequences, of stoic physics. It is these consequences that will ultimately foreshadow Descartes.

Pelagianism: a problem of Trinitarian theology?

To see what the Pelagian controversy is about we must consider *why* Augustine thought Pelagianism should be deemed heretical. Augustine's characteristic rebuttals to the Pelagian position as he sees it support the position argued here: that the Pelagians rupture the unity and mediation of Christ and sacrifice the immutability and transcendence of the Trinity.[10] The first of Augustine's standard responses is christological. Nature, construed in Pelagian terms, "renders the cross of Christ void."[11] This response takes on added ontological weight when refracted through a second that invokes the gratuity of the trinitarian economy, "that grace which begins with us is not grace."[12] Together the remarks echo the *De Trinitate's* understanding of Christ as the visible manifestation of triune love. And we can infer from them that whatever it means to nullify the cross of Christ, it will somehow nullify creation's participation in the divine love and, conversely, that a rupture in participation will rupture Christ's mediation.

Given the integral relationship between creation and soteriology within the *creatio, conversio, formatio* scheme, a compromise of Christology and the trinity will entail within it a compromise of the doctrine of *creatio ex nihilo*. Indeed it is not too strong to say, with proper qualifications, that soteriology is for Augustine simply the fulfillment and intensification of creation.[13] Augustine employs Psalm 100.33 to reassert the point in his response to the Pelagian position on the origin of faith, eliding the gift of faith with the gratuity of creation.

> Accordingly it is said to the Church, in the Song of Songs: "Thou shalt come and pass by from the beginning of faith." Was it we ourselves that that gave it to us? Did we ourselves make ourselves faithful? I must by all means say here, emphatically: "It is He that hath made us, and not we ourselves."[14]

Augustine's elision of creation and sanctification into a single economy is important for several reasons. First, one must recognize the interrelationship between these two aspects of Augustine's thought in order to avoid the error of artificially bracketing "theological" issues from "cosmological" ones, a tendency we have already considered. Secondly, this interrelationship will become important in the next section when we examine the "mechanics" of this economy. It will become clear there that the grammar governing the "mechanics" of creation *ex nihilo* is identical to that governing the doctrine of grace.

More immediately, however, it says something of the ultimate stakes of the Pelagian logic. One will recall from our "aesthetic" reading of *De Trinitate* that Augustine configured the gift of faith as an intention toward a future and final *exemplum*, one which presupposed its sacramental activity as first cause and principle. The effect was to invest intentionality with the *eros* of faith, and to locate this *eros* within the reciprocity and mutual delight between the Father and the Son, the *forma* of God. This gratuity is consummated in the creature as the fulfillment of creation which is *esse magis* as it participates fully in the love between Father and Son. And this participation is manifest, and manifest doxologically, as the perfection of our likeness to God in and through the image which is the Son.[15]

Consequently there is a philosophy of volition latent in this scheme. We began considering it in the last chapter, and will develop it more fully in this, but already one can see that this philosophy is a function of a broader understanding of creation consummated in communion with God.

By contrast, the essence of Pelagius' teaching, as conveyed by Augustine, consists in his understanding of the relation of volition to grace according to a scheme which divided the good act into *possibilitas*, *voluntas*, and *actio*, and which restricted grace to the order of *possibilitas*.[16] Intrinsic to this scheme is a denial of the traducianist formulation of original sin, formulated fully in Augustine and held in common, at least implicitly, by Cyprian and Ambrose.[17] The traducianist perspective insists that Adam's fall precipitated a contagion of defect which was more than merely a mimetic failure to come to grips with the demands of the law.[18] The Pelagian position also entails an inverse affirmation: that the "graced" state in which individual humans subsist is, a priori, a state of indeterminate possibility regarding sin and their *telos* for good, a state over which potentially autarkic agents hold sway.[19] Augustine perceived that these claims, quite apart from undermining the case for the necessity and efficacy of infant baptism, had profound ramifications for Pelagius' construal of nature, grace, personhood and volition.

Augustine's early criticisms of the Pelagian position, though vigorous, were relatively muted and stopped short of attacking Pelagius personally. In the anti-Pelagian tract from 412, *De Peccatorum Meritis et Remissione*, Augustine acknowledged Pelagius' holiness.[20] In *De Gratia Novi Testamenti* (*ep*. 140) and *De Spiritu et Littera*, both written in that same year, Augustine refrains from mentioning the Pelagians by name. He remarks further that even though some enemies of grace do not attribute their goodness to God, they still deserve praise for their good works as they nevertheless live temperately and do not believe in a false Christ.[21]

This spirit, though already in decline at the time of the writing of *De Natura et Gratia*, all but disappears after the second of the anti-Pelagian trials, at Diospolis in Palestine, in 415.[22] Despite a catalogue of condemned errors, Pelagius himself was acquitted of any charges.[23] The dissonance between the acquitted man and his condemned propositions disturbed Augustine, for a couple of reasons. Not only did Augustine think that the Pelagian affirmation of grace which led to the acquittal was disingenuous— as he would charge when the matter was turned over to Rome—but also the dissonance displayed a more troubling confusion. Pelagius' affirmation obscured the extent to which terms the two men held in common, such as *natura* and *gratia*, masked vastly different referents when deployed in their respective schemes.[24]

Augustine's anxiety corroborates our contention that the very meaning of *natura* is at stake here, and it should give pause to those who would insulate Augustine's doctrine of grace from the broader scope of his thought.

What most vexed Augustine, however, was how this difference in usage occluded the supreme stakes of the debate. At stake is how Pelagian grace, construed as "knowledge of the law" "endeavors to overthrow the foundation of the Christian faith: 'By one man death, and by one man the resurrection of the dead; for as in Adam all die, even so in Christ shall all be made alive.'"[25]

Pelagianism, in other words, is a threat to orthodox Christology, though we do well not to let modern compartmentalism relegate this point to a theological ghetto. Augustine's use of the same Pauline passage, in *De Trinitate* IV.12.15, suggests that his christological preoccupations are more cosmic in scope. In that context, this passage works to juxtapose the mediation of life to the mediation of death, and in the last chapter we saw how Augustine works out the harmony between Christ's single death and resurrection and our double death. Augustine then concludes that the ratio of single to double everywhere signifies *this* ratio. The *magis* and *minus esse* distinction, and the convertibility of the transcendentals in God's triune *esse*, only further corroborate the importance of this point. For Augustine, life in the historic Body of Christ, with its increase in knowledge and love of the good (in both senses of the genitive), is tantamount to an increase in being.[26] It is therefore grossly anachronistic to view this christological preoccupation through the distorting bifurcation of reason from revelation or the disjunction of nature and grace, just as it is anachronistic to attempt to separate what is discretely "philosophical" about this question from Augustine's "particularist" theological concerns. Incommensurable understandings of *natura* and the christological threat are not separate facets of the Pelagian problematic; *they are the Pelagian problematic.*

At issue, in other words, is whether *natura* will finally be understood christologically.[27] The *exercitatio mentis* of *De Trinitate* makes this plain. These are christological exercises through and through and a function of our participation, through the unity of Christ, in the Father's delight in his Word. To fail to see that is to not simply to fail to grasp the Pelagian problematic; it is to fall into it. "[W]ith what face," asks Augustine, "can this writer on hearing that 'God is love' persist in maintaining that we have of God only one of those three, namely, 'the capacity,' whereas it is of ourselves that we have 'the good will' and 'the good action?'"[28]

We can thus begin to see in Augustine's criticism of the Pelagian *cognitio legis* a bit more of what it will eventually mean to render the cross of Christ void and how these diffuse concerns are interrelated. Everything turns on what it means to be *in Christ*, that is, within the delight shared between the Father and the Son as mediated to us through the union of the two natures.

Our reading of the *De Trinitate* demonstrated the fundamental importance of beauty for understanding both the intelligible love of the Trinity and our participation in it through the *fides quae per dilectionem operatur*. We saw how *dilectio* and *delectatio* were integral to this understanding. Just as in

77

the *De Civitate Dei*, where *bonum* is the only motive for, and the principle and end of, creation, so also *delectatio* in the beauty of God served as both principle and end of the generation and procession of the Son and Spirit.[29] These terms helped further to distinguish the one movement from the other and to demonstrate the convertibility of appetibility and intelligibility in God's triune simplicity. Moreover, we saw how Augustine understood this life of trinitarian delight to be manifest as a doxological economy of gift in Christ's sacrificial self-donation, with "our own" worship—at once this gift's reception and transfer—being both a sign of our participation in this economy and a visible, if distant, manifestation of God's beauty.

This economy was itself "located" *in* the two-natured Christ and the reciprocal intention of the Father for the Son, and was refracted through the distantiated unity of the *scientia/sapientia, exemplum/sacramentum* pairs. First, the *forma* or the *species* of the Father was made materially visible in Christ as *exemplum*, and conveyed "horizontally" across time through his body the Church. Secondly, the very intelligibility of this *forma* insinuated in turn an erotic, intentional distance between us as seeking agents and the exemplary object, which would not be sought but for its beauty. Yet this "infinite distance" was actually a plenitude, that is, a distance without lack which presupposes this "object" as both first and final cause and so invokes, "vertically," the mediatory gift of Christ as *sacramentum*. Thus we were able both to identify our apprehension and desire for God as a gift of the Holy Spirit, the simultaneous giving and delight proceeding from the Father and Son, and to demonstrate the trinitarian difference while simultaneously maintaining the indivisibility of the works *ad extra*.

This account was the rather technical explication we gave to that Pauline phrase from *De Trinitate* which is ubiquitous throughout the anti-Pelagian writings: "*fides quae per dilectionem operatur*." As a consequence of the infinite distance at once opened and filled by this faith and its motive, we saw that this understanding entailed a philosophy of volition and indeed insinuated a vestigial, doxological form of the Trinity, however remote and debased it might become, in the distance intrinsic to any action. Intentionality is intrinsically erotic and *eros* intentional, with our intentional objects being—to borrow again Aquinas' words—last in the order of execution and first in the order of intention.[30] Our actions thus vestigially manifest the image of the Father's love for the Son; whether this image passes over into likeness is contingent less upon a difference of operation than of object.[31]

Among those propositions condemned at Diospolis was one which equated "knowledge of the law" with "that grace of which the Scripture says: 'Who shall deliver me from the body of this death? The grace of God through Jesus Christ our Lord.'"[32] If we take Augustine's latent theological background into account, there turns out to be more to this objection than immediately meets the eye. Affirming the *possibilitas, voluntas, actio* schema, denying the aprioricity of grace and its cooperation in *voluntas* and *actio*, and maintaining instead that the necessary conditions for a free act resided in the indeterminacy of *possibilitas*, requires of the Pelagians, if they are to affirm grace, that *gratia* assume a definition quite at odds with Augustine's. Either grace must be restricted to the conditions of *possibilitas* or attributed simply to the pedagogical apparatus of the law.[33]

Each option is problematic. The first marginalizes baptism and renders the incarnation superfluous.[34] The second, as we shall see, institutes *voluntas* as a kind of reified choice, a motiveless choosing of motives that renders both action and the agent incoherent. At present, however, we are interested in why these options present christological problems and how they bear on trinitarian theology and the cosmology of creation. Just what is it that Augustine is rejecting by denying that grace is tantamount to knowledge of the law? And just how does this aspect of the issue relate to "the grace of God through Jesus Christ our Lord" which rescues from "the body of this death?"[35]

The accusation appears elsewhere in *Contra Duas Epistulas Pelagiorum*, only this time the crux of the complaint is more specific.

> But those enemies of grace never endeavor to lay more secret snares for more vehement opposition to that same grace than when they praise the law, which, without doubt, is worthy to be praised. Because, by their different modes of speaking, and by variety of words in all their arguments, they wish the law to be understood as "grace"—that, to wit, we may have from the Lord God the help of knowledge [*a Domino Deo adiutorium cognitionis habeamus*], whereby we may know those things which have to be done,—*not the inspiration of love* [*non inspirationem dilectionis*], that, when known, we may do them with a holy love which is properly grace. For the knowledge of the law without charity puffs up, does not edify, according to the same apostle, who most openly says, "Knowledge puffs up, but love edifies." Which saying is like to that in which it is said, "The letter kills, but the spirit makes alive." For "Knowledge puffs up," corresponds to "The letter kills": and "Love edifies" to "The spirit makes alive"; because "the love of God is diffused in our hearts by the Holy Spirit who is given to us."[36]

This remark fuses Augustine's moral, psychological, christological and trinitarian concerns. Let us allow his comments in *De Spiritu et Littera* to interpret them further. Commenting upon the Pelagian understanding that "God both created man with the free choice of the will, and by commandments, teaches him, Himself, how man ought to live," Augustine writes:

> We, however, on our side affirm that the human will is so divinely aided in being made just, that (beyond man's being created with a free will and beyond the teaching by which he is instructed how he ought to live) he receives the Holy Ghost, by whom there is formed in his mind a delight in, and a love of, that supreme and unchangeable good which is God even now while he is still "walking by faith and not by sight" in order that by this gift to him of the earnest, as it were, of the free gift, he may conceive an ardent desire to inhere in his maker, and may burn to enter upon the participation in that true light, that it may go well with him from Him to whom he owes his existence.[37]

Together these two remarks contain almost the entirety of the *De Trinitate*.[38] One will recall from *De Trinitate* that Christ mediates for us because he opens an erotic distance as *exemplum* between our intention and its object which was filled by his gratuity as *sacramentum*. The erotic distance opened and filled by these pairs was the gift of our *particeps* within the delight integral to the Father's generation of the Son, the Son's seeing of the Father, and the procession of the Spirit common to them both.

The account of the *fides quae per dilectionem operatur* in *De Spiritu et Littera* conforms to this formal structure and locates the agent within the ambit and anteriority of the gift. The law is to be praised, not simply because it is the law, but because it provokes in us an earnest delight without which there is no action. Yet the promise of an erotic distance and of a faith not yet sight are already gifts, already a movement in us of the beauty of the gift itself.[39]

This interpretation is further warranted by two moves within *De Natura et Gratia* and *De Spiritu et Littera* which also recapitulate this trinitarian structure and which testify to our location within the unity of Christ and the anteriority of his gift. The first, which recapitulates the *exemplum*, is Augustine's *rehabilitation* of the law, now elided into Christ himself and the doxological economy manifest in him.[40] The second, which recapitulates Christ's mediation as *sacramentum*, attributes the efficacy of this law to a faith which is moved by delight in its object. This structure recapitulates exactly both the erotic, aesthetic distance between faith and its object explicated in our reading of *De Trinitate*, and the filling of that distance by a delight in the object which serves as the anterior motive, the first cause and principle, of our seeking of it.

> By the law we fear God; by faith we hope in God: but from those who fear punishment grace is hidden. And the soul which labors

under this fear, since it has not conquered its evil concupiscence, nor from which this fear, like a harsh master, has departed—let it flee by faith for refuge to the mercy of God, that He may give it what He commands, and may, by inspiring into it the sweetness of His grace through His Holy Spirit, cause the soul to delight more in what He teaches it, than it delights in what opposes his instruction. In this manner it is that the great abundance of His sweetness—that is, the law of faith,—His love which is in our hearts, and diffused, is perfected in them that hope in Him, that good may be wrought by the soul, healed not by the fear of punishment, but by the love of justice.[41] *from On the Spirit and the Letter*

Augustine has elided the motive, the *inspiration dilectionis*, with a *delectatione* which he attributes to the gift of the Spirit. Simultaneously, he implicitly incorporates the delight that provokes our intention of the law who is Christ into the delight intrinsic to the Father and Son's mutual intention and seeking of one another. The location of our intention within the interval of the trinitarian intention is evidenced further by two subsequent moves: the linking of this delight with Christic mediation and the elision of this mediation and the intrinsic *eros* of faith with the Son's vision of the Father.[42] As a consequence Augustine will claim in *De Dono Perseverantiae* that "Christ altogether with his members is—for the Church's sake, which is his Body—the fullness of Him."[43] And thus the precise aptness of the formulation: who shall deliver me from the *body* of this death? The grace of God through Jesus Christ our Lord.[44]

The argument thus far should suffice to establish *that* there is an intrinsic relation between the problems presented by Pelagius and Augustine's Christology, trinitarian theology, and theological anthropology. One can infer from this relationship an answer to the original question of just why the Pelagian controversy should be controversial and Pelagianism condemned as heretical. If indeed it should be condemned, this is because it contradicts what had become orthodox trinitarian theology and what would soon be codified as orthodox Christology. Precisely how does it do so? Part of the answer no doubt resides in the restricted scope of a Pelagian grace limited to *possibilitas* and the *cognitio legis*. More crucial still is the way that the *actio* of the Pelagian agent ruptures Christ's mediation, severing our participation in the delight between the Father and the Son. The implications of such a rupture are not simply moral, but ontological. However, in order to substantiate this we must elaborate on the relation between creation and sanctification, the grammar of creation and its bearing on Augustine's theological anthropology.

Creation and the mechanics of grace

On creation as grace

Augustine was insistent that grace, far from violating free will, established free will. To understand this one should first understand how *not* to try to establish the relationship between the two. The point is not merely methodological, for it is integral to understanding Augustine's Christology as the context for creation's unfolding and for seeing how this context determines his doctrine of grace. It is thus a crucial point for grasping the ontological stakes of the Pelagian controversy.

Few contemporary analyses of Augustine's doctrine of grace acknowledge the ontological stakes of the question, just as few analyses of Augustine's ontology consider the relevance of his doctrine of grace.[45] As a consequence, the former almost inevitably turn on the attempt to dissect the willed movement into action and passion, delineate the human from the divine contribution and, quite predictably, protect the human contribution from violation by the causality of grace.[46] Abstracting Augustine's ontology from his Christology results in different problems, as it either leaves the agent locked in a dialectic with God above the flux of history and materiality or presumes a definition of "the human" apart from determination to Adam or Christ, or both.[47]

These attempts share more in common with the preoccupations and ontological presumptions of the Pelagians than with those of Augustine, as we shall eventually see.[48] The essential problem with this endeavor is one endemic to any attempt to treat the doctrine of grace in isolation from Augustine's Christology and his trinitarian "ontology." Presuming that the ontic and ontological status of humanity, nature and God are self-evident, it then implicitly reduces God to one object among others, dialectically juxtaposed to creation. Coextensive with this reduction is the reduction of grace to an immanent causal force, in an impoverished view of causality, whose precise connection to its effects is presumed to be accessible.[49] This manner of framing the issue has the a priori effect of making God less than transcendent and immutable, and thus less than Augustine and Christian tradition understands God to be. Briefly put, this attempt to delineate and make discrete the respective contribution of the "two agents" is simply bad theological grammar.

We are therefore warranted in viewing the Pelagian problem within the context of the larger question of causality. By articulating the grammar of divine action within which human action is set, we can better articulate the presuppositions and implications of Augustine's doctrine of grace. Moreover, there are several good reasons to view the Pelagian problem as a subset of this larger question of the causal grammar relating creature to Creator. First, if one locates the Pelagian controversy within the onto-logical setting of the doctrines of the Trinity and creation, it becomes evident that the problem dividing Augustine from the Pelagians is not very different from two other, typically Augustinian, concerns. The first is the principle of inseparable operations.[50] The second is a problem Augustine confronted in the opening chapters of *Confessiones* XI and indeed throughout the final three books of the *Confessiones*: the question of how the transcendent Word uttered immutably from all eternity can be understood to create temporal effects.

Secondly, within the *creatio, conversio, formatio* schema of creation from *De Genesi ad Litteram*—wherein *esse magis* is to participate in the God who is transcendent charity—the line which demarcates creation and sanctification into discrete categories or operations is difficult to sustain. On this view there can be no sheer *being*, no existence deprived of all form, no mere quantum, to which the transcendentals good, beautiful, and true are simply accidental qualifications. Hence sanctification simply is the consummation of creation: to be is finally to participate in one's measure in the goodness which is the love and beauty of God.[51] Augustine's figural reinterpretation of Genesis 1 in the *Confessiones* as a doxological and ecclesiological text corroborates this view.

Finally, and perhaps most importantly, the formal structure of the question of creation is identical to the problem posed by the Pelagians. Indeed it is the peculiar requirements entailed in the Christian understanding of a God who creates *ex nihilo* that make the Pelagian position so troublesome. These requirements contain both positive and negative implications that regulate our understanding both of the causal relationship between God and creation and of the nature of both terms in that relationship.

Negatively, these requirements produce what is really a single qualification viewed slightly differently under the respective aspects of creation and sanctification.[52] The doctrine of *creatio ex nihilo* entails the notion of divine immutability as a corollary. Creaturely existence or prime matter can have no prior claim to God's activity without locking God into a real relation to his creation (to use Thomistic language).[53] Hence the relation of divine cause to created effect cannot be dialectical. This compromises God's transcendence and immutability, and, ultimately, his status as creator.[54] Rather, God's causality of temporal effects cannot in any way be thought to effect a change in God's own agency or a compromise of God's simplicity.[55] It must be understood as sheer gratuity even though, paradoxically, it is internally reciprocal.

Augustine's incessant rebuttal of the Pelagian position, that grace cannot originate with us, simply transposes this logic into the category of sanctification. Human merit cannot be antecedent to the activity of grace without similarly rendering the divine act finite and reactive.[56] The point is one Augustine insists upon differently in numerous contexts, and it is necessary to protect not only God's transcendence but also his goodness. The

83

alternative, as Augustine would insist against Julian, is finally Manichean.[57] For it makes evil ontologically necessary and indeed integral to the good, celebrating it as the occasion for virtue's exercise. "And thus do you act, Lord God, for You love souls with a greater and deeper purity than we can, and are more incorruptibly compassionate because no sorrow can reach to wound you."[58] It is this incorruptible compassion, this plentiude of giving, which will make charity the ground of the only genuine virtue in *De Civitate Dei*, which is to say that we must understand our possession of this virtue as itself a gift. It is this plenitude, giving being in an act of sheer delight, that in fact constitutes the ontological difference (and constitutes it for the first time in Judaism and Christianity.) For this delight, this generosity, knows no opposite, not even non-being.[59]

Positively, however, the insistence upon this immutable plenitude means that God cannot be properly thought of as "cause" in any conventional sense, a kataphatic assertion which places apophatic limits on our theoretical capacities. Since the ontological difference is a consequence of the doctrine of creation, it follows that, "by implication, the difference between creation and Creator is beyond our comprehension."[60] There is no proper analogy by which a "causal mechanism" for creation from nothing can be brought into view. Creating, as opposed to merely causing, remains mystery in the most profound sense.[61]

This difference is made explicit in *Confessiones* XI, when Augustine makes the utterance of the transcendent Logos quite "other" to the alterations of time.[62] In so doing, he identifies creatureliness with time, change and alteration—to surprising effect.[63] Far from suggesting the usual pejorative contrast between the mutability of creation and the immutability of the divine life, this identification actually establishes a similitude, however remote, between them: "Time in all the beauty of its changefulness holds on its appointed course . . ."[64] The movement of history is once again a sacramental reflection of the beauty of God.[65]

Several crucial points follow. The divine Beauty, the *forma* of God, functions as a mediating concept in several respects. Here it establishes this similitude with God in the very *difference* of created reality from God; subsequently in our argument it will play a mediating role between cosmology and creation on the one hand, and subjectivity or moral psychology and grace on the other. Consequently, it will be at this point, the point of our differential participation in the beauty of the Son, that Pelagian thought will rupture mediation. Meanwhile, however, the crucial point repeats one made in the previous chapter's discussion of the positive ratio of time to eternity. In establishing this differential similitude, the category of beauty helps to reconfigure the way in which both terms in the causal relationship, and indeed that relationship itself, are understood.[66]

The insistence on God's immutable generosity means that the relationship of Creator cause to created effect can neither be represented

84

dialectically nor considered as a simple hylomorphism. The Creator/creature relationship cannot be dissected into action and passion with its parts subsequently attributed to an active agent and passive patient, or even to the interaction of two agents. God is not *an* agent. That is, God is not one actor alongside others, whose agency can be treated as an efficient quantifiable force in relation to the force of other agencies. Nor are creatures patients awaiting actualization prior to God's gift of being. Prior to this gratuity they are simply nothing at all. None of the usual binaries are adequate to the representation of the act of *creation*. Indeed creation, properly speaking, cannot be *represented* at all.

However, the most critical point—the point which undoes the Pelagians and the reason for rehearsing the positive ratio of time to eternity—follows from the manner in which change and mutability exhibit the creative act of the God whose goodness is immutable love and delight.[67] Since creation is an act of utter gratuity which does not merely impose a hylomorphic form on a passive "substrate" by immanent force, but brings being out of nothing, this "causal" activity is manifest in the creature as effect, *precisely in the creature's own actuality and activity*.[68] Consequently, a strict dichotomy of action and passion—the precondition for the Pelagian opposition to Augustinian grace—will simply have no place here.

It is true that Augustine conceives of a certain "formless matter" capable of receiving form along with the heaven of heavens in the *principio* before the beginning of days, and he even offers in *De Natura Boni* XVIII a Christian definition of *hyle*, probably derived from the *khora* of Plato's *Timaeus*.[69] Yet its "passive" character and its characterization as a substratum need to be qualified by its place within the *creatio*, *conversio*, and *formatio* of *De Genesi ad Litteram* and the role given to form within a doxological ontology wherein *magis esse* is tantamount to *magis amare deum*.

Augustine's acceptance of a primordial *hyle* is probably attributable to two factors: general philosophical commonplace and the need to contend with the formless world of Genesis 1.1. Hence Augustine characterizes the *hyle* in virtue of its formlessness and its capacity to receive form (*capacitas formae*). One will recall here Augustine's equation of form and beauty, and indeed Augustine understands this *capacitas* as potentiality for conversion towards the one whom he describes in *De Vera Religione* as "*qui est forma infabricata atque omnium formosissima*."[70] Still, Augustine asserts, this *hyle* is not to be called evil, for if form is a good thing, "so that those who have a superior form are called beautiful," then "doubtless even capacity for form is a good thing."[71] Augustine thus asserts, as Harrison puts it, that "the beauty of creation, which is intrinsic to its existence and synonymous with it from the moment of its creation, cannot therefore be denied."[72] The implications of this conclusion are important.

To assert that *hyle* is good in its very capacity to receive form is already to invoke its participation in the good explicated earlier as simultaneously an *intentio* and *responsio* of love.[73] The *hyle* is thus already interposed in the interval between the Father's intention of and delight in the Son and the Son's response to and vision of the Father, and it is by virtue of this location that the *hyle*, along with formed matter and "spiritual corporeal compounds," can be understood to participate in the conversion to form.[74]

Three further facets of this logic help to clarify this point and to reform our characterization of the *hyle*. First, Augustine is adamant in *Conf.* XIII.33 that there was no interval of time between this *hyle* and its acquisition of form, which forbids thinking of a formless *hyle* existing prior to its being informed.[75] The assertion is immediately preceded by an echo of Psalm 58: "Your works long to praise you, to the end that we may love you, and we love you to the end that we may praise you."[76] Given the *creatio, conversio, formatio* schema, the coincidence of the two remarks hardly seems coincidental. This brings us to a second facet of the *hyle* which Augustine insists upon in this remark, that its goodness—logically, though not temporally—precedes its reception of form.

When we recall that Augustine has located the *hyle* within the triune intention and delight, we can see the upshot to these two observations. The "gap" between the *hyle* and its form should be understood, not as a gap between an active and passive principle conjoined, or, as Hankey would have it, between the form and its formless "substrate."[77] Rather the distinction serves to locate the division *within* the creature itself as a proportion within a single "extension" so as to make a certain inequality intrinsic to the creature itself. This inequality is consistent with much of what we have already seen from Augustine: his conception of the soul and the soul–body relationship as composed of various numeric proportions; his conception of temporality as a numeric proportion within a cosmic poem, analogous to the sounding of notes within the unity of an overall score; his preoccupation in *Confessiones* X with the memory of his forgetfulness, the inequality between himself as a product of history and himself as remembered; and his insistence in the *De Musica* and elsewhere that nothing in time is ever equal to itself.[78]

Judged from one angle, this inequality can be viewed with anxiety as loss and lack, as Augustine indeed does when he grieves over the death of Nebridius and laments his failures of memory in *Confessiones* X and his *distentio* amidst the cares of the *saecula* in Book XI.[79] Hankey follows suit in fretting that such an inequality would forever postpone the union of human and divine. Yet, as I shall argue against Stephen Menn in Chapter 5, this anxiety should not really be coupled with a "movement into the self as *against* the sensible."[80] This view suffers from the double fault of being premised upon an unsustainable dualism and of neglecting the positive role played by sensible beauty in Augustine's Christology. Instead this entropy should be attributed to a failure in one's *use* of the sensible, owing to willful conformity with Adam's original misuse.[81]

Judged from another angle, however, there emerges a positive aspect to
this inequality, which brings us to the final facet of this logic. The view
under the first aspect situated the creature within the Father's intention of
and mutual delight in the Son who mediates the temporal *extensio*.[82] In
consequence, it is possible to view this division *within* the extension of the
creature differently, as a distance denoting not a lack, but a plenitude of
intention, delight, and gift which both recapitulates microcosmically within
the creature the mediating plenitude of Christ as *exemplum* and
sacramentum and constitutes her place within that plenitude.[83] The
proportional inequality of a creature to itself, though mutable and subject
to dissolution, loss, and lack under sin, is also susceptible, in other words,
to being construed positively as an ecstatic *surplus* of the creature to itself,
just as the very process of change which is our dying is also our coming to
be.[84] This surplus is held out as promise in the Son and is wrought through
his gift, which manifests both the indivisibility of the trinitarian operations
ad extra and the *theologia ad intra*. Numerous features of the *Confessiones*
witness to this surplus: the dual sense of *distentio* in *Confessiones* XI, its
interplay with *intentio*, Augustine's exclamation in *Confessiones* X, that he is
a "life varied and manifold mightily surpassing measurement," and that he
"cannot comprehend all that I am."[85]

To claim that the creature's inequality to itself manifests its participation
in divine charity is to claim that created reality is at once *intrinsically
constituted* in an extension toward an *exemplum* and moved by its beauty as a
principle. And so created reality is constituted in the union of *viam* to the
patriam, in Christ's act of mediation.[86] We can see this in the case of the *hyle*.
For the fact that the *hyle* already participates in the Good, in the Father's
delight in the beautiful *forma* of the Son and the Son's responsive vision of
the Father, means that the very *capacitas formae* by which the creature may
become equal to, and indeed surpass, itself in its reception of *forma* should
itself be understood as a kind of active reception, a capacity and movement
to "respond" to the *vocatio* to form constitutive of this participation. Yet
inasmuch as its future telos lies anterior to it in the gift from the *principio*,
the response itself must be moved and mediated by the call.[87] Thus even the
hyle is not purely passive as its activity consists precisely in its proper
response to the Word, moved and mediated by that same Word.

This conclusion disrupts the dualism of the sensible and intelligible, and
the subsequent need to beat an absolute retreat from *sensibilia*. Though it is
true that this language pervades the Augustinian corpus, the logic of
Augustine's view of creation thoroughly subverts it. For this logic contextual-
izes this language within an ontology in which such dualism can find no
final resting place.[88] The *hyle*'s active reception of the divine intention,
rather than instituting a dualism between matter and ideal form, renders
matter itself, in some sense, *ideal* and *active*.[89] "Matter participates in something belonging to the ideal world, otherwise it would not be matter."[90]

87

Emilie Zum Brunn's testimony to the "tightness of the bond that links the body's fate to that of the soul," supports this anti-dualistic inference.[91] It also helps us to understand Lewis Ayres's move to locate the *exercitatio mentis* of *De Trinitate within* the two-natured person of Christ. For it helps us to locate the *caesura* between *sapientia* and *scientia*,—and the created economy's diverse signification and manifestation of him—not between sensibility and intelligibility, form and matter, or action and passion.[92] Instead the caesura appears at the point of the ontological difference between a transcendent God who creates from nothing and the creature whose entire existence, both form and matter, witnesses to the goodness of that Creator. Within a doxological ontology, wherein *magis esse* is tantamount to *magis amare deum*, wherein not just the soul but the cosmos "bears witness to the metaphysics of conversion," a dualism of time and eternity or of activity and passivity, cataloged discretely to spirit and matter, simply has no final application.[93]

If Augustine's doctrine of grace is a function of his trinitarian theology and Christology, and if these doctrines are definitive for understanding the relation of creature to Creator, then the problematic of regeneration posed by the Pelagians is subordinate to the question of this relation and is a "grammatical" issue for the notions of causality adequate to such a conception. Having demonstrated in the previous section the trinitarian character of this problem, and having now shown how an understanding of creation in the Son transfigures the terms in question, let us consider this causal grammar.

The mechanics of grace

The Father's generation of the Son is at once an intention of the good and a delight in his beauty; the Son's filiation is constituted actively in a response which, together with the Father's delight, makes up the third term. Creation's participation in this immutable beauty and reciprocal generosity was denoted by a kind of similitude, by *its* active response to that same beauty, moved by the gratuity of that beauty itself. There is no room in this understanding for a simple interchange of activity and passivity. Transcendence and immutability preclude this opposition from God's side. Both the created similitude and this understanding of *creatio ex nihilo* preclude it from ours: there is nothing passive prior to God's bringing us into actuality for God to act upon.

Hence the grammar of causality intrinsic to this conception is akin to one David Burrell attributes to Aquinas, where causing an effect is properly construed, not as a quantum of force, but as a non-reciprocal *relation*. Whatever is in act, or, in Augustine's terminology, whatever simply and immutably *est*, "whose will is part of its very substance," need do nothing beyond being to become a cause. "Therefore just as in the beginning you have known heaven and earth without change in your knowledge, so too, 'in the beginning you have made heaven and earth' without any change in your activity."[94]

No "causal connection" is posited for this activity by which the respective agencies may be "conjoined." Rather causality here is simply said to have occurred when something new appears where before there was nothing, when the activity of the object changed can be described in terms similar to those describing the active power of the primary "agent." This is precisely what the trinitarian similitude in us does, however analogically remote it remains from its origin.[95] With no real reciprocal relation between the related terms, there is no causal connection, no immanent force, and thus no immanent exclusivity or competition, between cause and effect. Rather we must understand creatures to exhibit their status as creatures, as received effects, in their active response to the call to form from the divine *vox*. Paradoxically, this movement is utterly distinct and yet utterly indistinguishable from the movement of the *vox* in them. In consequence, it is a response, a movement which fully belongs to creatures *precisely insofar as it belongs to God*. It is a conversion to form, to actuality, to beauty, precisely to the extent that it is a participation in the doxology, the intention, delight and gift which is the *forma* of God. Thus we actually become fully human, fully ourselves, as we pass through a doxological offering which is at once ours *and* a gift of the Holy Spirit, as we pass from the similitude to the image *in which* we are created: the *principio*, from whom, with whom, and in whom our creation occurs.

A grammar thus emerges from reflection upon the doctrines of the Trinity and creation that is identical in structure to the grammar which governs the doctrine of grace. I shall call this logic of divine causality proto-Chalcedonian for two reasons. The first is that the divine and human contributions can neither be neatly delineated nor represented as a "Nestorian" conjunction.[96] The second is that these "contributions" occur within the unity of the two-natured Christ who is the beauty and end of creation in his doxological response to the Father. He incorporates us into this offering in the gift of the Holy Spirit who moves us to desire him with the desire by which we can truly be said to move ourselves.

This proto-Chalcedonian logic is apparent in Augustine's replies to the Pelagians. In *De Spiritu et Littera*, for example, Augustine asserts that "whatever [the soul] possesses, and whatever it receives, is from God; and yet the act of receiving and having belongs, of course to the receiver and possessor."[97] Augustine affirms the activity of receiving and that the two aspects of this logic are distinct; yet this active reception makes it impossible to distinguish them. In things created to manifest the beauty and the image of the one who *is* as the act of generative *caritas*, there is simply no pure passivity, no way of delineating action from passion and thus no way to isolate a mechanism by which to distinguish the activity of the "cause" from the activity which, precisely as activity, is the effect. For apart from participation in this gift, there is finally nothing.

> For before I was, you were, and I was nothing to which you could grant being. Yet, behold! I am, because of goodness, which preceded all that you made me to be, and out of which you made me.[98]

The enterprise which ignores either the ontology of creation or the apophatic limits that creation places on ontology, and which attempts to delineate in the graced act a distinction, whether conjunctive or disjunctive, between two autonomous agents, is doomed to failure or misrepresentation. God is not *an* agent, and *creatures* unfolding within the divine gift are not freestanding and autonomous objects. They and their agency cannot be dialectically juxtaposed to the giver and gift of their good existence and they are not in a position transcendentally to survey the relation they have to their Creator. (If they were, they would *be* the creator, as Aquinas implies.)[99] In claiming that grace establishes free will, Augustine nowhere posits the causal connection between the gift of grace and our good acts. And his treatment in *De Gratia Christi* XII–XIII of "the grace which conducts [*perducit*] all who are predestined and called according to the divine purpose," a grace which consists simply in our doing what ought to be done, should not be read as attempting to offer one. Nowhere in his treatment, where grace is understood to be present precisely *as* my performance of the good work, is there space for a mechanism distinguishing the respective contributions of the "two agents," whether from God's side a causal mechanism, or from the creature's, the intervention of my "choice."[100] In claiming, therefore, that grace conducts the predestined, Augustine is not providing a mechanism for delineating the inviolable divine and human contribution. Rather he is stating the conditions under which any contribution I might make can be genuinely human at all.

These conditions subsist ultimately in Christ, and his mediation of this gift implies a certain philosophy of action without which the soul, on Augustine's terms, becomes unintelligible. It is the task of the next section to demonstrate how the Pelagian conception of action threatens to rend asunder both this ontology and this intelligibility.

Augustine's doxological self

"'In the Beginning (*principio*) God created the heavens and the earth,' that is, in his Word, coeternal with himself, God made intelligible and sensible, or spiritual and corporeal creation."[101] This entire movement of *creatio ex nihilo* occurs, for Augustine as with Christian tradition more generally, in the Father's delight in his Word. That creatures should therefore be constituted precisely in activity is a consequence of having this effusive love as their origin, and their conversion to form—their coming *esse magis*— is a consequence of the Father's love of the Son (which is also the Son's love of the Father), being more fully realized in them. "We see all these things, and we see that they are very good, because you see them in us, who have given to us your Spirit, by whom we might see them and in them love you."[102] If it is in this image, from this principle and with this likeness that we are created, and if it is for this image that the elect are destined, then it is only *in* the Word, *in* Christ, in the "hypostatic union" which is the complete realization of the cause in the effect, that one is *magis esse*. Hence this complete realization of the cause in the effect is really the complete realization of the effect in itself. There is no "outside" to that economy.[103] In attempting to jump outside it, to flee it, one simply consigns oneself to the incoherency of a remote *regio dissimilitudinis* which is *esse minus*.[104]

Selfhood is doxological. It is only through delight in Christ, a gift of the mutual delight between the Father and the Son, that "I" can finally be myself. It is the purpose of this section to bring this understanding to bear on Augustine's doctrine of grace and to begin to show the ominous consequences of the Pelagian introduction of another kind of self, alien to this economy, into Christian thought and practice. The stakes from Augustine's side are already clear. In claiming that the *cognitio legis*, quarantined from *voluntas* and *actio*, negates the cross of Christ, Augustine effectively charges the Pelagians with compromising both the nature of creation and the Trinity itself.[105] The incoherence of the Pelagian self, and the account of the conditions and motives of its action, is but a by-product of this compromise. Robert Dodaro's commentary upon Augustine's position, which recalls the christological union of *scientia* and *sapientia*, helps us begin to see why.

> When Augustine charged the Pelagians with reducing divine assistance (*adioutorium*) to knowledge of the law (*cognitio legis*), he understood them to be equating grace with knowledge of *scientia* without mediation. Missing from the Pelagian explanation of moral knowledge was *inspiratio dilectionis*, the love of God (in both senses of the genitive) which informs moral understanding and will.[106]

The analysis of the last chapter illuminated one sense of the genitive *Dei*, of the love which is both God and the gift of God, and showed how Augustine conceives its manifestation in us as a function of Christ's unity and the indivisibility of the trinitarian operations. We saw how intelligible desire is intrinsic to even the most mundane of actions, and how, for this very reason, all action implied the "anterior" mediation of the desired. The object of intention, the "final cause" must also be the "first cause" whose beauty entices us to act for its sake, a movement which we have been at pains to locate within God's intention of the Good and love of the Beautiful which God is.[107] We have seen, moreover, that the mechanics of this mediation are "proto-Chalcedonian;" there is no "conjunction" of discrete and mutually exclusive contributions, as there would be in Nestorian Christology.[108] Both the anteriority of the divine love and its futurity are exhibited precisely in my love and are indeed the very preconditions for this love being "mine."

Consequently the latter sense of the genitive, my love for God, is both derivative of and coextensive with the first. This reflects the "aesthetic functions" of Augustine's Christology in both manifesting and incorporating us into the beauty and love of God. Christ is as at once the *exemplum* of God the Father whose *profunditas* exhibits a certain distance and elicits desirous attention, which he fills gratuitously as *sacramentum* (sending the Spirit with the Father) in the *eros* of a "faith which is able to 'pass over' into its object."[109] Augustine's understanding of intelligible action, in other words, is isomorphic with his articulation of Christ's mediation of divine love. It follows, as Dodaro's remark suggests, that to break with this moral psychology is to break with this Christology and ontology. At long last, we may now appreciate what the Pelagians substituted for Augustine's doxological ontology.

In *De Civitate Dei* IX, Augustine reduces the various schools of pagan moral philosophy to a single, broadly stoic, moral psychology. The failure of Pelagian moral psychology, according to James Wetzel, is the result of a flaw that it shares with this stoicism, which leads him to conclude that "Augustine's best challenge to Pelagian theology lies in his rebuttal of pagan philosophy."[110] In contrast to Augustine, who includes repentant grief within wisdom, the reconstructed pagans equate beatitude with an impassible virtue, and are thus left with a common conception of beatitude as a condition of *apatheia* achieved through reason's mastery over the passions.[111] This will prove to be its undoing as a moral psychology, but the crucial point—which Wetzel does not address—is how the Pelagian failure is a function of its inadequate Christology, a failure attributable to those stoic debts and the ontological baggage they bring. In employing a conception of self-hood and agency whose original ontological register was the immanentist and monist cosmology of the stoics, the Pelagian self will carry into Christian thought and practice the tensions intrinsic to this cosmology, tensions incompatible with divine transcendence, the conflation of *esse* and *dilectio* and the gratuity of *creatio ex nihio*.[112]

Wetzel's analysis is nevertheless important for several reasons. Confirming the earlier view of Gilson, he concludes, in contrast to Stephen Menn and others, that the concept of will as "the power of choice" is a Pelagian "fiction" and counters that "there is no *faculty* of will, distinct from desire, which we use to determine our actions."[113] Our analysis of *De Trinitate* concurs for (at least) two reasons: because will always entails memory and intellect, and because delight is integral to the intelligibility of our actions while "choice" is not.

To accept this point is to see that Augustine is not discovering or inventing *voluntas* as the capacity for a "reified choice" superadded to the *ratio* of our affections. And it allows us to begin to see, at the psychological level, what we have already considered at the ontological level: how "irresistible" grace can coextend with freedom. This is a matter of immediate importance in countering the Pelagians, but it also has long-term implications for the narrative of continuity between Augustine and Descartes. For the line from Augustine to Descartes to be an unbroken one, both Augustine's God and the Augustinian agent will need to become voluntarists, to exercise *arbitrium* as power or choice unqualified by other essential divine predicates and without motive beyond power's exercise.[114] The refusal of a "faculty of choice" rebuts this reading and counteracts the tendency to misread "temporal dislocation," that phenomenon whereby past actions are habitually carried over into present willing, in this voluntarist direction.[115] As we shall see, it is precisely this voluntarist aspect of Pelagianism that Augustine opposes. Augustine's particular take on the phenomenon of *akrasia*, where our action for the good is not always equal to our knowledge of it, does indeed seem to be original and does not ultimately redound to a simple failure of judgment.[116] Yet it does not follow that this recognition is the origin of "our modern notion of will" understood as "sheer volition, regardless of its origin either in cognition or emotion," and only a positivist abstraction of "Augustinian humanity" from Augustine's ontology could make it so.[117]

Augustine's seamless treatment of acting according to an intelligible good will leaves no space for this voluntaristic faculty or the account of choice which attends it.[118] In the "aesthetic" realm of *magis et minus esse*, where *natura* is an eschatological term denoting a restoration convergent with a semblance of affection, consent is merely the *ratio* expressed in the act itself and already testifies to a prior desire.[119] Choice between alternatives is not a sign of the will's freedom to choose but its bondage to an internal division in desire. Augustine's recollection of his own divided will in *Confessiones* VIII illustrates this conclusion in exemplary fashion.

Freedom for Augustine consists not in unqualified *arbitrium*, but in a single-minded love of the good where the need for choice never arises.[120] In this case, "consent" merely denotes our acting at last with the continence of a unified desire toward that which supremely attracts us. And to the degree that the act consented to accords with the good of doxology, it denotes the restoration of the trinitarian image in us.[121] From this perspective—which grounds the integrity of our willing in our ontological integrity as creatures—any alternative is destined to produce profound incoherence.

Augustine's reduction of all pagan moral psychology to a species of stoicism in Books IX and XIX of *De Civitate Dei* contains an attack on (at

93

least) three fronts: on the conception of beatitude as *apatheia*, wherein reason rules undisturbed by the passions, on the conception of virtue which is correlative to this conception, and on the ontological presuppositions, reflected in pagan practices of worship, that support them both.[122] This three-pronged attack allows him to depart from the stoic conclusion that virtue and grief are incompatible, a conclusion which he thinks untenable anyway for reasons we shall soon discover.[123] Reconfiguring the emotions as forms of will, that is, as forms of desire, Augustine recasts the question of disruptive passions in accord with the new definition and with the Christian understanding of the good. The important question becomes not whether one suffers certain passions, but whether our suffering of these passions is appropriate to the contingent circumstances, in the light of this good.[124]

In both books, Augustine deploys anecdotal evidence to render the stoic position untenable. In Book IX he relates a tale from the *Attic Nights* in which a stoic sage caught in a tempest at sea was reduced to a brief instance of panic before regaining his composure.[125] Similarly, in Book XIX, Augustine ridicules Varro's contention that a wise man might justifiably commit suicide in the face of unremitting evil.[126] The first anecdote illuminates a division of desire within the sage's judgment; both aid Augustine's assault upon pagan beatitude by making this division in desire intrinsic to the life of virtue itself. As Wetzel remarks, Augustine's very translation of *sophrosyne* as *temperantia* denies "the philosophers the purity of their practical reason," makes temptation *intrinsic* to the virtuous life, and thus implicates our vices in our capacity to reason.[127]

This same condition of irascibility holds good for the other virtues. The very presence of justice, for instance, implies the need for discrimination because injustice is an ever present threat.[128] Augustine does not quite suggest here the rather Nietzschean conclusion that "virtue is always reactive: it always secretly celebrates as its occasion a prior evil, lives out of what it opposes," but elsewhere he does, as we have already seen.[129] This is important, for as his critique of pagan virtue passes over into a critique of the pagan cult, it becomes clear that Augustine weds the failure to manifest virtue as charity to the "ontological" failure to recognize charity as the transcendent ontological reality. Pagan civic virtue conceals the civic celebration of a transcendental violence.

As a consequence of this unmasking, Augustine lays a dilemma at the feet of the philosophers which keenly illustrates the interrelation of the three fronts of Augustine's attack and which most constitutes its force. The sage's contemplated suicide exemplifies this dilemma well: "Either this belief involves a massive equivocation on the meaning of beatitude, or it is a betrayal of the virtue of fortitude."[130]

Wetzel characterizes Augustine's relationship to stoicism more as an orientation to a generally pervasive cultural attitude, one probably imbibed from Cicero's *De Finibus* and Varro's *De Philosophia*, than a direct rebuttal of

94

specific doctrines as they were held by historic stoics. So it is perhaps fair to class Augustine with a host of the stoa's antique critics who remained rather unaware of some of the nuances of their ethical doctrine. In critiquing stoic reason's claim to mastery over the passions, Augustine may not have known that the passions had already come to be entailed in judgments and vice versa in the passage from Zeno to Chrysippus; indeed Augustine's own formulation may be unwittingly indebted to it. Numerous contemporary reconstructions of stoic moral psychology have emphasized this point, and it is not necessary to rehearse them here.[131] Still Augustine's depiction in *De Civitate Dei* Book IX of stoic practical reason is correct in its essential features. He describes the stoics account of how , in our *horme*, or striving, we either give or withhold assent to *phantasiai* which impress themselves upon the *hegemonikon* involuntarily. Our actions are "up to us," because it is in our power to give or withhold this assent, and this power is freedom. The fact that the *phantasiai* already contain judgments by virtue of their appearing under the aspect of "*x*," a point crucial to the contemporary reconstruction of stoic passion, is beside the point from Augustine's perspective and immaterial to the success of his case.[132]

The contemporary reconstructions, which admit that the intrusions of the *phantasiai* do not come under the control of the *hegemonikon* only either push the problem exposed by Augustine back one remove to a "pre-rational" level or, ironically, implicate vice in reason more deeply.[133] In either case, they fail to perceive the depths of the disorder that Augustine wishes to expose, for, as we showed in the last chapter, Augustine understands that the will is entailed in vision or apprehension itself.[134] He therefore insists, rightly, that the "irrational" *phantasiai*, even those rejected by the sage, would not even elicit attention if they did not already attest to an "anterior" division in desire. If we did not assume such a division, we would have no way to account for their claim upon us. This insistence undermines both the sage's claims for the sufficiency and ultimacy of virtue, for it negates the claim that "a person possessed of wisdom and virtue would never experience a genuine conflict between will and world."[135]

So the dilemma persists, despite the contemporary rehabilitation of stoic thought, and it is this dilemma that constitutes the force of Augustine's case. Either horn of the dilemma is unsavory. Insist upon reason's control of the passions and one ends up, as we shall see, with an incoherent account both of how the self lives its life in time and of how we are moved to action. (Wetzel is right on this score to insist that "pagan otherworldliness" is Augustine's real target here.)[136] Admit the passions into reason, and one opens a breach in the beatific *apatheia* of the stoic sage that its moral psychology was designed to prevent.[137] And this we have already seen. Pagan happiness, it seems, cannot be sustained without sacrificing pagan virtue. And pagan virtue cannot be sustained without sacrificing pagan happiness.

Conceiving of beatitude wrongly, the pagans thus conceive of virtue wrongly. For with virtue itself now agonized, it clearly cannot suffice as the highest good. Taken as its own end, virtue merely testifies to the "stupefying arrogance of those people who imagine that they can find the Ultimate Good in this life and that they can attain happiness by their own efforts," and to the cruel trick the philosophers have perpetrated on themselves in assessing their actual condition.[138]

Augustine appears to have the stoics in a bind whether or not he "misreads" them. For the dilemma posed by Augustine *requires* them to adopt something like a moral psychology of reason's mastery over the passions if they have any hope of sustaining the goal of *apatheia*. This is to say, sustaining *apatheia* in this life, or better, its illusion, will *require* that the sources of conflict be externalized, even at the "pre-rational" level of the intrusion of *phantasiai* into the citadel of consciousness.[139] And this requirement purchases its beatitude at the price of restricting the realm of the voluntary to what we can *control*, not to what we *want*. This opens the floodgates for Augustine's criticism, and its effects are far reaching. For the ultimate result of this restriction is a correlative shift in the image through which to model the relation of the will to its object: from the relation of lover to beloved to that of cause to effect.[140]

For Augustine, by contrast, the scope of the voluntary appears, to a modern point of view, at once both broadened and narrowed. It is broadened, as is our culpability, because *volo/velle/voluntas* express our capacity to act, and our actions embody and give expression to our desires. Hence Augustine "internalizes" the conflicting sources of motivation for our various actions.[141] This scope is narrowed, as is our capacity to act for the good, precisely because our actions express these desires and not the power of unqualified *arbitrium* between alternatives.

We have already seen the positive side of this understanding of the voluntary. Freedom consists not in the capacity to withhold assent to external intrusions; the need for such strength is for Augustine a sign of our enduring unfreedom. Rather it consists in the single-minded love of God, our happiness. The negative counterpart to this idea is the notion of involuntary sin, and, inasmuch as the stoic conception of freedom requires them to deny it, they remain blinded to the depth of their disorder.[142]

We can see this conception of the voluntary in Augustine's consideration of whether faith is any longer "in our power" (*in nostra potestate*) when given gratuitously by God. Augustine asks us to consider more closely the meaning of that phrase.

> We are not accustomed to saying that someone who acted unwillingly acted under his own power. Although, if we should attend to the matter more precisely, even what someone is forced to do he does by means of his will if he does it at all. But since he

would prefer to do otherwise, he is said for that reason to act against his will; in other words, he acts unwillingly. Obviously some evil compels him to act in that he does unwillingly what willingly he would avoid or remove from himself. For if his will were such that he should prefer not acting to not suffering the evil, no doubt he would resist the source of compulsion and not act. And so if he does act, even without a full or free will, he acts nevertheless in no other way than by means of his will. And because his will issues in effect, we cannot say that the power for acting was lacking to him.[143]

Both the positive and negative aspects of this understanding are latent in this explanation. Our actions are "free" when they realize our desire for the good, enslaved when they do not. And our lives in time express this condition of enslavement. We are "internally" compelled to sin; we do not "choose" it, and this internal compulsion, which literally sets the soul against itself, threatens to become ontological dissolution. Yet these actions "are up to us," to use the old stoic phrase; they are *ours*, because they nevertheless express *our* desires.[144] We want them. And to the extent that we both want them and do not want them, we can be hopeful, at least for the later Augustine of *De Spiritu et Littera*, that our ontological dissolution is being overcome by grace.[145]

The broadened scope which Augustine gives to the voluntary combines with the notion of involuntary sin to illuminate the weaknesses of the stoic equivocation on sources. As Wetzel explains, the hope for reason's mastery over the passions relies on a misunderstanding of the passions, which must somehow entail our capacity to reason in order to account for their claim on us. Yet if this is admitted, the integrity of reason is compromised. Reason cannot cast out rebellious passions without, as Wetzel puts it, "dividing its own house." For this reason, "the basis of pagan moral psychology—that of two distinct sources of motivation, only one of which emerges from reason—is therefore corrupt."[146]

One can already see how the Augustinian perspective diagnoses this corruption. The detachment of the two sources of motivation from one another is the undoing of the unity of knowledge and love in creatures created in the image of the Trinity.[147] The implications are even clearer if one recalls that the creature's status as image is not merely a matter of resemblance, but of participation in the divine love.[148] More immediately, however, Augustine's expansion of the voluntary illuminates two fatal weaknesses of the stoic moral psychology. The first was the stoic inability to cope with the phenomenon of involuntary sin, a weakness exposed by Augustine's anecdotal evidence. This inability has profound implications both for how one conceives of life in time and for the ability to live out the moral life under temporal restraints. Not least among these is the extent to which the externalization of our conflicting sources of motivation clouds the agent's self-knowledge, a point we shall return to shortly. The second weakness of the stoic moral psychology is its failure to account, not only for how we are moved to sin involuntarily, but how we might even be moved to desire beatitude. It is also here that the Augustinian alternative begins to emerge and the groundwork is laid, at the level of moral psychology, for the claim that grace is the necessary and sufficient condition for the will's freedom.

In the *De Trinitate*, Augustine asserts that blessedness consists in two things: willing rightly and having what one wills.[149] If involuntary sin reflects the negative side of Augustine's expanded view of the voluntary, the positive side, and the corrective to the weaknesses of the stoic view, consists in the philosophy of volition latent in these remarks.[150] Augustine's identification of *voluntas* and desire issues in the notion of positive freedom we have already discussed. Transposed into the language of action theory or moral psychology, this means that freedom consists precisely in our actions giving expression to the desire that qualifies those actions as "ours." Or, to put it differently, "our actions are genuinely ours [and so genuinely free] if our motives fully account for our having committed them."[151] This is why a will torn between irreconcilable desires is ultimately unfree.

Of course this begs many questions that a contemporary philosophy of action would want to ask. What, for instance, does one mean by "motive?"[152] By what criterion of identity does one render descriptions of the acts for which the motive is supposed to account or of the motive apart from the action? What kind of descriptions are these? Are there any rules for this derivation and, if so, rules for application of the rules? What sense does it even make to speak of motives when the proximate ends and means of an act can be elided into a description of the remote end?[153] Does the invocation of motive not invoke the kind of self knowledge, and indeed the kind of self, which I have been at pains to deny as having its origin in Augustine?

I do not claim to address all of these questions adequately, but there are a number of implications to this position that at least indicate a reply. First, we should remember that all knowledge, though not to be equated with "thought," is, for Augustine, knowledge of time remembered.[154] This is true even of "present" knowledge. Memory is "the condition in which the mind is present to itself."[155] From this it follows that the *attribution* of motives to oneself is always a matter of narrative re-description, just as "being moved" to act is always a matter of narrative enactment, that is; it is always situated within the *ordo amoris* put into action by a *civitas*.[156] It is neither necessary to detach the motive as "a cause" apart from or prior to the action nor to identify one's motives with the sort of introspective "mental contents" that Anscombe ridicules.[157] This identification between thought and motive will prove problematic on Augustinian terms. The identification of one's "true motives" with one's prospective mental contents is always subject to revision under the formality of a higher desire, as evidenced by Augustine's recollection in *Confessiones* II of his motiveless pear theft, which when "represented under the good of his own creation, [loses its] intelligibility."[158] Furthermore, the loss of self in memory is a central preoccupation of *Confessiones*, which can be understood as an attempt to re-describe more truthfully in retrospect, under this formality, motives and desires embodied in action which were prospectively unavailable. It is because of this necessity for *confession* in all its senses that it is so monumental that Augustine admits grief over past sins into the life of wisdom. The externalization of miscreant affections by the stoic sage does not simply hide himself from his own view. Rather it makes impossible the attempt to render oneself intelligible by means of what Alasdair MacIntyre calls the "narrative unity of a human life."[159] In so doing, it extricates the sage from life in time.[160] This is a theme to which we shall return.

One can employ this same point against a second, "Foucaultian" line of criticism.[161] It does appear, at first glance, that the "internalization" of conflict occasioned by "involuntary sin" sets Augustine further down the path than the stoics toward a phenomenologically unified—and ontologically original —subject burdened with anxieties and requiring technologies for his own self mastery. Yet I shall contend, more in the subsequent two chapters than here, that the opposite is the case and that it is those traditions of Christian thought and practice which draw upon stoic moral psychology that are instrumental in giving birth to this creature. The crucial difference is exhibited in Augustine's evolving interpretation of Romans 7 and the important place it comes to occupy in his thought.[162] This internalization of motive means that "I do not understand my own actions, do not do what I want and do the very thing that I hate." But whereas this once would have demarcated the distinction between life *sub lege* and life *sub gratia*, for the Augustine of *Ad Simplicianum* and the Pelagian controversy the conflict testifies to the anterior operations of grace. Paul's condition testifies to a soul once again turned inside out, for whom interiority is already radically exteriorized. It means that any border which would rigidly demarcate interiority from exteriority loses its intelligibility. This renders the unity of the soul's self identity and self-knowledge provisional.

The *Confessiones* never ceases to exhibit this provisionality. Even after the climactic events of Book IX, Augustine remains a mystery to himself, "a life varied and manifold and mightily surpassing measurement."[163] Partly, this is because of this anteriority, because Augustine himself is constituted in God's gift, is most fully himself in giving and knows even himself apophatically as a consequence of this kataphatic acknowledgment.[164] To reify himself in the appropriation of this gift is to risk "becoming a *simulacrum* of himself which passes away just as he abstracts or distills it."[165]

As we saw earlier, there are both positive and negative aspects to this instability. Each is reflected in Book XI of the *Confessiones*. The movement to "internalize" the source of conflict in irreconcilable desires is one with the *distentio* of *Confessiones* XI.29. It signals the *enkratic* and *akratic* dissipation of this subjective unity, and the intrinsic inequality "between that self which is the sum of his historical experiences and the self which is the sum of his remembered experiences."[166] Yet the positive side to this inequality—the surplus, as it were—is indicated by the solution to this *distentio*, invoked in the same passage. For it is here that Augustine invokes christological mediation as the answer to his own dissipation. This move once again situates both the self and its knowledge within the ambit of trinitarian gift, and makes the means to the acquisition of that knowledge neither a self-objectification nor a sacrificial self-negation, but a sacrifice of praise and thanksgiving.[167] To recover oneself in this sense, however, is only to further the soul's ecstatic reversal by opening it in charity to the Body's participation in the doxological sacrifice of its Head.[168] The gaze of the *Confessiones* is not the gaze of subjectivation, destined "ultimately to constitute subjects that will generate their own gazes—gazes that will envelop them with a continuity and thoroughness that the gaze of another could never sustain."[169] Augustine's continual revision and dissipation testifies to that. Rather selfhood, insofar it is to become selfhood, is, once again, *ecclesiologically* constituted. This is the concluding lesson of *Confessiones* XIII.

By contrast, it is the stoics, and those Christians who draw upon a stoicism unchastened by Augustine's criticisms of pagan virtue, who must expel the source of miscreant passions beyond the circumference of the soul and who must implicitly erect that soul as an originary and autarkic citadel to protect it from the loss of its identity. It is no accident that *charity* assumes a paramount importance in the Augustinian tradition and *discretion* in the latter, nor that *delight* in the one case and *assent* or *choice* in the other are the corresponding terms in their respective philosophies of action.[170] The terms denote divergent ontological contexts within which selfhood, action, and virtue are construed.

For Augustine, these terms are determined by christological mediation, apart from which any alternative is destined to be finally incoherent. It is here that we can at last join the two strands of our argument, the proto-Chalcedonian mechanics and philosophy of action. We are also finally in a position to see how Augustine's rebuttal to pagan philosophy passes into a two-front assault on Pelagian Christology, anthropology, volition and freedom.

In the case of the stoics, we have already seen one facet of this alleged incoherency in the sage's inability to render a coherent narrative of himself. Even more germane, however, is the consequence Wetzel draws from Augustine's critique of the "two distinct sources of motivation" in pagan philosophy. The need to assert reason's mastery over the passions results in an incoherent account of freedom and action.

Recall that our acts can only be attributed to us, we are only genuinely free, we can only enter beatitude, and the soul can only finally be itself if our acts are accounted for by our motives, if they embody and express the desire that moved us to act in the first place. The incorporation of *ratio* into the passions, *pace* the stoics, is crucial in that it then makes possible the fundamental role which *delectatio* plays in meeting this condition.

There are two aspects to this role. First, *delectatio* provides the middle term necessary to connect our act to its end and so to meet the condition of attribution. We *are moved* to action by what is judged to be desirable.[171] "It is neither to him that wills nor to him that runs, but to the mercy of God. But we would by no means be able either to will or to run, unless excited and moved by him."[172] We are moved by delight in what attracts us, which is to say we are moved by what has the character of the beautiful. Delight in the end, which invokes the mediation of the object of delight in our action, is for good or for ill the principle of our movement and embodied in it. Of course one must qualify this in terms of the distinction between remote ends, proximate ends and the use of means, so as to be able to variegate this moral psychology.[173] We may, for instance, do something repulsive for the sake of something in which we delight. But that does not cease to make the role of delight fundamental. The sage tossed at sea would not recoil if the storm had not threatened something he valued.[174] Augustine's observation here presupposes a latent conviction that he shares with Aquinas: "there is no other passion of the soul that does not presuppose love of some kind."[175]

It is no accident that this formal account of action is so similar to our earlier treatments of the trinitarian generation and procession and to its economic manifestation in the incarnation of Christ. Nor is it accidental that this account requires that action be open to the mediation of the Son as form of God and sender, with the Father, of the Spirit. For that is the second role of delight. It is because *delectatio* meets this condition of attribution that Augustine is able to make freedom and grace coextend; indeed it is because of this *delectatio* that freedom is able to be freedom. For our motives are able to account for actions, which have the good as their formal object, precisely to the extent that we are moved by the good.[176] This is Augustinian grace.[177] In short, grace establishes freewill through the mediation of the object of delight by incorporating our realization of the remote end, that which is supremely delightful and for whose sake we pursue lesser goods, into the delight shared between the Father and the Son in the procession of the Holy Spirit. "For to be drawn to Christ is to receive the gift of the Father, which is to believe in Christ."[178]

The logic of Augustine's position is fairly succinct. If we are only genuinely free and only genuinely ourselves to the extent that our actions express our desires, and if this condition obtains only to the extent that we are moved in our pursuit of proximate goods by delight in that good for whose sake this pursuit is undertaken, then insofar as this good must be the

God who is love (the argument of *De Civ.* XIX.4), then we can only be free to the extent that we are moved by love. We can therefore only be truly free, only truly ourselves, as a consequence of sharing in the delight of the Father for the Son. Freedom must therefore coextend with grace, and the form which this freedom takes is the erotic love of the beautiful, for the beautiful, the source of which is at once us and the beauty which moves us.[179] The name given to this beauty is Jesus Christ and his body, the love of which is his gift to us.[180]

Irresistible attraction to the beauty of Christ, the form and exemplar of God, moved by the delight which the Father takes in the body of his Son, is therefore both the necessary and sufficient condition for Augustinian freedom and the consummation of nature. The contemplation of this beauty "is promised to us as the end of all actions and the eternal perfection of joy."[181] Apart from this all other action, in retrospect, will be revealed not even to have been free, indeed not even to have qualified as action.[182]

Yet the Pelagian scheme of *possibilitas*, *voluntas* and *actio*, which follows the stoics in conceiving of freedom as the power of assent and negation, intends to secure against the irresistibility of this erotic attraction and thus reinstitutes a kind of mitigated stoic autarky.[183] At the level of moral psychology, we can already see why Augustine must reject this Pelagian view. To reject *delectatio* is to reject the very thing that qualifies our actions as ours.[184] The Pelagian tripartite schema of *possibilitas*, *voluntas* and *actio* has an ontological effect as well. It inserts a *caesura* between our pursuit of proximate ends, lesser goods and the last end or highest good for whose sake these lesser are pursued and from whom we derive our being. If our pursuit of proximate ends is severed from our motive for doing them, they fail not only to meet the conditions for free acts but, ultimately, to attain to the weight of being.[185]

This Pelagian conception of volition implies a conception of the agent who acts. From an Augustinian viewpoint, both must be incoherent. By eliminating *delectatio* and insulating against the irresistibility of divine attraction, the Pelagians eliminate the locus of our participation in God and the very thing Augustine thinks is crucial to making our actions intelligible. Moreover, the restriction of grace either to the indeterminacy of *possibilitas* or to the *cognitio legis*, separated discretely from *voluntas*, re-institutes two discrete sources of motivation. We just saw how the Pelagians, severing the agent from participation in the delight between Father and Son, drive a wedge between proximate and remote ends. Something similar occurs "within" the agent when viewed from close range. For the insinuation of two discrete sources of motivation, with its resultant notion of "freedom," drives a wedge between the act and its motive and institutes a motiveless choosing of motives in the breach) "When the right action and the true aim has begun to appear clearly, unless it also be delighted in and loved, there is no doing, no devotion, no good life."[186] With this wedge driven between the act and its motive, with movement of the will by attraction sealed off, the Pelagian cannot provide a moral psychology to account for how knowledge of this law can pass over into its object, even in a simple act of obedience to the law.

Augustine is quite explicit in linking this philosophical failure to a breach in participation, to a failure in understanding Christ's role in a trinitarian economy. When, in *Contra Duas Epistulas Pelagianorum*, Augustine faults the Pelagians for omitting the *inspiratio dilectionis* from their praise of the law, he is not merely offering platitudes, but indicating how the incoherency of the Pelagian account of human action is a problem of trinitarian theology.[187]

He also locates agents squarely within the christological mediation of the trinitarian gift economy that we saw in our reading of *De Trinitate*. It is precisely this that the phrase "faith working by love" expresses. One can see still further the convergence of this account of erotic love for the beautiful with this Christology in this remark from his commentary on John:

> You are drawn, not merely by the will, but what is more, by pleasure. What is it, to be drawn by pleasure? "Delight in the Lord, and he shall give you the requests of your heart" (Ps 37.4) . . . Moreover if the poet had leave to say, "*Trahit sua quemque voluptas*," not necessity, but pleasure, not obligation, but delight; how much more strongly ought we to say that a man is drawn to Christ, when he delights in truth, delights in blessedness, delights in everlasting life, all of which Christ is?[188]

We may ask, by contrast, where the tripartite schema leaves the Pelagian agent. Wetzel has already faulted the stoics because their moral psychology causes the sage to disown his past, and thus extricates him from time. But there is another sense, not sufficiently explored by Wetzel, in which this schema begins to sacrifice time. To begin from the indeterminacy of potentiality means, on the one hand, that the Pelagian is committed, in principle, to being able to identify and isolate a discrete *moment* of choice, of opting for the good, something which Augustine's *memoria dei* denies in principle. For upon recollection, one finds both that one has always already anticipated the good and been anticipated and overcome by it.[189] And yet, on the other hand, precisely inasmuch as the refusal of participatory grace drives a wedge between the act and its principle and forces upon us a motiveless choosing of motives, this isolated moment—which is so important in the reduction from potentiality to act—becomes utterly uncharacterizable as occurring within temporal sequence, or rather, becomes characterizable only as purely indeterminate spontaneity, unconditioned by mediating influences, descending from a discrete, original "presence" which "I" possess.[190] It becomes, at the risk of committing an anachronism, *noumenal*.

103

This may seem a stretch, and we are admittedly a long way from the reduction of space and time to the a priori forms of pure intuition which are the conditions of possibility for subsequent sense experience. But we are not so very far from the subject of the transcendental unity of apperception whose freedom in giving the law to himself cannot be rendered intelligible save for its abnegation in duty and its ability to go against its perceived interests—a point as true of the stoics as it is of Kant. Both stoic autarky and Kantian noumenal freedom can only be displayed in their own negation. Any positive alternative would require that they revise their conception of freedom to make it compatible with determination. Yet the problem of a noumenal freedom visible only in its self-abnegation creates precisely the problem of how actions are to be attributable to their agents. Given the fact that "one of Kant's central failures had been the failure to provide a psychology which could explain how this complete setting aside of one's own particular goals and interests was possible," the comparison is not as outlandish as it seems.[191]

The logic of negation thus set in train by the Pelagian self is foreboding, and appeared more than once in subsequent history. Once human agency is no longer constituted by its participation in the doxological agency of God; once, subsequently, one's status *in Christ* is reduced from participation in the hypostatic union to *mere* mimesis or imitation (and Christ himself from the *Logos* of the Father and *forma* and fulfillment of the new humanity to a sage); once we are no longer understood to be moved to action by the Father's delight in the Son; then *voluntas* ceases to name a relation of love between lover and beloved but rather a "Cartesian" relation of cause to effect.[192] It can only then be construed as an unqualified and unrepresentable projection into the void, and grace—to the extent that it can appear at all—can only appear as an extrinsic and delimiting qualification of an opposing force, which one passively accepts. Grace becomes merely the a priori duty and capacity to obey law.[193] And the sacrifice of praise and thanksgiving is eclipsed, in its logic at least if not yet fully in practice, by a sacrifice of a more ominous kind: by the recovery of the self through its annihilation.

Augustine's repeated refrain, "that grace which begins with us is not grace," can thus be read as a remarkable criticism of Pelagianism's incipient "modernism" and its attendant metaphysics.[194] It declares that Pelagian pietism subtly and ironically establishes itself as its own origin and ground, and is thus deconstructable into a form of *superbia* whose incoherence is as predictable as that resulting from any sin. For, as we have seen, it is precisely the function of the *fides quae dilectionem operatur*—now the implicit form and last end of all our actions—to locate knowledge and action themselves within the love and delight between the Father and the Son. The distance of faith opened up between the agent in Christ and Christ as *exemplum* was filled and moved, made to pass over into its object, by the desirous seeking given by Christ in the Spirit as *sacramentum*. Delight in the Father's beauty manifest in and mediated by Christ was the very form of our participation in the divine life and of the ratio of time to eternity. To extract oneself from time is to extract oneself from this economy, no longer to conceive of one's life as *in* Christ, and thus, in God. This is why Augustine responds to the Pelagians with christological and trinitarian doctrine and why his rebuttal of pagan philosophy extends to the Pelagian cause. From an Augustinian point of view, Pelagianism's failure as a moral psychology is a consequence of its failure as a theology. And the restriction of grace to the indeterminacy of *possibilitas* or to the *cognitio legis* leaves the Pelagians, in spite of their apparent piety, in precisely the same position as the pagans: "philosophizing without a mediator."[195]

4

THE SUBTLE TRIUMPH
OF PELAGIANISM

On winning the battle and losing the war

In the previous chapter I argued that the Pelagian conception of selfhood and volition smuggles into Christian thought an attendant ontology at odds with the doctrine of the Trinity, causing it to sacrifice both what would become orthodox Christology and the doctrine of *creatio ex nihilo*. For this same reason I shall maintain in this chapter that this heresy contains certain metaphysical features that can be characterized as proto-modern.

The ensuing section will demonstrate those proto-modern features and their origin. Since the "stoic" self employed by the Pelagians derives its original intelligibility from stoic cosmology, I shall first situate this self within its original register and contend for the nihilistic implications of this cosmology. I shall then show how the Pelagian conception of grace implicitly depends upon some of stoicism's most basic cosmological assumptions, and, consequently, transmits these implications into a Christian context. This will impinge upon the doctrine of the Trinity and the Augustinian construal of creation derived from it. It is finally here that we can isolate certain features of the Pelagian self that foreshadow modern subjectivity, features that derive from the loss of a trinitarian economy.

The claim that Pelagianism smuggles stoic cosmology into Western Christian thought and practice comprises only half the thesis of this chapter, however. The second half, elucidated in the final section, is that the Pelagian controversy both occasions the refinement of an independent tradition of "stoic" Christianity, unchastened by the criticisms of stoicism in *De Civitate Dei, and* infects the transmission of *Augustinianism,* in the generations after Augustine's death, with the tensions inherent to stoic immanentism. The latter provides antecedents for later voluntaristic transformations to the Augustinian inheritance. The former constitutes a crucial, though often overlooked, contribution to the advent of modern thought. For as we shall see in the next chapter, Descartes' debts both to this tradition of stoic Christianity and to the neostoicism of the Renaissance

106

give a decisive color to his alleged Augustinianism and to the advent of a metaphysics that realizes the nihilistic implications of the stoic first principle.

We shall consider the second aspect of this thesis in the final section, by examining the so-called Semi-Pelagian controversy and the treatment of grace in the ascetic theology of John Cassian. The abbot is both crucial to the future course of Western monasticism and important as a vehicle for the transmission of stoic thought into Western Christendom.[1] This aspect of the argument requires numerous qualifications at the outset, however. While it is necessary to emphasize the importance of the ongoing struggle occasioned by the Pelagians, both for the reception and subsequent transmission of Augustine and for the constitution of Christian asceticism in the West, it is equally important not to mischaracterize it.[2] Though I shall locate certain stoic features of Cassian's thought which create problematic tensions, my concern is neither to resuscitate the misleading seventeenth-century charge of "Semi-Pelagianism," to burden the great Abbot with heresy, nor, conversely, to isolate Augustine as the lone ranger of Western theology. Cassian, it has been argued, was a student of Augustine's work.[3] His stoicism is counterbalanced by a profound theology of prayer which is compatible with Augustine, at least in spirit, and the subject implied by a stoic conception of volition is contextualized within a communal discipline and ordered to this prayer as a goal. This arguably undermines his formal logic of volition and staves off its negative implications. For this, Cassian could just as easily be seen as a hero.

Cassian was no Pelagian. Indeed, he would tar Nestorius with the Pelagian brush himself, a move, as Ralph Mathisen notes, which had become a popular rhetorical tactic.[4] Contrary to the once commonplace notion that the Thirteenth *Conference* is a rejoinder to Augustine, R. A. Markus has even ventured that it is indeed an *anti-Pelagian* treatise, albeit one that reflects a pre-Augustinian tradition.[5] Moreover, the *Conferences* as a whole clearly seek to articulate a gift economy, and at least two modern scholars, Peter Munz and D. J. Macqueen, have contended that his teachings on grace and free will can be made more or less to coincide with Augustine's. The latter goes so far as to assert that "the dispute between the two leaders emerges as a tragedy of mutual misunderstanding with few parallels in the annals of ecclesiastical history."[6] We shall see.[7]

Despite all of Cassian's salutary contributions to the subsequent development of Christian monasticism in the West, his teachings on grace nevertheless contain serious tensions which, if carried to their logical conclusions or abstracted from those mitigating features of his broader thought and practice, hold serious implications for how one can subsequently conceive of the relationship between creation and God. Now speculative theology was not where Cassian's talents lay.[8] One should perhaps make allowance for the fact that the *Conferences* were written for

107

paraenetic purposes, and it may well be that the practice promoted by them is better than the theory used to justify the practice. Still, both Augustine's proposals for the monastic life and his doctrine of grace are coterminous with his ontology. And to the extent that this relationship does not follow so easily for Cassian, and indeed for the broader monastic culture of South Gaul, a possibility is opened up for theoretical perversion when the practice which gives the theory its point and purpose deteriorates.

It is my hope to illuminate this dissonance in this chapter. Cassian's advocacy of grace is not in question. Rather, the question is whether his "pre-Augustinian" conception of grace, indebted to Origen and the stoicism of Evagrius Ponticus and unreformed by Augustine's "ontological" critique of pagan virtue, is coherent and consistent with his otherwise orthodox affirmations.[9] Inasmuch as these debts to stoic virtue entail debts to the stoic ontology which renders that virtue intelligible, we can expect to discover tensions between this ontology and the Christian view which Cassian professes.

These assumptions provide part of the latent backdrop to the reception of Augustine's thought in the monastic culture of South Gaul. As important as Cassian was, both as an alternative to what were perceived to be the unsavory consequences of Augustinianism and as a major shaper of subsequent events, our concerns extend beyond him to the question of this reception. In other words, we are not simply concerned with Cassian's alleged Semi-Pelagianism, but rather with the subtle "pelagianization" of *Augustine* as his thought was received into an intellectual context whose first principles were incommensurable with his own.[10]

From the perspective of Augustine's doxological ontology and proto-Chalcedonian mechanics, the questions *whether* grace or nature, *whether* grace or free will, and the problem of how one may delineate the respective divine and human contributions in the act for the good, cannot finally be intelligibly stated. Hence the primary problem consists not so much in Cassian's response to the concern that grace destroys free will, though this answer will indeed present problems. Rather it consists in the very attempt to answer questions which, on Augustinian terms, there should have been no good reason for asking.[11] Cassian, though a crucial figure, is not alone here. This attempt would last a century, and the same charge could be leveled against some of Augustine's defenders, such as Prosper of Aquitaine.[12]

Yet if the questions cannot be intelligibly stated within the terms of Augustinian thought, then the very attempt to address Augustine to Pelagian or stoic questions will inevitably bring about a "Pelagianization" or "stoicization" of that thought. The very formulation of the question, in other words, will move the issue onto the home turf of Augustine's opponents. The decisive move will have been made in the very formulation of the question. If our earlier analysis is correct, and Pelagian stoicism is premised upon a breach in the trinitarian economy and an impoverished Christology, then this move cannot be made without effecting a fundamental reconfiguration of the metaphysical geography between creature, creator, and their union in Christ.

Our task in the next section is to visit the ominous consequences of this breach.

Duelling cosmologies

The modernity of stoicism

In the previous chapter, I attempted to show how Pelagianism renders human nature and action incoherent through a failed moral psychology and to show further, how, from an Augustinian viewpoint, this follows as a consequence of its failure to grasp Christ as the *forma* of the trinitarian God, in whom we must participate if we are finally *to be* at all. I have also advanced an Augustinian alternative which has participation in trinitarian delight as its form and condition of possibility. I now wish to demonstrate more fully a thesis which is correlative to these observations and which I have already intimated. It is that the "mitigated stoicism" reintroduced into Christianity through the Pelagian problematic entails within it a latent stoic metaphysics which sacrifices participation and transcendence and thus requires an unthinking of the doctrine of the Trinity, the "aesthetics of salvation" and the proto-Chalcedonian "mechanics" of *creatio ex nihilo*.[13] I shall suggest, moreover, that it is only within the conceptual space made possible by this "unthinking" that modern subjectivity and its onto-theological double-founding, alleged by Alliez and others to be intrinsic to Augustinian Christianity, can ever arise. Modern subjectivity, in other words, is predicated on the de-trinitization of God, though this argument will not be complete until the next chapter.

The Pelagian institution of a sort of proto-modernity or the modern realization of a variant, Pelagian strain of stoicism is complicated by several factors, including the number of stoicisms originally on offer.[14] Zeno, Cleanthes, and Chrysippus, to the extent that their thought can be reconstructed from the fragments largely preserved in the writings of their critics, all seem to diverge on some key points of both cosmology and moral psychology.[15] And, as many scholars have shown, Augustine's own relationship to stoicism is diffuse and complex, and on some points seemingly more faithful to stoic cosmology and ethics than Pelagianism.[16] Augustine's erotic and aesthetic cosmology, whose mechanics of transcendence subvert the borders between interiority and exteriority, arguably contains a kind of vitalism and transcategorical eclipse of atomic substance that is at least superficially analogous to the stoic theory of surfaces. If it were not for Augustine's need to defend grace against Pelagian nature, one could legitimately say that an *Augustinian* agent acting for the good acts in harmony with nature—a claim clouded by the incommensurable language games which determine the Pelagian and Augustinian uses of the word *natura*.[17] Despite his pains to refuse the restriction of grace to nature as possibility, Augustine never really relents on this point, even when arguing against the very sufficiency of nature.[18] Of course the difference consists in the fact that finally to fulfill one's nature, *magis esse*, is to be in Christ and to remember, know, and love God.

The grammar of divine simplicity; Augustine's insistence upon the radical transcendence and absolute difference of the Trinity; the refusal of any passivity in the generation and procession of the Son and Spirit; and the location of the *imago dei* in the active participation in divine love, all serve to differentiate the "mechanics" of *creatio ex nihilo*, from the cosmogony of the stoics.[19] Earlier we saw that the indivisibility of the trinitarian works *ad extra* combined with this grammar to deny a real relation (in Thomistic terminology) between creator and creature and so any competition between divine and human "agency." The result was a mechanics which I termed "proto-Chalcedonian," such that both God and the agent are utterly distinguished by the greatest possible difference and yet utterly inseparable into "parts." My good action is, once again, fully mine and God's and indeed *more* mine for its being God's. We suggested furthermore that it is precisely in this very difference from God, a difference that constitutes our need, that the image of God is manifest in us.[20] Hence humility, coming to terms with the dependence implied in the "downward participation" of God's condescension to us, is intrinsic to this manifestation.[21] The resultant conception of the ontological difference, and our inability to survey that difference, meant that this mechanics could not be represented within a dichotomy of the active and the passive without in fact compromising the difference and idolatrously rendering the "divine agency" on an immanent continuum with human agency. Instead the divine agency was registered precisely in the positive activity of human agency, and it was precisely on this presumption that Augustine could account for human actions in terms of human motives which were themselves the work of grace.[22]

Stoicism was a thoroughgoing materialism, and the importance of Augustine's discovery of the *libri platonicorum* is usually associated (as he himself suggests) with his newfound ability at last to conceive of God in spiritualistic terms, an ability which is frequently cataloged to a Platonic dualism between the sensible and intelligible.[23] The absolute infinity of Augustinian transcendence does indeed differ profoundly from the more "modern" infinity of Stoic "mathesis," conceived either as an infinitely divisible finite magnitude or an equally divisible, though inconceivable, infinite magnitude.[24] This infinite turns out to be less than absolutely infinite, for while it may be infinitely divisible or extended, it is finite at each divided point. For Augustine, by contrast, the transcendence of God entails the regulatory idea of his simplicity, meaning that God's truth is everywhere entire and indivisible, wholly present, unconsumed and unexhausted by those who are present to it. Paradoxically, this conception makes God's infinity both wholly knowable as apprehensible and yet fully incomprehensible.[25]

Confessiones VII seems to distinguish between these two infinities fairly clearly.[26] However, several features of Augustine's thought which we have already considered preclude our crudely plotting this point of difference onto a dualism of the sensible and intelligible: the operation of the soul in sensibility, the "ideal" character of Augustinian matter as it "responds" to the *vocatio* to existence, and the beauty of *forma* with its antecedent and consequent participation—*magis* or *minus*—in the truth, goodness, and beauty of the creative *Verbum*.[27] Instead we should locate the distinction in the difference between a metaphysics of creation from a transcendent source (which can really provide no metaphysics at all) and that of an immanentist monism.[28]

Indeed monism and immanentism are the twin pillars on which stoic physical theory and the theory of first principles are based, especially in their Chrysipian form. These pillars are held together by the central concept of *pneuma*, a physical field which pervades the universe and is the carrier of all the specific properties, the nature (*physis*) and state (*hexis*) of both organic and inorganic material bodies.[29] These bodies are construed less as distinct surfaces occupying a topical plane than as "tensional" arrangements of this pneumatic medium, that is, as figures whose physical structure and cohesion is derived from the tensional motion (*tonike kinesis*) or self-opposing force of pneuma itself, and its relative degrees of tautness or slackness.[30] Intrinsic to the unity and coherence of *pneuma* itself and constitutive of its capacity for this motion are two inseparable principles: an active one identified with the qualities hot and cold and the "elements" fire and air, and a passive one, similarly identified with wet, dry, earth, and water.[31]

Rather like the Fichtean super-ego or Nietzsche's Dionysian will-to-power (particularly in its Deleuzian version), the Chrysippian *archai* are, or rather, *pneuma* is, simply through oscillatory activity on its own passivity.[32] This perhaps seems no more significant than Todd's observation "that this is simply to claim that body that acts on itself does so in virtue of its having an aspect that does not act."[33] This would then mean that the passive element simply functions as the medium through which the active passes. However, the physical monism requires "a specific physical theory to explain the immanence of the primary element," a role filled by a cosmogony of the primal elements, articulated first by Zeno as the *pyr teknikon*, the "self-crafting" fire, and later modified by Chrysippus in his theory of pneuma.[34] And it is this union which exposes the strains in the theory.

111

The stoics' dual commitment to immanence and monism means, first, that the physical theory must be an expression of the theory of first principles, and second that the agent of immanence in the universe cannot be separable from its medium. Yet the very notion of pneumatic oscillation which accounts for the generation of physical bodies implies that, in the case of pneuma itself, there is a physical separation between body and medium.[35] This causes the immanent *tonikos*, the tensional motion, to break, instituting a logic of negation, inconsistent with the monistic character of the doctrine, between the active and passive principles. As a consequence, the void, long banished to the outer circumference of the material *plenum* constitutive of God and the universe, returns interposed between the two principles. Both Lapidge and Todd seem to credit this tendency merely to the grafting of the Chrysippian doctrine of *pneuma* onto the Zenoian cosmogony of the *pyr teknikon*, in which the active tensional arrangement and mutual coherence of earth, air, fire, and water progressively tends toward *ekpyrosis* or conflagration, that point at which "the fiery element" reaches its maximum at the expense of the passive.[36] Todd even suggests that, *sans* Zeno's cosmogony, Chrysippus might have been able to retain the theory of first principles in a broadly Spinozistic fashion.[37]

This is not self-evident, however, and one may ask whether any doctrine of immanent first principles with a strict dichotomy of action and passion must not inevitably conclude in *something like* the Zenoian cosmogony, insofar as the tensional force which sustains their interrelation implies opposition and juxtaposition. Furthermore, we may ask whether it is the destiny of a Zenoian cosmology, in fracturing these immanent principles, to fragment into a dualism akin to the nihilistic juxtaposition of subject and object, the former of which proceeds ultimately from nothing, the latter of which is obliterated in the encounter. The alternative, it seems, is stalemate, or perhaps, *stabilitas*, a mere cease-fire at any rate. Does not the "ethical" position of the sage reflect this ontological position, as he scrupulously patrols the circumference of the *hegemonikon* against "involuntary" incursions from alien *phantasiai*, assenting to them and, particularly later, with Descartes, negating them through assertions of will? Can we not see in this logic shades of Kant's transcendental ego, arguably less Kantian than Fichte's absolute I?[38] Jacobi, after all, thought it a short step from Spinoza to Kant and Fichte; indeed he saw them as but two faces of a single coin.[39] And one can pose questions to the stoic theory of *archai* analogous to those that Jacobi poses to Spinoza (via Mendelssohn) and Fichte. What *is* this passive principle—and what can it be —except either an antagonistically related "other," a separate body which insinuates a dualism inconsistent with stoic monism, or a mere receptacle for the active principle's assertion and delimitation of itself, a receptacle whose own criterion of identity must be negated in the movement?[40] The former option fractures the system apart. The latter, which is arguably the logical conclusion of either option, renders the passive principle into *nihil*. Yet with the passive thus annihilated, what can the active be but a self determining projection into the void by something like a transcendental ego which is through its own negation?[41] For on inspection the passive principle (τὸ πάσχον) and the void (κενὸς τόπος) as a receptacle for activity appear virtually synonymous.[42]

We can press Jacobi's line of questioning even further.[43] As Lapidge notes, there is a problem in stoic cosmology accounting logically for *ekpyrosis* and its subsequent *palingenesis* or cosmic regeneration.

> [A]t ekpyrosis the universe is said to resolve itself into creative fire; but cosmic regeneration or palingenesis requires, as we have seen, the interaction of this creative fire with precosmic moisture. If the universe dissolves into fire alone, whence comes the moisture?

Citing Diogenes Laertius and a report on Chrysippus from Plutarch, Lapidge continues.

> After *ekpyrosis* the fire is at length contained by moisture; the fire and moisture then set about creating the next universe. But no Stoic provides any explanation as to why the fire should be quenched. It would seem consistent with Stoic theory that *ekpyrosis* would imply not merely the dissolution of the created universe, but also the dissolution of the four created elements back into primal substance (*ousia*) that, as we saw, had two aspects: active/fiery and passive/watery.[44]

This only seems to push the problem back one remove. Since the active principle only *is* through its tensional arrangement with the passive, and yet since the passive is rendered as nothing precisely by this arrangement, whence the active? Taken to this conclusion, this logic seems to invert *creatio ex nihilo*, insinuating instead a *nihil* which creates. This conclusion suggests that immanentism cannot indeed be saved from a nihilistic cosmology, and the fact that the Chrysippian doctrine of *pneuma* seems to have been advanced partly as a solution to the cosmological inadequacy of Zeno's theory of immanence only underscores the point.

The relationship between stoic ethics and physical theory is complicated to say the least, and since neither the Pelagians nor Cassian and his followers reproduce this relationship in its entirety, only certain isolated features are relevant to this aspect of the analysis. The crucial features, apart from those we considered in the previous chapter, concern the

113

interrelation of this immanent materialism and the theory of judgment. As we saw in the last chapter, judgment is an act of the *hegemonikon* and its faculty of assent in response to presentations or *phantasiai*, though this act is admittedly complicated by prior judgments which affect the tensional composition of the individual soul and the forms under which the presentations appear.[45] There is some disagreement about the mechanism of this presentation. Earlier stoics such as Cleanthes thought it a literal "depression and protrusion" like a signet ring in wax, while Chrysippus considered it a multifaceted "modification" (*heteroiosis*) of the soul, a conception that both accommodates the simultaneity of diverse impressions and perhaps better emphasizes the contiguity between the soul and the pneumatic medium. Nevertheless, the Stoa seem generally agreed that the involuntary impressions were themselves the result of the movement of pneuma.[46] It is the capacity to assent or to withhold assent that makes these actions "up to us." I do not wish to revive the age-old arguments about whether this notion is compatible with fate, or whether the latter is tantamount to fatalism. I am convinced that Chryssipus' distinction, conveyed by Cicero, between perfect and principal causes on the one hand and auxiliary and proximate causes on the other is sufficient to deflect this fatalist charge. Not all antecedent causes (e.g., *phantasiai*) are perfect and principal, and thus do not of necessity bring about their effects.[47]

What is of concern, rather, is the way that stoic physical theory informs the notion of judgment itself. Because of the disjunction of action and passion, the *pneuma* forcibly impresses itself on the soul, which passively receives the modification, though the agent's causal activity can reverse this. The actions of irrational creatures, who cannot be praised or blamed for committing them, are caused by these externally induced impressions.[48] The mark of rationality, by contrast, is fundamentally negative, a consequence compounded, as we saw in the last chapter, by the stoic conception of the *hegemonikon* as unitary and incapable of division.[49] The soul can assert its unity, integrity and power *primarily* because it can "interrupt the causal chain of impulsive impression" by negating those impressions, by withholding assent.[50] We have already considered the cogency of this as an account of volition. At the ontological level, the result, or rather the presupposition, is a persistent antagonism between the passive rational agent and the medium of his action, an antagonism reflective, I suggest, of the Stoa's inability to sustain the unity of the active and passive principle at the cosmological level.

Pelagian nihilism

Pelagian grace presupposes a similar antagonism, and though the conceptual demonstration of this point does not require the demonstration of a historical debt to stoicism, their reception of some aspects of this philosophy through Rufinus the Syrian, Evagrius of Pontus and the *Sentences* of Sextus does underscore it.[51] The restriction of grace to possibility reflects the fact that the Pelagians cannot conceive of the interaction of human and divine agency save antagonistically. This presupposition entails the corollary that they conceive of agency *per se*, whether human or divine, on the model of a univocal *force* within an immanent theater of operation.[52] It also means that human and divine agency have implicitly been brought into real relationship with one another. The antagonistic character of their interaction implies that force is here understood to occur within a strong dichotomy of activity and passivity, which have come apart from one another, as in the stoic *pneuma*. As a consequence, human agency, which can only be passive in the face of God's agency, is set in dialectical opposition to the activity of the God whose transcendence is at once rendered finite and exiled to an abyssal "beyond," extrinsic to the finite, from which it "intervenes."

Divine transcendence is not all that is lost, however. Though the Pelagian rejection of original sin and praise of nature is typically thought to assert the goodness of nature against Augustinian pessimism, the opposite is in fact the case. The Pelagians claim that each person is born with an intrinsic, ineradicable possibility of sinlessness, and, subsequently, that agents become sinners by mere imitation of Adam and not by a contagion of defective desire which *is* a defect in nature. This sustains the Pelagian agent in a state of reserve, unconstrained by the necessity and the determination which either a seductive good or a contagious defect implies. As a matter of philosophy of volition, we have already criticized such a conception for being implicitly "noumenal," and thus unintelligible as an account of how our motives account for our actions. We can press this criticism further. For to define *natura* as a state of *possibilitas,* and make the correlative assumption that both virtue and sin are merely matters of *imitatio*, is implicitly to define *natura* indifferently with regard to its *telos*. This drives a wedge, not simply between an act and its motive, but between *esse* and the good, the beautiful and the true. Hence the primacy accorded to indeterminate potentiality and the rejection of the compatibility of freedom and participatory grace do not simply divorce the volitional from the natural and pronounce nature potentially "good enough" to will its ends. Rather they *institute* that nature as an autonomous and indifferent fact. On the one hand, this makes nature immanently self-contained and subsistent apart from erotic determination within the economy of gift. On the other hand, nature becomes immediately locked into an antagonistic mechanical relation with tensional forces deemed intrinsic to any determination. The assumption of stoic mechanics brings with it the simultaneous need to exert one's independence from them and indifference to them.

A certain irony is emerging here which will perhaps not be fully realized until the advent of German idealism.[53] J. B. Schneewind has argued that Kant's conception of the "indifference of the natural world to rational human concerns," "his loss of confidence in the rational order of nature" marks a decisive break with a stoic physics and metaphysics with which he otherwise has some affinities.[54] On the contrary, we can see that it was the Pelagian defense of a nature teleologically indifferent to formal goodness and beauty and of a freedom allied to the physics of stoic immanentism which anxiously foreshadows Kant's third antinomy. And it does so precisely insofar as it finally sacrifices nature on the altar of a failed and frustrated *apatheia*. This irony would not have been lost on Augustine. He was adamant, despite the protestations of Julian of Eclanum, that it was in fact Pelagian logic that reproduced the Manichean dualism.[55] We can now see why. To drive a wedge between *esse* and the transcendentals—goodness, beauty and truth—is to destroy creation as sanctification, that is, as *creatio*, *conversio*, and *formatio*. That is to say, to drive a wedge between *esse* and the transcendentals is to take creation "outside"—and to set it over against the delight between the Father and the Son. It is to institute in its stead a rupture which has proved ominous. For to set creation over against God is to complete and fulfill the anxiety of "escape," to institute a space in which self-hood, a rigorous policing of its borders, or an abnegatory sacrifice in the face of God can occur.

Such a move is, needless to say, not without subsequent ramification. To institute this rupture is to deprive theology of the key terms through which the doctrine of the Trinity, and our participation in the trinitarian life, can be explicated. To carry this logic through to its conclusion would thus be both to *institute* nature as the autonomous realm of the finite, ontologically undetermined in its finitude by any qualitative predicates, and to render being, and the very categories of finitude and infinity in which it is now primarily registered, ontologically prior to these same predicates.[56] Moreover, since finitude and infinity cannot be concurrent, it is to lock them into real relation with one another, and hence to render this finitude in juxtaposition to an infinity divisible by finitude itself, an infinity which, to an Augustinian point of view, turns out to be finite after all. Hence to carry this logic through to its conclusion would thus be to commence a radical and, from an Augustinian point of view, idolatrous reconfiguration of the ontological context in which terms such as God, humanity, and creation find their intelligibility.

There is one seemingly insuperable obstacle facing this argument for the stoic and Pelagian origins of this contextual shift. Stoicism as a school did not survive the train wreck of antiquity. Pelagianism was vanquished. By all accounts both conceptual and historical, Augustine is supposed to have won this battle. It is the burden of the final section to show that in winning this battle he may have lost the war.

116

Pelagianizing Augustine

Cassian's Christian stoicism

Augustine's campaign against Pelagian concerns was not a single controversy at all, but rather a series of engagements against a handful of opponents. Whether spearheaded in its first generation by Pelagius and Caelestius, or in the second by Julian of Eclanum, Pelagianism as a "movement" was taking its last gasps by 427 when Augustine entertained Cresconious and Felix, two monks from the North African monastery at Hadrumetum. They had traveled to Hippo Regius to seek the bishop's help in a controversy that had arisen in the monastery over Augustine's teachings on grace. Of particular concern was the Letter to Sixtus (*Ep.* 194), which Augustine had written in 418. In brief, their worry was that Augustine's insistence that our good deeds were the work of an anterior gift of grace undercut the rationale for the monastic life and undermined the quest for perfection.[57] The visit elicited from Augustine two letters to the abbot Valentius and the treatise *De Gratia et Libero Arbitrio*, written "because of those persons who, by thinking that free choice is denied when the grace of God is defended, defend free will in such a manner as to deny the grace of God."[58] This seemed to have the desired effect of quieting things for a time, until Augustine got wind of a new problem, a monk who justified his refusal to accept his superior's rebuke by appealing to Augustine's teachings. This prompted another treatise, *De Correptione et Gratia*, which appears once again to have quieted the controversy at Hadrumetum.

This treatise contains a number of salient features that support the case for the trinitarian and christological stakes inherent in Augustine's teaching on grace. The argument insists upon the importance of the *fides quae per dilectionem operatur*, the aprioricity of grace and hence the doctrine of election.[59] It incorporates the saints into the dialogue between the Father and the Son, equates predestination with Jesus Christ and our freedom with the *non posse peccare*.[60] Latent in each of these replies is the conviction that *esse major* is to be fully incorporated into the gifting delight of the Father and Son, an understanding that eliminates any antagonism between the "imposition" of this gift and the integrity of the creature.

The tract is not without other problems that would come to haunt the history of Augustinian theology, and more immediately, the reception of Augustine's teaching in Gaul. The refuge that Augustine takes in Romans 11.33 while deferring the mystery of election—"O the depths . . ."—can make Augustine's God appear arbitrary, like the God of Ockham and the voluntarists who are often said to follow him.[61] More than one Gallic commentator would prove anxious over this very point.[62]

There are numerous problems with this interpretation. As we have seen, the primary analogue for displaying *voluntas* in Augustine's theology is not "monistic" or "dyadic;" it is not the relation of cause to effect, but rather of lover to beloved. This analogy assumes further that the beauty and intelligibility of the beloved is already *in* the lover as the principle of the love's "movement." In other words, it presupposes triune simplicity constituted as the infinite determination of intelligible love and beauty to itself, which incorporates the intelligible object of intention, the "beloved," into the will's act. Secondly, we saw that this beauty was indeed intelligibly and iconically manifest through the *modus*, *species* and *ordo*, and the *mensura*, *pondus* and *numerus* of the creature constituted actively as a response to the divine *vox*. Because God of his very essence is both giver and gift, *electio* is at once a gratuitous donation *and* an ontological designation—making the meaning of "covenant," were this to be a prominent category, very different from late medieval covenantal theology.[63]

To become a voluntarist, Augustine must be relieved of his trinitarianism and his Platonism, a feat that has been achieved more than once by opponents and apologists alike. The result is always an *electio* that is more Pelagian than Augustinian and a God who looks like Pelagian man writ large. Yet if we resituate Augustine's *electio* within its trinitarian home, an alternative interpretation of Romans 11.33 emerges. In this case, the text functions in close parallel to Augustine's insistence, in the realm of trinitarian theology *per se*, that our *similitudo* to the divine essence gives us no foundation on which to ground an analogy of proportion between the Trinity and its image.[64] In that event, the Pauline exclamation would be tantamount to the admission, at once kataphatic and apophatic, that human perceptions of justice cannot plumb the depths of divine justice, but can nevertheless conceive of how the salvation of some would prove merciful and the reprobation of others just.[65]

This may not eliminate all problems surrounding Augustinian *electio*, but it does relocate them.[66] If there is a problem here, it is not whether Augustine's conception of *voluntas* is voluntaristic or his freedom coherent. The first option extracts the will from its trinitarian context; the second makes the stoic assumption "that love is authentic only when it admits of being refused."[67] Rather the question is whether his conception of justice, which insists with his opponents on a limited atonement, is consistent with his ontology.[68] Can the doctrine of eternal reprobation be reconciled with the doctrine of gratuitous creation?[69]

This was not the question that would be asked, however, as the controversy made its way into the monasteries of south Gaul.[70] Though debate over Augustine's teaching was evidently underway before the advent of this treatise, the arrival of *De Correptione et Gratia*, which had calmed the little squall in Hadrumetum, only intensified it across the Mediterranean.[71] Perhaps with diminished confidence in their ability to defend Augustine, Prosper and Hilary, two laymen, sought the bishop's assistance directly through a pair of letters that articulated the points of agreement and divergence.[72] The resulting tracts were the last two completed works of Augustine's life: *De Praedestinatione Sanctorum* and *De Dono Perseveratiae*. There is little evidence that these efforts helped matters.

Undoubtedly, there are several reasons for this reaction. Perhaps the real questions at issue in Augustine's position were not available to the monks, since they too were committed, albeit differently, to a doctrine of limited atonement. Though Augustine does insist that Christ himself *is* predestination and that we finally are as we are constituted as his Body through the Spirit, perhaps he is unsuccessful in these treatises in making the ontological stakes of the question clear.[73] Most fundamentally however, the monks' hostile reaction and their failure to grasp the trinitarian and christological basis of Augustine's view suggest that the first principles latent in the monastic endeavor, principles which would govern the interpretation of Augustine's theology upon arrival, were in fact quite different from Augustine's own. This would insure not only a degree of misunderstanding of Augustine's theology but also a transformation of it.

Indeed much has been made of the difference between the African and Gallican contexts in the scholarship of the last thirty years or so, and the dawning discovery that Pelagianism had not extended this far only underscores this difference.[74] The ecclesiastical culture of South Gaul early in the fifth century was dominated by two great monastic foundations: the island monastery of Lerins and the monasteries of St. Victor in Marseilles, the latter of which were founded by John Cassian.[75] Ralph Mathisen has demonstrated a persistent antagonism between these powerful orders and the comparatively weak episcopacy in the region, whose increasing social responsibility in the disintegrating empire marked the Bishops as compromised in the eyes of the monks. An increased tendency after 380 on the part of those outside the monastery to invoke the assistance of Rome lent another ingredient to a recipe for conflict. As a result, perhaps, of this and the geographical distance between South Gaul and Hippo Regius, Augustine was accorded less than the unbridled deference apparently shown to him by the monks of Hadrumetum.[76]

These factors alone are not sufficient to explain the difference between the two settings, however. For North Africa was in similar turmoil and worse, and Augustine himself had fostered and upheld the monastic life, even bringing about his own version of the "'monastization of the clergy."[77] Rather, embodied in the two practices were presuppositions so incommensurable with one another that it calls into question whether each party was contending over the same subject matter.[78] In fact, the differences between these forms of monasticism can tell us something about the varied theoretical speculations embodied in their respective practices.

Consider, for example, the function of obedience in each context. "Augustine and Cassian both gave obedience supreme importance; but for different reasons. For Augustine, it constituted the unity of the community.

For Cassian, it was the monk's first step on the way to perfection."[79] For Cassian, in other words, obedience and thus community are necessary because without them "a solitary has no superior to eradicate his self-will."[80] He remains bound by the eight principle vices, and the road to perfection never commences. For Augustine, by contrast, obedience is set within the broader "socialism" of the heavenly city, on a par with the restriction or abolition of private property.

> Renunciation of private property is, naturally, central to this conception of monastic living; fasting still has its place, and chastity is assumed without question; but comparison with existing monastic practice leaves no doubt that Augustine shifted much of the stress previously laid on asceticism towards the values of communal living and the virtues which foster it.[81]

Markus sometimes gives the impression that Augustine had boxed himself into a corner and assumes this stance by default, that his battles with the Donatists forever blocked the "way of perfection" to him.[82] Perhaps there is something to this. However, it is also true that Augustine's position is coextensive with his ontology, with the doxological and christological constitution of both the self and city, and their place within the *creatio, conversio, formatio* schema of creation.[83] In Cassian's case, the situation is a bit murkier, for, as we shall see, this alternative role for obedience attests to a profoundly different conception of will and personhood.

As I stated in the introductory section of this chapter, Cassian was no Pelagian. He would have denied the condemned Pelagian propositions, affirmed their contraries and was inclined to malign his enemies with the stigma of Pelagianism.[84] However, he appears to have shared a common genealogy with the Pelagians that included Evagrius of Pontus, Rufinus the Syrian, and, ultimately, Origen.[85] In some respects that we shall soon consider, moreover, his debt to stoicism is more obvious and more thorough than that of the Pelagians. Marcia Colish even concludes that "it was Cassian more than any other single figure who monasticized Stoicism in the west and produced one of its most original and durable formulations in this period."[86]

Probably because Jerome attacked the concept so mercilessly, attention to the question of Cassian's stoicism has tended to focus on the role played in his thought by Evagrian *apatheia*, which he renames "purity of heart."[87] It remains one of the most controversial preoccupations among Cassian's interpreters.[88] On the one hand, there is a definite stoic element to the concept. Purity of heart, the *skopos* of the monk whose attainment leads him to his *telos* in the kingdom of God, demands the elimination of the mundane attachments to the world that manifest themselves in eight principle vices, whose unity and interrelation is also stoic in character.[89]

Cassian subdivides these into natural vices that require bodily mani-festation, such as gluttony, and unnatural vices that do not, such as avarice.[90] This division makes it clear that the attainment of this purity requires a rigorous *ascesis*. On the other hand, it is also clear, as Phillip Rousseau argues, that the attainment of this *skopos* is not simply a passive, hermetic endeavor, but an active, coenobitic labor that encompasses a life of practical activity.[91] Moreover, Cassian views the *telos* which is the end of this endeavor as a contemplative union so intimate that the distinction between God and supplicant virtually disappears in the gratuity of inter-trinitarian love.

> For then will be brought to fruition in us that prayer of our Savior when he prayed to his Father on his disciples' behalf when he said: "That the love with which you have loved me may be in them, and they in us." And again: "That all may be one, as you Father in me, and I in you, that they also may be one in us." Then that perfect love of God, by which "he loved us first," will have passed also into our heart's disposition upon the fulfillment of this prayer of the Lord, which we believe in no way can be rendered void. This will be the case when every love, every desire, every effort, every under-taking, every thought of ours, everything that we live, that we speak, that we breathe, will be God, and when that unity which the Father now has with the Son and which the Son has with the Father will be carried over into our understanding and our mind, so that, just as he loves us with a sincere and pure and indissoluble love, we too may be joined to him with a perpetual and inseparable love and so united with him that whatever we breathe, whatever we understand, whatever we speak, may be God.[92]

These hardly sound like the words of a heterodox Christian, and the corresponding affirmation of grace is of the same spirit as the emerging tradition, despite the customary Semi-Pelagian appellation. D. J. Macqueen is right to insist on this point.[93] Cassian is adamant "that the beginning of a good will is bestowed upon us at the Lord's inspiration."[94] He affirms that "God is not only the one who suggests good things but also their patron and promoter, such that he sometimes draws us to salvation even involuntarily and unbeknownst to ourselves."[95] He contends that "it is clear that the origin not only of our good acts but even of good thoughts is in God. He both inspires in us the beginnings of a holy will and grants the ability and the opportunity to bring to fulfillment the things that we rightly desire."[96] Clearly Cassian wishes to articulate an economy of participation and an economy of gift. His assertions may even be a covert argument against the Pelagians, as Markus supposes.[97]

Where then do the problems arise? The tensions occur because the ontological presuppositions implicit in the stoic moral psychology Cassian employs in his explication of the ascetic means to this end are not easily reconciled with the assertion of participatory grace. The presence of this psychology is exhibited in the paramount position *discretio* comes to occupy within the table of virtues that lead to purity of heart, or charity.[98] "[N]o other virtue can be perfectly attained or endure without the grace of discretion . . . For discretion is the begetter, guardian and moderator of all virtues."[99] The preeminence of *discretio* stands in contrast to Augustine, for whom charity, the anterior gift of God, makes all other genuine virtue possible. As in their respective uses of obedience, it signals profound differences in their respective conceptions of the self, its knowledge and its relation to God that will emerge more fully as we proceed.[100] This virtue of *discretio* is materially Christian, but its formal structure is that of stoic judgment. In Cassian, the formal problem of stoic assent to the intrusion of *phantasiai* returns in Christian guise as the *discretio spirituum*.[101] These spirits or thoughts have three possible origins: God, ourselves and the devil.[102]

Discretion traces our thoughts to these origins and prevents our deception by those ideas that take their beginning from the latter two.[103] In principle, it is an act of either affirmation or negation, but, as a rule, Cassian lays the stress on the withholding of assent, or the negation of these deceptive phantasms—an emphasis he shares with the stoics who emphasized the withholding of assent to the impressions made upon the soul as a means of demonstrating autonomy within the causal nexus of fate.[104] Insofar as these deceptions originate in the soul, and all vice, all attachment to these phantasms does originate there, then their negation amounts to a self-negation. As a negative judgment, *discretio* is therefore programmatically linked with the rigorous *ascesis* whose purpose is to expunge the eight principal vices that spring from our mundane attachments to the world.[105] In short, it is linked to a "self-naughting," a dialectical process which negates the self, and arguably the world, in order that the genuine self may be recovered, ultimately, *as* God.[106]

It is primarily this capacity for self-abnegation that Cassian means when he says that our actions are "up to us."[107] There is no corresponding logic of negation in Augustine, and his diagnosis of its presence in the stoics revealed a conception of the voluntary which differed from Augustine's by restricting it from what we want to what we can control. This conception was pronounced incoherent on two grounds. The first was that it insulated our actions from the desires which move us to execute them. This followed as a consequence of the second, that such a conception located the agent outside of Christ's mediation of inter-trinitarian delight, which "solves" the *aporia* of volition and completes the desire for the good intrinsic to any action.

We see a similar tension in Cassian, one that both impinges upon his conception of the relationship between grace and free will and ultimately raises questions about the adequacy of his Christology. Augustine's conflation of *voluntas* and desire invoked Christ's mediation in his dual but unified role as both *exemplum* and *sacramentum*, which located our desire within the anterior gift of the Spirit. Cassian, as we have seen, wants to affirm a prior gift as well, and his contemporary apologists are adamant that his conception preserves that gift intact. Effort and grace are not alternatives but the latter simply compounds the former.[108] According to MacQueen, the charge of Semi-Pelagianism results from the misinterpretation of a distinction occasioned by the practical, monastic setting of the *Conferences*: the fact that that Cassian sometimes ascribes the origins of virtuous thoughts and actions to God and at others attributes them, *simpliciter*, to human effort. The interpretation, he argues, fails to take note of Cassian's understanding of sin, which essentially prefigures the later distinction between venial and mortal sins. The latter all but destroys the divine image and severs friendship with God, and it requires "a prior inspiration *ex parte Dei*," without which desire for the good is not even possible.[109] By contrast, the disciplined life of the monk is already evidence of this inspiration; so the monk's "venial" struggles along the royal road to perfection are not evidence of a severed relationship to grace. Thus, in the controversial terminology of the thirteenth *Conference*, when God, seeing the rudiments of a good will in us, kindles it to greater ardor, this is simply the addition of grace to grace.[110]

Intent is one thing, execution quite another. These claims for Cassian would be much easier to sustain if he, like Augustine, were to equate *voluntas* and desire. Yet having already located freedom in the capacity to withhold consent from phantasms, Cassian will locate the will elsewhere. Like Augustine, Cassian understands the Pauline distinction between spirit and flesh to designate two forms and objects of desire.[111] Augustine recognized each as forms of will, and the persistent struggle between them as signs of a will divided against itself in involuntary sin that is symptomatic of the creature's potential ontological dissolution. The reverse side of this position is of course our dependence upon God and ontological completion in God. Cassian, by contrast, appears to follow the stoics in insisting upon the a priori unity of the soul, and he places free will in the position of the stoic faculty of assent—in a tensional position between the two poles of desire.[112] "Between these two desires, then, the free will of the soul occupies a somewhat blameworthy middle position and neither delights in the disgrace of vice nor agrees to the hardships of virtue."[113] It remains to be seen whether this signals a changed ontological position.

In the stoics, it was the assertion of a capacity for choice free from determination by desire that rendered their account of volition incoherent. With the Pelagians, this conception was shown to sever our participation in Christ's mediation of inter-trinitarian delight, to set the agent outside of the divine economy by severing Christ's exemplary and sacramental functions. We can see a similar tension resulting from this conception in Cassian.

Cassian's stoic conception of what "is up to us" leads him to treat will, like them, as a power for causation.[114] Yet, as we saw earlier with the stoics, the only way to secure the autonomy of this power, to distinguish it from the causal nexus, is a negative one, by establishing first the power *not* to cause. There are two consequences to this. First, Cassian has a tendency to define freedom negatively, as indifference, despite other remarks to the contrary.[115] "Consequently, there always remains in the human being a free will that can either neglect or love the grace of God."[116] Secondly, Cassian's conception of the will's freedom in causation forces him into an attempt to delineate the respective divine and human contributions in a manner not possible from the vantage of Augustine's proto-Chalcedonian mechanics.[117] The result is an account of grace which accords remarkably with a stoic conception of the causal nexus conveyed by Cicero, with God who generates the impression playing the part of the antecedent (though not perfect) cause of the effect (the agent's assent), and the free will of the agent playing that of the auxiliary cause in the giving of assent.[118]

> It would be very odd indeed if in every work and practice of discipline there were only a beginning and an end, and not also something in the middle. Accordingly, just as we know that God offers opportunities for salvation in different ways, so also it is up to us to be either more or less attentive to the opportunities that have been granted to us by God. For just as "leave your country" was a matter of God's beckoning, so the leaving was a matter of Abraham's obedience.[119]

Without a genuine transcendence, the antecedent and auxiliary causes operating within stoic immanentism are correlated in a forceful tension with one another. In its positive form, this tension is manifest in a cooperation between "joint causes" (*synaition*) in the production of the effect, a conjunction, as it were, between the impression forged from without by *pneuma* and the power of assent.[120] In the case of human causality, however, this tension tends to be rendered as a competition of forces, as the negative emphasis on the withholding of assent shows. Cassian's attempt to solve the "interaction" between grace and free will belies a similar assumption about this antagonistic relation and suggests that his stoic moral psychology carries with it some unwanted ontological baggage. Weaver, thinking herself an apologist for Cassian, does damage to his case when she notes his "careful distinction between the work of grace and the work of free will," and, treating these as mutually exclusive alternatives, concludes that "between the beginning and the fulfillment, however, the responsibility lies with the human agent."[121]

A question by Abbot Germanus frames the problem: does grace nullify human effort? From an Augustinian perspective, the question is poorly phrased. Still, Abbot Chaemeron answers, using the example of a farmer who toils at his labor and yet needs divine assistance to insure the prosperity of his farm. "From this," he replies, "it is clear that the origin of good acts but even of good thoughts is in God." "But," he replies in the next breath, "it is up to us to conform humbly to the grace of God that daily draws us on."[122]

There is nothing objectionable about these remarks a priori. Precisely because our actions express our desires, one can say the same thing in Augustinian terms, even when what we want is seemingly beyond our control or when our wants are moved by God's beauty. In the latter case, the will's movement simply is the movement of grace, and is finally all the more ours, for being God's. Cassian's Chaemeron takes a different approach, however, instituting what Chadwick famously calls "the successive theory of free will and grace."[123]

It is true, as Weaver notes, that the manifestation of grace is variegated for Cassian.[124] Sometimes it anticipates us; sometimes it conducts us without our knowledge; sometimes it reacts upon its own gift of a good will. Yet it is also true that Cassian is only able to conceive of the relationship of divine and human agency as an *inter-action*, according to a first–then form. This is evident in the famous cases of Zaccheus, the thief on the cross, Paul and the Centurion.[125] Of the last Cassian says, "it would not have been praiseworthy or meritorious if Christ had singled out in him what he himself had given."[126] He writes further of Peter, "[Grace] anticipates a human being's will, then, since it is said: 'My God will go before me with his mercy.' On the other hand, our will anticipates God when he lingers and stands with a salutary intent of testing our will . . ."[127]

We can be charitable here and treat these examples, with Munz and Macqueen, not as the stirrings of an autonomous Pelagian will, but as the manifestation of a prior grace. The real question, however, is not whether grace is first, but whether Cassian's appropriation of stoic assent and the subsequent need to delineate divine and human agency do not simultaneously render the divine agency finite, on the model of an immanent force, and inadvertently extract the human agent from the divine gift economy. For the very need to delineate the respective contributions to the good act implies, in spite of Cassian's insistence on God's transcendence, that the "two agencies" have implicitly been drawn into a real "tensional" relation to one another.[128] Insofar as this relation is positive, God and the agent can be said to be "conjoined," or to cooperate, in the production of the desired effect, though the need for their respective contributions raises the worry that a competition of forces underlies this cooperation. In the end it matters very little; either compromises the genuine participation of Augustine's proto-Chalcedonian "mechanics." Cassian can affirm our necessity for grace; even its prevenience. But he is unable to say, this side of the *telos*, that my good action simply is the act of God in me and all the more mine for that reason.[129]

In considering the rupture in the trinitarian economy which ensues from the *possibilitas, voluntas, actio* schema, we saw that the insulation of the act from its motive resulted in a "noumenal" conception of the will's act: a reified "moment" of the will's reduction from potentiality to act which could not be represented in temporal categories. Such a moment is retrospectively absent from Augustinian *memoria*. Yet Cassian's need to isolate a moment, albeit one bounded by grace, at which the will executes an assent to the beckoning impressions, a moment all its "own" distinct from that beckoning itself, comes perilously close to reproducing this problem. In the Pelagian case, this moment of "noumenalization" is ultimately traceable to a christological defect that implicitly reduces Christ to his exemplary function and misconstrues the hypostatic union. We need not go so far as Munz, asserting that Cassian "thought of Jesus mainly as an educator," who "founded the search for perfection—not the visible church" in order to recognize the striking absence of either the *corpus Christi* or the sacramental gratuity of Christ in the *Conferences*.[130] On Augustinian terms, these omissions indicate not just a failure to attend to crucial theological *loci*, but a failure to comprehend the meaning of human nature and action.

Formally, then, as an account of volition, Cassian's version of stoic subjectivity seems to institute within Western Christianity a conception of self-hood whose distinguishing features are recognizably proto-modern: a self in tensional relation to that which is not the self, will as a causal power, and freedom as indifference realized through a process of negation. Of course these features of his thought are offset by his material Christian commitments, which forestall their negative implications and perhaps even redeem them. His conception of the *telos* is perfectly orthodox, and is compromised only by its problematic relationship to the means. And even here, the practical employment of the means tends to redeem the deficiencies in the theoretical apparatus that justifies them. Contrary to Foucault's charge that Cassian institutes a "microcosm of solitude," which results in a "subjectivation . . . an indefinite objectivation of the self by the self," it should be maintained that *discretio*, within the context of coenobitic monasticism, is predominately a *communal* virtue that affirms, rather than negates, a particular orientation in the world.[131] "The vision of God, like the will of God, is mediated through fellow ascetics."[132] This alone undermines the autarkic unity of the monk for, as Talal Asad argues against Foucault, "there is no longer a single point of surveillance from which the self examines itself, but an entire network of functions through which watching, testing, learning teaching can take place."[133] For the full implications of these stoic debts to emerge, the form of the logic and the matter of its embodiment will have to be disjoined.

If one accepts the thirteenth *Conference* as a rejoinder to Augustine's understanding of grace, then one must grant that the Cassian's stoic holdings have conditioned his interpretation of the question. If one treats this text as the outworking of a pre-Augustinian position, then one could expect the presuppositions of this tradition to govern the interpretation of Augustine upon reception. Indeed, this is evident in the history which follows.

The contagion

Cassian's shadow looms large over this history, though his importance as a vehicle for the transmission of stoicism remains underappreciated by historians of philosophy.[134] His subsequent influence took several forms. His particular version of Christian asceticism would constitute a major alternative to Augustinianism and leave a lasting impression on subsequent monasticism in the West.[135] The *Regula* of St. Benedict bears its imprint. And, as the development of Prosper's own thought shows, Cassian's influence would color the subsequent shape of Augustinianism, even leading to several syntheses of the two positions.[136] This was made possible in part by certain changes taking place on the ground.

The greater part of the next century was characterized by a blurring of the boundary, so integral to the original controversy, between the "desert" of the monastic life and the city.[137] As the century passed, that tension between powerful monasteries such as the one at Lerins and the congregation or episcopacy would take up new residence *within* the persona of a new figure: the monk-bishop.[138] Both Faustus of Riez and Caesarius of Arles would exemplify this transition. Gregory the Great's ascent to the papacy would mark its consummation, and Cassian's stamp on his thought or, rather, the curious synthesis—though by no means the first—of Cassianite and Augustinian thought is obvious. Gregory would extend the Augustinian paradigm of the two cities.[139] He would further the cult of saints, advance the progress of Purgatory, and accord the sacrifice of the Mass a constitutive role in the "social miracle" of Charity.[140] Yet he would meld his generally Augustinian view of the Body of Christ and the sacraments with a stoic, "tensional" stability, taken over from Cassian, against "external" sources of sin.[141] He would retain the sense that obedience negates the individual will and the notion of virtue as a mean.[142] Consequently, one finds in Gregory an insistence on the priority of *discretio*, which complements a conception of the will primarily as a faculty of "choice" locked in a "successive" relationship to grace.[143] Cassian's thought would become codified in Gregory's Augustinianism.

While Cassian's influence on the Pope is evident, Gregory's thought occurs, as Carole Straw notes, within the possibilities generated by the "soft-Augustinianism" that triumphed at the Council of Orange in 529.

The Council had reversed the more pro-Gallican conclusions reached by the councils of Arles and Lyons in 473 and 474.[144] Orange would be taken as the definitive last word on the controversy until Gottschalk and the ninth-century Synods of Quiercy.[145] Little is known of the earlier councils, save that they condemned the extreme predestinarianism of Lucidus and prompted Faustus to write *De Gratia* in their aftermath to explain the councils' conclusions.[146] The Council at Orange, convened at the behest of Bishop Caesarius of Arles, modified what it took to be the Augustinian position on grace and free will by allowing for the restoration of *arbitrium voluntas* after baptism and meritorious works after the gift of unmerited grace. The result of this "soft-Augustinianism," if not an equally outright endorsement of "soft-Cassianism," at least left the door open for Cassian's conception of will as the faculty of choice and freedom as indetermination.[147]

The development is perhaps as significant for what it does not say as for what it does. That the Council saw the need for any modification of the received Augustinianism suggests that some of Augustine's friends, the *predestinati* as they would come to be called, were often at least as damaging to the cause of Augustinian theology as his opponents. Indeed some whom previous generations of scholars have taken to be Semi-Pelagian opponents of Augustine, notably Vincent of Lerins and Faustus of Riez, have been shown by more recent scholarship to be quite appreciative of Augustine on a number of points.[148] Perhaps this too says something about the sort of Augustinianism with which they were confronted.

Prosper's own writings, though they insist on our location in Christ, do not give clear evidence of a thorough apprehension of the connections Augustine had made between human action and desire, Christology, and the indivisible work of the trinitarian *personae*.[149] When Prosper accuses Cassian of instituting some "unformed third thing" between will and grace that satisfies neither the Pelagians nor Augustinians, it is not clear that his understanding of their "inter-action" is any more nuanced than Cassian's "successive" notion. Indeed it appears to be simply the reverse side of it. Furthermore, Prosper tells in his *Chronicle* of a group of "predestinarians" from as early as 417 who had badly misunderstood Augustine's teachings, and there would later appear a certain Monimus from Africa who seems to have fitted this description.[150] In Gaul the predestinarianism of Lucidus is attested by a letter of Faustus, written in advance of the Councils of Arles and Lyon, entreating him to recant his extreme views on grace.[151] The description of the *predestinati* is attested more generally in Vincent's *Commonitorium*, and though it is impossible to know whether the opponents here are real or caricatured the description nevertheless sheds great light on how Augustinianism was being received.

They dare to promise and to teach that in their Church, that is, in the small circle of their communion, there is a sort of great, special, and wholly personal grace of God such that without any labor, without any zeal, without any effort, even if they neither ask, seek, or knock, those who belong to their number are so divinely arranged that, borne by angelic hands, i.e., preserved by angelic protection, they can never dash their foot against a stone, that is, they can never be scandalized.[152]

Prosper's *Pro Augustino responsiones ad capitula objectionum Gallorum calumniantium*, while adding little new to the controversy, likewise preserve a series of Gallican objections to the Augustinian theology of the moment which are otherwise lost. Again, this may or may not tell us of these Augustinians, but it certainly does tell us something of how Augustinian theology was perceived among Gallicans who might otherwise be favorably disposed toward Augustine. The concerns range over a variety of pre-destinarian topics but the sixth article captures the overarching anxiety. "Free will is nothing in man; it is God's predestination that is operative in all men, whether for good or evil."[153]

There may well be problems with Augustine's doctrine of predestination, as we have seen, or rather, with his doctrine of eternal reprobation.[154] The violation of the creature's integrity and the will's freedom are not among them, however, unless one is trying to make Augustine's answers fit the presuppositions behind Pelagian questions. To act as if grace could violate the will, whether from the "Augustinian" or Gallican side, is to fail to grasp the ontological difference between creature and creator. It is to substitute the "proto-Chalcedonian" mechanics of transcendence with the mechanics of stoic immanence, and thus to misunderstand both transcendence and immanence. It is a failure to grasp the mediation of Augustine's Christ, and so it is a failure to grasp the indivisibility of the trinitarian operation and our location within it. It is to privilege the indeterminacy of choice over the determination of love, and thus inadvertently to privilege the nothing from which we are made over the plenitude of infinite determination who makes us. It is finally to open a breach within the gratuity through which we participate in the economies of creation and salvation, though it will take a millennium for this breach to become a rupture.

If we accept that Pelagianism was perceived to be just as problematic as Augustinianism, then Cassian's teachings on grace can be seen as an attempt to repair the breach. There would be others. Faustus of Riez, once thought to be a Semi-Pelagian opponent of Augustine, can now be seen to be attempting in his *De Gratia* something of an Augustinian synthesis in an effort to avoid the pitfalls of either a *sola gratia* or *sola labore* approach.[155] The results of Faustus' efforts resemble those of Cassian. Faustus stresses the gratuity of the first grace, the unity of God's work as creator and redeemer, and "the fundamental continuity of God's gifts to humankind, whether in creation as the array of positive capacities and orientations entailed in the *prima gratia* or *imago dei*, or in redemption as the *auxilium* given in and by Christ."[156] If the effect of the Pelagian "praise of nature" is in fact to devaluate it through indeterminacy, Faustus can be seen through this double stress to move toward a repair of that breach.

The result of these stresses upon the *prima gratia* and creation, says Thomas Smith, is not the elevation of an autonomous nature but rather a blurring of the distinction between grace and nature. "To be in the divine image is to receive grace."[157] The differences from Augustine's elaboration of the same point are significant, however. For Augustine, our status as *imago dei* had to do with our participation, through the *fides quae per dilectionem operatur*, in the gratuitous delight between the Father and the Son.[158] It had to do with our determination to the good, convertible with *esse*, which was the indivisible operation of that good in us. Since there is no *esse* apart from *bonum*, the *non posse peccare* of those finally brought to fruition in the second Adam perfects the image beyond the *posse non peccare* of the first; to be incapable of sin is finally what it will mean *to be*. For Faustus, however, the connection between the eternal filiation of the Son and our status as image is less clear; so too, then, is the connection between being and goodness.

> Thus, it was not fitting that he [Adam] be completed or perfected to the image of him through whom what was lost had to be repaired, lest under the name of the coming physician the ruin of the fall should be predicted in the very time of blessed origins. It is therefore more reasonable that humankind, to whom the reality of grace, not of nature, is handed on by God in the very likeness, image should rather be called what is received from one who is higher and superior, and likeness is better understood as conferred from the truth that the Father rightly communicates with his Son by nature.[159]

The movement from *imago* to *similitudo*, presumably, is simply registered as the movement from grace to grace. Yet the question remains to be asked, in what then does the original *imago* consist? On the one hand, Faustus insists that it entails a positive orientation toward the good.

> Do you see that the good of belief is not a new privilege, but an old one, and that in the very beginning of the world's establishment the human mind was endowed by the most high Author not only with intellect and reason, but also with faith? In fact he had already given a knowledge of himself to the soul then, when he agreed to commit his image to it.[160]

On the other hand, however, Faustus has rejected any determinate reference of the image to Christ, and thus, by extension, to the filiation of the Son from the Father. Rather, "the image of God functions as a summary term for the whole complex of capacities and aptitudes consequent upon the creation of humankind."[161] The formulation is risky, because it threatens to prize indeterminacy. Smith, seemingly alert to this possibility, argues that the inclusion of aptitudes means that "the inner gift is much more than a mere capacity; it is a positive datum."[162]

The question, once again, is not "whether grace," but rather whether grace as conceptualized sustains the unity of *bonum* and *esse*, the ontological difference, the triunity of God, and Christ's mediation. The answer is ambivalent. Insofar as this image bears some resemblance to its archetype, one could ask whether image as indeterminate capacity undermines Faustus' insistence on God's goodness, indeed whether it reopens the door to the divine caprice that Faustus thinks he has slammed shut.[163] Conversely, insofar as the image is understood as a residual datum, we can ask whether this conception does not begin to rend asunder the unions both of grace and nature and being and goodness and render divine agency finite. In Book II, Faustus equates the *imago dei* with *libertatem arbitrii*, the very thing which drove a wedge between being and goodness for the Pelagians. One can likewise begin to see them coming apart here, as the *imago dei* seems less determined by our residual participation in God's goodness than by our capacity to exercise the power of choice free from the determination of this goodness. Carried to its conclusion, this logic again opens the space either to conceive of nature and *esse* as neutral in relation to the good, or to conceive of the latter merely as a qualification of the former.

> They err, therefore, who regard justice and the other virtues as the substance of the soul, without which it could subsist anyway by the vital power of its nature, without which even the devil is seen to remain in his nature. These virtues are manifestly shown to have been added when they are stripped away by the intervention of sins. Only the power of choice and immortality (which is even implanted in evil people) are not removed . . . Insofar as it pertains to freedom of choice and immortality, then, even evil people can possess the image of God, but only the good can possess the likeness.[164]

The second concern, that this configuration renders divine agency finite and juxtaposes it to human agency, is magnified in Faustus' treatment of the will's freedom and its relationship to predestination and divine foreknowledge. Like Cassian, Faustus treats the will's freedom as equivalent to the capacity for choice.[165] He insists furthermore that the creature's movement of itself is something quite separate from the movement of God within the creature. As Smith notes, the chief argument of II.2 is that "divine foreknowledge 'forcibly urges human wills neither toward just pursuits nor toward their opposites.' Put differently, divine foreknowledge in no way intrudes upon or usurps the prerogatives of the human will."[166] The phrase, "*humanas violenter urgeat voluntates*" is interesting in itself, because for Augustine the idea of forced willing is an oxymoron.[167] This was because *voluntas* named not a faculty of choice but the desires embodied in our acts that qualify them as ours—even when those acts are compelled or involuntary. Compelled willing could never, by definition, be "my willing," and conversely my love of God is still mine even if it is "moved" by God himself. Thus our love of God could be at once both God's and ours without contradiction.

However, Faustus, conceiving of will and its freedom negatively in terms of the indeterminacy of choice, can only conceive of human and divine agency as an "inter-action" with the potential to violate the integrity of this choice.[168] Hence Faustus appears to perpetuate unwittingly a kind of ontological rupture which at once institutes and elevates the human subject and immanentizes the divine. For when we combine the conception of the divine image as a positive datum and a capacity with his doctrine of foreknowledge, a familiar set of assumptions begins to emerge. The assumption that the will's self-movement must be characterized independently of the divine movement is both the assumption of a strong active–passive dichotomy between immanent agents exercising efficient force and an inability to think of the movement of God within us as finally anything other than a violation of the integrity of the agent. The divine image as a deposit supplies this immanent criterion of identity, and the successive structure of the grace/will relationship is further testimony of this conclusion. Hence Faustus can say that creation in the image of God is good. He can say that grace precedes the exercise of free will, even that free will is grace. But he cannot say that my desire for God is the desire of God for God in me, and more fully mine for being most fully God's. And because he cannot say this, he has not grasped the profundity of Augustine's christological and ontological achievement.

Thomas Smith is on the mark when he concludes that Faustus' *De Gratia* should not be seen "simply as an exemplary species of the genus of Semi-Pelagianism, but as one part of a broad and variegated reception of Augustine in the fifth century."[169] The relationship of each of these recipients to his Augustinian inheritance differs, with a vague and circuitous border seeming to demarcate those who would number themselves as disciples of the Bishop of Hippo without qualification from those who would qualify their allegiance or perhaps profess none at all. Yet protagonists on each side of this border seem united by a common concern: to provide adequate answers, be they Augustinian or not, to Pelagian questions which from an Augustinian viewpoint there could be no good or intelligible reason for asking. Hence this reception, whose structures of intelligibility were so thoroughly informed by the monasticism of south Gaul and its borrowings from stoic philosophy and pre-Augustinian tradition, was also a transformation. The Augustinianism which emerged from this encounter, codified in the Council of Orange and institutionalized in the Christendom of Gregory the Great, was one therefore implicitly reliant upon the metaphysical underpinnings of a pagan virtue which it had been Augustine's great achievement to refute. Both the staying power of the lingering controversy and the emerging hybrid theology represent a failure to apprehend the scope of that achievement. For Augustine had not simply opposed virtue with virtue, but had opposed virtue's bearer, the autarkic soul damned to securing itself perpetually against outside incursions, with the God who gives us our life—and gives it again—by giving us his life in an act of utter gratuity. Augustine's great achievement was to press the implications of creation at the hands of the God who is charity into the very meaning of creaturehood.

The juxtaposition of the Augustinian and the unreformed stoic self is really then a juxtaposition between the creature whose integrity reflects the utter gratuity of its origins and one forced to secure itself perpetually against the machinations of its origin. The two could not be synthesized without one inflicting damage upon the other, though it is not inconsistent with the nature of this damage to remain hidden. Put differently, the stoic self, the persistent by-product of an active force acting tensionally upon its own passivity, ultimately to the point of its self-negation, could not be imported into Christianity without having a correlative, if subliminal, impact upon Christian assumptions about God. We saw the poison fruits of that reconfiguration in the first section, as the Pelagian self was taken outside Christ's mediation, outside the gratuity of the transcendent Trinity and set in opposition to a de-trinitized "God" reduced to an immanent causal force. We saw the lingering effects of this poison in this section, as the repeated attempts to launch grace against the Pelagians from the perspective of stoic assumptions shared in common with them repeatedly landed in failure.

Yet this failure was neither complete nor total. The practices which sustained the doxological self and its christological and trinitarian constitution would flourish as the sacramental practices of the greater Church formed the backbone of the ecclesial *Corpus Christi*, instantiating, albeit imperfectly, the social miracle of charity.[170] Within the monastic world, the very practices and ends that transmitted the stoic inheritance also staved off its most deleterious consequences. It was only as the formal account of will and subjectivity embodied in these practices was freed from this setting and directed toward a different set of ends that the soul which masters itself through its own negation would attain mastery over God and the world through *their* negation. The full realization of this logic would have to wait until the seventeenth century and the philosophy of René Descartes.

5

AN AUGUSTINIAN PARODY
Descartes and modern stoicism

An overlooked chapter in the story of
modern origins

"[W]here or how shall the Trinity manifest itself?"[1] In Chapter 2 I contended that this question animated the speculations of the *De Trinitate* and provided the conceptual center of Augustine's thought. The answer to this question was distributed throughout the created order (and indeed only through it) in a series of microcosms which manifest the Father's love for and delight in the beauty of the Son.[2] High among these, of course, was the triad of memory, intellect and will in the human soul, and yet even these did not suffice as an image of that beauty apart from the worship of it. This worship required, in turn, a proper orientation toward other constituents of that order, an orientation, namely, of charity, and, when regarded from its point of view, "every creature and every kind of movement that can be considered by the human mind speaks to us for our instruction."[3] Yet the priority of worship indicates that the beauty of these creatures, and of the soul itself, are both penultimate in relation to the full beauty of the created order and somehow a microcosm of that beauty in its fruition. That beauty was the one Christ, Head and Body, in whose unity and sacrifice the love, gift, and delight of the Father are manifest. Creation is finally realized as it manifests this generosity, which is to say that, for Augustine, creation is finally realized in and as Christ. Consequently, any account of an Augustinian "flight from the world" that neglects this integral role of created beauty in eliciting desire for the Father and manifesting his joy fails to ascend to the Augustinianism of Augustine.[4]

Contrast to this René Descartes' orientation to the beauty of creation. "I will now shut my eyes, stop my ears, and withdraw all my senses. I will eliminate from my thoughts all images of bodily things, or rather, since this is hardly possible, I will regard all such images as vacuous, false and worthless."[5] Descartes' radical skepticism has been seen by Michael Allen Gillespie as a genuine skeptical crisis provoked by a radically voluntarist God, by Stephen Toulmin as the reflection of cultural anxiety prompted by

134

the Thirty Years War, and by some as a response to the Pyrrhonism represented by Montaigne. Stephen Menn, Jorge Secada, and others view it simply as a heuristic device employed to defeat Scholastic existentialism in the name of an Augustinian essentialism.[6] It is not necessary to resolve that debate here. Whichever is the case, the difference from the Augustinian stance is more than rhetorical.

Encapsulated in this contrast are two antithetical economies, two vastly different understandings of the self, the God to whom it is ordered, and the role of the world in facilitating that order. At the root of these opposing economies are two fundamentally irreconcilable conceptions of will, both human and divine. We have seen them both before. In the one, *voluntas* is the site of our erotic participation in an anterior gift, and it is at once self-moved and moved by the beauty of that gift. Here will, whether human or divine, is constituted in a relation of love for the beloved, and its freedom is established in dispossession. In the other, will names an inviolable power, and freedom consists in demonstrating this inviolability, through the double negation both of itself and of created beauty.

In Chapter 1, we considered how Charles Taylor has provided the architecture for a grand story of modern origins now taken as axiomatic by thinkers who otherwise have little in common. Augustine's place in this narrative is crucial as one of the great pillars of the "Western metaphysical tradition" that concludes in the birth of Cartesian subjectivity, a tradition which has fallen into disrepute in the wake of Nietzsche, Heidegger and their disciples. Since Augustine is the father of the Western Church par excellence, the discrediting of this tradition as intrinsically nihilistic is thought, by those inclined toward such unmaskings, to expose the intrinsic nihilism of Christianity.

At the point of these contrasting economies, we are at last in a position, not simply to challenge Augustine's place within this narrative, but to recast this story in theological terms. From an Augustinian perspective, the transformed relation "between the cosmos, its transcendent source, and its human interpreter" will consist in a "de-trinitization" of God, an eclipse of the christological fulfillment of humanity, and the exchange of a gratuitous and beautiful creation for a pure *natura*.[7] If one takes *this* as the grand drama of the West, then the question of continuity between Augustine and Descartes takes on a decidedly different shape, and the nihilism occasioned by the advent of the *res cogitans* results not from the intrinsic contradictions of Christianity, but from the triumph of a philosophy whose first principles Christianity once presumed to criticize. For intrinsic to the Cartesian economy is a stoic conception of will that Augustine rejected in the name of Christ and the Trinity. Inasmuch, then, as Descartes is determinative for transformation, modernity can be understood to effect the substitution of the stoic *pyr teknikon* for the Christian Trinity, accompanied by all the destructive machinations unfolded in the previous chapter. This chapter will argue this conclusion, first by examining the question of Descartes' debts to stoicism, secondly by revisiting Augustine's aesthetic soteriology and showing how it prevents him from being proto-Cartesian, and finally by showing how Descartes' *res cogitans* realizes the nihilistic implications of stoic subjectivity.

This claim is more modest than it appears. I do not wish to suggest, as genealogical enterprises tend to do, either that modernity is a singular event that can be reduced to one characterization, or that this event can be reduced to a single point of "corruption." John Bossy's contention, that the introduction of the fork was a monumental event in Christian history, is a useful reminder that many of the crucial factors determining this event are not philosophical at all, at least as that term is conventionally understood.[8] A more complete analysis would have to take greater account of how the rise of the new philosophy and its subject corresponded to changes "on the ground:" the transformation of the universities and of the traditional religious orders that had originally sustained them, alterations within traditional sacramental practice, and the assertion of civil power over ecclesiastical power in the genesis of the modern state.[9] There were of course elements of philosophical and theological justification behind all of these transitions, but the isomorphism between the practical embodiment of an ideology and its theoretical justification is never perfect.

A move has been underway recently to reevaluate Descartes' dependence upon late Scholasticism, particularly Suárez, even as he attempted to supplant it. Nothing in the argument offered here invalidates this general endeavor. I have no stake in restricting the influences upon Descartes, be they pernicious or not. Indeed much of the groundwork both for Descartes' conception of will and his untrinitarian essentialism had been laid by late-medieval scholasticism, and especially by the Franciscans, who arguably had their own tradition of misreading Augustine.

Duns Scotus, for instance, had denied—against Thomas, the Dominicans and a good bit of the Patristic tradition—that the diverse emanations in God were predicated upon relations between the *personae*. At the very least, he could think of no grounds for such a claim beyond the appeal to authority.[10] Though he had invoked *De Trinitate* VI.27—"*Spiritus Sanctus est communis unio (vel communion) Patris et Filii*"—he departed from Augustine in making the divine essence, distinct from the other two *persona* and infinite in a way that the *persona* were not, the object of the Spirit's love.[11] The ground of this divergence is another un-Augustinian move sheltered within the general rubric of Augustine's trinitarian formula. Scotus claims that the trinitarian *personae* (along with the principles of intellect and will) are formally distinct from the divine essence.[12] Though he is trying to sustain the equi-primordiality of the essence and the *personae*, this is precisely the problem, for it presupposes a distinction between the *personae* and the essence considered apersonally. This then lends itself both to an overly psychologized interpretation of these emanations *and* to a (causal?) essentialism, in which the essence is "communicable to many by identity" prior to its differentiation.[13] This is not yet Descartes' causal God, but it has arguably moved the Augustinian conception of the Trinity in that direction.[14]

There are perhaps other viable interpretations, and I do not deny them outright. One might argue that since the divine essence, being utterly particular already, has no *haecceitas* formally distinct from itself, the formal distinction of each person from the essence—which is not the distinction of a *haecceitas*—is the attempt simply to posit the Trinity *as* the utter unicity of God.[15] Yet this latter possibility does not eliminate the former, and it is certainly true that by Descartes' day, one could speculate on divine simplicity, a causal essence, and the distinction between the divine intellect and will with no mention of the trinitarian relations whatsoever. Descartes' voluntarism follows and radicalizes Scotus, and particularly Ockham, both in treating the human and divine volition univocally and in uncoupling the will from the formal object *bonum*, and it is instrumental to his launch of the *epoche*. The voluntarist "concept of omnipotence allows Descartes to connect two Ciceronian hypotheses, the non-existence of the world and the deceiving God."[16]

Just as this insistence on an integral stoicism in Descartes does not deny an integral scholasticism, it does not even deny that Descartes exhibits a certain "Augustinianism." No thinker in the seventeenth century could have escaped Augustine's enormous shadow, and Menn, Janowski and others have rightly called attention to its influence in Descartes' case.[17] Yet this begs a crucial question. If Descartes is an Augustinian, *what kind* of Augustinian is he?[18] Scotus' account of the trinitarian processions is suggestive of a very different Augustinianism from the one offered here. We have already seen Augustinianisms transformed by stoicism into their opposites in the fifth and sixth centuries, and a similar phenomenon was prevalent in the seventeenth, as the lines demarcating Augustinianism and stoicism were frequently transgressed and blurred.[19] Even if we grant Janowski's thesis—that the *Meditations* are an Augustinian theodicy worked out against the backdrop of seventeenth-century debates over divine and human freedom—this only confirms my thesis,[20] for, as we have seen, this is a Pelagian question which assumes in advance that freedom means indeterminacy. Though Janowski gives a somewhat traditional assessment to Descartes' low estimation of "the freedom of indifference," it is only because "human freedom is the reverse side of his conception of Divine freedom," *defined precisely as freedom of indifference*.[21] God's indifference, Zanowski makes plain, is an absolute sovereignty stemming from God's unity, undetermined by any end, unconditioned by any good.[22]

As an account of divine freedom, Cartesian omnipotence has its roots in the voluntarism of Ockham. As a conception of human freedom, its roots are fundamentally stoic. Formally the two are the same, differing only in the extent of their reach.[23] Both depart radically from Augustine's view by freeing *voluntas* from its trinitarian home. This departure will explain "how the Augustinian ideas that largely shaped the intellectual countenance of Western (Latin) Europe for centuries were transformed in the hands of Descartes into forces that led to its destruction."[24] Though this omnipotence is supposed to insure that our freedom consists in the assent to truth, the Cartesian subject will retain the image of this God, with the real result being the reverse: the submission of God to the will of the *res cogitans*. Cartesian freedom thus masks the more fundamental antagonism, intrinsic to stoicism, between the will and an immanent, antagonistically related first principle. Out of this tension emerges the *cogito*'s nihilation of God and world.

This argument for Cartesian stoicism is fundamentally theoretical. Still, a number of possible historical sources lend credence to it. There are of course the various Augustinian and stoic syntheses prompted by the great neostoic movement of the Renaissance. Anthony Levi has included Charron, Montaigne, Francis of Sales, and even Descartes himself in this category.[25] This movement revived (and modified) stoic sources and stoic theories of nature somewhat unmediated by Christian gloss, though Justus Lipsius and others perpetually attempted to integrate the two.[26] In Du Vair, Charron and Francis of Sales, this revival profoundly shaped a new account of the passions, and it paved the way for Descartes' own conception, which bears their impress.[27] Furthermore, the stoic emphasis on the withholding of assent accords primacy to a sort of *epoche* within stoic ethics, making it ripe for alignment with a skeptical theory of knowledge. Justus Lipsius would eventually fuse the two in his *Manuductio*.[28] The result, at least formally, is remarkably proto-Cartesian, as "the wise man 'uses the *epoche* and reserves his assent'" when confronted with impressions which are less than certain.[29]

There is perhaps a stoic inspiration behind the physics themselves, though here again the relationship is complicated and should not be overstated. Certainly Descartes' ambition to derive a science of ethical behavior as the crowning conclusion to a mechanistic physics, if not exclusively stoic, is at least compatible both with the original stoics and with Lipsius.[30] It is true that Descartes' "Platonic" geometrical essentialism is constructed to oppose not simply the "real qualities" of the scholastics but the "vital spirits and occult qualities of Renaissance natural philosophy" which partly owe their inspiration to the neostoic revival.[31] Yet any reaction preserves traces of what it opposes, and several aspects of the Cartesian program may betray stoic influence: the notion of God as a direct, immanent cause acting on inherently passive matter, the subsequent importance of the concept of *force*, and God's immutable action preserving a constant quantum of motion and thus a material *plenum*.[32]

Without discounting these influences, however, I want to focus on one final source for Cartesian stoicism. That is Descartes' religious education at the hands of the Jesuits at La Flèche, where Descartes spent nearly nine years from 1607 to 1615. This source is crucial for two reasons, the first of which is the access it provided to the stoic influences already noted. Ignatius' commitment to the humanist study of letters was embodied in the pedagogical structure of the new Jesuit colleges, and their advent coincides with a revival of Christian neostoicism. Seneca and Cicero figured heavily in Jesuit rhetorical training, and in the final year of the educational program the course in metaphysics was accompanied by a study of ethics which also emphasized stoic sources.[33] Descartes, reflecting this training, would later recommend Seneca's *De vita beata* to the young Princess Elizabeth. And "when in part 3 of *Discourse on the Method* Descartes articulates provisional rules of ethics without giving them any theoretical foundation, he borrows the third maxim from the Stoics: 'I shall attempt to master myself rather than fortune, to change my desires rather than the order of the world.'"[34] As we shall see, the *Meditations* are at least in part a method for this self-mastery.

There is a second reason, quite apart from its humanist content, why Descartes' Jesuit education is important: its form. Extending the question of Augustinian-Cartesian continuity beyond the cogitarian arguments, Stephen Menn has argued that Augustine and Descartes are united by a common "*discipline* for approaching wisdom . . . and therefore also the series of intellectual intuitions produced by this discipline."[35] The wisdom sought is the Plotinian wisdom of God as *Nous*, and the method, appropriately, is a Plotinian "turning to *oneself*" that is also a retreat from the sensible.[36] The next section will examine the latter point from the Augustinian side; still, the claim raises immediate questions. If this identification with Plotinian *Nous* were as central as Menn claims, one would expect Descartes to go to as great a length explicating the divine essence as *summe intelligens* as the *summe potens*.[37] Yet he does not. Similarly, if God as *ens summe perfectum* were equivalent to Plotinian *Nous*, and if *Nous* were indeed the first name of the Cartesian God, then one would expect this demonstration to be like the demonstration of the infinite, established logically *before* the truths of mathematics, not among them.[38]

Nevertheless, the idea of a "spiritual discipline" leaving its tracks in the *Meditations* is an intriguing one. It is only odd that Menn overlooks the religious discipline of Descartes' youth in his zeal to locate antecedents in Augustine. For at least one set of footprints in the *Meditations* leads to the *Spiritual Exercises* of Ignatius, and from there to Cassian and the stoic account of volition embodied in the tradition of Christian *ascesis* considered in the previous chapter. Descartes would have been intimately familiar with the *Exercises*. Like all the students at La Flèche, he undertook extended Ignatian retreats annually.[39] Other scholars have noticed this connection;

yet even those with an eye toward an Ignatian influence upon Cartesian thought tend either to lump the *Spiritual Exercises* into an amorphous "tradition of spirituality stemming from St. Augustine" or to oppose them to Descartes' "Augustinianism" on grounds that they employ an Aristotelian account of cognition.[40]

There are of course crucial differences, and I by no means wish to suggest that Descartes is a faithful follower of Ignatius, or that the *res cogitans* is the inevitable conclusion of Ignatian spirituality. The two disciplines are clearly directed to different ends. The *Exercises* have the will of God as both their first cause and their final object, while the *Meditations* seek finally to establish a lasting foundation for the sciences.[41] Accordingly, the *Exercises* retain a unity of theory and practice that is putatively absent from Descartes, who distinguishes sharply between "the conduct of life and the contemplation of truth."[42] He consigns the former, with matters of faith, to the realm of things perceived only obscurely, thus leaving the latter to the adjudication of his fundamental principle. The difference from Ignatius is ultimately traceable to differences in, or rather Descartes' neglect of, a Christology. One must remember, moreover, that the *Exercises* are instructions for those who *direct* the course of weeks, not for the *exercitant* who undertakes them. Though they have as their avowed intent (their *skopos?*) "the conquest of the self and the regulation of one's life in such a way that no decision is made under the influence of any inordinate attachment," there is a profound sense in which, for Ignatius, as for Cassian before him, self-mastery is no longer *self*-mastery.[43] To this extent, Descartes' program to demolish "the large number of falsehoods that I had accepted as true since childhood," which would include the negation of input from any exterior director, any inherited tradition, any common endeavor, is profoundly *anti*-Ignatian.[44]

Much has been made of the alleged "modernism" of Ignatius' exercises, and it seems true that the relative autonomy and mobility they accord to the individual in comparison to the older, mendicant orders whom the Jesuits were rapidly displacing does indeed attest to the massive shift in ecclesial practice and cultural upheaval characteristic of a transitory period.[45] Yet I am willing to grant, despite whatever tensions this modernism occasions, that "the goal [of the *Exercises*]—the glory of God (*ut laudet Deum*)— intrinsically transforms the very method of attaining it," thus inverting "the modern ideal of self-realization" and preserving a genuine transcendence.[46] It is rather what is most ancient in Ignatius that is the source of the trouble.

In the last chapter we saw how Cassian baptized the formal features of the stoic theory of judgment, recasting the problem of assent to phantasms which intrude upon the *hegemonikon* as the *discretio spirituum*, a move that elevated *discretio* to pride of place among the virtues. *Discretio* determines the origins of thought from among three possibilities, God, ourselves or the devil. The will, in a "tensional" position between these extremities, executes an act of judgment, primarily by negating the latter two. This negative emphasis was especially crucial for the Stoa, since positive assent fails sufficiently to establish relative autonomy within the immanent causal nexus, and Cassian had retained a measure of this tension.[47] This understanding also recast humility primarily as the will's habitual abnegation, a negation that often includes the world within its scope. This notion would have a long career in Christian thought and practice.[48] The charge of Pelagianism crept in, of course, at the point in the act of assent where the respective contributions of the divine and human were delineated.

Ignatius imbibed this scheme and many other facets of the ancient ascetic tradition of Cassian, Evagrius and the Desert Fathers, in part through Abbot Cisneros of Montserrat, who in 1522 gave Ignatius a handbook of spiritual exercises that would serve as a primary source for his own discipline.[49] The "general examination of conscience," the judgments that initiate the first week of the *Exercises,* recapitulate both the three causal origins of our thoughts and the *discretio spirituum*.[50] Indeed it is precisely through "delicate discernment of the movements of the soul," terminology that Descartes will appropriate to define the passions themselves, that the exercitant "finds the will of God." This finding, achieved in part through prolonged meditation on the life of Christ, is then executed in an act of election.[51] Like Cassian, Ignatius sometimes conceives of the will in a sort of tensional position between alternatives, counseling that "I must be indifferent, without any inordinate attachment, so that I am not more inclined or disposed to accept the object in question, than to relinquish it, nor to give it up than to accept it."[52] Though Ignatius immediately insists that "I should beg God our Lord to deign to move my will," and concludes that "the love that moves and causes one to choose must descend from above, that is, from the love of God," his discipline would nevertheless elicit the charge of Pelagianism from the Dominicans much as Cassian's had from Prosper.[53]

There is thus both a historical connection and an intellectual debt between the discipline of Cassian and the Benedictines and Ignatius' *Spiritual Exercises.* And the *Exercises* therefore provide a mediating link between the stoic mechanics latent in this discipline and those of Descartes' *Meditations*.[54] For notwithstanding other divergent sources, vast differences in their respective ends and in the role of the director in facilitating the *exercitant*'s discernment, the *Meditations* mimic this discipline on key points of both aim and method.[55] One might even say that the *Meditations* are a kind of secularized, theoretical perversion of the *Spiritual Exercises* and that Cartesian judgment is a variation upon the examination of conscience and discernment of spirits. A comparison of their respective methods and aims reveals this.

The deceptive origins of the malign spirits imbue *discretio* with a special function. Discretion alone can "keep a monk permanently unharmed by the snares and deceptions of the devil."[56] *Discretio* prevents deceit, both from the *cogitationes* internal to a disordered soul and from those which have their origin outside the self and in the devil.[57] Menn recognizes the stoic origin of Descartes' *cogitationes.* "Cartesian ideas are Stoic *phantasiai* or impressions" which the will either affirms or denies by actively withholding assent.[58] Yet he fails to recognize how Descartes' fundamental principle entails a revised form of *discretio* and employs, in a slightly disguised form, the Cassianite and Ignatian categories for attributing our ideas to their respective causal origins. The meditator easily recognizes himself as a possible origin of some thoughts. "As to my ideas of corporeal things, I can see nothing in them which is so great as to make seem impossible that it originated in myself."[59] Descartes will specify this more fully in the *Passions,* which will follow both the ascetic tradition and the stoics in diversely allocating responsibility for these perceptions to both the soul and the body.[60]

The deceits of the devil return in the guise of the *deus malignus,* who confronts the meditator with the possibility that his thoughts of the world and his body are mere delusions.[61] The meditator resists this deceit first by withholding his assent from these perceptions; he defeats the deceiver by asserting the fundamental principle. "Let him deceive me as much as he can, he will never bring it about that I am nothing so long as I think that I am something."[62] Save for the mechanistic biology, Descartes' advice in the *Passions* for dealing with such unsettling "disturbances" might have been written by Cassian himself.

> The soul can prevent itself from hearing a slight noise or feeling a slight pain by attending very closely to some other thing, but it cannot in the same way prevent itself from hearing thunder or feeling a fire that burns the hand. Likewise it can easily overcome the lesser passions, but not the stronger and more violent ones, except after the disturbance of the blood and spirits has died down. The most the will can do while this disturbance is at full strength is not to yield to its effects and to inhibit many of the movements to which it disposes the body.[63]

Discernment of the third class of *cogitationes,* those of divine origin, occupies a special place, however, both in the ascetical tradition and in Descartes. Materially, this discernment differs profoundly in the two accounts. Formally speaking, it is the goal of both the *Exercises* and the third *Meditation,* which ostensibly sets out "to prove, not merely that our chosen effect has some cause, but that this cause is God."[64] Similar discernment of "effects in the soul which can have God alone as their cause" is an explicit goal of the *Exercises,* in the "consolation without previous cause."[65] Descartes' attempts to establish the idea of God as a cataleptic idea caused by an uncaused (or self-causing) God arguably mimic this Ignatian notion, which in turn bears a formal resemblance to stoic *cataleptic* impressions. The formal similarity between the means to these ends underscores this conclusion. Just as Ignatius advises the *exercitant* in a period of desolation to be most watchful and even to act contrary to the *motio* exciting the soul, so the meditator refuses those unclear perceptions while in a state of doubt.[66]

Ignatius may even have provided Descartes with inspiration for his conception of certainty. Descartes faulted humanists like Charron for failing to include it within *sagesse.*[67] As we have seen, Augustine implicitly smuggled faith into knowledge. Descartes might easily have missed that, but even so, Augustinian certainty lacks Descartes' causal concern. Descartes' cataleptic idea of God, unveiled through the long process of hyperbolic doubt, commends itself, by definition, indubitably.[68] The intervention of Cartesian ideas and their objective reality qua representation, which has the effect of *heightening* the anxiety over causal origins, will place this understanding at one remove from the immediacy of Ignatius' notion. Still, there appears to be a formal family resemblance between the certainty of this cataleptic idea and the "consolation without previous cause" which can have no other cause than God. Karl Rahner concludes that Ignatius' "Rules for the Discernment of Spirits maintain that there are mental movements whose origin from God is certain."[69] Hugo Rahner modifies this somewhat by emphasizing "the external judgment of the director as a means for controlling inward illumination."[70] This remains one of the most controversial aspects of Ignatius' thought. Whatever the final determination, the notion was initially regarded with enough suspicion to get Ignatius labeled an Illuminist or *Alumbrado.* And this charge, whether true or not, was sufficient to preoccupy subsequent generations of Jesuits with the task of vindicating their master. In short, whether or not Ignatius actually proffered a certainty that could inspire and prefigure a Cartesian variant, enough people read him that way that the capacity for inspiring the Cartesian notion depends little on Ignatius' actual intent.

In formal and programmatic terms, then, we can see first, Ignatius' historical debt to Cassian's stoicism, and secondly strong family resemblances, further suggested by historical familiarity, between this tradition and the method of Descartes' *Meditations*. As we proceed, particularly in the final section, the material similarities between stoic assent and the Cartesian will become more evident. Yet already these similarities should caution us against assuming that Augustine could be proto-Cartesian. The ensuing section will show why he cannot be.

Why Augustine is not a Cartesian

According to Stephen Menn, Augustine and Descartes' common pursuit of wisdom produces a common discipline and, consequently, a set of shared intuitions.[71] Since the wisdom in question is the Plotinian wisdom of God as *Nous*, the method, appropriately, is a Plotinian "turning to *oneself*" that is also a retreat from the sensible.[72] This turn, this "contempt for the sensible," lies at the root of the claim for continuity between the Augustinian and Cartesian selves.[73] Yet it is precisely because these "turns" are the expression of two markedly different wills, ordered finally to two dramatically different Gods, that the claim cannot stand.

The claim of continuity obscures this point from the outset. So in Menn's case for instance, the common quest determines not only Descartes' relationship to Augustine but also Augustine's relationship to Christianity; "'conversion' for Augustine is not the passage from one religious allegiance to another, but the soul's *conversio* or turning to God."[74] Menn thus follows a well-established tradition in according *Confessiones* VII, with its praise of the *platonicorum libri* and its distinction between the *via* and *patria*, a central, organizing role in his portrait of Augustine. The delineation fits nicely with the Cartesian disjunction of theory and practice.[75]

For Menn, Augustine's full rapprochement with Plotinus and Descartes is possible because he offers "no irreducible Christian intellectual content unknown to pagan philosophy."[76] For Wayne Hankey, as we saw in the first chapter, it is precisely *because* of Augustine's Christianity that he foreshadows Descartes. Though he praises Menn for grasping "what is positive in the intellectual union of the human and divine," Hankey criticizes him for failing to differentiate adequately between Augustine's "modification of the Plotinian hypostatic spiritual trinity" and the Plotinian original.[77] According to Hankey neither "Menn nor Augustine are interested in the One in its distinction from Nous," and this neglect causes Menn to fail to see crucial differences between Augustine and Plotinus which would actually strengthen Menn's claim for continuity.[78] This is because

> [F]or Plotinus, being and will do not belong to the One in an act of self-reflexion. Such an act would divide the One, placing it above and below itself, as if it received itself from itself as from another. What is true of the soul which exists from another, and needs above all to know this alterity, cannot be true of the One. There is no reflexive self-othering in the One.[79]

Given that the Plotinian self is established in the One, the absence of "reflexive self-othering" in the One means that "a self-reflexive knowing cannot be carried to the root of the self," rendering self-identity doubtful.[80] Only with the Christian and Augustinian transformation of the Platonic inheritance in the direction of the simplicity and equality of the trinitarian hypostases does one arrive at a "reflexive self-othering" in the first principle. [81] Accordingly, argues Hankey, neglect of this transformation causes Menn to miss how Augustine generates the self "constituted in relation to the divine as a mirror of the trinitarian divine self-relation, and possessing in that mirrored self-relation at once both a self-identity and a relation to the divine."[82]

Though the two approaches initially seem to be opposed to one another, each partakes of the same fundamental failure to grasp the implications of Augustine's elaboration of the trinitarian *personae* and its necessary relationship to his Christology. This failure is arguably endemic to any claim for continuity. Moreover, they fail to see how the gratuity of the trinitarian *donum* transfigures the meaning of self-presence, "the turn" and ultimately the self.[83] In Menn's case, this failure has several manifestations. The identification of Descartes' God and Plotian *Nous* is now rendered questionable both by Hankey's criticism of his Plotinus and by the relatively modest role Descartes attributes to God as *summe intelligens* in comparison to *summe potens*. Beyond that, however, his deployment of the distinction between *via* and *patria* from *Confessiones* VII involves him in a curious double maneuver. On the one hand, it allows him to relegate Augustine's Christology, so integral to his explication of the trinitarian *personae* and the divine will as a relation of love, to a merely practical realm. This is convenient, since Descartes has no Christology of which to speak. On the other hand, this move allows him to impose a Cartesian voluntarism, undisciplined by the strictures of trinitarian theology, back *onto* Augustine, so that when Christology makes its return in his brief mention of Jesus' passion, the divine will—"not naturally directed toward what is good and appropriate for the divine nature, but a will capable of encompassing its own humiliation"—appears as the spontaneous Cartesian capacity for self-negation.[84]

Whereas Menn's is a sin of commission, Hankey's, as we have seen, is a sin of omission. His Augustine, locked in an atemporal dialogue with God and a temporal dialogue with Plotinus and Descartes, simply has no Christology and passion, no ecclesiology and no soteriology in any distinctly Christian sense.[85] His "reflexive self-othering" contains a lot more reflexivity than othering, and his critique of Rowan Williams neglects the understanding of the Holy Spirit, not simply as *nous eron* but as *donum*. Not only did this invest the Christian God with an intrinsic gratuity and reciprocity unavailable to the One, but it effectively reconfigured the convertible transcendentals as love and creation as an act of benevolent generosity, as the Father brings forth creation in his love for the Son and creatures, ultimately, in the Body of Christ.[86]

This of course presented its own problems of self-identity. This is not because the unity of God and soul is forever deferred—Hankey is partially

145

correct here—but because this union of creator and creature, a union more intimate than self-identity, forever makes the soul both more *and* less than itself.[87] This is illustrated wonderfully by the dual sense of *distentio* in *Confessiones* XI.29 as the earlier sense of the *distentio animi*, of the mind's excess to the passage of time, gives way to the sense of sundering apart or dissipation and loss in "times whose order I do not know."[88] Yet Augustine's presence to self is not only attended by the absence that threatens to undo him and render the subject of his confession incoherent; it is also anticipated and intended as a surplus of gift. This is the position of a creature whose similarity to God is grounded in an ever greater dissimilarity and who exists gratuitously suspended between being and nothing.[89] "But 'your right hand has upheld me' in my Lord, the Son of man, mediator between you the One and us, the many, so that by him 'I may apprehend in whom I have been apprehended.'"[90] Distention in time elides into the intention of God who is other to time, and who gratuitously assumes our nothingness.[91]

Thus even in the most immediate presence to self of *De Trinitate* X, whose form is this very activity of knowing, remembering and loving, the soul while present to itself as a whole was nevertheless not necessarily wholly present.[92] It required for its self-presence, as other passages make clear, the gift of the mediator whom its every act intends as the ultimate object of its seeking.[93] Since the principle of delight is beauty and since delight "is the only possible source of action," this very seeking requires the manifestation of Christ the *forma* of God.[94] It is no coincidence that Augustine praises the *pulchritudo doctrinae* in commending self-know-ledge.[95] For this phrase indicates the trajectory along which *De Trinitate* is tending: to the conclusion that self-knowledge, self-recollection, and self-love finally occur in the beauty of Christ's dual status as *exemplum* and *sacramentum*, which is to say, in the convertible love and delight of the trinitarian *personae*. To the extent that our knowledge, memory, and love of ourselves turn out to have been true, we recognize that this self-giving love has been there all along, going before us.[96] This is the heart of Augustine's trinitarian theology, his Christology, and his doctrine of grace. This insight penetrates to the depths of what it means for Augustine to exist in time, to remember, to know and to will.

This conclusion expresses what the contemporary arguments for con-tinuity miss: how the christological union of time and eternity, creator and creation, intelligible and sensible is the locus for the revelation of the Trinity as both the beautiful and the love of the beautiful. This in turn distinguishes creation from mere causality and transfigures all of the terms in question.[97] The locus of this transformation, and the crucial point both for distinguishing the Augustinian *mens* from the Cartesian *cogito* and for redefining just what makes the "modern Western self" modern, is the concept of *will*.

Situated within Christ's unity, actively drawn by the beauty of the *exemplum* and receiving the gift of *sacramentum*, *voluntas* is neither exactly active nor exactly passive.[98] Here one *can* say, with proper qualifications, that this will "mirrors" the divine will just to the extent that it participates doxologically in trinitarian delight. Though again, it mirrors this delight precisely in its differentiation from it, just as the Son is at an infinite distance from the Father as a function of his *unity* with the Father's self-giving. This is because Augustine has made *voluntas* and *dilectio* synonymous in God, and love for the beauty of the Son the will by which the Father creates gratuitously in the Son.[99]

This understanding is reflected in the complexity of the Augustinian "turn." This complexity is evident even in *De Libero Arbitrio*, which is significant since it is not overtly "about" the Trinity and since Descartes' is alleged to be a "*De Libero Arbitrio* Augustinianism."[100] Menn refers to the Plotinian "turning to soul" straightforwardly as a "turning to oneself," though he nevertheless adverts in passing to its "aesthetic" character: "it considers sensible beauty and traces it back to its intelligible source."[101] He then draws upon the "ascent" of *De Libero Arbitrio* II to suggest that Augustine foreshadows a proto-Cartesian turn from the sensible, prefigures Cartesian *mathesis* by conflating number and wisdom, and perhaps even anticipates a proto-Cartesian doctrine of judgment. In doing so, he invokes a key Augustinian text.[102]

> Wherever you turn, [Wisdom] speaks to you by certain traces that it has imprinted on its work, and, when you have fallen back to outward things, calls you back within by the very forms of outward things, so that, whatever delights you in body and lures you through the corporeal senses, you will see that it is numerical; and you will ask whence it is, and return into yourself, and understand that you could not approve or disapprove what you reach through the senses of the body unless you had in you certain laws of beauty to which you refer whatever beautiful things you sense outside.[103]

In fact, the passage suggests a very un-Cartesian orientation toward *sensibilia*. This orientation indicates the profound difference between the Augustinian and Cartesian economies, and it becomes more evident if this passage is situated within some of the broader concerns of the work. This first is the issue of idolatry, foretold in Book I by the distinction between one who uses temporal things well and one who "clings to them and becomes entangled with them."[104] This echoes Augustine's famous distinction between use and enjoyment. It is perhaps easy to miss this concern, as it remains at points rather subterranean. Yet it is quite a prominent theme in *De Vera Religione*, a work commenced after Book I and roughly contemporary with Books II and III.[105] The second, more famous, concern

" uronus / fructus "

complements the first. It is Augustine's need to vindicate the goodness of both God and creation against the Manichees. Augustine completes this task in Book III by showing how even evil does not compromise the harmonious beauty of the whole.[106]

The relationship between the concern for right desire in Book I and the vindication of God and creation in Book III is evident in Augustine's discipline for right judgment and the equation of Wisdom and number in Book II. We can already see a key aspect of that relation in the passage invoked by Menn. In this instance, the turn inward is itself occasioned by delight in the beauty of "outward things," and the point of the so-called ascent of Book II is not *simply* "to bring Evodius to recognize this Truth [of *Nous*] for himself" separate from the soul and *sensibilia*.[107] In the context of Book I's concern for idolatry, and Book III's vindication, it becomes clear that a proper *regard* for the soul *and sensibilia* is intrinsic to our capacity to intuit the standard and judge by its light.[108] Carol Harrison observes a complex *double turn* in this regard that eludes Menn and integrates the passage in question with the broader concerns. "There is a simultaneous turning away from Creation and looking beyond it to its Creator, *and* a turning *towards* it, and looking in and through it for its Creator, in Augustine's thought."[109] To a soul possessed of such regard, *sensibilia* are no longer mere *sensibilia* but *revelabilia*. "Indeed, if you regard them carefully and piously, every kind of creature and every movement that can be considered by the human mind speaks to us for our instruction."[110]

Hence, unlike the Cartesian turn which we shall consider in the subsequent section, the Augustinian (double) turn effects neither the *negation* of the sensible nor, strictly speaking, is it the precondition for our knowledge of it.[111] Rather this turn is made possible by the trinitarian beauty of Wisdom, which, because it transcends both the soul and sensibilia, is *both* present in the soul *and* manifest *in* sensibilia: "Wisdom . . . calls you back within *by the very forms of outward things*."[112] The positive role accorded to these forms reflects the multivalent microcosmic/macrocosmic relationships discussed in Chapter 2. The fulfillment of this turn is our *conversio* to God made possible by the *exemplum* of Christ and the sacramental gift of the Spirit.

Created beauty is thus crucial to the success of *De Libero Arbitrio*, both for the attainment of wisdom and for vindicating God against the Manichees. In a similar vein, James O'Donnell insists that "revelation of the goodness of created things" is integral to the success of the Plotinian "ascent" of *Confessiones* VII.17.23, another text of fundamental importance for Menn.[113] Yet as the transition from *Confessiones* VII.17.23 to VII.18.24 shows, "It is not that [Augustine] discovered that the Plotinian method did not work; he discovered that it did work, and that it was not enough."[114] Augustine's conflation of number and wisdom must be understood in the context of this vindication and the economy that attends it. This suggests a second, antithetical difference from the Cartesian view, whose *mathesis* expels final causes and effectively makes "good" and "beautiful" incidental to the understanding of essences or existence.[115] For Menn's Augustine, "number" is important because "it can lead us up from mutable bodies to an immutable truth," and he therefore suggests that the moral of *De Libero Arbitrio* II is that "the wisdom or intelligence that should govern human life is shown to have the same divine source as the numerical order or intelligibility that governs the physical world."[116] These remarks are not so much false as empty, and they are misleading insofar as they suggest a precursor to Cartesian *mathesis*.[117]

By conflating number and wisdom and eliding these further into beauty, Augustine invests number itself with "a qualitative dimension and a mysterious inexhaustible depth" which is absent from Descartes' "grey ontology."[118] This conflation defies—in a manner perhaps now unimaginable to us—the disjunction of "quality" and "quantity." Augustine knows no such disjunction, and he does not consign the qualitative perfections of things to a merely noetic realm subject to the ego's powers of "amplification."[119]

This is not just theodicy (the category under which Menn treats it) but cosmology. For it is in this union of quantity and quality that "terrestrial things are joined to celestial, and their time circuits join together in a harmonious succession for a poem of the universe."[120] Number, in other words, is not simply concerned with quantity (and hence extension and motion), but rather the way in which "sheer diversity is ordered and directed toward unity," a unity unfolded as the infinite differentiation of love.[121] And by referring our judgment of *sensibilia* to certain "laws of beauty" within us, Augustine suggests that judgment is itself an aesthetic category concerned with delight in and apprehension of this unity, because the truth of things consists in their relationship to the divine unity.[122] In short, number and its judgment (or more precisely *numeri iudiciales)* are concerned with *harmonia*—with manifesting it *and* apprehending it. In Chapter 2 we discussed some of the ways that Augustine reflects this understanding, microcosmically and macrocosmically, in his cosmology and exegesis.

To say that number is concerned with *harmonia* is to say that number is intrinsically "aesthetic." Indeed insofar as Augustine makes number synonymous with *forma*, it is synonymous with beauty itself.[123] And to make number aesthetic is to deny that the inward turn is, *simpliciter*, inward. We have seen this reflected in Augustine's "erotic" conception of *voluntas* and mediation. For the very movement of this turn entails a proper orientation toward, a proper appreciation of—a well-ordered delight in—the sensible. This recognition invokes the complex of mediated relations that we have seen repeatedly in Augustine's trinitarian theology, anthropology, and his cosmology. The last being aesthetic, elides doxologically into his ecclesiology. Gerhart Ladner sums up these relations well.

Augustine's number symbolism, based as it is on an arithmology of numerically ordered multitude as a reflection of a unity implies, first, a vindication of the corporeal world, but only insofar as it is ordered toward the spiritual; secondly, of the periods or "ages" of history insofar as they are a prelude to eternity; and thirdly, of the multitudinous and societal life of rational creatures on earth and in heaven insofar as the common good of this *Civitas Dei*, is ordered toward the supreme good, God.[124]

In the *De Trinitate*, all three concerns terminate in the "hypostatic unity" of Augustine's Christ. Christ harmonizes our double to his single and thus creates harmony out of sin. In the unity of Christ's Body, with Jesus the Head, creation is restored as beautiful, showing forth the delight and love between Father and Son. Christ, the visible beauty of God delights and moves the will as both sacramental principle and exemplary object. This movement of the will, entailing recognition and thus those laws of beauty, at once both appropriates the *donum* of Father and Son and reflects the *harmonia* of creation by participating in the delight between Father and Son.[125] Once we saw this, we could see both how salvation was aesthetic and how the trinitarian similitude of memory, intellect and will fit within this understanding: the likeness becomes the image through doxological participation in the life of the Trinity. In short, when one understands the aesthetic function of *voluntas*, one understands how Christ saves us and what this salvation consists in: the love of God, in both senses of the genitive, which "alone distinguishes the sons of the eternal kingdom from the sons of eternal perdition."[126]

Given this relationship between Augustinian *voluntas*, Christology and trinitarianism, it follows that a failure to apprehend the Augustinian turn will produce deficiencies in the last two areas. This is clear enough in Descartes, who has no Christology, and whose specification of the divine will and essence differs markedly from Augustine's. The same can be said for the proponents of Augustinian-Cartesian continuity. For instance, Menn, who admits that "it is obscure precisely how Augustine thinks the Incarnation works in bringing about salvation," must walk a very narrow path. In order to sustain his thesis, he must read *Confessiones* VII as *both* asserting an essential continuity between Augustine and Plotinus *and* as foreshadowing the third *Meditation*. The former commits him to a "strong" reading of Augustine's appropriation of the *libri platonicorum*, and a certain *modern* hermeneutic posture toward the *Confessiones* as a whole, treating it simply as an "autobiographical report of the process by which [Augustine] came to a true understanding of God." This interpretation makes the genre of confession adventitious to its meaning.[127] The latter commitment requires that he overlook what *is* properly Plotinian in the "discipline" of *Confessiones* VII.17—that it has been occasioned by "the beauty of bodies"—

and how this discipline might be consummated christologically *beyond* Plotinus.[128]

Menn's attempt to clarify this soteriological point magnifies the obscurity by imposing post-Cartesian distinctions onto Augustine's text which it had been the achievement of Augustine's Christ to overcome: rigid distinctions between reason and faith, "natural theology" and "revealed religion," and speculation and practice. Each is underwritten by a hard distinction between *via* and *patria*.[129] This not only occludes how Augustine's Christology and trinitarianism inform his conception of *voluntas*, but it aids and abets the substitution of a Cartesian voluntarism for the Augustinian notion.

Augustine does make a distinction between *via* and *patria* in *Confessiones* VII.20–1, where he asserts that "it is one thing to behold from a wooded mountain peak the land of peace . . ." and "a different thing to keep to the way that leads to that land."[130] And a superficial reading of this distinction might lend itself to the conclusion that "the Platonists know all about the Fatherland, but lack only the Way to get there."[131] Yet the specificities of Augustine's Christology must be central to the meaning of this distinction, and its clarity here is complicated by the idiosyncrasies intrinsic to the confessional genre and the particular point in the narrative where it appears. The Augustine represented at this stage of the *Confessiones* is an Augustine on the near side of baptism. Hence, as O'Donnell reminds us, it is unclear at this point just how well the Augustine who is the subject of the narrative understands either the Fatherland or the Way, and it is likely that Augustine the narrator intends us to recognize this inadequacy. O'Donnell suggests further that in the narrative structure of the *Confessiones* as a whole, and thus in the structure of Augustine's self-narration, incarnation precedes Trinity.[132] All of this defies the attempt to determine the meaning of this distinction in isolation from Augustine's broader purposes. Indeed, if we wish to consider just how Augustine's Christology configures the distinction between *via* and *patria*, we would do better to look elsewhere.

We have already seen this relationship. In Chapter 2, we saw how the christological union of *sapientia* and *scientia* "hypostatically" joins the two poles in this distinction: "The one and the same Christ is *via and patria*."[133] "Therefore Christ is our knowledge, and the same Christ is also our wisdom."[134] This conclusion made speculation dependent upon the particularity of Christian doxological practice and vice versa.[135] "He himself implants in us faith concerning temporal things, He himself shows forth the truth concerning eternal things. Through him we travel to him: we stretch through knowledge to wisdom, yet we do not withdraw from one and the same Christ."[136]

Though he recognizes the indispensability of the *via* for Augustine, Menn nevertheless rigidifies this distinction, treating *via* and *patria* not as a "hypostatic unity," but as a "Nestorian" conjunction. This, importantly, allows for the possibility of their disjunction. This serves two advantages for his thesis. First, it allows him to uphold the essential continuity with Plotinus, by consigning the Christian contribution to Augustine's Platonism to the "practical" realm. "Platonism gave [Augustine] the vision of God, while Christianity gave him the path; but the vision was what inspired him to seek the path."[137] Second, it allows him to posit an Augustinian antecedent for the Cartesian disjunction of speculation and practice. Though his method arguably transgresses the distinction, the disjunction "between the conduct of life and the contemplation of truth" is firm and mandatory for Descartes. This is because truth and falsity in speculative matters are a function of the will's giving or withholding assent to clear and distinct ideas while practical matters or matters of faith are perceived only obscurely.[138]

This *via* and *patria* distinction permits Menn to deploy Augustine's Christology so as to maintain both speculative continuity with Platonism and anticipation of Descartes, while still accounting for Christ's function within Augustine's thought. In attempting this feat, Menn seizes on Augustine's rebuke of the Platonists for their rejection of the incarnation, noting that "[I]t is precisely Christ's 'humility' (meaning, ultimately, his descent into the flesh) that gives us a way to ascend to the *patria*."[139] By contrast pride prohibits the Platonists themselves from seeking Christ.

So far, this is largely unobjectionable. The problem arises in the relationship between humility and will.

> The Incarnation, so understood, presupposes that God has a *will*, which is not reducible to God's knowledge or to the capacities of other things to receive God's influence . . . For the Platonists, God rules in accordance with the natures of things . . . But it is not at all in accord with the nature of the recipient that Nous itself should descend into a human body: this requires a will in God, and not a will naturally directed toward what is good and appropriate for the divine nature, but a will capable of encompassing its own humiliation for the sake of the elevation of fallen human beings.[140]

This explanation cries out for theological interrogation. What does it say about the relationship between the Father and the Son? How does it correspond to Augustine's designation of the Spirit as *donum* or his rejection of propiatory sacrifice? Can it be reconciled with such Augustinian commonplaces as the grammars of simplicity, substantive and relative predication and the doctrine of impassibility? Menn's account of Augustine's "turn from the senses" omits the beautiful harmonies of creation, and thus the key orientation *toward* sensibilia that reaches its apex in the incarnate visibility of God.[141] His account of Augustinian humility entails a correlative omission: its stated relationship to charity.[142] The neglect of these concerns suggests that Augustinian soteriology is not really the point. This becomes

apparent only later, as Menn contends that Descartes "adopts the Augustinian description of the will" in his theory of judgment.[143] The passion is
important, in other words, because it provides an Augustinian antecedent
for the voluntarism—albeit a radicalized voluntarism—of Descartes'
· God.[144] This voluntarism, as we shall see, is integral to the launch of
hyperbolic doubt and to the doctrines of judgment and eternal truths. It is
thus central to Descartes' entire project.

Descartes emerges well after the scholastic controversies over the status
of universals, which nominalists saw as impinging upon the sovereignty of
God.[145] Though Cartesian voluntarism is neither identical nor reducible to
that of Scotus and Ockham, which cannot be reconciled with each another,
it is indebted, uneasily, to both.[146] Like each, however, Descartes accords
the divine will primacy over intellect.[147] And in denoting God *substantia
infinita*, he follows Scotus in conceiving of "God in terms of infinity,
interpreted as the unconditioned a priori of all conceptualization."[148]
This definition is the basis for the first proof of the third *Meditation*, and
Jean-Luc Marion has questioned whether it can be reconciled with the
definitions at the basis of the other proofs. We shall take up these questions
more fully below. Already, however, this designation and its use put
Descartes at odds with Augustine, on at least two fronts.

First, Augustine does not typically list infinity among the divine
attributes and, on those rare occasions when he does, it is certainly not
preeminent.[149] This is perhaps due to his neoplatonic prejudices. To speak
of God as infinite (ἄπειρον) on Plotinian terms is to place God's essence
beyond form, beyond being, and so finally to make it, strictly speaking,
unspeakable.[150] All talk of infinity on Aristotelian terms, even those of motion
or time, is dependent upon and reducible to an aspect of quantity.[151] Since
a perfection on these terms can only be finite and determined, to speak of
infinity is to speak only of potency and thus of an imperfection. This
accounts for the assertion by some theologians prior to 1250 that God
in his essence is *not* infinite. The "prejudice" against infinity, whether
neoplatonic or Aristotelian, would remain with the West for nearly a
millennium.[152] Traces of this indeterminacy remain in Descartes' borrowings from Scotus and Ockham, providing Marion with ammunition for his
argument against the coherence of Descartes' understanding of the divine
attributes.[153] Only with Bonaventure does infinity become a prominent,
and positive category in the West, and his absolute infinite an "intelligible
sphere whose center is everywhere and whose circumference is nowhere" is
quite a different animal from the Cartesian infinite, which will turn out not
to be *theologically* infinite at all.[154] Of course as Leo J. Sweeney notes,
Augustine's understanding of God's presence as *ubique totam* implies (along
with the *totus Christus*) what would become the Bonaventurian conception,
but Augustine is much more generous in proffering these notions than he is
in attaching "infinity" to them.[155]

Second, though Augustine is notorious for lacking a technical vocabulary and sometimes refers to God colloquially as *substantia,* in non-colloquial speech he explicitly rejects the designation of *substantia* as improper, instead preferring *essentia,* since the former term implies that "God subsists, and is a subject, in relation to his own Goodness."[156] Descartes will also affirm the conventional identity of essence and existence in God, and a certain construal of this identity is integral to his understanding of the identity of divine will and intellect, to the notion of God as uncaused or as *causa sui,* and, subsequently, to his direct apprehension of his own essence as a *res cogitans.*[157] However, Augustine's objection to *substantia* as a divine predicate serves the altogether different function of denying any substratum of substance somehow analytically or ontologically prior to the differentiation of trinitarian *personae.* Augustine rejects this term in order to insist that God is *essentially triune,* and the convertibility of divine goodness and *dilectio* demonstrates the point. Consequently, Augustine's rejection of this term can be read as a warning that its use will almost invariably bring the loss of a trinitarian understanding of this goodness with it.

Descartes' voluntarism thus implies a departure from Augustine's account of the divine essence. We can elaborate this difference further and see how it informs the retrospective Cartesianism that Menn reads back onto *Confessiones* VII, by considering Descartes' answer to the problem of God's knowledge of things "outside God himself." As Menn notes, Descartes follows Scotus in concluding that God knows these things by "*scientia libera,*" that is, not by diversely knowing his own perfections in the manner of Aquinas, but by knowledge of his will; his ability to know his creatures depends only on his power to produce them as he wills.[158]

The very fact that Menn frames the question of God's knowledge of particulars as knowledge of things "outside God" suggests that a decisive move has already been made *away* from the transcendence of the Augustinian infinite and *away* from will as *dilectio* between the Father and the Son in whom creation occurs.[159] Further examination bears out this conclusion. The will of Menn and Descartes, unlike Augustinian *dilectio,* is "de-finalized." It must be if the sixth *Meditation* is going to succeed in eliminating final causes.[160] The will's act is neither elicited by beauty nor determined by its relation to its proper object, the good.[161] Instead Descartes will define it—and Menn will follow suit—as either the undetermined power of choice, the power to effect causation, or both.[162] This de-finalization is obvious from Descartes' assent to "extreme voluntarists theses, e.g. 'God could have willed that four and four are not eight'."[163] If it is difficult to further characterize this power, it is for reasons enumerated in Chapter 3. Utter, undetermined spontaneity defies characterization.[164]

One might object at this point that Descartes does in fact preserve more of the tradition of a positive freedom than this reading admits. After all, he does assert

> that the indifference I feel when there is no reason pushing me in
> one direction rather than another is the lowest grade of freedom; it
> is evidence not of any perfection of freedom, but rather a defect in
> knowledge or a kind of negation. For if I always saw what was true
> and good, I should never have to deliberate about the right
> judgment or choice; in that case, although I should be wholly free,
> it would be impossible for me ever to be in a state of indifference.[165]

This "positive freedom," though ostensibly Augustinian, must be understood in the light of Descartes' method. Otherwise, if we admit Descartes'
fidelity to the tradition on this point and assume that the Cartesian will is
not "de-finalized" after all, we are forced to admit a contradiction. If we
take this remark as an indication that Descartes does smuggle a formal
object, *bonum*, back into his conception of will and *delectatio* back into the
form of its movement, then this contradicts both his assertion that the will is
without constraint and his claim, in the *Passions*, that the will chooses
between its passions—including the love which properly joins the soul to an
object.[166] If there remains any doubt, one need only turn to his claim, also
in the *Passions*, "that sadness is in some way primary and more necessary
than joy, and hatred more necessary than love."[167] From the perspective of
Augustinian moral psychology, such a notion is incoherent.

How then are we to make sense of this positive freedom and this denigra-
tion of indifference if Descartes conceives of will as a faculty of causation
and of freedom as indeterminacy? Descartes asserts in the passage immediately following that "the scope of the will is wider than that of the intellect,"
that "it easily turns aside from what is true and good, and this is the source
of my sin and error."[168] Notice the elision of sin into error; Descartes is
transposing this apparent Augustinianism into his method for judgment.

> If, however, I simply refrain from making a judgment in cases
> where I do not perceive the truth with sufficient clarity and
> distinctness, then it is clear that I am behaving correctly and
> avoiding error. But if in such cases, I either affirm or deny, then I
> am not using my free will correctly.[169]

The freedom of indifference is not a defect because it marks a disorder in
our love, a division in the self, or because it compromises the full comport-
ment of our acts and desires. Rather, indifference is a defect because it is
simply the state of the Cartesian will prior to the attainment of certainty. It
is the state of doubt; yet, precisely for this reason, it is not a state of
unfreedom, but a "lower stage of freedom" to be overcome precisely
through its own exercise. For doubt is not merely the opposite of certainty,
but the means to it. The ominous consequences of this conclusion will
become clearer below.

Menn's own analysis helps to bear out this interpretation. As we have seen, the power of the Cartesian will exceeds that of the intellect. This understanding underwrites Descartes' notion of judgment as an act of will assenting to or dissenting from phantasms passively received.[170] In Menn's account, this notion appears to be univocally applied to God in the act of creation, less the passive faculty. (Hence the identification of will and intellect in Descartes' God, which is more properly the *subsumption* of intellect to will, thus construed.) This univocal transfer of predicates is in fact *warranted* in Cartesian terms, because Descartes identifies the infinite freedom of his will with that of the divine will.[171]

> For although God's will is incomparably greater than mine, both in virtue of the knowledge and power that accompany it and make it more firm and efficacious, and also in virtue of its object, in that it ranges over a greater number of items, nevertheless it does not seem any greater than mine when considered as will in the essential and strict sense.[172]

"[I]f God is to give me freedom," Menn notes, "he must give me an unlimited freedom, indeed as much freedom as he himself possesses."[173] Indeed Descartes asserts in the same passage that it "is above all in virtue of the will that I understand myself to bear in some way the image and likeness of God." Univocal with the divine will, the human will, unlike the intellect, is formally infinite.[174] Menn notes wryly that this "infinite will . . . seems to exhibit itself chiefly in my errors."[175] Yet this is not entirely correct, since, "nothing compels me to deviate from the divine standard. I am still capable of not assenting to irrational impulses, and restricting my assent to the things that my intellectual nature irresistibly determines me to assent to."[176]

Janowski recognizes in this a very stoic conception of freedom. "The importance of Chryssipus' considerations for the understanding of Descartes' argument is that Chryssipus realized that the foundation of human freedom is the freedom not to assent to perceptions."[177] This is a direct function of Descartes' conception of will. Precisely because the will is infinite, and its scope is thus "wider than that of the intellect," this freedom is best registered negatively, in withholding assent from those ideas which are not clear and distinct. This accounts for the priority Descartes accords to the passions of repulsion over those of attraction. In short, the will's freedom is established and demonstrated primarily in its own negation and in the negation of the world through doubt. The "higher freedom" occurs as a consequence of this negation, in the will's recovery of itself in the higher synthesis of certainty.

We can now begin to shed some light upon the "humiliation" of the divine will, a notion that Menn attributes to Augustine. There is a clear similarity in structure between this humiliation and this freedom of negation. Like the human will, the divine will, "not a will naturally directed toward what is good and appropriate for the divine nature," apparently has no proper object. It thus appears as either a "faculty" of arbitrary choice, an infinite power for causing "extrinsic" effects, or both. "Not reducible to God's knowledge," this will appears either to have primacy over the divine intellect or to have subsumed it, until negated in and through the incarnation and crucifixion of Christ.[178] Suspicion intensifies as Menn attempts in later analysis to ground Descartes' voluntarism in Augustine's own thought.

Descartes had in fact invoked Augustine's authority for his voluntarism in order to place the "eternal truths" of mathematics at the basis of his physics and to argue that these are dependent upon the simplicity of the divine will.[179] In a letter to Mesland, he takes Augustine's remark at the close of the *Confessiones*, that "because you see these things, they are," as warrant for his "Scotist" subordination of the divine intellect to the divine will, understood as sheer *arbitrium*.[180] This is partly in consequence of his appropriation of the Scotist notion of objective being, which shifted the question of truth for Descartes away from the Augustinian criterion of the conformity of things to their divine *exemplars* to a property of judgments in assenting to mental representations.[181] Menn acknowledges that this is a distortion of the passage. Augustine does not equate God's seeing with willing (in a causal sense, at least); rather God sees the goodness of creatures "as uncreated paradigms within his own essence."[182]

What Menn fails to consider is how God's vision of goodness in creating might require trinitarian reflection or how this in turn might impinge upon his conception of *voluntas*.[183] In an earlier chapter of *Confessiones* XIII, Augustine asserts

> We have seen that things taken one by one are good, and that together they are very good, in your Word, in your Only begotten, both heaven and earth, the head and the body of the Church, in your predestination before all times, without morning and evening . . .
>
> We see all these things, and we see that they are very good, because you see them in us, who have given to us your Spirit, by whom we might see them *and in them love you*.[184]

These remarks transfigure the question. While Menn is right to note that God's vision of goodness hinders Descartes' attempt to recruit Augustine for his subordination of the divine intellect to will, he does not completely grasp how the trinitarian context of this vision alters the latter's meaning.[185] The issue is not simply whether "God's essence precedes *ratione* any act of God's will."[186] Rather the issue is whether that essence is understood as Trinity and whether "will" is conditioned by that understanding to express a relation of love between trinitarian *personae*.

157

There is a tension, in other words, between Menn's univocal treatment of the concept of will and the trinitarian implications of his best insight. To recognize that God creates from "seeing the goodness" of creatures as "uncreated paradigms within his own essence" is to recognize that the divine will does in fact have a proper object as its "motive." Consequently, the relation of the divine will to its objects is *not* primarily that of an undetermined *arbitrium*, nor even of cause to effect, but of lover to beloved.[187] *Voluntas* as a union of love, and creation "by the will of God" are consequences of the Father's delight in the Son in whom creation occurs and is finally manifest as doxology. This is evident in Augustine's interpretation of Jesus' passion. It is borne out in both *De Trinitate* and *De Civitate Dei*, as Augustine elides *voluntas* and *dilectio*, and in the anti-Pelagian treatises as Augustine accords delight priority over assent, or, rather, refashions assent as a species of delight.[188] In the case of the divine will, this union is at once identical with the divine essence and convertible with the love and delight between Father and Son which each are this essence, and are this essence together.[189] In the case of the human will, this union is the locus of participation in the divine love even in its difference from it, and it invokes the mediation of the Son and the reciprocal gift of the Spirit.[190]

Descartes, however, relegates this union to the mere passion of love. Like all passions, it is subordinate to the "higher" faculty of will. Free from all determinations apart from its necessary self-affirmation, the will then either assents to this union or negates it.[191] Descartes thus inverts the Augustinian perspective, and Menn appears to have followed suit in his account of divine humiliation. Menn is therefore half right to recognize that Descartes has radicalized Augustine's alleged voluntarism. Certainly it is radical, but the original is in fact a Cartesian voluntarism superimposed back onto Augustine himself. Not only does this obscure their vast differences, but it fails to illuminate how the Christology of *Confessiones* VII functions within the context of its argument, and within its proper ontological setting.

Resituated within these contexts, the subject of *Confessiones* appears in a remarkably un-Cartesian light. If the argument for Augustine's doxological self is correct, then the point of the *Confessiones* is not separate from its execution, and the genre of confession is not adventitious to its meaning nor merely autobiographical.[192] Rather, the *Confessiones'* doxological execution is *constitutive* of who the subject of this narration understands himself to be at the time of the telling. This is important for two reasons, one "literary," the other theological. As Paula Fredriksen puts it,

> Augustine's account of his conversion in the *Confessions* is a theological reinterpretation of a past event, an attempt to render his past coherent to his present self. It is, in fact, a disguised description of where he stands in the present as much as an ostensible description of what occurred in the past.[193]

Hence abstracting the narrative of *Confessiones* VII from the "present" ends that inform it will inevitably distort its meaning. This literary or hermeneutical concern elides into the theological one. If the genre of the *Confessiones* is indeed constitutive of their subject, then the performance of the work itself falls within the anteriority of gift and the aporias of mediation. Augustine lays this bare in the opening paragraph of I.1. "Lord, grant me to know and understand which is first, to call upon you or to praise you, and also which is first to know you or to call upon you?"

Two further consequences follow upon this. First, the "anachronistic" character of conversion narratives that Fredriksen describes is not simply a literary device, a machination that "manipulates the past time of history by the present time of narration."[194] This description only holds on the positivistic assumption that there *is* a "past time of history" with an independent and intelligible facticity, apart from its intelligibility in the mind of God. The *Confessiones* perform a *theological* rejection of that thesis, with their dissonance between the recollected and recollecting Augustine and with their hope of finally apprehending "in whom I have been apprehended."[195] The anteriority of grace will *entail* this anachronism. "There will always be, given the means of grace, a temporal dislocation between human recollection of God and God's recollection of humanity."[196] When this dislocation becomes apparent, the discrete origin by which one might say that "the [Platonic] vision was what inspired [Augustine] to seek the path" disappears.[197] This inspiration has no discrete origin because it sounds from all eternity, as the aporias of Book I once again attest. The *Confessiones* narrate the outworking of this call, retrospectively, in time.[198]

This means, secondly, that for Augustine there is no *immediate* first person narration, and Augustine could not be a simple *autobiographical* subject.[199] The "retrospective self," to use Fredriksen's term, is necessarily a self whose selfhood and self-knowledge are mediated.

This is evident in two quite different, but related, features of the *Confessiones*. First, while wandering in the *regio dissimilitudinis*, Augustine is on his own terms a divided and unintelligible soul—in a way that Descartes, importantly, could not be—even though this description is not prospectively available.[200] Since *voluntas* is primarily the bond uniting lover and beloved, one's self-hood and self-knowledge are always mediated by the soul's conjunction with the objects of one's love (an appropriately microcosmic take on the argument of *De Civitate Dei* XIX.24)—hence the real danger in the mind's "lovingly and intimately [connecting] itself with these images [of material things]."[201] We saw this concern for idolatrous entanglement in *De Libero Arbitrio* I. One recognizes here, in first person form, the mediation of death through the false love that Augustine describes in *De Trinitate* IV.[202] Through recollection, however, Augustine renders his life apart from the true mediator intelligible, and yet with the mediator he remains a mystery.[203]

voluntas/dilectio

Second, this mediated self-hood exhibits itself in Augustine's "typological" self-understanding. So too do the broader purposes of the *Confessiones*. Fredriksen demonstrates the importance of Augustine's evolving conceptions of Paul's conversion for his own self-understanding, and vice versa.[204] More fundamentally, Frances Young shows us how this understanding plays out in an Augustine "typologically" constituted at the conjunction of intertextual interstices. It is this, according to Young, which accounts for the oscillation between first and second person in Book XIII and for the transition between the first nine books and the last four.[205] The effect of these typologies is quite opposite to the "inward turn:" "to show how one might turn *away* from the self to become more God-centred."[206] Young argues that this must condition how we understand the *Confessiones* as a whole, and to the extent that these are spiritual exercises they are profoundly at odds with Descartes'.

> The theme of *The Confessions* is the quest for truth, and the discovery that we do not know God; rather God knows us. . . .
>
> With these clues, it is possible to revise one's whole view of Augustine's purpose. The episodes in his life which he earlier chooses to narrate are illustrative of the themes he discusses at length, themes which can appear digressive and tedious if we imagine the principal interest is in giving an autobiographical account. Of course there is an apologetic element. . . . But there is also a didactic thrust, and the overall perspective is on human existence and God's providence. Augustine points away from himself to God, but to do that he has to demonstrate how God has led him to appreciate the fact that true knowledge is ignorance. By doing this, Augustine makes himself an instance of the universal human story, and the work is fundamentally typological.[207]

What place might the *platonicorum libri* hold within such an understanding? Could these books—which Augustine subsumes within Scripture—be an exceptional type of that true but inadequate knowledge of Romans 1.20, wherein God is "understood and seen through the things that were made?"[208] This would serve the anti-Manichean polemic of this book, showing that evil is merely privation. Yet it would also allow Augustine to advance the clear conclusion of VII.9.14: that Platonism is still idolatry, albeit a noble one.

Nothing in this precludes Augustine's positive debts to Platonism, though this hardly comes as a revelation. Augustine is not the first or only Father to plunder the Egyptians' gold.[209] However, it does preclude an overly neat separation of faith from reason and contemplation from practice. It prohibits a "Nestorian" disjunction of *via* from *patria*. It prevents the relegation of Augustine's Christianity to a practical ghetto. It does justice to the richness and complexity of the *Confessiones* and to the breadth of the Augustinian corpus. It allows Augustine's aesthetic soteriology and his doxological ontology to emerge into the light of day.

And thus it clarifies the reasons why Augustine cannot be a Cartesian.

Why Descartes is not Augustinian

A clash of wills

Augustine cannot be proto-Cartesian because the Augustinian self is only completed doxologically, by participation in the love and beauty of the Trinity through the mediation of Christ and his Body. This conviction is built into his very understanding of self-hood through an erotic, aesthetic conception of *voluntas* and through the corresponding doxological constitution of the self manifest in the genre of confession. Already this is sufficient to distinguish Augustine from Descartes, but it does not go far enough in demonstrating just how far Descartes departs from and indeed inverts the position of his alleged forefather. To see this, we must look at the issue from the Cartesian side and show why Descartes cannot be Augustinian.

Though we will briefly consider the difference between their respective "cogitarian" arguments, the relationship between these arguments is only peripheral to my case. In the main, I concur with Jean-Luc Marion, that "the search for precursors remains legitimate and fruitful, but concerning what is essentially at stake, empty."[210] More fundamental is the function of these arguments within their respective programs, what each implies for the very meaning of thinking and willing, and how each thereby determines the self's relationship to God and creation.

As we have already begun to see, Descartes' "Augustinianism" is infected by an equally un-Augustinian stoicism. With the Pelagians we saw that the appropriation of stoic ethics brought with it some unwelcome baggage from the immanentism which was its original home. A similar result is detectable in Descartes. Insofar as his account of thinking is essentially stoic, he reproduces, albeit more ambiguously and metaphysically, the Pelagian antagonism with an immanentized God, a problem Augustine had overcome.[211]

Descartes' theories of thought, action and judgment are at least formally stoic.[212] "Cartesian ideas are Stoic *phantasiai* or impressions," which the will either affirms or denies by assenting or withholding assent from them.[213] This appropriation of stoic impressions complements Descartes' consummation of the change in the meaning of "idea," away from the Augustinian notion of an exemplar in the divine intellect to an image in the human intellect representing extra mental reality, *caused*, in the case of eternal truths, by the will of God in a manner which perhaps mimics the immanent stoic *logos*.[214] This notion of causality and this definition of an idea underlie the third *Meditation*'s endeavor to prove God's existence from an idea of God that is *cataleptic*, an idea which bears the imprint of its cause and thereby commands its own assent.[215] Consequently, the all-important "clear and distinct ideas" appear to be of stoic inspiration as well.[216]

This relationship between the will and these impressions lies at the basis of Descartes' theory of judgment, and it presupposes a distinction between two faculties or capacities in the soul which presupposes in turn a strong dichotomy between activity and passivity. "Now there is in me a passive faculty of sensory perception, that is, a faculty for receiving and recognizing the ideas of sensible objects; but I could not make use of it unless there was also an active faculty . . ."[217]

Later, in *The Passions of the Soul*, Descartes explains this distinction in greater detail. After discretely segregating things proper to the body to a mechanistic realm, he asserts that the soul is concerned strictly with thoughts, which are either active or passive. "Those I call actions are all volitions," and are characterized as such because they proceed strictly from the soul. He then further subdivides those volitions into two classes: those that terminate in the soul itself, as "when we will to love God," and those that terminate in the body, as when we will to walk.[218] Passions, in contrast, are "the various perceptions or modes of knowledge present in us."[219] These also have either the body or the soul as their cause, and in the latter case are both an action and a passion: passions insofar as they are objects of perception, actions insofar as they entail volitional activity.

When we analyze this Cartesian variant of stoicism from the perspective of the Augustinianism elaborated in the first three chapters, it appears deficient in two respects: first for its coherence as a philosophy of action, and secondly for how it configures the relationship between the *res cogitans* and God. These two concerns will occupy us for the remainder of the chapter.

Notice first the subtle dissociation of will and love noted in the previous section. If we love God ("or, generally speaking, apply our mind to some object that is not material"), we do not love God, strictly, *with* the will, nor is the will itself identical to this love.[220] Rather, *we will to love God*; this love is subsequent to the will's assent or negation. Stanley Rosen calls our attention to the deleterious and far-reaching effects of this understanding, though this pertains more to the second of our concerns. "The activity of the soul is willing to think rather than simply thinking, which thus becomes a passive instrument of the project to master nature."[221]

Descartes cannot identify the will with love, because doing so would raise the specter of dividing it among diverse objects of desire. This division is perfectly intelligible from the point of view of the *Confessiones*, because its subject is "not yet in his life." He is, in Wetzel's words, a "self who is not yet."[222] Augustine's conflation of *dilectio* and *voluntas* will reflect that understanding, as the self becomes itself and realizes its freedom by attaining to the love that is the source and goal of all desiring. As we shall see, however, both Descartes' fundamental principle and the theory of judgment will preclude this division, each for similar reasons. Augustine's view reflects his understanding of the image of the God who is a Trinity of love, completed doxologically through participation in that love. Descartes, by contrast, understands the *imago dei* to consist in our reflection of that sovereignty which flows from God's unity. Hence the will of the *res cogitans*, here separated from love, must be one.

Thus "there is in us but one soul, and this soul has no diversity of parts: it is at once sensitive and rational too, and its appetites are all volitions."[223] Departing from Augustine, Descartes follows the stoics in asserting the unity of the soul, and in particular the will, which functions as a faculty or power of assent.[224] Consequently, love and its divisions must be subordinate to the unity and integrity of the will, which Descartes—like Cassian—places in a "tensional" position "between" the contradictory motions of the animal spirits.[225] Descartes does not deny the *feeling* of a divided will, but this is a misnomer. In reality this division is attributable to the pressure that the animal spirits put upon the pineal gland, a mechanizing echo perhaps of the old spirit/flesh dichotomy. The will is always free to reject the movements of these animal spirits.[226] Indeed judgment as doubt will consist precisely in these rejections. For "love is an *emotion* of the soul caused by a movement of the spirits, which impels the soul to join itself willingly to objects that appear to be agreeable to it."[227] Moreover, love and hatred— with their corollaries, attraction and repulsion—"usually contain less truth than the other passions." Consequently they "are the most deceptive of all the passions."[228] Since "the scope of the will is wider than that of the intellect," false judgments and sin result directly from the will's assent to these deceptions.[229] Delight, the very form of *voluntas* for Augustine and the *locus* of our participation in the *dilectio* of God, is no longer to be trusted.

Descartes' rigid distinction between speculation and practice appears to be unraveling here. The conflation of sin and error perhaps suggests as much. In appropriating a stoic theory of judgment and insisting on the will's unity, Descartes appears to have transposed the problem of reason's control of the passions onto a theoretical plane, with the Meditator as stoic sage and the will cast in the role of the *hegemonikon*.[230] One can perhaps even see a trace of the old stoic *tonos* in the way in which the animal spirits and the will each apply opposing, tensional force to the pineal gland.

Inasmuch as Descartes reproduces the stoic sage in the theoretical realm he reproduces the problem of intelligibility in his account of volition. For on the view just outlined, the will must *choose* which of its loves will motivate it. Indeed it is this very *potentia* for choosing or causing that defines the will for Descartes, and the result of this stoic formulation is a very stoic

163

conception of volition. What is "up to us" is once again what we can *control*. Two aspects of Descartes' definitions of will make this clear. The first appears in the *Mediations*.

> It is only the will, or freedom of choice, which I experience within me to be so great . . . so much so that it is above all in virtue of the will that I understand myself to bear in some way the image and likeness of God."[231]

The second Descartes states in the *Passions*.

> But the will is by its nature so free that it can never be constrained. Of the two kinds of thought I have distinguished in the soul—the first actions, i.e., its volitions, and the second its passions, taking this word in the most general sense to include every kind of perception—*the former are absolutely within its power* and can be changed only indirectly by the body, whereas the latter are absolutely dependent on the actions which produce them, and can be changed by the soul only indirectly, except when it itself is their cause. And the activity of the soul consists entirely in the fact that simply by willing something it brings about that the little gland to which it is closely joined moves in the manner required to produce the effect corresponding to this volition.[232]

Descartes' definition of will has issued in the very understanding of volition that Augustine had once presumed to criticize. Augustine, too, had used the old stoic phrase. Yet in conjunction with his rereading of Romans 7, he had redefined the voluntary not as what we can *control*, but as what we *want*, a maneuver that had the paradoxical effect of at once broadening and limiting its scope. This redefinition served as the basis for Augustine's ridicule of the stoics, and of pagan virtue generally, in *De Civitate Dei*.

From Augustine's perspective, the stoic conception was incoherent on two, interrelated, grounds. First, stoic autarky required an insistence upon the integrity of reason and judgment, which had the effect of driving the source of our miscreant passions outside the bounds of the *hegemonikon* and instituting two distinct sources of motivation.[233] Augustine ridiculed this conception as it appeared in the *Attic Nights* which demonstrated its failure to come to terms with involuntary sin. The phantasms that had provoked the sage's fear at sea would have had no claim on his attention if his desires were not already entailed in their recognition, and they would have had no power to induce fear if they did not already threaten the sage with the loss of some object of delight: all of which portended a more profound depth of internal division than the stoics were willing to admit. At just the point where the Augustinian conception of the voluntary broadens, the stoic is too narrow. At just the point where the Augustinian conception narrows, the stoic is too broad.

The second weakness follows from the first. To externalize the source of conflict within the soul is to deprive us of an account of how any object of delight could move us in the first place. In other words, the "definalization" of *voluntas*, the segregation of will and delight, drives a wedge between the voluntary act and its motive. The result is an inability to attribute actions to their agents and an incoherent account of volition.

Descartes repeats this incoherence, and this signals his difference from Augustine. Augustine's identity of desire and volition breaks the latter's identity with autarky. Augustine can afford this rupture, because, in the time of involuntary sin, the will's unity and true freedom is an eschatological condition dependent upon the gift of grace. Augustine simply has no interest in defending the sort of freedom that Descartes will find so crucial. Thus, unlike Descartes, Augustine allows division into the will itself, and the later interpretations of Romans 7 demonstrate this.[234] Descartes' theory of judgment and his fundamental principle can admit of no such division. As the stoics are committed to unity of the *hegemonikon*, Descartes is committed to the absolute oneness of the soul. As the stoics are committed to the autarky of the sage, Descartes is committed to a will "so free that it can never be constrained," a freedom exhibited *negatively* in doubt. This freedom serves as the foundation for attaining autarky, and Descartes converts it into a method, with consequences beyond anything the stoics could imagine.[235] It is unsurprising then to find Descartes, like the stoics and Pelagians, instituting two discrete sources of motivation and externalizing the sources of sin and error beyond the circumference of the will. "It is to the body alone that we should attribute everything that can be observed in us to oppose our reason."[236]

As we have seen, Descartes identifies the unrestrainable freedom of the will with the sort of freedom that God has. This liberty marks the image of God in us.[237] Whether in doing so he appropriates a voluntarist notion of divine freedom as a counterpart to his stoicism or projects his stoic subjectivity onto the divine is historically interesting, but theoretically unimportant. The important point is their mutual confirmation of one another. Descartes' voluntarism de-finalizes the divine will. Without the good as a proper object, unmoved by delight in beauty, the divine will is utterly inscrutable. It must be, if Descartes is to launch hyperbolic doubt. If we take Descartes at his word when he identifies human and divine freedom, we can conclude that the human will, like the divine, has no proper object. Its freedom consists in its capacity to assert itself spontaneously. Yet, on Augustinian terms, this deprives us of the means to qualify this assertion as "mine." From this perspective this freedom is not only delusory, but it is not really freedom at all. Cartesian freedom is the very epitome of Augustinian servitude, a figure of deficient causality.[238]

165

Taming the omnipotent God

Augustine's theories of freedom and will are a function of his doctrine of grace; which is to say, they are a function of his trinitarianism and his Christology. In previous chapters we saw that the stoic and Pelagian failures to attain to this understanding wrought some fairly ominous consequences for their respective understandings of God and creation's relationship to God. The logic of stoic monism and immanentism, for instance, tended to fracture into a bifurcation of the active and passive principles with the subsumption of the latter under the former. The Pelagian conception of grace produced a similar fracture, ultimately juxtaposing God and the creature as univocal agents. We have now seen that Descartes' "Augustinianism" is informed by a stoic anthropology and moral psychology antithetical to Augustine's, with incoherencies that are analogous to those of his forbears. Can we therefore expect an analogous fracturing and antagonism at the ontological level, in the relationship between the Cartesian *cogito* and the Cartesian God?

This question about the relationship between the Cartesian *cogito* and the Cartesian God prompts what little I have to say on the relationship between Descartes' and Augustine's "cogitarian" arguments.[239] The similarities between Augustine's *si fallor, sum* and Descartes' fundamental principle cannot be denied.[240] In the main, however, I concur with Jean-Luc Marion that "Descartes' original contribution does *not* consist in advancing the proposition 'I think, therefore I am' but in interpreting it as the discovery of a first principle—Descartes will even say, of a substance," and that this innovation "makes the search for Augustinian antecedents empty."[241] This attitude is warranted for several reasons, the first among them being that it is Descartes' own. When told by Colvius of the similarities between his argument and Augustine's, Descartes replied

> I am obliged to you for drawing my attention to the passage of St. Augustine relevant to my [*I think, therefore I am*]. I went today to the library to read it, and I find that he really does use it to prove the certainty of our existence. He goes on to show that there is a certain likeness of the Trinity in us, in that we exist, we know that we exist, and we love the existence and knowledge we have. I, on the other hand, use the argument to show that this I which is thinking is an immaterial substance with no bodily element. These two are very different things.[242]

Taken in isolation from their broader contexts, the similarities between the two arguments are striking, and we can take Descartes' professed ignorance of Augustine's argument with a grain of salt. Descartes' knowledge of the Augustinian corpus is now well established, and his project provides him with a vested interest in disavowing traditional authorities (though he will apparently admit congruence strictly for pragmatic purposes).[243] Still, Descartes is right to assert that his and Augustine's conclusions "are very different things," and in noting how Augustine "goes on to show that there is a certain likeness of the Trinity in us, in that we exist, we know that we exist, and we love the existence and knowledge we have" he indicates how profound the difference is. After situating the arguments of *De Civitate Dei* XI.26, 28 and *Med*. II in their broader contexts, Jean-Luc Marion comments upon this difference, noting that Augustine's argument emphasizes our status as creatures and is bracketed by the quest for a distant and vague *imago dei*. It is worth quoting him at length.

> [T]he argument intends to construct in man three terms liable to be recognized *ad imaginem Dei*: Being, knowing that one is, loving that one is. Self-certainty thus leads self-consciousness back to the inner consciousness of God, which is found to be more essential to consciousness than itself. For the *si fallor, sum* does not aim at the *ego*, nor does it come to a halt in the *res cogitans*, seeing as the *interior intimo meo* transports it, as a derived image, toward the original exemplar. The *si fallor, sum* remains the simple, though first moment of a path that, in two other more rich moments (knowing one's Being and loving it), disappropriates the mind from itself by the movement of reappropriating it to its original, God. The *si fallor, sum* does not assure the mind of having its principle in itself, since it does not grant it Being in itself nor saying itself by itself (like substance). On the contrary, *si fallor, sum* forbids the mind to remain in itself, exiled from its truth, in order to send it back to the infinite original. The mind is retrieved only insofar as it is exceeded.[244]

The Augustinian and Cartesian "cogitos" are two very different things indeed, because they emerge from two dramatically different ontological contexts and issue in vastly different "exercises." Subtle but profound differences indicate these diverse locations. One feature that differentiates the *si fallor* from the *ego cogito* is the *fallor* itself. This indicates an apparent or possible lack (and an excess to this lack), while the *cogito*, taken in itself, does not.[245] (It is important here that Descartes takes the crucial step in making thinking itself formally indubitable *before* recognizing that doubt constitutes a lack.)[246] For Augustine, this bountiful "lack" triggers the simultaneous "disappropriation" of the mind from itself and its "reappropriation to God." This double movement is the gesture of an erotic, doxological will: delight in the beauty of an end that is other to it as the form and principle of its every act.

Other attributes of the Augustinian *cogito* signal this double movement and indicate a second crucial difference from Descartes. In *De Trinitate* the "mind's knowledge of itself" is accompanied necessarily by the memory and love of itself. Consequently knowing oneself and loving oneself (a feature absent from Descartes) are in the same class of ideas, and the desire for happiness is accorded the same degree of certainty as the knowledge of existence.

This is an altogether different kind of certainty from the founding certainty of Descartes. If the mind never ceases to understand itself, this is inseparable from the fact that it never ceases to remember and love itself. Yet its love of itself must entail delight in its beauty, which implies a certain distance compounded by the temporal distance of memory. This is important for several reasons. First, the entailment of memory locates self-love within the *successio saeculorum*, within the sequence of referrals of end upon end, and thus within either of the two cities, mediated truly by Christ or falsely by the devil. Self-knowledge is always already contextualized by an historical *ordo amoris* and its language, even as it transcends these in a crossing of the vertical and horizontal axes that we have now seen repeatedly. Second, to say that self-knowledge is inseparable from self-love is to assimilate the mind's knowledge of itself to an intention of itself which must have the beauty of God as its formal end and first mediating cause. Thus Rowan Williams is right: "There is nothing that can be said of the mind's relation to itself without the mediation of the revelation of God as its creator and lover."[247] This is how one can reconcile Augustinian "self-certainty," exhibited in the claim always to remember, understand, and love oneself, with the claim which immediately follows it: "He who knows how to love himself, loves God."[248]

In other words, our self-knowledge—if it is to be self-knowledge—occurs in Christ, in whom *sapientia* and *scientia* are indivisible. Both the temporal and intentional aspects of this conclusion are further visible at a "phenomenological" level, and at the point where Augustine is thought to be most Cartesian. Hankey, for one, sets great store by the proto-Cartesian character of Augustine's refutation of the skeptics of the New Academy in *De Trinitate* XV.12.22. Yet Augustine, unlike Descartes, adverts here to the temporal character of the utterance "I exist."[249] Though self-surety is alleged to be the form of the mind's presence to itself, there is not a strict identity between the "I" uttering and the "I" uttered. The latter is a product of the former's memory, and memory, as we recall, is "the condition of the mind's presence to itself."[250] Yet, as the things which the mind knows of itself—even that it lives—are brought forth in a word from memory, it becomes much more difficult, in a way that is not difficult for Descartes, to tell precisely where one might draw the line not simply between *scientia* and *sapientia*, but between the three classes of knowledge: what the mind knows through itself, through the senses, and through historical testimony.[251]

For what the mind knows of itself through memory, it must return to, in time, through love. It has to *seek* and *desire* it, in some sense to intend and remember *the future* by analogy with the past. Yet this locates the surety of self-knowledge once again, not in an act of closure, but in that temporal referral of ends, in that longing for the happiness that is held out as promise and awaits completion. This is the significance of Augustine setting the desire for happiness on equal footing with the certainty of existence. For us, to exist, to know, *is* to desire happiness. For us, to desire happiness is not yet to be fully happy. Still the mind could not seek what it does not in some sense already know, though, paradoxically, the mind could also not know this happiness unless it sought it. The seeking of the end presupposes the mediation of the promised end as principle and gift, and so we see reproduced at the point of self-knowledge and our alleged certainty the same temporal and intentional distance and the same aporia that provokes Augustine to invoke christological mediation in the *Confessiones*. Self-certainty is close to being assimilated to the *eros* of faith and hope.

The surety of the *homo interior* can never be isolated from the mediatory activity of the *magister interior*, whose sacramental and sapiential character can never be fully divisible from the exemplary *signa* which manifest his beauty and which call us to him. Similarly, the fact that it is a *word* which is brought forth from memory in our intention and recollection of ourselves makes the border demarcating the interior from the exterior difficult to sustain. As self-knowledge comes to be assimilated to the *eros* of faith, so too does the *sapientia* in which we know ourselves come to be identified with a word remembered in time, and thus with the *dispensatio similitudinum* and the *cognitio historica* transmitted through Christ's historical body.

From Augustine's side, then, we can conclude that the doxological configuration of *voluntas* is part and parcel of a more fundamental difference between the Augustinian and Cartesian "cogitos" in relation to their respective Gods. To better grasp this difference from Descartes' side, however, we must determine, first, the meaning of Descartes' fundamental principle and its relationship to Cartesian voluntarism and, second, how these relate to Descartes' determinations of the divine essence.

Determining the meaning of *cogito ergo sum* requires that we consider the relationship between thinking and willing for Descartes, at least in his later works.[252] Already we have seen that his voluntarism subsumes the divine intellect under the divine will. And we have noticed a similar move in his treatment of judgment. Though judgment entails both the will and the understanding, the latter plays a merely passive role. Indeed in his *Comments on a Certain Broadsheet*, Descartes remarks:

> For I saw that over and above perception, which is a prerequisite of judgment, we need affirmation and negation to determine the form of the judgment, and also that we are often free to withhold our assent, even if we perceive the matter in question. *Hence I*

> *assigned the act of judging itself, which consists in assenting (i.e. in affirmation or denial) to the determination of the will rather than to the perception of the intellect.*[253]

This redefinition of judgment as an act of will is crucial to the meaning of Descartes' *cogito*. In his description of the will in the *Principles,* Descartes includes a cluster of actions including doubt, affirmation, denial, love, hate, desiring and refusing.[254] Michael Allen Gillespie observes that each of these forms of will, except doubt, are paired opposites.[255] This is unsurprising given Descartes' identification of will with choice; for each member of the pair represents one side of a choice. Yet doubt has no opposite, and this suggests that it is more fundamentally integral to the meaning of the *cogito* than the other forms of will.

The opposite of doubt is certainty, the very essence of understanding, and Descartes does indeed pair doubt with understanding in the second *Meditation*'s description of the *res cogitans*.[256] As Gillespie notes, however, the relationship between the two sides of this pair is more complex than the others. For while doubt appears to be the opposite of understanding, it is not, as in the other pairs, simply one of two possible choices. Rather doubt itself sets the standard for certainty and, furthermore, as an act of will that negates all that is not indubitable, doubt is the very means and activity through which certainty may be attained.

Consequently, any certain understanding inherently presupposes a prior negation. This signals a fundamental difference between the Augustinian and Cartesian wills and their respective relationships to the world and to God. Unlike Augustine, for whom the beauty of created form occasions what is a paradoxical double turn to God, at once both toward *and* away from the world, Descartes must first destroy the world in order that the ego may recover it, reconstructed as a clear and distinct idea. The ego must annihilate even itself in order to recover itself as object. Hence, where love of a prior gratuity is the first act of the Augustinian will, an act which is always a response, this annihilation is the first act of the Cartesian will, and the first act in the will's recovery of itself—and the world for itself—in the higher synthesis of certainty.

Without an Archimedean point, however, the will's freedom to annihilate the world is "the freedom of the void."[257] The meditator appears to be in this Promethean position at the beginning of the second *Meditation*, though how much one should read into the meditator's laments here depends perhaps on whether one follows Gillespie in attributing a genuine skeptical crisis to Descartes or follows Menn and Secada in denying one. Nevertheless this quest for "just one firm and immovable point," this hedge against the caprice of the evil demon, is crucial both for further determining the meaning of the *cogito* in its relation to the *sum* and, later, for understanding the God who emerges from this reconstruction.[258]

Importantly, both the quest and the discovery of this point come *before* the conclusion that God cannot be a deceiver. They likewise come *before* the conclusion that the good God and the soul are both better known than bodies. Yet even when Descartes has reached these conclusions, he never relinquishes the Archimedean point or the method by which he arrived there. This presents a problem. As we have seen, it is precisely Descartes' voluntaristic supposition of divine omnipotence that permits him "to connect the two Ciceronian hypotheses: the non-existence of the world and the deceiving God."[259] It is this God that helps give birth to the *cogito* amidst the ruins of the world's and will's annihilation. In other words, the *cogito* is utterly *dependent* on the deceiver God even as his birth is a hedge against divine caprice. The vindication of God in the third *Meditation* then raises a crucial question: "if there is this dependence between doubter and deceiver, why is the doubting self any less imaginary than the fiction used to define it?"[260] Why indeed, unless the real God of the *Meditations* is not the one whose existence the third *Meditation* sets out to prove?

The *res cogitans* who emerges in the midst of the second *Meditation* is generally taken to restate the fundamental principle of the earlier *Discourse* and later *Principles*.[261] An analysis of one therefore suffices as an analysis of all three formulations, and a great deal of attention has been paid to the status of the *ergo* in the famous *cogito ergo sum*.[262] At first glance, the principle as a whole appears to be the minor premise and conclusion of a syllogism, and commentators have spilled plenty of ink attempting to supply the suppressed major premise.[263] Descartes rejects this interpretation in his *Replies*, however, and suggests in the same passage that the principle is a simple intuition.[264] Yet it had been the inadequacy of the theory of intuition as a basis for truth in the *Rules* which set him on the path to the *Discourse* and the *Meditations* and required Descartes to prove that his clear and distinct idea of God was a *cataleptic* impression.[265] And though it is true that Descartes *later* contends that "my perception of the infinite, that is, God, is in some way prior to my perception of myself," this is precisely in virtue of God *as infinite,* and thus, at this stage of the argument, still a potential deceiver. For as we shall see, the idea of God as infinite arises with the *cogito* as the a priori background and horizon for all possible experience in a way in which the idea of God as perfect does not.[266] Syllogistic reasoning, intuition, and the idea of the infinite God all fail to secure the veracity of the fundamental principle; indeed, Descartes seeks this principle as insurance against this God's guile. What then secures the status of *cogito*?

In both the *Discourse* and the *Principles*, Descartes characterizes this fundamental principle as a *judgment*.[267] And as such, it is an act of will, of affirmation. Gillespie makes an important distinction here.

> It is necessary to distinguish between the proposition that is at the heart of the principle and the recognition and assertion of this

proposition *as* the fundamental principle. The truth of the principle resides not in its logical *form* but in the *act* of judgment or will that establishes it as fundamental.[268]

This *act* gives the *cogito* its fundamental status. The verb expresses "the performatory character of Descartes' insight; it refers to the 'performance' (the act of thinking) through which the sentence 'I exist' may be said to verify itself."[269] Though Austin's "performative utterance" is an anachronistic term, something like it appears central to Descartes' own understanding of his achievement.[270] "[T]his proposition *I am, I exist,* is necessarily true *whenever it is put forward by me or conceived by my mind.*"[271]

In the context of the *Meditations*, this is not just any "whenever." The assertion of this principle follows upon the negation of all that can be negated, including body, world and any predicates traditionally proper to God except incomprehensible power. This affirmation is thus a projection into a void. The performance that establishes the fundamental status of the *cogito* consists in the fact that it is a self-grounding, self-constituting assertion of the I, revealed in its essence as a *res cogitans.* This assertion depends upon the negation of all that is not the I.[272] Thus the self-negation effected by the will as doubt is in fact a self affirmation through which the ego constitutes itself in a "higher" synthesis. For the rebirth of the will out of its own destruction is the rebirth of a will inviolable and impervious to the ruses of a deceiver God, a will possessed of all the freedom of God himself. It is a will that may now achieve mastery both over itself and over a nature now recovered for the will as "idea," precisely through its own (and the world's) negation. It is a will capable of becoming God.

• Despite appearances, the Cartesian *cogito* could not be less Augustinian. Both the self recalled in the *Confessiones* and the self recalling are "not yet." Augustine "is not yet in his life, but the source of his life is present to him, as are all the many beings that have come from that source. God and world, but no self."[273] This self requires the mediation of the *inspiratio dilectionis,* in both senses of the genitive. The Cartesian *res cogitans,* who is perhaps even more fundamentally a *res volens,* inverts and perverts its Augustinian ancestor, grounding itself in its own assertion and becoming a figure of that *superbia* which Augustine is consistent in opposing.

The wages of sin is incoherence.[274] This was the conclusion of Pelagian attempts to characterize freedom apart from grace, and from an Augustinian perspective it is the destiny of the Cartesian *res cogitans,* the univocal image of the voluntarist God. Moreover, if Augustine's estimation of the relationship between knowledge and desire is correct, then we inevitably reproduce our sins in our speculations. One could therefore expect the incoherence of the Cartesian will to migrate into his speculations about the "God" apposite to that will. In fact, this incoherence allows us to reconcile the effects of the Cartesian will, the enthronement of the *cogito* as God, with

Descartes' stated *intent* to prove that his cataleptic idea of God and true mathematical knowledge must have a good God as their cause.[275] This brings us to a second issue in this question of the relationship between the *cogito* and God: how the will of the *cogito* relates to Descartes' determinations of the divine essence.

Taken together, these determinations will prove mutually incoherent.[276] But this incoherence *as a theology* derives finally from their coherence as an expression of Cartesian *superbia*. In short, Descartes maintains two incompatible determinations of the divine essence as omnipotent and infinite, on the one hand, and as the most perfect being, on the other.[277] The former allows him to negate the God of Augustine and the orthodox tradition, in order to establish the *res cogitans* as a self-grounding will. The latter allows him to reconstruct this God as a clear and distinct idea subordinate first to the will of the *cogito* and its project to master the world through science and, secondly, to the principle of reason embodied in Descartes' causal principle. If one recognizes here the redoubled gesture of onto-theology—a being founding itself in Being, understood flatly as cause, while requiring this Being as the presupposition to its self-founding—one should also recognize in this gesture the long shadow cast by the stoic and Pelagian problematic, which both produces an immanent opposition between tensional active forces—decided, in this instance, to the advantage of human agency—and presupposes a causal reliance upon the activity of a first principle now evacuated of content.[278] In other words, the tension between an incomprehensible, immutable deceiver, and an assertive will constituted both by that deception and in opposition against it signals once again the elision from creation out of nothing to a nothing that creates. Descartes repeats this gesture by negating and reconstitutiong God as a clear and distinct idea for the ego. This requires a cause with more formal reality than Descartes himself possesses, but one which submits to the principle of reason in fulfilling this obligation.[279] As a *pathos*, the logic is perfectly intelligible and diagnosable in Augustinian terms as a variation of the *libido dominandi*, one that "bears testimony to the intoxication of the ego, 'master and owner' of the world reduced to evidence."[280] From the perspective of a theology, the beauty of whose object is the principle and end of creation's movement, it is incoherent.

In the *Meditations* and *Replies*, Descartes gives three fundamental determinations to the divine essence corresponding to three proofs for God's existence. These are the notions of God as *idea infiniti* (*Med.* III), as *ens summe perfectum* (*Med.* V) and of *causa sui* (*Replies* I, IV). The corresponding proofs are the proof by means of effects (*Med.* III), the so-called ontological argument (*Med.* V) and the principle of reason (*Replies* I, IV). Importantly, however, these proofs and definitions do not all possess the same status or produce the same effect.

The determination of God as *Deus infinitus* is both logically and sequentially prior to the other determinations; it is, in consequence, "the highest Cartesian determination of the essence (and therefore the existence) of God."[281] It must be in order to fulfill the various functions it serves within Descartes' arguments. The first of these functions is as a catalyst for the entire Cartesian project. The defining characteristic of the infinite qua infinite is its incomprehensibility.[282] Thus the primacy accorded to this determination is compatible with, and indeed definitive of, God's omnipotence, which is alone among predicates listed early in *Meditation* III in eluding hyperbolic doubt.[283] As we have seen, this incomprehensible omnipotence is actually instrumental in *inducing* hyperbolic doubt. Thus the God whose essential character transcends the skeptical component of the project is one for whom the traditional predicates which inform the meaning of divine power—good, beautiful, just and true, for instance—have *already* been negated, and this a priori negation is doubly essential in getting the whole project underway. "The undefined malign spirit can only be imagined insofar as the concept of God, while invoked, remains fundamentally indeterminate."[284]

The primacy of this determination is further underscored by the second function of the infinite, which emerges in the course of Descartes' reconstruction in the third *Meditation*, as an a priori which "precedes the finite in that it renders possible both experience and the objects of experience."[285] This function performs an important "bridging" step in the transition between negation and subordination. It makes God obey the principle that "for a given idea to contain such and such objective reality, it must surely derive it from some cause which contains as least as much formal reality as there is objective reality in idea."[286] In short, this function facilitates the transition from the infinite to causal power, which requires the infinite's a priori subordination to the principle of causality.

The two determinations derive from two irreconcilable strands—a Scotist and an Ockhamist strand—in Descartes' thought. To Marion's mind, this forces a choice between the mutually exclusive alternatives of conceiving God as incomprehensible infinity and as most perfect.[287] It is partly Descartes' refusal to choose that leads Marion to pronounce the union of these determinations incoherent. To maintain both determinations, Descartes will have had to subordinate perfection to incomprehensible infinity. Without denying this, I wish to add an observation consistent with the two sides of our "stoic" problematic and much of Marion's own work: that this subordination is likewise crossed by a subordination of the infinite to the most perfect in the interest of subordinating God to the will of the *ego* in the order of ideas.

This latter subordination should be seen within Descartes' need to neutralize this monster he has unleashed, a point which returns us momentarily to the question of the various functions of the infinite. While the omnipotent deceiver is instrumental in birthing the *cogito* and enables his negation of the world, he also obstructs the overall aim of the *Meditations* to provide a sure "foundation" for the sciences.[288] The infinite God is an obstacle and a competitor to Descartes' plans to master nature. He must therefore be negated.[289]

The first moment of this negation occurs in the realization of the *cogito* itself and indeed *prior* to it. Thus, just as the Cartesian subject repeats the earlier incoherence of the Pelagian self, so here it repeats an earlier metaphysical implication of the Pelagian self in relation to God. Descartes recognizes elsewhere that "all limitation is a negation of the infinite."[290] This is precisely what the *res cogitans*, understood essentially as a *res volens*, does. The power of the *res volens* to ground and assert himself is his power to delimit the power of the infinite God: "let him deceive me as much as he can, he will never bring it about that I am nothing so long as I think that I am something."[291]

Notice, however, that for the will of the finite *cogito* to negate the omnipotence of the infinite God, *finite and infinite must already have been brought into real relation to one another*.[292] While Descartes' God may be infinite and omnipotent, his infinite is a "bad infinite" and not the transcendent God of Augustine, a transformation perhaps reflected in the rhetorical shift from *creator* to *causa*. Hence while Descartes completes the finitization of God in the subordination of the *idea infinitii* to the *ens summe perfectum*, this finitization is in fact encoded at the outset into the relationship between the Meditator and his divine foil, just as a certain voluntarism is encoded into the *aliquis Deus*, who escapes doubt in the second *Meditation* and precedes determination in the third.[293] Descartes thus gives us a priori testimony that his loss of mediation entails a loss of transcendence, that his infinite is not infinite, that his God is not God.

This initial negation of the infinite God, while it eliminates divine caprice, is not sufficient to guarantee the veracity of the clear and distinct ideas of the world that this God helped Descartes to obliterate. The reconstruction of God as *ens summe perfectum* is sufficient; yet it also completes the subordination of the infinite God to the Cartesian method. To see this, one must understand the different status of the two designations of the divine essence and the two proofs. The proof in the third *Meditation* for the infinite and the proof that God cannot be a deceiver are in fact two distinct proofs at two different points in the argument. The first establishes the infinite, always thought in and with the thinking of the *res cogitans*, as the a priori condition of possibility for any experience, including the perception of oneself. Still, the proof for an object corresponding to the idea of the infinite only establishes God as limitless, immense, and incomprehensible; it does not establish that God is not a deceiver.[294]

This demonstration follows from the idea of perfection. Descartes has this idea within him, and yet his own doubt demonstrates that he himself is not intrinsically perfect. According to the aforementioned principle of causality, he himself could not be the cause of such an idea; therefore a being possessing all such perfections as he conceives in this idea must exist in reality. The difference in status consists in this: whereas the idea of the infinite is the a priori possibility for any experience, the idea of perfection is one among the order of innate ideas, apprehended through Descartes' attention to one of his activities. And as such, it is subordinate to the principle of reason and the order of causes.[295] Hence in the fifth *Meditation*, the idea of God is compared to the simple natures of other innate ideas, leading Marion to remark, "This is a stupefying declaration: the idea of God is found to be on the same footing, at least in me, as the idea of a triangle; therefore, God becomes an idea in the same manner as the simple natures."[296]

Since Cartesian infinity implies incomprehensibility, immensity and limit-lessness, and perfection implies "a certain determinate nature, essence, or form," there is an incompatibility between these two designations and their corresponding proofs and, moreover, a subordination of the latter to the former.[297] God as incomprehensible infinity surpasses God as the sum of comprehensible perfections.[298] However, precisely inasmuch as the idea of God as perfection is reconstructed as clear and distinct and subordinate to the principle of causality, it is possible to see in it a strategy for subordi-nating and domesticating the omnipotent God to the will of the *cogito*. Again it is crucial that the designation of God as *ens summe perfectum*, unlike the *idea infinitii* which occasions hyperbolic doubt, can only occur *after* this doubt, after the self-founding of the ego. On this view, then, God, who is now "required to respond to a principle that is stated as a *dictat* of reason," becomes a mere representation within human thinking, thought in and with every act of the *cogito*.[299] "I will God to be God in the same act that I will myself to be I. In so willing, I establish a realm for myself that is beyond the sway of God."[300] Implicitly, then, I can become God.[301]

This is Gillespie's position, and there is little doubt that this is the historical effect, as Jacobi would later recognize in attacking both the Spinozistic and Fichtean offshoots. Gillespie's remarks here, which speak both to the function of these proofs relative to one another and to their nihilistic destiny, are poignant.

> The unpredictable and transrational God of nominalism is revealed as rational and predictable when he is seen within Descartes' bastion of reason and certainty. God's infinite and all-powerful will proves in the end not to endanger human will and power, but, on the contrary, to enable it to achieve a universal mastery of nature.
>
> This conclusion points to the underlying meaning of Descartes' proof. It is not meant to demonstrate the existence of God but to show that God is irrelevant for human affairs, to show that even if

there is an infinite and omnipotent God, he cannot be a deceiver, a *genius malignus*. If we can know with certainty that there is no *genius malignus*, then we cannot doubt the truths of mathematics. If we cannot doubt mathematics, then *mathesis universalis* depends only upon our capacity to avoid error, and error can be largely avoided by means of the method. We thus can come to know everything actual and possible with certainty; we can produce a perfect universal science and with this science we can master and possess nature. In short, because God cannot be a deceiver, we can become God.[302]

One can view this outcome in either of two ways with respect to the Augustinian tradition. We can see it as this tradition's logical conclusion and destiny, as having always been entailed in its *rationes seminales*. We can thus we rejoice with Nietzsche at Christianity's nihilistic destiny and the absurdity with which the highest values devalue themselves. Or we can view this outcome, this *Deus* without *Trinitas*, this *arbitrio* without *dilectio* and *delectatio*, as a contingent perversion of that tradition. From the perspective of the Augustinianism elaborated here, these Cartesian developments are incoherent not simply because they attempt to affix incompatible divine predicates to one another, though that is true enough. The root of its incoherency as theology does not even consist in its illicit, a priori finitization of the infinite, though that too is true enough. The deeper incoherency derives from the deeper pathology that drives the project. The loss of *Trinitas* from *Deus*, of *dilectio* from *arbitrio*, is inevitably, from this perspective, the loss of the mediation of the God-Man, a rupture of the union binding *scientia* to *sapientia* and time to eternity. As the stoics and Pelagians, the *civitas terrena* and even Augustine's own youth demonstrate, this loss is always accompanied by the substitution of another figure: the Man-God who generates a different kind of incoherency, one not liable to qualify as philosophical within the narrow limits of that term in a post-Cartesian age. From the perspective of a secular history, or a genealogical viewpoint, the developments instituted by Descartes are bound to appear as either a pure *novum* of a peculiarly *modern* kind, or as a signal moment within the perversely providential destiny of the metaphysical tradition. The Augustinian perspective, however, would claim to encompass all three of these perspectives with one that has seen these developments before, and locate them as instantiations of a different sort of tradition, a tradition that is more than philosophical, a tradition at once new and sadly all too familiar: the *tradux peccati*.

POSTSCRIPT
Modernity in Augustinian hindsight

Descartes' *cogito* is an idea, but its birth is more than an event in the history of ideas. The Augustinian self who is its alleged precursor helps us both to understand this event in theological terms, and to see in more profound depth just what was dying as this creature was born. Although Descartes is often credited with rigidifying an Augustinian dualism between mind and body, his *res cogitans* is symptomatic of an altogether different *caesura* already well underway by the seventeenth century. Now the individual will – distinct and separated from the love of beauty, the longing for God, or the praise of Christ – becomes a will to power, and it is set over against *God*'s body, which must be placed under house arrest. One need only consider the attempts to police the Church by the early modern political philosophy at the root of our own political arrangements to bear out this view.[1] One need only consider Christianity's contemporary confusion and domestication to see how successful it has been.

Louis Dupré has called modernity "an event that has transformed the relation between the cosmos, its transcendent source, and its human interpreter."[2] Eric Alliez claims to diagnose the nature of that transformation. "It is the nature of Christianity to be delivered up to this new immanence."[3] We can now see, however, that the new immanence owes a great deal to the old immanence, having made its way back from an exile that was never really complete. This immanence, born of the desire for mastery, has in turn gained mastery over us, gripping us in its agonistic machinations and confirming the Augustinian diagnosis.[4] Here I would wish partly to join forces with Alliez, and to see in the machinations of capital speculation, in the effacements of exchange value and in the form of empire, the trace of a god and its disobedient subject, though not the God of Augustine, but the god Augustine fought to overcome.

The prescription, in these terms, is not a kind of philosophy which inscribes those machinations in advance and thus aids and abets them, but rather an alternative form of desire which is also an alternative truth, a desire and a truth that cannot be separated from its sacramental embodiment.[5] The new immanence may blind us to its splendor, which again only

178

confirms Augustine's diagnosis.[6] But it is never too late, precisely because it is always too late. "Too late have I loved you . . ." The hope is not nostalgic; there can be no simple return. The new paganism prohibits that, as does the nature of the hope. It is, after all, both "ever ancient and ever new."[7]

To the extent that we still find ourselves able to long for that which *seems* absent, there is still grace. Most frightening about this new immanence, some four hundred years after the evacuation of being, after the Cartesian disjunction of quantity and quality, is how little of this longing seems to remain. This beauty is increasingly among "the things we are learning not to hope for."[8]

It will no doubt seem a pious retreat to offer the prayer of the Church as response to the event that Descartes helped to create. That it cannot but seem a pious retreat is evidence of the depths of our loss. Nevertheless, the prayer urged here is not the unthinking antithesis to knowledge, not in Augustinian terms. It is the very form of a knowledge whose consummation quenches the anticipation of faith but does not quash it, and I urge it, not because God might hasten his descent to help us—though perhaps he might—but rather because only God's body can save us from the nothing of this new immanence. If we are to genuinely learn anything from Augustine that we do not already want to know, it is that this response which is always a response to God's prior call to us, is perhaps the only genuinely political, the only genuinely ontological, indeed, the only fully human act.

And a graceful act indeed.

179

NOTES

INTRODUCTION: THINKING WITH AND ABOUT AUGUSTINE

Notes to pages 1–5

1 I do not intend by this to suggest either that the "religious" aspects of Augustine's thought are separate from the philosophical or political aspects or that there is a realm of specifically "religious" concerns. I use the term simply to denote those specifically Christian features of Augustine's thought typically omitted or neglected in philosophical treatments.

1 A GRIM PATERNITY?

Notes to pages 6–26

1 See for instance, Eric Alliez, *Capital Times: Tales from the Conquest of Time*, trans. Georges Van Den Abbele (Minneapolis: University of Minnesota Press, 1996), pp. 88–9, 95–7, 107.
2 Zbigniew Janowski, *Cartesian Theodicy: Descartes' Quest for Certitude* (Dordrecht: Kluwer Academic Publishers, 2000), p. 21.
3 I would suggest that it is this cultural concern that prompts popular works like Garry Wills, *Augustine* (New York: Penguin, 1999).
4 Nor it it always obvious which is which. Phillip Cary's *Augustine's Invention of the Inner Self: The Legacy of a Christian Platonist* (Oxford: Oxford University Press, 2000) is one such example. Cary's book is to be located within the general story told by Charles Taylor, which we will discuss below. (For Cary's relationship to Taylor, see pp. 65, 168 n. 12.) At first glance, Cary's would appear to be the "theological Augustine," or rather his intent is to sustain the Augustinian unity of theology and philosophy. (Certainly Cary's own concerns are theological.) He attributes the invention of the "private" inner-self, in part, to the self-enclosure of sin (pp. 107–9), and he is critical of Augustine's Christology "of the heart" on the grounds that it ultimately effaces Jesus' "life-giving flesh" (pp. 49–51). I would take issue with quite a number of points in Cary's account (including his account of Platonism); what is interesting here is how the commitment to seeing Augustine as a "Christian Platonist," with "Christian" as the adjective and "Platonist" as the noun, affects his organization of Augustine a priori. Peripheral to his account, if not absent altogether, are any treatment of the generation of the Son and filiation of the Spirit, any account of Christ's passion or his unity of *sapientia* and *scientia*, any sense of how talk of Christ "in the heart" is counterbalanced by an

181

ecclesiology which sees Christ as the head of his ecclesial body. He writes at the end that "the great limitation of this book is that I have not had the space to discuss the positive relation between inner and outer in Augustine's thought." This limitation is coextensive with his theological limitations for, if he had begun with the latter, he would have had to qualify the turn "in then up" and conclude that these aspects of Augustine's thought disturb the distinction between "inner" and "outer," just as he rightly recognizes that the "inner space" is not a space and that transcendence implies immanence (p. 103).

5   I think here of MacIntyre's "disquieting suggestion" at the outset of *After Virtue* in which the catastrophe which afflicts his hypothetical civilization occurs before the invention of academic history, "so that the moral and other evaluative presuppositions of academic history derived from the forms of the disorder which it brought about." See MacIntyre, *After Virtue* (Notre Dame: Notre Dame Press, 1981), p. 4.

6   I qualify "Platonism" to indicate my agreement with Wayne Hankey, James O'Donnell, and indeed Augustine's own self-assessment, in noting the extent to which Augustine either transforms, criticizes or simply disavows Platonism: in his Christology, his articulation of the trinitarian personae, his account of history and elsewhere. I rather mean to draw attention to the suspicion which Augustine's alleged Platonism has drawn since the Reformation.

7   Charles Taylor, *Sources of the Self* (Cambridge: Harvard University Press, 1989), p. 127.

8   Ibid., 129; Augustine, *De Vera Relig.*, XXXIX.72.

9   See Etienne Gilson, *The Christian Philosophy of Saint Augustine*, trans. L. E. M. Lynch (New York: Random House, 1960), pp. 41–2 for a list of Augustine's proto-cogitarian arguments.

10 Stephen Menn, *Descartes and Augustine* (Cambridge: Cambridge University Press, 1998), pp. 281–93. I will consider Menn's case more thoroughly in the final chapter.

11 Taylor, *Sources of the Self*, p. 138; Charles Kahn, 'Discovering the Will: From Aristotle to Augustine,' in J. Dillon and A. A. Long (eds.), *The Question of Eclecticism: Studies in Later Greek Philosophy* (Berkeley: University of California Press, 1988), pp. 234–59; Albrecht Dihle, *The Theory of Will in Classical Antiquity* (Berkeley: University of California Press, 1982).

12 Taylor, *Sources of the Self*, p. 135.

13 Ibid., p. 138.

14 Ibid., p. 150. We will consider Descartes' treatment of the passions and its relationship to the Cartesian will more fully in the final chapter. The final status of this dualism, which on Taylor's reading derives from Platonic and Aristotelian components of Descartes' thought and not stoic materialism, is debatable. Descartes, *Replies* II; CSM II, p. 106; AT VII, p. 149; *Meditations*, IV; CSM II, pp. 40–1; AT VII, pp. 57–60. See also Stanley Rosen, "A Central Ambiguity in Descartes," in Bernd Magnus and James B. Wilbur (eds.), *Cartesian Essays* (The Hague: Martinus Nijhoff, 1969), pp. 30–2.

15 Alliez, *Capital Times*, pp. 76–137. We will consider Alliez below.

16 Stanley Hauerwas and David Matzko, "The Sources of Charles Taylor," *Religious Studies Review*, 18, 4, October 1992, pp. 286–9 (287).

17 "The parallels with the Christian doctrine of the Trinity, particularly with the Father's begetting of the Word, need no stressing. But what is striking here for our purposes is that man shows himself most clearly as the image of God in his inner self-presence and love. It is a kind of knowledge where knower and known are one, coupled with love, which reflects most fully God in our

lives. And indeed, the image of the Trinity in us is the process whereby we strive to complete and perfect this self-presence and self-affirmation" (Taylor, *Sources of the Self*, pp. 136–7). Taylor fails to note that Augustine at least twice denies that the mind is the *imago trinitatis* in its self-relatedness as such (*De Trin.* XIV.11.14, 12.15) but rather in loving God, and, consequently, neighbor. Unlike God, therefore, whose self-love is self-sufficient, the ground of our likeness to God is in fact our difference *from* God. Yet perhaps more crucial is the fact that he thinks the "parallels with the Christian doctrine of the Trinity need no stressing." See Rowan Williams, "Sapientia and the Trinity: Reflections on the *De Trinitate*," in B. Bruning, M. Lamberigts, and J. van Houten (eds.), *Collectanea Augustiniana: Melanges T. J. von Bavel* (Leuven: Leuven University Press, 1993), pp. 317–32.

18 Taylor, *Sources of the Self*, pp. 3–24; Augustine, *De Trin.* XIII.19.24.

19 Compare, for instance, *Conf.* VIII.5 and *De Civ.* I. *praef.*, each of which display, one microcosmically and the other macrocosmically, our domination by the lust with which we dominate. Compare Augustine's proto-Nietzschean diagnosis of the reactivity of virtue in *Conf.* III.2's analysis of the attraction of stage plays and the Empire's love of the "goddess Injustice" at *De Civ.* IV.15. See also the synthesis of the microcosmic/macrocosmic relation in Augustine's discussion of genuine peace in *De Civ.* XIX.24–8.

20 See Augustine, *De Civ.* XIX.5; XXII.29–30.

21 See Frances Young, "The Confessions of St Augustine: What Is the Genre of This Work?," *Augustinian Studies*, 30,1, 1999, pp. 1–16.

22 This is especially true of its eschatological completion, as the glory that is now partially shielded becomes fully visible. See Augustine, *De Civ.* XXII., 29–30.

23 Hauerwas and Matzko, "The Sources of Charles Taylor," p. 289.

24 James Wetzel, "Crisis Mentalities: Augustine after Descartes," *American Catholic Philosophical Quarterly*, LXXIV, 1, 2000, pp. 115–33.

25 Hauerwas and Matzko contend that Taylor is able to sustain his narrative unity only because he treats the constitution of the modern self primarily as the outcome of the history of ideas. Hauerwas and Matzko, "The Sources of Charles Taylor," p. 288.

26 See Gilson, *The Christian Philosophy of Saint Augustine*, pp. 38–43. Gilson's insistence upon a difference in spirit between Augustine and Descartes seems to have lost its force, however. See Menn, *Descartes and Augustine*, pp. 7–17.

27 Menn, *Descartes and Augustine*, p. 393.

28 For his dissatisfation with Gilson's conclusion of Descartes' anti-Augustinianism, see Menn, *Descartes and Augustine*, pp. 6–17, 393.

29 See Hankey, "Re-Christianizing Augustine Postmodern Style: Readings by Jacques Derrida, Robert Dodaro, Jean-Luc Marion, Rowan Williams, Lewis Ayres, and John Milbank," *Animus*, 2, 1997, Online. Available HTTP: http://www.mun.ca/animus/1997/vol2hankey1.ht Hankey, para. 55, 80–1; "Stephen Menn's Cartesian Augustine: Metaphysical and Ahistorically Modern," *Animus*, 3, 1998. Online. Available HTTP: http://www.mun.ca/animus/1998 vol3/hankey3.ht, para. 28, 59. See also "Between and Beyond Augustine and Descartes: More than a Source for the Self," *Augustinian Studies*, 32, 1, 2001, pp. 65–88. The specific targets are John Milbank and Rowan Williams, and, to a lesser extent, Lewis Ayres, Robert Dodaro and Jean-Luc Marion.

30 Hankey, "Re-Christianizing Augustine," para. 2.

31 Hankey, "Stephen Menn's Cartesian Augustine," para. 55–6.

32 We will consider this in more detail in Chapter 5. For these reasons, one would have to place Hankey's among the "Augustines of philosophical interest,"

even though he wants to attribute what is most damnable in Augustine (from a postmodern viewpoint and not necessarily his own) to what is specifically Christian in his thought.

33 Hankey, "Stephen Menn's Cartesian Augustine," para. 50, 47.

34 Ibid., 43.

35 Catherine Mowry LaCugna, *God for Us: The Trinity and Christian Life* (San Francisco: Harpers, 1991), p. 101.

36 Ibid., pp. 250–5, 266–78, 390–400.

37 Colin Gunton, "Augustine, the Trinity, and the Theological Crisis of the West," *Scottish Journal of Theology*, 43, 1990, pp. 33–58 (33–4, 58).

38 In this they follow characterizations of Augustine's 'conversion' to neo-platonism that were prominent earlier in the twentieth century. Among these, Propser Alfaric, *L'Evolution intellectuelle de saint Augustin* (Paris: E. Nourry, 1918); P. Courcelle, *Recherches sur les Confessions de saint Augustin* (Paris: E. de Boccard, 1950); O. du Roy, *L'Intelligence de la foi en la Trinité selon saint Augustin* (Paris: Etudes Augustiniennes, 1966). These have since become somewhat canonical, and Menn, too, will continue in this tradition. For the contrary view now emerging, see James J. O'Donnell, *Augustine Confessions: Commentary in Three Volumes* (Oxford: Clarendon Press, 1992), Vol. 2, pp. 413–16.

39 The distinction echoes Karl Rahner's famous axiom: "The economic Trinity *is* the 'immanent' Trinity and vice versa." See Rahner, *The Trinity*, trans. Joseph Donceel (London: Burnes and Oates, 1970), p. 22.

40 See LaCugna, *God for Us*, pp. 260–6. I have no stake in stoking the un-charitable relationship that often persists between Eastern and Western Christianity, and there is much that is admirable and profound in the work of Zizioulas, Vladimir Lossky and others. However, on the basis of the narrative to follow, and in contrast to that of LaCugna and Gunton, one could actually argue that it is the persistence of the sources of an Eastern form of asceticism, dependent upon a stoicism unmodified by Augustine's trinitarian critique of pagan virtue, that insinuates a 'modern' moment into the Western Christian self.

41 John Zizioulas, *Being as Communion: Studies in Personhood and the Church* (Crestwood: St. Vladimir's Press, 1985), p. 41, n. 35. See also p. 88: "The subsequent developments of trinitarian theology, especially in the West with Augustine and the scholastics, have led us to see the term *ousia*, not *hypostasis*, as the expression of the ultimate character and causal principle [*arche*] in God's being."

42 Augustine, *Conf.* I.1; *De Trin.* VIII.4.6–6.9.

43 Lewis Ayres, "'Remember That You Are Catholic' (serm. 52.2): Augustine on the Unity of the Triune God," *Journal of Early Christian Studies*, 8, 1, 2000, pp. 39–82.

44 Ibid., pp. 55–64; Augustine, *Serm.* 52.2.

45 In addition to Ayres, "Remember That You Are Catholic," see Sarah Heaner Lancaster, "Three-Personed Substance: The Relational Essence of the Triune God in Augustine's *De Trinitate*," *The Thomist*, 60, 1, January 1996, pp. 122–39. Lancaster's article is a direct rebuttal to LaCugna, and I am indebted to it here.

46 Augustine, *De Trin.* VII.6.11 (LaCugna's translation), "[I]n God to be is not one thing, and to be a person another thing . . . When we say the person of the Father, we mean nothing else than the substance of the Father. Therefore, as the substance of the Father is the Father himself, not insofar as he is the Father but insofar as He is, so too the person of the Father is nothing else

than the Father Himself. For he is called a person in respect to Himself, not in relation to the Son or to the Holy Spirit, just as he is called in respect to Himself, God, great, good . . ." She comments, "Earlier in the treatise Augustine had cited Father, Son and Spirit as relative terms, but in this passage he denies the relative character of a divine person and equates person with substance. The person of the Father is the same as the being of the Father. The person of the Father is thus absolute, without relation to Son and Spirit" (LaCugna, *God for Us*, p. 89).

47 See LaCaugna, *God for Us*, pp. 243–317.

48 LaCugna, *God for Us*, p. 106 n. 21; Gunton, "Augustine, the Trinity, and the Theological Crisis of the West," p. 38.

49 Augustine, *De Trin.* IV.10.13; see also *De Civ.* IX.15–16. See Ayres, "The Christological Context of Augustine's *De trinitate* XIII: Toward Relocating Books VIII–XV," *Augustinian Studies*, 29, 1, 1998, pp. 198, 111–39; Basil Studer, "History and Faith in Augustine's *De Trinitate*," *Augustinian Studies*, 28, 1, 1997, pp. 7–50.

50 Gunton, "Augustine, the Trinity and the Theological Crisis of the West," p. 37. He does not tell us what it might mean to say that God is *insubstantially* involved.

51 There is a certain imprecision to Gunton's terminology here. How could God be insubstantially involved, on Augustine's terms or any other? How could he act but with the Word if the operations are inseparable? See, for instance, *De Trin.* II.1.3, 5.9. What does it mean to refer to the Son as a *means*?

52 See Augustine, *Conf.* XIII.6.ff.

53 On the distinction between the incarnation and theophanies, see *De Trin.* II.6.11; on divine visibility, see *De Trin.* III.4.9–10. See also, Michel Rene Barnes, "Exegesis and Polemic in Augustine's *De Trinitate* I," *Augustinian Studies*, 30, 1, 1999, pp. 43–59.

54 See Augustine, *De Trin.* IV.1.2–2.4.

55 See *De Trin.* XV.17.27–9; Gunton, "Augustine, the Trinity, and the Theological Crisis of the West," p. 55. To the contrary, Rowan Williams suggests that Augustine is uniquely successful among the Fathers in "giving some account of how and why the Spirit is intrinsic to the trinitarian life" (Williams, "Sapientia and the Trinity," p. 329).

56 Gunton, "Augustine, the Trinity and the Theological Crisis of the West," pp. 53–4.

57 Ibid., p. 54.

58 See Augustine, *Conf.* XIII. So much for the criticism that Augustine foregoes the economy for a Plotinian view of creation. As we shall see, the Church, for Augustine, is creation par excellence.

59 Augustine's tendency, particularly during the Pelagian controversy, to complete the *fides quae per dilectionem operatur* of Gal. 5.6 with Rom. 5.5, "the love diffused in our hearts by the Holy Spirit who is given to us" is evidence of this conclusion. This pairing will prove crucial.

60 In addition, therefore, to the fact that it is anachronistic to speak of Augustine's "starting point," there is a second sense in which the key question for Gunton and LaCugna—that "the real question is whether one begins or not from the economy of salvation," in contrast to "the anthropological starting point," is false. A genuine appropriation of the economy recognizes no outside and therefore that the dilemma here is a false one. See LaCugna, *God for Us*, p. 97.

61 Further warrant for such an account follows from the fact that the *visio dei* on the part of the damned differs distinctly from that of the blessed. See

Augustine, *De Trin.* I.13.28–31; Matt. 5.8. One might suggest here that these criticisms are philosophically insufficient, or rather that they consign such questions to a philosophy which adjudicates what it means "to know" independently of theology. This is the reverse side of separating a doctrinal and a philosophical Augustine.

62 In this, too, they follow on the heels of Rahner, *The Trinity*, p. 17.

63 See Fergus Kerr, OP, *After Aquinas: Versions of Thomism* (London: Blackwell, 2002), pp. 162–206. Kerr's account provides a helpful survey of both sides of the question as well as an account of Aquinas' trinitarianism that rebuts accounts such as Gunton's.

64 Aquinas, *ST* I, 13, 11; 14; 20, 1; 26; 27. Kerr, *After Aquinas* (pp. 193–5), notes a tension in Aquinas between the "natural" conclusions of the trinitarian processions from the nature of divine unity, arrived at apophatically, and his desire to restrict knowledge of the Trinity to the Christian dispensation. The result, in any case, is to direct us to God's economic effects.

65 See Kerr, *After Aquinas*, pp. 167–72.

66 For a fresh discussion of this turn to the economy, of how it is and is not Aristotelian, and of the theological structure of the *Summa*, see John Milbank and Catherine Pickstock, *Truth in Aquinas* (London: Routledge, 2001), pp. 19–87. On the relation between virtues and gifts of the Spirit, see Paul Waddell, *Friends of God: Virtues and Gifts in Aquinas* (New York: Peter Lang, 1991).

67 See Kerr, *After Aqiunas*, pp. 163–8. Kerr usefully resituates the *Summa* and its purposes within its historical, practical and liturgical contexts.

68 And by Aquinas' too, since he conceives of Christ as both perfect law and perfect litergy. See Matthew Levering, *Christ's Fulfillment of Torah and Temple: Salvation according to Thomas Aquinas* (Notre Dame: University of Notre Dame Press, 2002).

69 Augustine, *De Civ.* X.6. We will have more to say about Augustinian sacrifice in the following chapter.

70 For more on the role of the Spirit in the Mass, see *De Trin.* III.4.10.

71 Augustine, *De Trin.* IV.9.12.

72 Though Augustine contrasts the forgiveness of sins to the perfection of virtue, I do not intend to suggest that medieval penitential machinery was of Augustinian origin. It emerges partly from the asceticism of the monasteries influenced by Benedict and Cassian, from the reform of monk-bishops like Gregory the Great, from Irish penitential manuals that began to flourish from about the seventh century and from the emergence of canon law. See James A. Brundage, *Medieval Canon Law* (London: Longman, 1995), pp. 18–43; John A. Gallagher, *Time Past, Time Future: An Historical Study of Catholic Moral Theology* (Mahwah: Paulist Press, 1990), pp. 5–28.

73 See Catherine Pickstock, *After Writing: On the Liturgical Consummation of Philosophy* (London: Blackwell, 1998), pp. 158–66; Michel De Certeau, *The Mystic Fable*, tr. Michael B. Smith (Chicago: Chicago University Press, 1992), pp. 82–5; Henri de Lubac, *Corpus Mysticum: L'Eucharastie et L'Eglise au Moyen-Age* (Paris: Aubier-Montaigne, 1949), p. 281.

74 See John Bossy, "The Mass as a Social Institution 1200–1700," *Past and Present*, 100, August 1983, pp. 29–61 (52).

75 See *De Civ.* XIX.27 and XXII.29 where we, "in our measure, are made partakers of peace in ourselves, peace among ourselves, and peace with God, according to our standard of perfection." William Durandus commenting on this sequence in the *Rationale divinorum officiorum* (Naples, 1859), p. 249, offers a similar hope "that we may pass from exterior peace, through the peace of the heart, to the peace of eternity." Cited in Bossy, "The Mass as a

Social Institution," p. 54. One could even argue that the *"ecce"* and subsequent elevation substitute the host for one of Christ's crucial functions in *De Trin*.

76 On the transition from the virtues and sins to an ethic of command and its relationship to the loss of ritual kinship, see John Bossy, *Christianity in the West 1400–1700* (Oxford: Oxford University Press, 1985), pp. 35–42, 99. For pictoral representations of virtues, acts of mercy and vices in English churches, see Eamon Duffy, *The Stripping of the Altars: Tradtional Religion in England 1400–1580* (New Haven: Yale University Press, 1992), figures 22–8. I certainly do not mean to imply a necessary antithesis between the Decalogue and an ethics of virtue (or of Law and Gospel). Aquinas, for one, thought they could be harmonized by understanding each subsequent commandment as a further specification of the first which, in essence, enjoins charity, in conformity with the Augustinian conception of virtue. See Aquinas, *ST* I–II, 99, 2; 100, 10, ad.2. Nor do I mean to suggest, as a historical matter, that the transition from an "ethics of virtue" to an "ethics of law" is attributable simply to the Reformer's emphasis on the Word. Underlying it also is a formalization of abstract power within the Church facilitated in part by the expansive growth of Canon Law and the Renaissance retrieval of Roman law and also by new conceptions of will which would pass from Scotus to Occam, through Descartes and Hobbes to Kant. See Alisdair MacIntyre, *Three Rival Versions of Moral Inquiry: Encyclopaedia, Genealogy and Tradition* (Notre Dame: Notre Dame Press, 1990), pp. 154–5.

77 See Mervyn E. James, "Ritual, Drama and Social Body in the Late Medieval English Town," *Past and Present* 98, 1983, pp. 3–29.

78 On the first part of this thesis at least, Alliez and Wayne Hankey are in agreement. See Alliez, *Capital Times*, pp. 77–83, 93.

79 "As for Augustinianism, it will complete the accomplishment of its mission of dis-integration within the framework of the Reformation. Augustine, Descartes, and Kant are the major poles and privileged moments of this religious movement of emancipation that attains its acme with the Augustinian Renaissance of the Reformers . . ." (Alliez, *Capital Times*, p. 92).

80 "In itself, apart from its Christian recuperation—and from that retrospective optic that was ours—Neoplatonism does not belong to the West's dominant dynamics (One speaks of 'Oriental Influences')" (Alliez, *Capital Times*, p. 82).

81 Ibid., p. 9. For Marx on exchange value and Aristotle, see Karl Marx, "Capital I," in Robert C. Tucker (ed.), *The Marx-Engels Reader* (New York: Norton, 1978), pp. 333–4 n. 1.

82 Alliez, following Marx, attributes this predicament to Aristotle, but does not consider that it applies to his own case. See Alliez, *Capital Times*, p. 8. We will attempt a partial reconstruction of Augustinian *natura* in the following chapter.

83 Alliez, *Capital Times*, pp. 136, 82–3.

84 Ibid., p. 83.

85 Ibid., pp. 78, 135.

86 Ibid., pp. 82, 109–10, emphasis mine.

87 Ibid., p. 133.

88 Ibid., p. 100.

89 Ibid., pp. 84–5. Despite its postmodern drag, Alliez is actually quite conventional and liberal on this point. For a critique of this general position, see John Milbank, *Theology and Social Theory: Beyond Secular Reason* (Oxford: Basil Blackwell, 1990), pp. 398–408.

90 Alliez, *Capital Times*, p. 87.

91 Ibid., p. 99.

92 Ibid., pp. 106–7.

93 In this sense, it resembles heresy, that is, truth taken too far, though Alliez would undoubtedly disavow the Christian pretension of such a designation.

94 Augustine, *De Lib*. III.11–16.

95 "Far from expressing the refound unity of human nature with divine nature, the reconciliation takes place by the Son of Man's blood (Col. 1:20). If he had not been a man, Augustine writes mercilessly, he could not have been put to death. And a Christ absolved of all debt could not have redeemed us with his blood spilled gratuitously. Such, then, is the economy of the Redemption: the death of the Son of Man for the price of redemption. The reconciliation is not within us, for us, but 'in God,' that 'greedy usurer' [Nietzsche]. The expiatory sacrifice, the juridical logic of the unpaid debt, annulled by the second Adam who paid for us a debt that was not his . . ." (Alliez, *Capital Times*, p. 95). Augustine's answer to this is *De Trin*. XIII.10.13–15.19. We shall take this up in the next chapter.

96 Augustine, *De Civ*. XIX.27. On the kinship between Pelagianism and pagan philosophy, see James Wetzel, *Augustine and the Limits of Virtue* (Cambridge: Cambridge University Press, 1990), pp. 122–4, 177, 183.

97 Alliez appears to collapse the distance intrinsic to the ontological difference with the distance of sin. In fact, as we shall see in the next chapter, the former difference is constitutive of our similitude to God, whereas only the latter fundamentally effaces this similitude, and even that not absolutely. See Alliez, *Capital Times*, pp. 80–6.

98 Augustine, *De Civ*. XIX.22.

99 See William T. Cavanaugh, "Coercion in Augustine and Disney," *New Blackfriars*, 80, 940, June 1999, pp. 283–90.

100 Alliez, *Capital Times*, pp. 120–1. To secure this point, Alliez devotes significant attention to refuting Robert Jordan's caution against defining Augustinian time as such because Augustine's "relational conception of time" does not find its "foundation" until the commentary on Genesis in Book XII, as time comes forth from the hand of God. While I agree with Alliez that Jordan's provisional definition of time with reference to physical motion is inadequate, his final answer to Jordan's cautions consists of little more than repeating the question—*quid est ergo tempus?*—in a louder tone. See Alliez, *Capital Times*, pp. 273–4 n. 148; Robert Jordan, "Time and Contingency in St Augustine," *Review of Metaphysics*, 8, 1955, pp. 394–417.

101 "It will be noticed (a) that the excellence of the voice implies that Augustine dispossesses himself of his own writing in the course of a constant citational play where 'I' is able to write a book only in the Book where 'He' has already written, ever since the beginning—to the point of getting caught 'in the endless spiral that the "You" whom "I" addresses is none other than the "Me" that "He" constitutes in the very words that "I" pronounces and that he writes by rewriting the Book' (voice presents itself as consciousness only at the price of this engagement in the strategies of differance) . . ." (Alliez, *Capital Times*, p. 117).

102 Ibid., p. 115; Deleuze and Guattari, *Anti-Oedipus: Capitalism and Schizophrenia*, trans. Robert Hurly, Mark Seem, and Helen R. Lane (New York: Viking, 1977), p. 205.

103 This co-articulation of time and space too should be correlated to the economy of beauty neglected by Alliez. See Catherine Pickstock, "Soul, City and Cosmos after Augustine," in John Milbank, Catherine Pickstock, and Graham Ward (eds), *Radical Orthodoxy: A New Theology* (London: Routledge, 1998), pp. 243–77 (248). Augustine, *Conf*. XI.27; *De Mus*. VI.17.57.

104 Think, for instance, of the relationship between the pear tree incident and the fall, or the Paul of Rom. 7 and the Augustine of books VII and VIII.

105 Ludwig Wittgenstein, *Philosophical Investigations*, trans. G. E. M Anscombe (New York: MacMillan, 1957), para. 104.
106 Augustine denies this at *Conf.* XI.23, where he first offers time as a kind of *distentio*; the *distentio animi* comes at XI.26. See Alliez, *Capital Times*, pp. 108–13. In fact, the aporias of measurement extend beyond XI.26.
107 Alliez, *Capital Times*, p. 102.
108 Augustine, *Conf.* IX.1.
109 Wetzel, *Augustine and the Limits of Virtue*, pp. 29–30.
110 James McEvoy, "St Augustine's Account of Time and Wittgenstein's Criticisms," *Review of Metaphysics*, 37, 1984, pp. 547–77 (556). See also Robert Jordan, "Time and Contingency in St Augustine," *Review of Metaphysics*, 8, 1955, pp. 394–417 (409).
111 The phrase is Wetzel's. See Wetzel, *Augustine and the Limits of Virtue*, p. 30. Augustine, *Conf.* XI.28: "I am about to recite a psalm that I know. Before I begin, my expectation extends over the entire psalm. Once I have begun, my memory extends over as much of it as I shall separate off and assign to the past. The life of this action of mine is distended into memory by reason of the part I have spoken and into forethought by reason of the part I am about to speak. But attention is actually present and that which was to be is borne along by it so as to become past."
112 Augustine, *Conf.* XI.29. Note how the invocation of Phil. 3.12 reintroduces the question of standards.
113 See Augustine, *Conf.* IV.10, 12.
114 See Pickstock, "Soul, City and Cosmos after Augustine," p. 269.
115 Augustine, *Conf.* IV.10–11.
116 Consider, for instance, the various contingent and temporal manifestations of the eternal law in *De Lib.* I.6.
117 Is this not the necessary conclusion to draw from Augustine's conflation of creation and ecclesiology in *Conf.* XIII?
118 Alliez, *Capital Times*, p. 136.

2 *DE TRINITATE* AND THE AESTHETICS OF SALVATION

Notes to pages 27–71

1 See Ayres, "The Christological Context of Augustine's *De Trinitate* XIII.
2 The argument between Rowan Williams and Wayne Hankey is partly an argument over what *De Trin.* is about. Part of Williams's task is to extract the structure of Augustine's key argument (books VIII–IX) from its many digressions. In fastening onto Augustine's polemics against the skepticism of the New Academy (*De Trin.* XV.12.21) as a proto-Cartesian maneuver, Hankey makes what is marginal to Augustine's argument central. See Williams, "Sapientia and the Trinity." Menn, "Stephen Menn's Cartesian Augustine," para. 54.
3 Barnes, "Exegesis and Polemic in Augustine's *De Trinitate* I," p. 58. It falls to the next chapter for us to consider *theologically* "the content" of these two terms, material and divine, and how the latter affects Augustine's construal of the former. Suffice it for now to note that their sense is not being taken in positivist fashion as self-interpreting.
4 Ibid., p. 57.
5 I qualify "function" for methodological reasons which are theological: to avoid reducing Jesus to a formal exemplification of a prior general idea at the expense of the drama, contingency and historicity of the Gospel narratives. However, the internal logic of those narratives (as well as the letters of Paul) presents something of an aporia which makes a qualified use of the term

appropriate: the recognition of Christ as the revelation of God requires that one already participate in that which is revealed. ("Who do you say that I am?" Simon Peter answered, "You are the Christ, the son of the living God . . ." "Blessed are you, Simon son of Jonah! For flesh and blood has not revealed this to you, but my Father in heaven.") Augustine is highly attentive to that aporia, and, I shall suggest, avoids the errors of neglecting it through the unity of *scientia* and *sapientia*, which makes contemplation of the eternal and knowledge of temporal particulars mutually dependent.

6 In light of the earlier qualifications about the limits placed on ontology, it is perhaps important to bear in mind here that this latter concern is not a concern over the transcendentally valid conditions of our apprehension.

7 Carol Harrison, *Beauty and Revelation in the Thought of Saint Augustine* (Oxford: Clarendon Press, 1992).

8 Augustine, *In Jo. Ep.* IX.9. See Harrison, *Beauty and Revelation*, p. 232.

9 Augustine, *De Beata Vita*, 32–3; *De Vera Relig.* 66, CCSL, XXXII, 230–1. "datur intelligi esse aliquid, quod illius unius solius, a quo principio unum est, quidquid aliquo modo unum est, ita simile sit, ut hoc omnino impleat ac sit id ipsum. Et haec est ueritas et uerbum in principio et uerbum deus apud deum. Si enim falsitas ex his est, quae imitantur unum, non in quantum id imitantur, sed in quantum implere non possunt, ill est ueritas, quae id implere potuit et id esse, quod illud est. Ipsa est, quae illud ostendit, sicut est, unde et uerbum eius et lux eius rectissime dicitur. Cetera illius unius simila dici possunt, in quantum sunt, in tantum enim et uera sunt. Haec autem ipsa eius similitudo et ideo ueritas. Ut enim ueritate sunt uera quae uera sunt, ita similitudine similia sunt quaecumque similia. Ut ergo ueritas forma uerorum est, ita similitudo forma similium. Quapropter quoniam uera in tantum uera sunt, in quantum sunt, in tantum autem sunt, in quantum principalis unius similia sunt, ea forma est omnium quae sunt, quae summa similitudo principii et ueritas est, quia sine ulla dissimilitudine est."

10 Augustine, *Solil.* II.32; *De Fide et Sym.* 2; *De Vera Relig.* 35–6; *De Nat. Boni.* 18; *De Div. Q.* 83, 10. Harrison, *Beauty and Revelation*, pp. 36–9, trades in part on the etymological connection between *species/speciosus* and *forma/formosus*, drawing on von Balthasar and Du Roy. See Hans Urs Von Balthasar, *Glory of the Lord: A Theological Aesthetics*, Vol. 2, *Studies in Theological Style, Clerical Style* (Edinburgh: T&T Clark, 1982 and 1984), p. 115. Du Roy, *Intelligence de la foi en la Trinité selon saint Augustin*, p. 281 n. 4.

11 See Emilie Zum Brunn, *St Augustine: Being and Nothingness*, trans. Ruth Namad (New York: Paragon House, 1988), pp. 9–34. Brunn's analysis of the convertibility of the transcendentals in the divine *esse* and the consequent increase or decrease in the being of creatures coextensive with participation in the transcendentals, helps us to reunite aesthetics, ethics, and ontology. However, his theological grammar is perhaps not sufficient on this point. From the fact that Augustine uses the same term, *esse*, of both creatures and the God of Ex. 3.14, it does not follow that he uses the terms univocally of each, differentiating them merely by quantity. Augustine's rejection of an "analogy of proportion" which would underwrite such a use suggests rather just the opposite. See the following note for more on this issue.

12 Wayne Hankey contends that Augustine's identification of God and *esse* is cause for nervousness amongst "postmodern Augustinians" (particularly Marion) because it is vulnerable to the Heideggerian critique of onto-theology. (Hankey, "Rechristianizing Augustine Postmodern Style," para. 39.) Arguably, though, only the Christian and Jewish doctrine of *creatio ex nihilo* requires, discovers or attains to the ontological difference. Moreover,

Aquinas' real distinction of *esse* from *essentia*, with God, who *is* his own esse, understood as the giver of the created *esse* which creatures have in "composite" by participation, skirts this critique by engendering meaningful speech about a differential relation between creator and creature "which makes its appearance within the world as we know it and yet does not express a division within that world" (David B. Burrell, *Knowing the Unknowable God: Ibn-Sina, Maimonides, Aquinas* (Notre Dame: Notre Dame Press, 1986), p. 20. This makes possible a form of analogous predication which does not require as its basis a specifiable analogy of proportion—ruled out both by Aquinas and Augustine (*De Trin.* XV.7.12, 23.43; *Ep.* 169.6)—able to specify the degree to which created likenesses differ or correspond with their divine "archetype." Augustine writes of the correspondence of memory, intellect and will, "I do not say that these three things are in any way to be equated with the Holy Trinity, as if arranged according to an analogy, or according to a ratio of comparison. This I do not say" (Non dico ista illi Trinitati velut aeuanda, quasi ad analogiam, id es, ad rationem quamdam comparationis dirigenda: non hoc dico) (Augustine, *Serm.* 52.23, *PL* 38, 364). Lewis Ayres contends, and I concur, a) that the Augustinian grammar of divine simplicity and its corollary of radical transcendence performs a similar function to the real distinction, and b) that the Augustinian language of similitude (rather than analogy) at once expresses this grammatical possibility and denies an analogy of proportion. See Ayres, "The Fundamental Grammar of Augustine's Trinitarian Theology," in Robert Dodaro and George Lawless (eds), *Augustine and His Critics: Essays in Honour of Gerald Bonner* (London: Routledge, 2000), pp. 53–9, 68–70, 72 n. 8; "'Remember That You Are Catholic.'"

13 Harrison, *Beauty and Revelation*, pp. 36–47.

14 Augustine's exegetical habit of constructing a theological point from disparate biblical passages is interesting in its own right and indicative of the significance of the point in question wherever it occurs, particularly if a formulation is repeated throughout the Augustinian corpus. This will later prove true with the pairing of Gal. 5.6 and Rom. 5.5.

15 The "meaning" in question is the divergence in the vision of God between the just and unjust (I Cor. 13.12; I Jn 3.2; Ps. 17.4; I Jn 14.21; Matt. 5.8; Augustine, *De Trin.* I.13.31).

16 Augustine, *De Trin.* XV.5.7, *PL* 42, 1061. "Si ergo haec atque hujusmodi omnia, et ipsa Trinitas, et in ea singuli dici puissant; ubi aut quomodi Trinitatis apparebit?"

17 Though this distinction was arrived at independently of von Balthasar's theological aesthetics, its components correspond roughly with his distinction between a "theory of vision" and "theory of rapture," delineated according to a division of "subjective" and "objective" evidence. See Hans Urs von Balthasar, *The Glory of the Lord: A Theological Aesthetics*, Vol. 1, *Seeing the Form* (Edinburgh: T&T Clark, 1982), p. 125.

18 R. A. Markus, "St Augustine on Signs," in *Signs and Meanings: World and Text in Ancient Christianity* (Liverpool: Liverpool University Press, 1996), pp. 60–91.

19 This is partly why Alliez's positivism toward nature and his abstraction of the *distentio animi* from the "order of nature" are inadequate. See Alliez, *Capital Times*, p. 135.

20 There is no a priori conflict between the claim that Jesus is both the "highest expression" of God's creative act (and thus an Adamic archetype, first-born of a new creation, fulfillment of the old) and that he is utterly exceptional (historically, sacrificially, ontologically), and to this extent discontinuous with it. One would wish to argue instead that it is in virtue of this exceptionality

and this discontinuity that he can be the "highest expression." See Augustine, *De Trin.* II.6.11.

21 Ibid. II.6.11. Further warrant for this argument comes from the fact that Augustine equates the visible manifestation of the Son and the Spirit "to the sight of mortals in some corporeal form" with their missions in being sent, since it is true of each to say that "he was sent thither, where he already was." *De Trin.* III proem.3.

22 Augustine, *De Trin.* II.15.25, *PL* 42, 0862. "sed per subjectam, ut saepe diximus, creaturam exhibentur haec omnia visibilia et sensibilia, ad significandum invisibilem atque intelligibilem Deum, non solum patrem, sed et Filium et Spiritum sanctum, ex quo omnia, per quem omni, in quo omnia (Rom. 11.36); quamvis invisibilia Dei, a creatura mundi, per ea quae facta sunt intellecta conscpiciantur, sempiterna quoque virtus ejus ac divinitas (Rom. 1.20)." See also *De Trin.* III.4.10, *PL* 42, 0873, and generally all of Book III: "what wonder if also in the creature of heaven and earth, of sea and air, God works the sensible and visible things which he wills, in order to signify and manifest himself in them . . ." ("quid mirum si etiam in creature coeli et terrae, maris et aeris, facit Deus quae vult sensibilia atque visibilia, ad se ipsum in eis, sicut oportere ipse novit, significandum et demonstrandum . . .").

23 Ibid. III.1.4–9.19.

24 Ibid. III.9.16.

25 Ibid. III.9.18, "But He only is the creator who is the chief former of these things. Neither can any one be this, unless He with whom primarily rests the measure, number and weight of all things existing . . ." On the "unexceptional" character of miracles, see *De Trin.* III.6.11, "And who is it that restored to the corpses their proper souls when the dead rose again, unless He who gives life to the flesh in the mother's womb, in order that they may come into being who are yet to die? But when such things happen in a continuous kind of river of ever-flowing succession, passing from the hidden to the visible, and from the visible to the hidden, by a regular and beaten track, then they are called natural; when, for the admonition of men, they are thrust in by an unusual changeableness, then they are called miracles."

26 Ibid. III.4.9, *PL* 42, 0873, "Illic enim Dei voluntas . . . quibusdam ordinatissimis creaturae motibus promo spiritualibus, diende corporalibus, per cuncta diffundit, et utitur omnibus ad incommutabile arbitrium sententiae suae . . ."

27 Augustine, *De Trin.* IV.4.9.

28 It is this, more than the material exegetical content of the theophany passages, that is of interest here.

29 As we shall later discuss, this ratio does not imply a "real relationship" to creation from God's side.

30 Augustine, *De Doct.* I.2.2.

31 Ibid. I.3.3.

32 Alliez, *Capital Times*, p. 120.

33 Ibid., p. 135.

34 William S. Babcock, "Caritas and Signification in De Doctrina Christiana," in Duane A. H. Arnold and Pamela Bright (eds), *De Doctrina Christiana: A Classic of Western Culture* (Notre Dame: Notre Dame Press, 1995), pp. 145–63 (156, 147). Babcock also writes (p. 149) that "Augustine says nothing to indicate how the association between sign and thing is established in *signa data*," a fact that perhaps leaves him open to the charge that the association is arbitrary. In Wittgensteinian terms, one would say that the question of "the association" is ill-posed, precisely because of the relation between meaning and use which

Augustine seems to endorse. And this might provide a clue to an Augustinian "solution," how the "use" constitutive of the formal elements of language "corresponds," which is to say participates in the reality in which both it and its objects are grounded. This would be the ground for claiming, for instance, that Augustine's terms in *De Civ*. render a truer account of Roman politics than Rome's own, though there would be no grounds for "verifying" the claim apart from undergoing a "conversion" of one's habits of minds and language coextensive with a modification of desire.

35 Augustine, *De Doct.* I.35.39, *CCSL* XXXII, 29. "Omnium igitur, quae dicta sunt, ex quo de rebus tractamus, haec summa est, ut intellegatur legis et omnium diuinarum scripturarum plenitudo et finis esse dilectio rei, qua fruendum est, et rei, quae nobiscum ea re frui potest . . ."
36 Augustine, *De Doct.* I.3.3; I.31.34; I.2.2.
37 Augustine, *De Trin.* III.9.16; *De Gen ad Lit.* IV.4.9. See Harrison, *Beauty and Revelation*, pp. 101–10; O'Donnell, *Augustine Confessions*, Vol. 2, pp. 48ff.
38 Augustine, *De Doct.* I.2–3.4. See also Babcock, "Caritas and Signification," pp. 145–63.
39 Augustine, *De Doct.* I.35.39, *CCSL* XXXII, 29. "Omnium igitur, quae dicta sunt, ex quo de rebus tractamus, haec summa est, ut intellegatur legis et omnium diuinarum scripturarum plenitudo et finis esse dilectio rei, qua fruendum est, et rei, quae nobiscum ea re frui potest . . ."
40 Ibid. *De Doct.* I.35.39.
41 It is perhaps significant here that Augustine endorses, with the proper grammatical qualifications, Hilary's characterization of Father, Son and Holy Spirit as, respectively, eternity, form and use. Augustine, *De Trin.* VI.10.11.
42 One is reminded of Wittgenstein's characterization, ironically and wrongly, of *Augustine*. "These words, it seems to me, give us a particular picture of the essence of human language. It is this: the individual words in language name objects—sentences are combinations of such names.—In this picture of language we find the roots of the following idea: Every word has a meaning. It is the object for which the word stands." Wittgenstein, *Philosophical Investigations*, 1.
43 Augustine, *Conf.* XII. 28.
44 See Augustine, *Conf.* XII.25.34; *De Lib.* II.8–14. One is not, strictly speaking, a number but is rather the principle of number in which all other numbers partake. In this, one is to number as the point is to magnitude. See S. K. Heninger, *Touches of Sweet Harmony: Pythagorean Cosmology and Renaissance Poetics* (San Marino: Huntingdon Library, 1974), p. 78.
45 See Augustine, *De Trin.* II.2.4, Markus; *Augustine on Signs*, p. 71.
46 Augustine, *De Trin.* III.10.19–21.
47 "The whole series of times is timelessly contained in God's eternal Wisdom." Augustine, *De Trin.* II.5.9, *PL* 42, 0850. "id est, factum in tempore, ut incarnatum Verbum hominibus apparet; quod in ipso Verbe sine tempore erat, in quo tempore fieret. Ordo quippe temporum in aeterna Dei Sapientia sine tempore est." I have used Edmund Hill's translation here (p. 103), though I have retained the conventional pagination. Hill's footnote (pp. 123–4), which correlates the *De Trin.* to *De Gen. ad Lit.* is instructive here, and it contains at least one remark with which this thesis concurs: "Creation displays in a new mode (a spatio-temporal one, and thus a less perfect one, of course) the dramatic reality that is the divine tri-personal life." On history as sacrament, see Harrison, *Beauty and Revelation*, pp. 81–9; Studer, "History and Faith in Augustine's *De Trinitate*," pp. 32–6.
48 Michel de Certeau, *The Mystic Fable* : *Volume I, The Sixteenth and Seventeenth*

Centuries, trans. Michael B. Smith (Chicago: University of Chicago Press, 1992), p. 82. In a footnote to this remark (n. 16), Certeau continues, "This perspective insists on the *mysterium* (a problematics of the 'operation'), more than on the *sacramentum* (a problematics of the 'sign' and, before long, of representation). Lubac reminds us pertinently that 'a mystery, in the old sense of the word, is more of an action than a thing' it is a 'mutual relation' (Simonin), the operation of an exchange or of a communication between the terms distinguished" (*Corpus mysticum*, pp. 47–66). While Augustine's lexicon is obviously replete with the language of *sacramenti*, I hope it will be clear that, when both sign and thing collapse in the Son's filiation in love from the Father, that there need be no inevitable antithesis between the two terms or an inevitable conclusion in the metaphysics of representation.

49 Hence the price of Alliez's neglect of the economy of beauty. As we shall see, Augustine alternatively uses these terms in *De Trin.* III and XIII to describe the restoration effected in us by Christ.

50 See Catherine Pickstock, "Music: Soul, City, and Cosmos after Augustine," in Milbank, Pickstock and Ward (eds), *Radical Orthodoxy*, pp. 246–50; Gerhart Ladner, *The Idea of Reform: Its Impact on Thought and Action in the Age of the Fathers* (Cambridge: Harvard University Press, 1959), pp. 203–22. See also Augustine, *Conf.* XII.29.

51 Augustine, *De Mus.* VI.10.28.

52 Pickstock, "Music: Soul, City, and Cosmos after Augustine," p. 269.

53 Augustine, *De Trin.* IV.15.21, I.8.16, XIII.1.1–2.5. See also I.8.17, *PL* 42, 831. "Haec enim nobis contemplatio promittur actionum omnium finis atque aeterna perfectio gaudiorum."

54 Augustine, *De Trin.* IV.15.21; XIII.9.12–10.13, 16.21. Studer, "History and Faith in Augustine's *De Trinitate*," pp. 12–14, 44.

55 The idea recalls those of *De Util. Cred.* 19–32. One could arrive at a similar conclusion from *De Doct.* and *De Magistro*.

56 John Bossy notes the migrating senses of words in the early modern period such as "charity," "friendship," "society," and "state" as the abstract new political power and its attendant rites of civility displace ritual forms of friendship and kinship (both, ultimately, with Christ), as the origin and ground of the social body. So too "Christianity," from the late fifteenth century onward, ceases any longer to name a particular body of people—most of the people of Europe—and comes to denote, rather, an *-ism* or body of thought and belief. I am obviously deeply indebted to Catherine Pickstock; particularly to her brilliant reading of the *De Mus.* However, inattention to Bossy's observation is perhaps partially responsible for a latent tendency in Pickstock's *After Writing* to treat "doxology" as a genus and Christianity as a species, a tendency perhaps in tension with the book's masterful claim—that the Mass is the condition of possibility for all meaning. The result is such that at the end of the book she is left to ask, vis-à-vis Christianity's relationship to Platonism, "why Christianity?" The question is problematic insofar as it implies a vantage outside theology from which it could be answered. It suggests a category mistake. See John Bossy, *Christianity in the West 1400–1700*, pp. 167–71; Catherine Pickstock, *After Writing: On the Liturgical Consummation of Philosophy* (Oxford: Blackwell, 1998), pp. 267–73.

57 This would be apparent from a Wittgensteinian viewpoint, where meaning is correlated with use. Hence the very meaning of doxology would be bound to the practices of particular traditions in which it is embedded, and would vary as much across traditions as the meaning of the word "God" varies in a Thomistic and Cartesian usage. As should be apparent from our treatment of

De Doct., there is an affinity between the Wittgensteinian and Augustinian view. For hints of a greater affinity between Augustine and Wittgenstein than the early pages of the *Investigations* would lead one to believe, see Stanley Cavell, "The Availability of Wittgenstein's Later Philosophy," in *Must We Mean What We Say? A Book of Essays* (Cambridge: Cambridge University Press, 1976), pp. 44–72.

58 See Augustine, *De Trin.* X.5.7; *Conf.* I.13, 19; II.3, 9; III.3; VIII.5; *De Lib.* III.15.

59 My intent here is to think of "personhood" in theological terms without taking "human nature" in positivist fashion or emptying Christ of specific material content.

60 This understanding does not exclude the thesis that Jesus is also the superlative human, under the aspect of Adam's curse, in being uniquely *deprived* of that light on Good Friday and Holy Saturday, though obviously qualifications are required which do not compromise divine impassibility. See Hans Urs von Balthasar, *Mysterium Paschale* (Edinburgh: T&T Clark, 1990), pp. 168–74. During the formulation of orthodox Christology, often against the backdrop of various adoptionist formulations, it was necessary to insist upon a distinction between will and nature so as to avoid the conclusion that Jesus was made Son by virtue of his concord of will or obedience to the Father. After Desartes, however, when both *esse* and *essentia* are determined according to a *mathesis* reduced to a species of quantity, and when "quality" is reduced to the private life of the mind and put in problematic relation to the extra-mental world, it is perhaps necessary once again to conflate them, and recognize love and being as coextensive. This would preclude the adoptionist problem.

The next chapter offers an Augustinian conception of materiality premised upon the participation of the primordial *hyle* in the response of the Son to the Father, which renders matter itself "ideal" and makes its being coextensive with its capacity for "response" to the Father. If this capacity for response is what it means *to be*, then I would suggest that we think of God the Son assuming human *nature* in Christ, precisely in virtue of his *assuming* human nature in Christ. That is to say, Christ is fully human precisely in virtue of his being hypostatically united to the extension and return of the love which is God. This presents several advantages, apart from its amenability to an Augustinian conception of grace. First, it restores a theological cosmology wherein materiality is recovered for participation in the beauty of the divine love and where true, non-possessive knowledge of it follows from entering into that love. (For truth as defying possession, see *Conf.* XII. 25.34; *De Lib.* II.7–14.) Second, this formulation conspires with the entailment of love and knowledge in Augustine's thought to deny the fact/value distinction and makes Christianity, in contrast either to encyclopaedic, scientific or genealogical modes of thought, perhaps uniquely qualified to accommodate the intrinsically formal character of our terms of material description and uniquely capable of criticizing the orders of desire embodied in those terms. Thirdly, one can think both this cosmology and the incarnation without a positivistic hypostasization of "nature." Rather, "nature" itself is a pattern or "*forma*" constituted in participatory and ecstatic relation to that which is other than itself, and instantiated analogically as it is unfolded in time, an understanding that comports with the Augustinian doctrine of "seminal reasons." One could therefore *strengthen* the connection for which Ayres contends between the union of Christ's two natures and the participation of the members of his Body in that unity, without implying either an indefensible positivism or a totalizing circumscription of its referents.

61 Hankey, "Stephen Menn's Cartesian Augustine," para. 33–43, 49–57. The recognition of this complementary relationship requires that some form of time be imported into the *memoria* of eternity, just as the glorified bodies of Christ and the resurrected retain, in some fashion, the marks of their temporal existence. The crucial point here seems not to be temporality itself, but loss.

62 See Williams, "Sapientia and the Trinity," p. 329. This link is attested further in Augustine's "ecclesiological" interpretation of Genesis in *Conf.* XIII.

63 Augustine, *De Trin.* VIII.7.10, *PL* 42, 0956. "Quapropter non est praecipue vivendum in hac questione, quae de Trinitate nobis est, et de cognoscendo Deo, nisi quid sit vera delectio, imo vero quid sit dilectio."

64 Augustine, *De Trin.* VIII.7.10–11, *PL* 42, 0957. "Et pleraque alia reperimus in Litteris sanctis, in quibus sola dilectio proximi ad perfectionem praecipi videtur, et taceri de dilectione dei; cum in utroque praecepto Lex pendeat et Prophetae. Sed et hoc ideo, quia et qui proximum diligit, consequens est in ipsam praecipue dilectionem diligat. 'Deus *autem* dilectio est, et qui manet in dilectione, in Deo manet' (I Joan. IV.16) . . . Quapropter, ui quarent Deum per istas Potestates, quae mundo praesunt vel partibus mundi, aufereuntur ab eo longeque jactantur; non intervallis locorum, sed diversitate affectuum . . ."

65 According to Rowan Williams, Books IX through XIV constitute a long digression from this central point, necessitated by the fact that the analogy of love depends upon a relationship between the lover and an external object and is therefore inadequate as a similitude for the Trinity. Williams, "*Sapientia* and the Trinity," p. 323.

66 Augustine, *De Trin.* VIII.8.12, *PL* 42, 0957. "Nemo dicat: Non novi quid diligam. Diligat fratrem, et diliget eamdem dilectionem. Magis enim novit dilectionem qua diligit, quam fratrem quem diligit. Ecce jam potest notiorem Deum habere quam fratrem: plane notiorem, quia praesentiorem; notiorem, quia interiorem, notiorem, quia certiorem. Amplectere dilectionem Deum, et dilectione amplectere Deum."

67 Augustine, *De Trin.* XII.14.22, *PL* 42, 1010. "Verum Scripturarum sanctarum multiplicem copium scrutatus, invenio scriptum esse in libro Job . . . *Ecce pietas est sapientia; abstinere autem a malis est scientia* (Job XXVIII, 8). In hac differentia intelligendum est ad contemplationem sapientiam, ad actionem scientiam pertinere. Pietatem quipe hoc loco posuit Dei, cultum, quae graecia dicitur Θεοσέβια. Nam hoc verbum habet ista sentential in codicibus graecis. Et quis cultus ejus, nisi amor ejus, quo nunc desideramus eum videre, credimusque et speramus non esse visuros; et quantum proficimus *videmus nunc per speculum in aenigmate, tunc*, in manifestatione?"

68 Alliez is right to see that "It [is] no longer just the *Confessions* but the ensemble of [Augustine's] opus that [bears] witness to a 'metaphysics of conversion'" (Alliez, *Capital Times*, p. 80).

69 Augustine is not idiosyncratic among the Fathers in this regard. See Henri de Lubac, *Catholicism: Christ and the Common Destiny of Man*, trans. Lancelot C. Sheppard and Elizabeth Englund, OCD (San Francisco: Ignatius Press, 1988), pp. 25–47, 67–76.

70 Augustine is contemplating Jn 17.20–3 in this passage. Augustine, *De Trin.* IV.9.12, *PL* 42, 0896. "Non dixit, Ego et ipsi unum; quamvis per id quod Ecclesiae caput et et corpus ejus Ecclesia (*Ephes.* I, 22, 23), posset dicere, Ego et ipsi non unum, sed unus, quia caput et unus est Christus . . . quia in se ipsis non possent, dissociati ab invicem per diversas voluptates et cupiditates et immunditias peccatorum: unde mundantur per Mediatorem, ut sint in illo unum . . . per eamdem in eamdem beatitudinem conspirantem concordissimam voluntatem, in unum spiritum quodam modo igne charitatis conflatam."

See also Harrison, *Beauty and Revelation*, pp. 224–30. The thought is echoed in *En. Psa.* 119.7 (Studer's translation): "Because Christ's possessions reach to the ends of the earth, and [Christ's] possessions are all the saints, and the saints form one human being in Christ (since in Christ there is a holy unity), this one human being says: 'From the ends of the earth I have cried to you, when my heart was in anguish.'" See generally Studer, *The Grace of God and the Grace of Christ in Augustine of Hippo* (Collegeville: The Liturgical Press, 1997), pp. 39–65.

71 Augustine, *De Lib.* II.11, Wisdom 8.1. *CCSL* XXIX, 258: "quod adtingit a fine usque ad finem fortiter et disponit omnia suauiter." Part of the basis for this convertibility is the fact that all number "is named on the basis of how many times it contains one" (II.8) which, strictly speaking is not *a* number but the principle of all number, since any material thing we call one is in fact composite and multiple. The analogy between one and number and the modes of perception appropriate to them thus provide the grounds for convertibility between one, which is present within and contains all numbers, and wisdom (or truth), which "is one and present to all who think" (II.10). In *De Trin.*, this understanding easily modulates into the way distinct numerical series can unfold within the one *sapientia* of God.

72 Augustine, *De Lib.*, II.16.

73 "To this form it has been said, 'You will change them, and they shall be changed; but you are always the same, and your years will not fail.' By 'years without fail' the prophet means 'eternity.' It is also said of this form that 'abiding in himself he makes all things new.' From this we understand that everything is governed by his providence. For if everything that exists would be nothing without form, then that unchangeable form—through which all changeable things subsist, so that they complete and carry out the numbers of their forms—is itself the providence that governs them." Augustine, *De Lib.* II.17; Ps. 102.26–7; Wisdom 7.27.

74 Augustine, *De Trin.* IV.2.4, *PL* 42, 0889. "dum simplum ejus congruit duplo nostro."

75 Ibid., IV.6.10, *PL* 42, 0895. "Refertur autem ad illam rationem simpli ad duplum, ubi est coaptationis maxima consonantia."

76 *De Trin.* IV.4.7–6.10. Gerhart Ladner notes that this sort of numerology was widespread outside of a biblical context and suggests that Augustine may have been influenced by Varro here. See Ladner, *The Idea of Reform*, p. 217.

77 Augustine, *De Trin.* XV.7.2.

78 *De Trin.* XIII.9.12.

79 Ibid., XIII.10.13, *PL* 42, 1023. "ut istum modum quo nos per Mediatorem Dei et hominum hominum Jesum Deus liberare dignatur, asseramus bonum et divinae congruum dignitati."

80 *De Trin.* XIII.11.15, *PL* 42, 1025. "Omnia ergo simul et Pater et Filius et amborum Spiritus pariter et concorditer operantur . . ." As usual, however, Augustine does not remain within one technical vocabulary, using a variety of synonyms for "fittingness."

81 *De Trin.* XV.14.18, *PL* 42, 1028. "Numquid isto jure aequissimo diabolus vinceretur, si potentia Christus cum illo agere, non justitia voluisset? Sed post posuit quod potato, ut prius ageret quod oportuit."

82 *De Trin.* XIII.10.13, *PL* 42, 1024. "quam ut demonstraretur nobis quanti nos penderet Deus, quantumque diligeret?" See also *De Trin.* IV.13.16–18.

83 Augustine, *De Trin.* XIII.10.13–14; Gal. 5.5; Rom. 5.4–5.

84 *De Trin.* XIII.11.15.

85 Ibid., XIII.14.18. See David B. Hart, "A Gift Exceeding Every Debt: An

Eastern Orthodox Appreciation of Anselm's *Cur Deus Homo*," *Pro Ecclesia* 7, Summer 1998, pp. 333–49.

86 *De Trin.* XIII.11.15. See *De Civ.* XI.24, where Augustine asserts that the only motive of creation was goodness. We will give that a triune explication in terms of Augustine's understanding of the Trinity as love forthwith.

87 See Augustine, *De Civ.* XI.18.

88 *De Trin.* XIII.13.17. Augustine would agree with Balthasar that "to become man is for him, in a most hidden yet very real sense, already humiliation— yes, indeed, as many would say, a deeper humiliation than going to the Cross itself" (*Mysterium Paschale*, p. 23).

89 *De Trin.* XIII.13.17.

90 All of creation but the angels of the heavenly city, that is. I will suggest in subsequent chapters a possible inadequacy in the notion of justice attendant upon Augustine's understanding of hell.

91 Ibid., XIV.18, *PL* 42, 1028: "Solus enim a debito mortis liber est mortuus."

92 The *Carmen Christi* of Phil. 2, and especially 2.8, perhaps helps to frame a crucial distinction between the senses in which we should understand Christ's death: as "necessary" in one sense and pointless in another. "Rather he emptied himself, taking the form of a slave, coming in human likeness and, being found in human form, he humbled himself becoming obedient unto death, *even* death on a cross (Θανάτου δὲ σταροῦ)." The δὲ is the key term. Condescending to human form as the Son of Man means that Jesus' mission in "bearing our evils" necessarily entails becoming a "partaker in our mortality," not as a passive victim whose annihilation appeases the wrath of the Father, but as the active expression of the immutable love and power of the Father extended to the point of our ultimate estrangement from that power. "I have power to lay down my life, and I have power to take it again. No man taketh it from me, but I lay down my life that I might take it again" (Jn 10.17, 18; *De Trin.* IV.13.16; see also XIII.14.18). This active, donative character of Christ's kenosis is crucial, both ontologically and as a historical matter. Augustine lays great stress on the fact that Jesus gives his life "unindebtedly" (*indebite*). This is of course crucial to the assertion of Jesus' innocence, an integral factor in the *iustitia* which defeats the devil (*De Trin.* XIII.15.19). The ontological implications of this assertion confirm this point. For to say that Jesus' kenosis is an active, immutable donation is to say that it is not reactive. It does not celebrate a prior evil as the occasion of its exercise, and thus does not inadvertently rationalize the animosity of Jesus' persecutors' by converting it into a dialectical moment in the generation of a higher synthesis. Henri de Lubac indirectly supports this position by showing that, for Augustine, the *gratia Christi* would have been necessary for Adam even if he had not sinned, though a prelapsarian cross is unintelligible. "[I]t does not lead us further, but comes to seek us further away—and farther down" (Henri de Lubac, SJ, *Augustinianism and Modern Theology*, trans. Lancelot Sheppard [New York: Crossroads, 2000], pp. 48–9).

In this sense it becomes necessary to insist on the seemingly contradictory propositions that Christ's death was in equally profound senses both necessary *and* pointless: he was obedient unto death, insofar as the full gift of God to fallen humanity entails, by definition, God's entering into our death with us. Yet it was *even* death on a cross, an emphasis denoting a pointless death occasioned by the ultimate in human disorder and privation. This ultimacy is evidenced in the panoply of witnesses, whose presence signifies that "all of humanity's representatives, considered theologically, are integrated from the outset into guilty responsibility for Jesus' death" (Balthasar, *Mysterium Paschale*,

p. 114). It is only in view of the utterly active and donative character of the first point that we can assert the second, and it is this unique character of Christ's sacrifice, derived from the fact that Christ is uniquely priest, victim and recipient, that separates the Christian sacrifice from those pagan sacrifices and the cult of heroic glory which receive such scorn in *De Civ.*, and which do celebrate a prior evil insofar as they redound to the power of the empire and enjoin sacrifice for the sake of imperial glory.

On the problem of the celebration of a prior evil which results in a simulacrum of virtue, see Augustine, *Conf.* III.2; *De Civ.* IV. 15; XIX.7. See also, John Milbank, *The Word Made Strange* (Oxford: Blackwell, 1997), pp. 219–32; Hanby, "Democracy and its Demons," forthcoming in John Doody, Kevin Hughes, and Kim Paffenroth (eds), *Augustine and Politics* (Lanham, MD: Rowman and Littlefield, 2003). My understanding of the sense in which Christ's death is necessary is indebted to von Balthasar, *Mysterium Paschale*, pp. 11–83. However, it departs from him somewhat on the sense in which the crucifixion might be termed "accidental" (54).

93 *De Trin.* XI.9.16, *PL* 42, 0996: "Ubique tamen voluntas non apparet, nisi copulatrix quasi parentis et prolis."
94 Luke 23.46.
95 Augustine, *De Trin.* I.8.17.
96 Ibid., XIII.15.19–16.20.
97 See Alliez, *Capital Times*, pp. 94–5.
98 Augustine, *De Trin.* VIII.7.10, XIII.5.8.
99 On the *imago dei*, see Augustine, *De Trin.* XIV.12.15. *De Civ.* XII.1, XIII.1 and XIV.1 contain what are perhaps Augustine's clearest statements on the consequences of this deviation. He says of the difference between the blessed and fallen angels in XII.1, "We must believe that the difference had its origin in their wills and desires, the one sort persisting resolutely in that Good which is common to all—which for them is God himself—and his eternity, truth, and love, while the others were delighted rather with their own power, as though they themselves were their own good. Thus they have fallen away from the Supreme Good which is common to all . . ." In the later texts, he associates this with death.
100 Augustine, *De Trin.* IV.10.13.
101 On the mediator of death, see Augustine, *De Trin.* IV.10.13, 12.15–13.18; XIII.13.17. According to O'Donnell, the vices of 1 Jn 2.16 cited throughout the *Conf.*, *concupiscentia*, *curiositas*, and *ambitio saeculi* are the corresponding undoing of the triadic structure of *modus*, *species*, and *ordo*. He suggests, moreover, that Books II, III, and IV of the *Conf.* each roughly correspond to one of these vices. See James J. O'Donnell, *Augustine: Confessions*, Vol. 1, p. xxxv.
102 Augustine, *En Psa.* 127.8.
103 In the same way, it should be said, that they are not "one" in any ordinary sense either.
104 Studer, "Faith and History in Augustine's *De Trinitate*," p. 41.
105 Augustine, *De Trin.* XIII.17.22.
106 Augustine's insistence on the manner in which the damned partake of the *visio dei* confirms this negatively. "For whereas both good and bad shall see the Judge of the quick and the dead, without doubt the bad will not be able to see Him, except after the form in which He is the Son of man; but yet in glory wherein He will judge, not in the lowliness wherein He was judged. But the impious without doubt will not see that form of God in which He is equal to the Father" (Augustine, *De Trin.* I.13.28). Balthasar worries that "those

representations which see in the Cross of Christ a principle that founds, and holds together, the cosmos," might, though "does not necessarily abandon the terrain of Christian theology by making the Cross a 'general symbolic idea'" and the historical event merely the instantiation of a prior universal. That is not the case here; rather the universal and particular are—for us—codetermined. Christ's cross and resurrection are the definitive manifestation of divine glory, yet this manifestation itself presents us with an aporia of recognition that is crucial to Augustine and leads to the conclusion that it is only by the Spirit, and thus through participation in the prior economy of that beauty, that it can be recognized as such, just as any historical event, qua the structure of event, must have some analogical continuity (identity *and* difference) and recourse to formalities transcending the event to be so recognized (Balthasar, *Mysterium Paschale*, pp. 59–60).

107 Augustine, *Serm.* 27.6, cited in Harrison, *Beauty and Revelation*, p. 234.

108 Since the microcosm is a microcosm of charity, it requires a city by definition. Incidentally, this point likewise makes the disordered *mens* a microcosm of the *civitas terrae*.

109 Augustine, *De Trin.* IV.20.27–9; V.14.15–16.17; XV.17.27–9, 26.45–7.

110 Ayres, "The Fundamental Grammar of Augustine's Trinitarian Theology," pp. 51–76; "Remember That You Are Catholic," pp. 40–55. Of this last, see particularly *De Trin.* VII.5.10.

111 Williams, "Sapientia and the Trinity," p. 323. The qualifier "inasmuch" is crucial here as it emerges that our relation to the otherness of God is constitutive of the knowledge we have even of ourselves. As Williams remarks immediately after this point—in a remark which will prove crucial in the next chapter— "There is nothing that can be said of the mind's relation to itself without the mediation of the revelation of God as its creator and lover."

112 Augustine, *De Trin.* XV.6.10; see also VI.5.7. See Williams, "Sapientia and the Trinity," p. 323.

113 Augustine, *De Trin.* VI.10.11, *PL* 42, 0931. "Imago enim si perfecte implet illud cujus imago est, ipsa coaequanter ei . . . In qua imagine speciem nominavit, credo, propter pulchritudinem, ubi jam est tanta congruentia, et prima aequalitas, et prima similitudo, nulla in re dissidens, et nollo modo inaequalis, et nulla ex parte dissimilis, sed ad identidem respondens ei cujus imago est . . ."

114 I shall develop this theme below.

115 The Son's "response" recalls the assertion of II.5.9 that since the Son was sent by a Word, his being sent is constituted as the Son's activity: "His being sent was the work of both the Father and his Word."

116 *De Trin.* VI.1.11, *PL* 42, 0032. "Ille igitur ineffabilis quidam complexus Patris et imaginis non est sine perfruitione, sine charitate, sine gaudio. Ille ergo dilectio, delectatio, felicitas ve beatitudo, is tamen aliqua humana voce digne dicitur, usus ab illo appellatus est breviter, et est in Trinitate Spiritus sanctus, non genitus sed genitoris, genitique suavitas, ingenti largitate atque ubertate perfundens omnes creaturas pro captu earum, ut ordinem suum teneant et locis suis acquiescant." The last remark is reminiscent of the musical ontology of *De Mus.* Commenting upon the co-articulation of time and space within this ontology, Catherine Pickstock writes, "Thus, music, although initiated by the flow [of time] is not primarily a matter of flow 'over against' articulations. On the contrary, it is only constituted as flow by the series of articulations mediated by the silence which allows them to sound together. It is on the basis of this conception that Augustine can make the astonishing assertion at the end of the *De Musica* that the salvation of every creature consists in its being in

its own proper place as well as its time. [*De Mus.* VI.xvii.56.] Both aspects are equally necessary if there is to be a cosmic poem" (Pickstock, "Music: Soul, City and Cosmos after Augustine," p. 249).

117 Augustine, *De Trin.* IX.10.15. I do not intend to suggest that these "grammatical rules," derived from consideration of how we may know, recognize, and love a just man, may be applied univocally to speech about God and creatures. We have repeatedly denied, as has Augustine, that "analogy of proportion" which serves as the basis for such an extension. However, in this case, the extension applies superlatively to God as a consequence of the grammar of simplicity: God's knowledge, love, and delight must be convertible, as Augustine remarks so eloquently in the *Conf.* XIII.16: "Your essence knows and wills immutably, your knowledge is and wills immutably, and your will is and knows immutably."

118 Augustine, *De Trin.* VIII.4.5. It is pertinent to note that Augustine never actually resolves the aporia. Instead he will situate it within the mediation of that *forma* of justice which is both our interior and exterior *magister* in his dual function as *sacramentum* and *exemplum*. (Though as we shall see in both the next section and the ensuing chapter, this very formulation renders the distinction between "inner" and "outer" inherently unstable.) This mediation will deny Augustine a vantage point from which to survey the relation to his origin and thus deny him the vantage from which to resolve the aporia.

119 Augustine, *Conf.* IV.13.20. See also Robert Innes, "Integrating the Self through the Desire of God," *Augustinian Studies*, 28, 1, 1997, p. 93. "*Delight*, concluded Augustine, is the only possible source of action, nothing else can move the will." Innes's footnote 88 elaborates: "*De diversis queastionibus ad Simplicanum* (London: SCM, Library of Christian Classics, 1953), I, qu.ii.21: 'The will can by no means be set in motion unless an object be presented which delights and attracts;' cf. *De spiritu et littera* III.5: 'When the right action and true aim has begun to appear clearly, unless it also be delighted in and loved, there is no doing, no devotion, no good life.'" The dissimilarity between the created similitude and its archetype impose limits to the application both of these rules and of the language of motive. It is of course theologically unintelligible to ask "why" the Father generated the Son as if the eternal filiation were on a par with God's creation of the world. However, it is not inappropriate to employ a different sense of the question "why?": why must we understand it this way?

120 Augustine, *De Trin.* VI.10.12, PL 42, 0932. "In illa enim Trinitate summa origo est rerum omnium, et perfectissima pulchritudo, et beatissima delectatio. Itaque ill atria, et ad se invicem determinari, et in se infinita sunt . . . in illa summa Trinitate tantum est una quantum tres simul, nec plus aliquid sunt duae quam una. Et in se infinita sunt. Ita et singula sunt singulis, et omnia in singulis, et singula in omnibus, et omnia in omnibus, et unum omnia."

121 Augustine, *De Trin.* V.1.2, VI.1.1–8.9. This, in part, is why Augustine insists upon "the impossibility of any formal analogy" (Ayres, "Remember that You are Catholic," p. 63) between the operations of memory intellect and will and the Trinitarian persons that would render the *mens* a mirror for the latter, because in the Trinity "no one person performs a specialized mental act on behalf of all" (Williams, "Sapientia and the Trinity," p. 325). I would contend, however, that Augustine's demonstration makes a discrete delineation of the "specialized mental functions" of memory, intellect, and will equally difficult to sustain in human activity—which seems to be half the point of using the similitude in the first place. See also *De Trin.* XV.12.17.

122 Augustine, *De Trin.* VI.7.9.

123 Aquinas, *ST* I–II, 9. This also implies the procession of the Spirit in the generation of the Son from the Father, but more on that below.

124 We have had comparatively less to say about their convertibility with truth. But such is entailed in the maxim that one must know what one loves and hence in the Son as the intelligible Word of the Father who elicits this love and is intended by it. This entailment is also reflected in the inseparability of memory, intellect and will which renders true knowledge in part a function of right desire and vice versa.

125 Augustine, *De Civ.* X.6. "If then the body, which the soul employs as a subordinate, like a servant or a tool, is a sacrifice, when it is offered to God for good and right employment, how much more does the soul itself become a sacrifice when it offers itself to God, so that it may be kindled by the fire of love and may lose the 'form' of worldly desire, and may be 're-formed' by submission to God as to the unchangeable 'form', thus becoming acceptable to God because of what it has received from his beauty. . . . It immediately follows that the whole redeemed community, that is to say, the congregation and the fellowship of the saints, is offered to God as a universal sacrifice, through the great Priest who offered himself in his suffering for us—so that we might be the body of so great a head—under the form of a servant.'"

126 Augustine, *De Trin.* II.1.3; Jn 5.22, 27, 26, 19. Barnes remarks that it is precisely this distinction which allows Augustine to assert against the homoians the necessary "materiality" of the Son. Barnes, "Exegesis and Polemic," p. 57.

127 Augustine, *De Trin.* II.1.3, *PL* 42, "Restat ergo ut haec ideo dicta sint, quia incommutablis est vita filii sicut Patris, et tamen de est, id est de Patre, et inseparabilis est operatio Patris et Filii, sed tamen ita operari Filio de illo est, de quo ipse est, id est de Patre; et ita videt Filius Patrem, ut quo eum videt hoc ipso sit Filius."

128 Ibid. VIII.8.12.

129 Augustine, *De Trin.* II.1.3, *PL* 42, 0846–847. "Non enim aliud illi est esse de Patre, id est nasci de Patre, quam videre Patrem; aut adiud videre operandem quam pariter operari, non a se, quia non est a se."

130 Augustine, *De Trin.* XV.17.29, 26.47, 27.48.

131 Williams, "Sapientia and the Trinity," p. 327.

132 Augustine, *De Trin.* XV.19.36, *PL* 42, 1085. "Ita enim datur sicut Donum Dei, ut etiam se ipsum det sicut Deus."

133 Augustine, *De Trin.* XV.17.27–9.

134 In a manner that shall prove importantly integral to the articulation of the unfolding of creation within the two natures of Christ, Augustine reverses the typical patristic emphasis on *imago* and *similitudo* and makes the latter the higher term. See R. A. Markus, "'Imago' and 'Similitudo' in Augustine," *Recherches augustiniennes*, 10, 1964, pp. 125–43; Ladner, *The Idea of Reform*, pp. 185–203.

135 Augustine expresses his unease with the use of *personae* in *De Trin.* V.9.10, though there is another sense in which we would wish to say that personhood, insofar as it is thus constituted, is predicated *superlatively* of the divine hypostases and only secondarily of creatures. He states his unease with the language of *substantia*, preferring instead *essentia*, VII.5.10. The importance of this will become clearer in subsequent chapters.

136 Herbert McCabe, OP, *God Matters* (Springfield: Templegate, 1987), p. 221. Recognizing that it is the Son's "prayer to the Father that constitutes him as who he is" (p. 220), and consequently us as who we are, McCabe is following an Augustinian line. See Augustine, *En Psa.* 85.1, "It is one saviour of His body, our Lord Jesus Christ, the Son of God, who both prays in us, and is prayed to

by us. He prays for us, as our Priest; he prays in us, as our Head; He is prayed to by us as our God. Let us therefore recognize in Him our words, and His words in us." Cited in Harrison, *Beauty and Revelation*, p. 227. For another nice account of how this is borne out christologically, see Geoffrey Wainwright, *Doxology: The Praise of God in Worship, Doctrine, and Life* (Oxford: Oxford University Press, 1980), pp. 15–86.

137 The term in *De Trin*. II.1.3 (*PL* 42, 0846–847) is "est nasci" and is treated as synonymous with "est esse de Patre."

138 Augustine, *De Trin*. XV.21.40.

139 Williams, "Sapientia and the Trinity," p. 329.

140 Augustine, *De Trin*. VI.10.11, 12.

141 Ibid. IV.1.2. "And first we have to be persuaded how much God loved us, lest from despair we should not dare to look up at him."

142 This is one of the implications of the *privatio boni*. Its implications will become more prominent in the next section. I am grateful to D. C. Schindler for this way of putting the point; he has helped my thinking immensely here. It also follows from God's impassibility and thus the denial of God's real relation to creatures. The difference internal to God must by definition exceed the difference between God and creation.

143 Balthasar, *Mysterium Paschale*, p. 168. I avoid discussion of the "death of God" controversies that typically surround Balthasar's theology of Holy Saturday, to which this is indebted but not identical. I am attempting to think through both Jesus' death within the context of the Augustinian articulation of trinitarian love in a manner that both takes that death seriously and yet does not compromise the traditional insistence on divine impassibility. One crucial way to do this is to rethink the relation between death and Christ's entry into it, such that a preconceived death predetermines the meaning of Christ's descent into hell less than Christ's activity in dying transfigures the meaning of death in the direction of a kind of activity.

144 See again Ladner's interpretation of Augustinian creation, especially *De Gen. ad Lit*. Ladner, *The Idea of Reform*, pp. 167–85, 212–38.

145 One can see this in *De Trin*. III.2.7–4.9, in Augustine's discussion of the referral of proximate to remote ends. I shall address this more fully forthwith.

146 See Augustine, *De Civ*. X.6.

147 Augustine, *De Trin*. XV.4.6.

148 I qualify this term for the historical reason that the concept had not as yet been codified at the time of *De Trin*.'s composition. It is clearly operative theologically, however.

149 Ayres, "The Christological Context," p. 120.

150 Augustine, *De Trin*. I.6.12; Rom. 11.36.

151 Ibid. I.8.16; Col. 3.3, 4.

152 Ibid. I.1.16; 1 Cor. 13.12. This enigma he understands to mean *in similitudinibus*.

153 One could add the sensible and intelligible as well.

154 Augustine, *De Trin*. XIII.19.24, *PL* 42, 1034. "Scientia ergo nostra Christus est, sapientia quoque nostra idem Christus est. Ipse nobis fidem de rebus temporalibus inserit, ipse de sempiternis exhibet veritatem. Per ipsum pergimus ad ipsum, tendimus per scientiam ad sapientiam: ab uno tamen eodemque Christo non rededimus, *in quo sunt omnes thesauri* sapientiae et scientiae absconditi." This portion of my argument is greatly indebted to Ayres, "The Christological Context," pp. 118–31. Ayres translates "per ipsum pergimus ad ipsum," "through him we travel to him."

155 Augustine, *De Trin*. XV.11.20, 16.21.

156 See Certeau, *The Mystic Fable*, p. 83. Earlier we noted Certeau's distinction between the problematics of the *mysterium* which is that of an action and that of a *sacramentum*, which is that of the sign, tending toward the problem of representation. Our earlier discussion of *signa* in relation to use and the plenitude of charity denies this distinction, or that the problematics of *sacramenta*, of efficacious signs, inevitably conclude in representation.

157 See Augustine, *De Trin.* IV.18.24, for further remarks on the utility of temporal in manifesting things eternal.

158 Augustine, *De Trin.* XI.9.16.

159 Ibid. XI.6.10.

160 Augustine, *De Civ.* X.6.

161 See Ladner, *The Idea of Reform*, pp. 222–39.

162 Ayres, "Remember That You Are Catholic," pp. 58–61. Augustine, *Serm.* 52.23.

163 And this too is evident in the analogy between the ages of man and the days of creation. See Augustine, *De Gen. c. Manich.* I.23.39; Ladner, *The Idea of Reform*, p. 238.

164 Alasdair MacIntyre, apparently following Elizabeth Anscombe, demonstrates the priority of intelligible narrative action, which draws on the linguistic resources of a community, to action as such. The Augustinian entailment of intelligibility in appetibility descending from the inseparability of memory, intellect and will comports with this argument, for it too makes intelligible action logically prior to action as such, making the intelligibility of action dependent upon communal linguistic conventions. It is unsurprising that Augustine's analysis of the wise man's referral of proximate to remote ends, whereby he intends to show that the final end is also the first cause of the wise man's act, comports with MacIntyre's account (Augustine, *De Trin.* III.3.8–4.10). This account relates to our broader semiotics by making the formal elements, the "why" intrinsic to the intelligibility and applicability our term, depend upon the convergence of the *novum* of circumstance with ever new analogical modifications of a kind of civic intentionality. Yet an Augustinian view, following upon Book VIII, sets the intelligibility of the formal elements of the terms within the aporia of the *Meno* and makes that intelligibility dependent upon our ever new participation in that form. Christ as both *sapientia* and *scientia* is thus Augustine's "answer" to the dilemma raised by this aporia. MacIntyre, *After Virtue*, pp. 204–25. Anscombe, *Intention* (Ithaca: Cornell Press, 1957), pp. 35–45.

165 Augustine, *De Lib.* III.23.

166 For more on Christ as *viam* and *patriam*, see Studer, *The Grace of Christ and the Grace of God*, pp. 44–7.

167 Augustine, *De Trin.* XIX.24, *PL* 42, 1033.

168 To this extent, Alliez is right. Time is a distention. Carol Harrison notes (*Beauty and Revelation*, pp. 118–19), "[I]t is not surprising to find that on numerous occasions Creation is itself described by Augustine in terms of linguistic analogies—a fact which further establishes its nature as a 'sign' in his thought. This is most evident when Augustine reflects upon the transient, mutable nature of Creation and its beauty. It, like the words of a sentence or a poem, must pass for 'the whole beauty of things in their temporal sequence to be displayed.' (*De Vera Relig.* 21.41) Thus, Augustine can speak of time not just as something which stands in contrast to, and as inferior to eternity, but of 'time in all the beauty of its changefulness' (*De Vera Relig.* 40) and referring to corporeal beauty, comparing it with the example of a line of poetry, he can write, 'all this is not evil because it is transient. A line of poetry is beautiful in

its own way, though no two syllables can be spoken at the same time, although it consists of successive syllables of which the later ones follow those which had come earlier. In spite of this the verse is beautiful as exhibiting the faint traces of the beauty which the art of poetry keeps steadfastly and unchangeably'" (*De Vera Relig.* 42).

Catherine Pickstock's analysis of the Augustinian construal of creation as a *carmen universalis* and *concordia discors*, wherein time becomes a "moving image of eternity," concurs with Harrison's view. Pickstock, "Music: Soul, City, and Cosmos after Augustine." See also Heninger, *Touches of Sweet Harmony*, pp. 292, 364–90.

169 See Ayres, "The Christological Context," p. 126. Such a view is corroborated by *Conf.* XIII, where Augustine's interpretation of Genesis is ecclesiocentric and rife with eucharistic overtones.

170 Augustine, *De Trin.* XIII.20.25; IV.18.24, 19.25. It is worth noting the phrase "fullness of time" here.

171 It is here that Ayres locates the meaning of the *convenientiae* of the incarnation, that it is "fitting" to our condition, "because we cannot any longer perceive God through those things which were made 'in the Word,' the heavens and the earth (the structure of our incapacity), the Incarnate Christ provides 'smaller' signs and testimonies which will enable us to move to the 'bigger' signs and testimonies (the structure of the Incarnation)" (Ayres, "The Christological Context," p. 125). I do not think that this interpretation and the one I have offered for the function of *convenientiae* are mutually exclusive, and would only amend this remark by noting that to a vision christologically formed, "the heavens and the earth" are indeed for Augustine revelatory. "For not only does the authority of the divine books declare that God is; but the whole nature of the universe itself which surrounds us, and to which we also belong, proclaims that it has a most excellent creator . . ." (*De Trin.* XV.4.6). One could also elaborate on this "fittingness," in Ayres' sense, in terms of a variety of perennial Augustinian themes: the *forma serui, forma dei* pair, the *Christus humilis*, and the *Christus medicus*. However, as Carol Harrison shows, these are not mutually exclusive with the interpretation of *convenientiae* put forth here. See Harrison, *Beauty and Revelation*, pp. 214–24.

172 Augustine, *De Trin.* IV.18.24, 3.6, 10.13. See also Studer, "History and Faith in Augustine's *De Trinitate*," p. 12.

173 Augustine, *De Trin.* IV.3.6, *PL* 42, 0891. "Huic ergo duplae morti nostrae Salvator noster impendit simplam suam: et ad faciendam utramque resuscitationem nostram, in sacramento et exemplo praeposuit et proposuit unam suam. Neque enim fuit peccator aut impius, ut ei tanquam spiritu mortuo in interiore homine renovari opus esset, et tanquam respiiscendo ad vitam justitiae revocari: sed indutus carne mortali, et sola moriens, sola resurgens, ea sola nobis ad utrumque concinuit, cum in ea fieret interioris hominis sacramentum, exterioris exemplum."

174 See Ayres, "The Christological Context," pp. 131–4.

175 Augustine, *De Trin.* IV.1.2, emphasis mine.

176 See Harrison, "The Rhetoric of Scripture and Preaching," in Robert Dodaro and George Lawless (eds), *Augustine and His Critics*, pp. 223–9.

177 Jn 12.32.

178 Ayres, "The Christological Context," p. 133. It remains to be seen in the next chapter, however, how Augustine's construal of "the material" more fully permits this concern to square with materiality's revelatory capacity.

179 Augustine, *En Psa.* 127.8.

180 Augustine, *De Trin.* IV.19.25.

181 Robert Dodaro, "*Sacramentum Christi*: Augustine on the Christology of Pelagius," *Studia Patristica* XXVII, 1991, pp. 274–80 (279).
182 Augustine, *De Trin*. II.2.4.
183 Dodaro, "Sacramentum Christi," p. 277.
184 See Harrison, *Beauty and Revelation*, pp. 83, 101, 211–14. Studer, "History and Faith in Augustine's *De Trinitate*," p. 23.
185 Dodaro, "*Sacramentum Christi*," p. 279.
186 See Harrison, *Beauty and Revelation*, pp. 211–14.
187 Augustine, *Tract. in Jo*. XXXIV.4–5: "That Light which made the sun, was made, I say, under the sun for our sake. Do not despise the cloud of the flesh; with that cloud it is covered, not to be obscured, but to be moderated." *CCSL* XXXVI, 313: "Factum est, inquam propter nos sub sole lumen quod fecit solem. Noli contemnere nubem carnis; nube tegitur, non ut obscuretur, sed ut temperetur."
188 Pickstock, *After Writing*, p. 13.
189 Dodaro, "*Sacramentum Christi*," p. 275.
190 Dodaro, Harrison and Studer each considers in complimentary ways the meanings of these two terms. Harrison summarizes the general possibilities. "One might generalize and refer *exemplum* to Christ's life, acts, and words, and *sacramentum* to a religious mystery, symbol, or sacred rite based upon them." Considering Studer and Couturier, she continues, "Alternatively, they can be interpreted in the context of their literary and exegetical background and use, where *exemplum* would refer broadly to *narratio* and *historia*, and *sacramentum* to *allegoria* and *figura*, the implications of which [are] that temporal and eternal truths are held together in the same text of Scripture, as in the Incarnation" (Harrison, *Beauty and Revelation*, p. 204). It is the last part of this remark that is of most interest here. Adhering to the Augustinian principle (*Conf*. XII.31.42) that truth is polyphonic, I do not wish to deny the exegetical validity of either manner of interpreting these multivalent terms. I interpret them theologically in a manner which does not confine them to the arena of signification, or does so only under the understanding that in Christ sign and signified are one and the signified is itself transcendent generative *caritas*. Hence I would push the sense of *sacramentum* further in the direction of "an effective sign—not simply representing salvation but bringing it about. Again, the gap between sign and referent is saturated through the self-giving of the referent" (Frederick Christian Bauerschmidt, "Aesthetics: The Theological Sublime," in Milbank, Pickstock, and Ward (eds), *Radical Orthodoxy*, pp. 201–19 (212). See also Dodaro, "*Sacramentum Christi*," p. 277 n. 21; Studer, "*Exemplum et Sacramentum*."
191 Markus, "Augustine on Signs," p. 71.
192 Augustine, *De Trin*. XIV.15.21. "Certainly [t]he mind does not remember its own [prelapsarian] blessedness; since that has been, but is not, and it has utterly forgotten it, and therefore cannot even be reminded of it. But it believes what the trustworthy scriptures of its God tell of that blessedness, which were written by his prophet, and tell of the blessedness of Paradise, and hand down to us historical information of that first both good and ill of man."
193 Elizabeth Anscombe, *Intention*, p. 67. The invocation of Anscombe here highlights many questions about the role of "wanting" in action. We will attend to these more in the next chapter, and we can admit a variety of material actions which fall under the grammar of wanting, but suffice it for now that since on Augustinian terms, memory, intellect, and will entail one another, it is wrong headed to think of "desire" or "intention" as something placed before the action, operating like a causal mechanism. Rather it is

already entailed in the descriptions of our practical activity and thus is more like the "form" of action.

194 See F. H. Jacobi, "Jacobi to Fichte," *The Main Philosophical Writings and the Novel Allwill*, trans. George di Giovanni (Montreal: McGill-Queen's University Press, 1994), pp. 498–527 (514): "As surely as I possess reason, just as surely I do not possess with this human reason of mine the perfection of life, not the fullness of the good and the true. And as surely as I do not possess all this with it, and know it, just as surely do I know that there is a higher being, and that I have my origin in Him. My solution, therefore, and that of my reason is not the I, but the 'More than I'! the 'Better than I'!—Someone entirely Other."

195 Thus far we are only considering Christ under the aspect of *exemplum*; this language will require modification when we consider him as *sacramentum*. Nevertheless, there is one place where this construal of *eros* as entailing lack has no application, and that is in the divine Trinity itself. This is obviously because the Son as Image of God "perfectly fills the measure of that of which it is the image" (Augustine, *De Trin.* VI.10.11).

196 Not all "behavior" would qualify as "purposive" in Anscombe's sense. Which is to say, it would not all be susceptible to answering "why?" in the sense that she makes requisite to descriptions of intentional action. We shall see in the next chapter that Augustine's ontology and his concomitant notion of volition entail a much broader conception of the realm of the voluntary than is suggested by Anscombe's formulation. Yet she herself insists that "the possession of sensible discrimination and that of volition are inseparable" (Anscombe, *Intention*, p. 67).

197 The full import of this contention will become clearer in the next chapter when I contrast Augustinian and stoic moral psychology.

198 See Basil Studer, "History and Faith in Augustine's *De Trinitate*," p. 26. Augustine, *De Util. Cred.* 12.26. Perhaps Augustine's use of his mental image of the walls of Alexandria, which he has never seen, could be interpreted to insinuate this point. *De Trin.* IX.6.10–11.

199 See Augustine, *De Vera Relig.* 38.69.

200 Augustine, *De Trin.* X.7.10–10.16.

201 I take this point again, in the next chapter, in regard to what is thought in Augustine to be the "proto-Cartesian" certainty of our own existence. Suffice it for now, however, to say that this certainty is crossed out, at least as being Cartesian, by three factors: a) the role of love, of desiring to know oneself, and therefore faith entailed in the mind's knowledge of itself, b) consequently, the role of christological mediation in all of our knowledge and relations, including those we have to ourselves, and c) the inequality of the object of self-knowledge to itself, that is, the fact that a creature in time is never fully instantiated as a unity. See Augustine, *De Vera Relig.* 60: "No material thing, however beautiful, can possibly achieve the unity it aims it."

202 It is in part this which makes the notion of a *noumenal* freedom unintelligible.

203 Heb. 11.1.

204 I Cor. 13.13. I am grateful to D. C. Schindler for enriching my appreciation of the inadequacy of the traditional antithesis between faith and knowledge and the beatific obsolescence of faith and hope. As Stephen Menn points out, Augustine at various places appears to affirm this contrast. Yet both the logic of his account of attention and of the inter-trinitarian life undermine it, and he himself elaborates a more sophisticated account of the relationship at *De Util. Cred.* 24 (emphasis mine): "What then we understand, we owe to reason, what we believe, to authority, what we have an opinion on, to error. *But*

everyone who understands also believes, and also everyone who has an opinion believes; not everyone one who believes understands; no one who has an opinion understands." *De Civ.* XXII.29, *PL* 41, 0800, speaks of eschatological knowledge, and this must be taken as normative. "It will not be as it is now, when the invisible realities of God are apprehended and observed through the material things of his creation [so much for Augustine's contempt for the sensible!], and are partially apprehended by means of a puzzling reflection in a mirror. Rather in that new age the faith by which we believe, will have a greater reality for us than the appearance of material things which we see with our bodily eyes" ("ubi plus in nobis valet fides qua credimus, quam rerum corporalium species quam per oculos cernimus corporales"). Consequently, precisely because faith works through love and love is implicated in the distance intrinsic to all knowledge, faith is the form of knowledge and does not cease as knowledge is achieved.

205 See also Augustine, *Conf.* I.1.1.
206 Augustine, *Conf.* XI.29.39. On the parallel aporias of *Conf.* and *De Trin.*, see Hanby, "Desire: Augustine beyond Western Subjectivity," in Milbank, Pickstock, and Ward (eds), *Radical Orthodoxy*, pp. 109–26.
207 Augustine, *De Trin.* VIII.6.9, *PL* 42, 0956. "Homo ergo qui creditur justus, ex ea forma et veritate diligitur, quam cernit et intelligit apud se ille qui diligit: ipsa vero forma et veritas non est quomodo aliunde diligatur."
208 Rowan Williams explains this very well. "Love, Augustine proposes, arises from recognition, recognising in something or someone else a pattern (*forma*) of justice or goodness that we already know within ourselves as the source and norm of our own judgment (vi.9); we begin to understand the trinity as we understand love . . . We must be in love with loving, we must desire that there be love, in us and in others. This is what it is to want *justitia* . . . It is thus that caritas or *dilectio* itself provides a model of the trinity. Love loves love—which means that love characteristically loves the act of love or the condition of being in love with something further. We can only love love when it is actually loving (obviously); the love that is loved cannot be an abstract or objectless state, enclosed in itself: caritas therefore implies, in addition to itself as an act and a relation, a loved object and the love that is in that object to make it worthy of love" (Williams, "Sapientia and the Trinity," p. 323).
209 Augustine, *Conf.* IV.13. Hence, as Studer notes, the *fides qua* always entails a temporalizing *fides quae*, in which the universal is manifest in the form of a particular "elect" history, Studer, "Faith and History in Augustine's *De Trinitate*," p. 27.
210 Augustine, *De Trin.* IX.10.15; see also IX.5.8.
211 Gal. 5.6. This passage is of fundamental importance for Augustine, and will become increasingly so in the Pelagian controversy. See *De Trin.* XIII.20.26; XV.18.32.
212 Augustine, *De Trin.* XV.19.36.
213 Ibid., IX.8.12.
214 Ibid., XV.17.31, *PL* 42, 1082. "Spiritus itaque sanctus de quo debit nobis, facit nos in Deo manere, et ipsum in nobis: hoc autem facet dilectio Ipse est igitur Deus dilectio."
215 Ibid. V.16.17.
216 Ibid. VII.6.12, *PL* 42, 0946. "Non enim locorum intervallis, sed similitudine acceditur ad Deum, et dissimilitudine receditur ab eo."
217 Aquinas, *ST* I–I, 3, ad.5.
218 This point should be qualified in light of both the *corpus mixtum* and Augustine's own recollections in the *Conf.* The line distinguishing citizens of the two cities is not simply a line *between* agents, but *within* them.

219 See Augustine, *De Trin*. X.5.7; *Conf*. II.612–14; *De Lib*. III.13–15; *De Civ*. XII.1–9.

220 I shall take on this issue more fully in the next chapter.

221 Williams, "Sapientia and the Trinity," p. 323.

222 Augustine, *De Trin*. XIV.12.15.

223 Ibid. IX.8.12; X.5.7.

224 Ladner, *The Idea of Reform*, p. 279; Brunn, *St Augustine: Being and Nothingness*, pp. 9–34, 49–90.

225 Williams, "Sapientia and the Trinity," p. 326.

226 Augustine, *Conf*. XIII.35.49.

227 Augustine, *De Trin*. IX.7.8. As further confirmation of the "formality" of *fides quae per dilectionem operatur*, Augustine distinguishes at *De Trin*. XV.18.32 between uses of *dilectio* to distinguish Christian faith from the "faith by which 'even the devils believe and tremble.'" Henri de Lubac criticizes this position, arguing that it is a misunderstanding to "understand charity as an inverse concupiscence; as if between heavenly delectation which causes the soul to experience its true happiness, and earthly delectation which produces the illusive pleasures of this world, there were only a difference of object, not of nature." Surely this is to put the matter backward. If concupiscence is privative, then it is an inverse charity and not the reverse. If there is a difference "of nature" it is surely *because* of the difference in objects, one of which completes our nature in union with God, the other of which leads ultimately "to the distraction, dismemberment and collapse of the being which it possesses" precisely because its objects, apart from that union, are nothing. Lubac, *Augustinianism and Modern Theology*, p. 76.

228 Augustine, *De Trin*. XV.18.32. The first phrase is from Gal. 5.6, the second from Rom. 5.5.

229 Augustine, *De Trin*. XV.17.27–31.

230 Ibid. XV.5.7.

231 Ibid. VI.4.7–5.10.

3 CHRISTOLOGY, COSMOLOGY AND THE MECHANICS OF GRACE

Notes to pages 72–105

1 There are mitigated exceptions to this. See, for instance, John Burnaby, *Amor Dei: A Study of the Religion of St Augustine* (London: Hodder and Stoughton, 1938), pp. 158–79.

2 The ironic historical effect of these developments was to elevate the anti-Pelagian Augustine to a place of prominence heretofore unseen in the Middle Ages. See Eric Leland Saak, "The Reception of Augustine in the Later Middle Ages," in Irena Backus (ed.), *The Reception of the Church Fathers in the West: From the Carolingians to the Maurists* (Leiden: E. J. Brill, 1997), Vol. 1, pp. 367–404, and William J. Bouwsma, "The Two Faces of Humanism: Stoicism and Augustinianism in Renaissance Thought," in Heiko A. Oberman and Thomas J. Brady, Jr. (eds), *Itinerarium Italicum: The Profile of the Italian Renaissance in the Mirror of Its European Transformation* (Leiden: E. J. Brill, 1975), pp. 3–60. The former shows the complex heteronomy of origins for the Augustinian Renaissance of the Late Middle Ages, and how these appropriations are often overlain with an Aristotelianism with which it may be incompatible. The latter, though presenting a questionable interpretation of the relationship between Augustinianism and stoicism, does nevertheless show both how the political exigencies of this appropriation, particularly in

its Calvinist guise, require the attribution of a "Pelagian" concept of will to Augustine and how its conception of law and its rejection of "natural" theology are coextensive with the need to secure the autonomy of Geneva. Bouwsma thus echoes this thesis in locating a tension within Renaissance Augustinianism, but he locates that tension at a point virtually opposite the one argued here.

3 Rebecca Harden Weaver, *Divine Grace and Human Agency: A Study of the Semi-Pelagian Controversy* (Macon: Mercer University Press, 1996), p. 31. Emphasis mine. Weaver can phrase the matter this way because she ignores intellectual context, which is Augustine's antecedent *corpus*.

4 See Lubac, *Augustinianism and Modern Theology*, pp. 1–86. These pre-suppositions, which Lubac attributes in different form both to Baius and Jansenius, include the supposition of a "pure nature" and subsequent extrinsicist conception of grace. The result is a form of Augustinianism which is actually Pelagian.

5 "Augustine, *De Trin*. IV.19.12, *PL* 42, 896. "He did not say, I and they are one thing; although, in that He is the head of the church, which is His body, He might have said, I and they are not one thing, but one person, because the head and the body is one Christ . . ." "Non dixit, Ego et ipsi unum; quamvis per id quod Ecclesiae caput est et corpus ejus Ecclesia (Ephes. 1, 22, 23), posset dicere, Ego et ipsi, non unum, sed unus, quia caput et corpus unus est Christus . . ." A similar christological move can be seen in the early (*c*.400) *Ep*. 55.vi, in his treatment of Jesus' cry of dereliction (Ps. 22) from the cross.

6 This view of nature comports with Brunn's analysis of the *magis/minus esse* distinction, wherein to be is finally to love the one whom Ex. 3.14 describes as "He who is." Brunn, *St. Augustine: Being and Nothingness*, p. 41.

7 In claiming that Augustine's response to the Pelagians recapitulates the theology of *De Trin*. I do not intend to reject *tout court* the work of J. Patout Burns and others who restore many of the contours to the Augustinian land-scape and deny "the assumption that [Augustine's] early and later reflections on the efficacy of divine grace are in complete agreement and can be syn-thesized as the elaboration of a fundamental insight" (Burns, *The Development of Augustine's Doctrine of Operative Grace* [Paris: Etudes augustiniennes, 1980], p. 53). This would be to contradict Augustine's own recollection. Yet to concede this much as a *historical* point is not necessarily to concede it as a philosophical and theological point. First, Wittgenstein has forever compli-cated the relation between the "contents" of one's mind at any given point and the diachronic development of one's textual output, and Burns' "genetic" method is inadequate to this complexity. Second, the procedure results in pronouncements so general that they are virtually useless. For instance, he writes of Augustine's alleged conversion from Manicheanism to neoplatonism (p. 18), "Augustine fled this visible, temporal, and corporeal world to take refuge in the newly discovered spiritual realm." This begs a lot of questions. Finally, Burns is complicit in that tendency to confine the search for such "fundamental insights" to the texts dealing explicitly with the issue of grace as modern commentators construe them. The *De Trin*. is neglected despite the obvious repetition of its themes in the anti-Pelagian corpus.

8 But for a few notable exceptions, it is not commonplace to treat the Pelagian controversy primarily as a matter of Christology, and—by extension—trinitarian theology. Among the exceptions, with varying results, are: Robert Dodaro, OSA, "*Sacramentum Christi*: Augustine on the Christology of Pelagius," *Studia Patristica*, XXVII, 1990, pp. 274–80; J. McWilliam Dewart, "The Christology of the Pelagian Controversy," *Studia Patristica*, XVII.3,

1982, pp. 1221–44; and Basile Studer, "Sacramentum et exemplum chez saint Augustin," *Recherches Augustiniennes*, 10, 1975, pp. 88–141. It should be clear, given both the ontological implications and the gnosiological and practical implications of Augustine's Christology, that moral and practical issues, or questions of the grace–nature relationship, cannot be bracketed off from such "ontological" questions as the relationship between creation and the Trinity.

9 Wetzel, *Augustine and the Limits*, pp. 213–17.

10 It is often alleged that Pelagianism is itself an Augustinian invention, and its shelf life has undoubtedly been prolonged by Augustine's attention to it. However, as my concern is ultimately with the transmission and modification of *Augustinian* thought, this claim only reinforces my case.

11 Augustine, *De Nat. et Grat.* 2.2, 3.3, 7.7, 9.10, 40.47, 77.

12 Augustine, *De Praed. Sanct.* 6.II; *De Grat. Christ.* 34.

13 As noted previously, Augustine does not use the words *natura*, *gratia* and even *creatio* univocally. It is true that that these terms sometimes provide Augustine with a needed distinction between the effect of God's gratuity among the elect and among those outside, so that, as a matter of ordinary speech, it appears in talking about creation and about sanctification, or about nature and grace, that we are talking about differences in kind or about different moments in the life of God. However, this distinction should be nuanced by several factors intrinsic to the bulk of Augustine's thought. First, the understanding of these distinctions as marking different "moments" in the divine life is ruled out by God's immutability, and is rather made intelligible by the fact that the activity of the effect *qua* effect is displayed precisely in its activity. Second, the differences in kind are rendered suspect by the ultimate convertibility of *esse* and *beatus* within the *magis* and *minus esse* distinction. The recognition of some sort of specific distinction between the discrete "acts" of creation and sanctification, or between nature and grace, is only possible from the vantage afforded by a perspective which privileges a bare and naked *esse*, or a Cartesian infinite, over the categories of good, beautiful and true. The trinitarianism of the previous chapter rejects this, as do two somewhat opposed points observed by Emilie Zum Brunn: the elision of creation and ecclesiology in the *Conf.* and the continued existence and function of the damned within the economy of beauty and divine justice in *De Lib.* See Brunn, *St. Augustine: Being and Nothingness*, pp. 35–67.

14 Augustine, *De Gest. Pel.* XIV.34.

15 For the grammar governing Augustine's multifarious uses of the *imago dei*, see *De Trin.* VII.6.12.

16 Augustine, *De Grat. Christ.* III.4–4.5; *De Spir. et Lit.* XXX.52.

17 "[O]n the one hand, it is difficult to show that [the doctrines of original sin, the bondage of the will and predestination] were *expressly formulated even* in major Western thinkers like Cyprian or Ambrose and yet it is apparent, on the other hand, that *the state of mind* and *style of thinking* in the West tended to stress the common destiny of all men under sin and was ready to look for divine deliverance, arbitrary, perhaps, yet powerful. At least this is how the 'Pelagians' understood the situation, for both Rufinus the Syrian and Caelestius attacked the notions of hereditary sin and infant damnation before they became a matter of controversy, before they were even fully formulated . . . If there is anything that gives unity and emphasis to the 'Pelagian movement' it is this antagonism to the Western motifs of hereditary sin and infant damnation." Eugene TeSelle, "Rufinus the Syrian, Caelestius, Pelagius: Explorations in the Prehistory of the Pelagian Controversy," *Augustinian Studies*, 3, 1975, pp. 66–7.

18 This insistence reflects the inverse side of the conclusion of the previous chapter, that on Augustinian terms there is no such thing as *mere* mimesis, a conclusion which follows in turn from the convertibility of the transcendentals in God.

19 Eugene TeSelle attributes to Rufinus the Syrian, whom he speculates was a major influence on Caelestius, "an individualist theory of man," according to which it is in each individual's power to resist temptation. Rebecca Harden Weaver concurs and follows Guy de Broglie in recognizing, for Augustine, the priority of collective identity in either of the two Adams. "Moreover," she writes, "even Adam and Christ take on the character of being classes themselves, at least with regard to those persons who are members of each." This "generic" character of Christ comports with my earlier suggestion of how transcendent forms—in this case the form of all forms—are, on an Augustinian construal, mediated by a historical *tradux*. However, as previous criticisms would suggest, Weaver does not permit this point to disturb the anthropology which she brings to her reading of Augustine. TeSelle, "Rufinus the Syrian," p. 72. Weaver, *Divine Grace and Human Agency*, p. 26.

20 Augustine, *De Pecc. Mer. et Rem.* III.1.I

21 Augustine, *Ep. 140*, 37.

22 The first, held at Carthage in 412, involved Pelagius' alleged pupil, the more vociferous Caelestius.

23 For a complete recapitulation of the anathematized propositions, see *De Gest. Pel.* XXXIV.59–63.

24 See, for instance, *De Gest. Pel.* 41, *De Grat. Christ.* II.2; III.11; *Cont. Duas Ep. Pel.* IV.v.11. While it is undoubtedly reasonable to attribute the increasingly *ad hominem* character of Augustine's attacks to rhetorical conventions and to accidental circumstances as they occurred "on the ground," such increasing attribution of viciousness to the Pelagians is philosophically consistent, for, as we have seen, it is intrinsic to an Augustinian philosophy of language that such different linguistic economies as are displayed in the incommensurable uses of the words *natura* and *gratia* will inevitably be attended by different economies of desire. For Augustine, we reproduce our sins in our speculations.

25 Augustine, *De Gest. Pel.* XXXV.61, I Cor. 15.21–2. The attempt to rehabilitate Pelagius' reputation and to discredit Augustine's doctrine of grace has brought much attention to Augustine's exegesis of a similar passage in Rom. 5.12–19, and in particular to the phrase *in quo omnes peccaraverunt*, a poor Latin rendering of the Greek, better translated into English as "*Because* of one man, sin entered the world . . . and thus death came upon all men, *in that* all sinned." For a summary of this debate, and a defense of Augustine's position, see Philip L. Quinn, "Disputing the Augustinian Legacy: John Locke and Jonathan Edwards on Romans 5:12–19," in Gareth B. Matthews (ed.), *The Augustinian Tradition* (Berkeley: University of California Press, 1999), pp. 233–50.

26 This is not to deny a qualitative and doctrinal difference between reason and revelation, but rather to deny that the former is operative in an immanentist field of operation such that the latter can only appear as an intervention of extra rational data from outside. On the origins of this modern conception of revelation, which all too easily serves as an obfuscating grid through which to read Augustinian controversies, see John Montag, SJ, "Revelation: The False Legacy of Suárez," in John Milbank, Catherine Pickstock, and Graham Ward (eds), *Radical Orthodoxy*, pp. 38–63. On the origins of the division of nature and grace, viewed philosophically, see de Lubac. Interestingly, and perhaps

in telling contrast to the Protestant attempt to recruit anti-Pelagian Augustine to underscore the difference between nature and grace, de Lubac cites a tradition of criticism of pre-Thomist Augustinianism, dating back to Albert Magnus, alleging Augustine's *failure* to distinguish sufficiently between nature and grace, the very division he is often thought to have instituted. See Henri de Lubac, *The Mystery of the Supernatural*, trans. Rosemary Sheed (New York: Crossroads Herder, 1998), pp. 19–21.

27 Even Henri de Lubac, who recognized so clearly that Pelagianism is really about the natural and its supernatural consummation, does not sufficiently elaborate this point. See Lubac, *Augustinianism and Modern Theology*, p. 5.

28 Augustine, *De Grat. Christ.* XXI.22.

29 Augustine, *De Civ.* XI.23–4.

30 Aquinas, *ST* I–II, 1, 4.

31 This is exhibited not only positively in the "increase" of God in us (or rather the increase of us to ourselves in God), but also in the idea that sin is a perverse mimesis of the Trinity, wherein the trio of sins of 1 Jn 2.16 are the vicious counterparts to *modus, species*, and *ordo* manifesting our participation in the divine beauty. Augustine, *De Trin.* XI.5.8; *De Lib.* III.25; *Conf.* II.6. See also O'Donnell, *Augustine: Confessions*, Vol. 1, p. xxxv.

32 Rom. 7.24–5; Augustine, *De Gest. Pel.* XXXV.62.

33 Augustine, *De Grat. Christ.* I.2.–II.7; VI.

34 See Burns, *The Development of Augustine's Doctrine of Operative Grace*, pp. 53–9.

35 Rom. 7.24–5.

36 Augustine, *Cont. Duas Ep. Pel.* IV.V.11. The scriptural citations are, in order, 1 Cor 8.1; 2 Cor. 3.6; Rom. 5.5; Rom. 3.31. Emphasis mine. The passage also illustrates a point made previously, that terms shared in common by Augustine and the Pelagians mask incommensurable referents.

37 Augustine, *De Spir. et Lit.* III.5, *PL* 44, 203. "Nos autem dicimus humanam voluntatem sic divinitus adjuvari ad faciendam justitiam, ut praeter quod creatus est homo cum libero arbitrio voluntatis, praeterque doctrinam qua ei praecipitur quemadmodum vivere debeat, accipiat Spiritum sanctum, quo fiat in animo ejus delectatio dilectioq ue summi illius atque incommutabilis boni quod Deus est, etiam nunc cum adhuc per fidem ambulatur, nondum per speciem: ut hac sibi velut arrha data gratuiti muneris inardescat inhaere Creatori, atque inflammetur accedere ad participationem illius veri luminis; ut ex illo ei bene sit, a quo habet ut sit." I have altered the *NPNF* translation on several points, which I think affect the sense of the text in important ways most notably 1) translating the passive participle *faciendam justitiam*, as passive, rather than as the "pursuit of righteousness," 2) translating *praeter* as "beyond" ("more than" would suffice as well) rather than "in addition to" which sounds extrinsicist, and 3) translating *inhaere Creatori* as "inhere in" (lit. "stick into") rather than "cleave to," which is a better match for the concern about *participationem*.

38 This case for the recapitulation of *De Trin.* is underscored a few chapters later in *De Spir. et Lit.* XI.18, where Augustine's equation of piety with θεοσέβια echoes *De Trin.* XII.14.

39 Rom. 5.5. See *De Spir. et Lit.* XXXII.56, *PL* 44, 237: "Postremo haec est fides, quae per dilectionem operatur, non per timorem; non formidando poenam, sed amando justitiam. Unde ergo ista dilectio, id est, charitas per quam fides operatur, nisi unde illam fides ipsa impetravit? Neque enim esset in nobis, quantacumque sit in nobis, nisi diffunderetur in cordibus nostris per Spiritum sanctum, qui datus est nobis. Charitas quippe Dei dicta diffundi in cordibus nostris, non qua nos ipse diligit, sed qua nos facit dilectores suos:

sicut justitia Dei, qua justi ejus munere efficimur; et Domini salus qua nos salvos facit ; et fides Jesu Christi, qua nos fideles facit. Haec est justitia Dei, quam non solum docet per legis praeceptum, verum etiam dat per spiritus donum."

40 Augustine, *De Nat. et Grat.* I.1.

41 Augustine, *De Spir. et Lit.* XXIX.51 altered slightly from the *NPNF*, *PL* 44, 233: "Ex lege timemus Deum, ex fide speramus in Deum: sed timentibus poenam absconditur gratia. Sub quo timore anima laborans, quando concupiscentiam malam non vicerit, nec timor ille quasi custos severus abscesserit; per fidem confugiat ad misericordiam Dei, ut det quod jubet, atque inspirata gratiae suavitate per Spiritum sanctum faciat plus delectare quod praecipit, quam delectat quod impedit. Ita multa multitudo dulcedinis ejus, hoc est, lex fidei, charitas ejus conscripta in cordibus atque diffusa, peficitur sperantibus in eum, ut anima sanata non timore poenae, sed amore justitiae operetur bonum." See also *De Trin.* IV.9.12, *PL* 42, 896: "posset dicere, Ego et ipsi, non unum, sed unus, quia caput et corpus unus est Christus."

42 *De Spir. et Lit.* XXVIII.48; XXXIII.59.

43 Augustine, *De Dono Pers.* VII.14. In the previous chapter we saw two other instances of this understanding, in *De Trin.* IV.9.12 and *En. Psa.* 119.7. See also Studer, *The Grace of Christ and the Grace of God*, pp. 57–8.

44 I intentionally emphasize *body,* in conjunction with Augustine's interpretation of Christ's ecclesial body, to draw attention to possible resonances between the two *social* bodies of either of two Adams, or either of the two mediators discussed in *De Trin.* Given the importance of Christ's social body to Augustine's thought, the "body of this death" could well pertain to the body of the first Adam, adherent to the mediator of death.

45 James Wetzel gives a nice summary of contemporary treatments of this question: *Augustine and the Limits of Virtue* (Cambridge: Cambridge University Press, 1992), pp. 197–234.

46 We have already seen such an approach from Rebecca Harden Weaver. Wetzel faults Eugene TeSelle and John Burnaby on similar counts. Wetzel, *Augustine and the Limits*, pp. 200–1.

47 Weaver's account of the problem fits the first mold; Kant's account of radical evil, offered in deliberate rejection of the *tradux peccati*, fits the second. The underlying problem finds its most poignant articulation in Kant in the antinomy between freedom and causality in the First Critique. The Augustinian text lurking in the background of Kant's doctrine is *De Pecc. Mer. et Rem.* III.7,14. See Emmanuel Kant, *Religion within the Limits of Reason Alone*, trans. Theodore M. Greene and Hoyt H. Hudson (New York: Harper, 1960), pp. 27–39.

48 Wetzel, *Augustine and the Limits*, p. 200.

49 That Augustine does presume the "causal connection" to be inaccessible is evident from *De Trin.* III.10.21. That the reduction of the four forms of Aristotelian causality to efficient causality is characteristically modern is a well-established fact, though I do not intend to suggest that Augustinian causality, as exhibited in the priority of a sound to its melody in *Conf.* XII.29.40, for instance, is identical to the Aristotelian view. See Amos Funkenstein, *Theology and the Scientific Imagination* (Princeton: Princeton University Press, 1986), pp. 35–42. Within stoic immanentism, however, causality is variegated in a different way, owing largely to the manner in which the material *plenum* of the cosmos and the constitution of material coherency by pneumatic tension eclipse Aristotelian *topoi*. See Samuel Sambursky, *Physics of the Stoics* (London: Routledge and Kegan Paul, 1959), pp. 60, 80–97.

50 Lewis Ayres, commenting on Augustine's pre-*De Trin.* theology (Ep. 11) concludes, "Augustine's governing concern is to defend and explain the doctrine of the inseparable operation of the three persons. This he has inherited as a fundamental axiom of Catholic Christianity. *Comprehending* this doctrine is interwoven with comprehending the function of the Incarnation and the nature and purpose of Scripture" (emphasis mine). Ayres, "Remember that You are Catholic," p. 55. That the comprehension of this doctrine is a christological problem will prove to be quite germane to the question at issue in the battle with the Pelagians.

51 Harrison, *Beauty and Revelation*, pp. 3–53, 140–91, 230; Zum Brunn, *St. Augustine: Being and Nothingness*, pp. 9–36; Ladner, *The Idea of Reform*, pp. 167–85.

52 Much of the historical confusion and ensuing ontological disarray surrounding the relation of grace to nature has a two-fold conceptual root in 1) the failure to consider the profound implications of creation *ex nihilo* for the construal of the form/matter–space/time relationship, and 2) inattention to theological grammar which makes it appear as if "creation" and "sanctification" were names which referred to two different "processes" in God and not to two different ways of speaking about what must, in God, be simple. Though Augustine's doctrine is clear, it is less clear that his grammar was always immune from the latter mistake.

53 Useful here perhaps is the distinction which Graham White employs to distinguish Ockham's anti-Pelagian concerns from Luther's. Noting Ockham's concern to protect divine immutability, White distinguishes between an "ontological anti-Pelagianism" and a "pragmatic anti-Pelagianism." This distinction probably does justice to the preoccupations dividing Augustine and Pelagius, as it does Ockham and Luther, and I concur with White to a point that ontological anti-Pelagianism can in principle countenance a morality which is similar to its opponents. To a point, for while we will see in Chapter 3 that Augustine and his later "semi-Pelagian" opponents can in fact endorse similar practices, certain ascetic acts for instance, I will maintain that Augustine's ontological anti-Pelagianism does in fact promote a somewhat different practice, with charity at its center. Finally, the usefulness of White's distinction shouldn't be overstated: Ockham's God differs from Augustine's in that his will is not even constrained by the formality of his own good nature—though more on this in Chapter 4. See Graham White, "Pelagianisms," *Viator: Medieval and Renaissance Studies*, 20, 1989, pp. 233–54.

54 Augustine, *Conf.* XII.15. "Will you claim that those things are false which Truth with a strong voice speaks in my inner ear concerning the true eternity of the creator,that his substance is in nowise changed by time, and his will is not outside his substance? For this reason he does not will this, now that, but once and all at once, and forever he wills all that he wills. It is not again and again, now these things, now those. He does not will later on what he once willed against, nor does he will against what he previously willed to do. Such a will is immutable and no mutable thing is eternal. But our God is eternal."

55 I formulate this as a matter of how creation can be understood, as an intentional reference to the inadequacy of our composite way of speaking so as to follow Aquinas' cautions in *ST* I–I, 13. That these same cautions are generally Augustinian I take to be entailed in Augustine's treatment of the terms used to designate perfections and of substantive and relative predication in *De Trin.* V.9.10–16.17. However, despite this attention to theological "grammar," and despite my use of the term "regulative principle" to describe the doctrine of divine simplicity, I do not intend to uphold a rigorous distinction, as do

Nicholas Lash and George Lindbeck, between reference and description or description and regulation. Proper qualifications are of course in order, since God is not an object of description. But inasmuch as the distinction *may* suggest a Kantian split between the noumenal and phenomenal, the distinction is problematic. If indeed language is already a participation in the "object of description," the sense/reference distinction ceases to be adequate, and God's indescribability comes to be correlated to his plenitudinous excess to our language, not to the transcendental conditions of our reception. This does not rise to a charge against Lash and Lindbeck, but to a concern. To enter more fully into this argument would take us too far afield. See, Nicholas Lash, *The Beginning and End of Religion* (Cambridge: Cambridge University Press, 1996), pp. 132–6; George Lindbeck, *The Nature of Doctrine: Religion and Theology in a Postliberal Age* (Philadelphia: The Westminster Press, 1984), pp. 104–8. I am indebted here to John Milbank's argument. See Milbank, "A Critique of the Theology of Right," *The Word Made Strange: Theology, Language, Culture* (London: Blackwell, 1997), pp. 7–35.

56 Augustine, *Conf.* XII.7.7; XIII.2.2–3.
57 Augustine, *Cont. Jul.* I.7.34–46; V.16.59; VII.26.53. Contemporary commentators who see Manichean residue in Augustine's two cities or his doctrine of election fail to grasp this point. See, for example, Elizabeth Clark, "Vitiated Seeds and Holy Vessels: Augustine's Manichean Past," in Karen L. King (ed.), *Images of the Feminine in Gnosticism* (Philadelphia: Fortress Press, 1988), pp. 367–401.
58 Augustine, *Cont. Jul.* III.2. Augustine employs the same formal argument in *De Civ.* IV.15 and XIX.6 to decry the secret celebration of evil in Roman "justice," even mockingly suggesting that "foreign injustice" be elevated to the Roman pantheon since she is so instrumental to the success of the empire. Inasmuch as the Roman celebration is bound up with the civic cult of glory, the point indicates the different economies of sacrifice which distinguish the heavenly and earthly cities.
59 I am indebted to David B. Hart for this point.
60 Ayres, "Remember that You are Catholic," p. 66.
61 I distinguish between creation and causality to indicate the irreducible character of newness and the inaccessibility of the power which brings it about, not to imply that there is a "simple" causality that is somehow transparent. Indeed, I would insist that no genuine effect, that is, no genuine *novum* (which is always individuated and temporally singular), is reducible to its causes, be they formal, efficient or material, and therefore there is no simple cause which does not entail the mystery of creation. I would insist, in other words, that causality apart from creation is inherently flawed. By contrast, to insist upon creation is to doubly insist first upon the irreducibility of effects to causes and therefore upon the inherently mysterious character of effects, and, secondly, that the failure to recognize this point is ultimately the failure to admit any genuine novelty and, therefore, anything actually genuine. Only the insistence upon creation, therefore, finally prevents our mastery over the effects, and an objectification of those effects which reduces them ultimately to death.
62 Augustine, *Conf.* XI.5.–17.9. I prefer the formulation "other" to time to such phrasings as "outside" of time because the latter has a transcendental ring to it which runs afoul of the logic of transcendence. As we have seen, that logic destabilizes the demarcation of such borders as inside and outside. Precisely as transcendent, God is at once most immanent *and* most extrinsic to creation.
63 Ibid. XII.6.

64 Augustine, *De Vera Relig.* XX.40. See also Ladner, *The Idea of Reform*, pp. 202–22; Pickstock, "Music: Soul, City and Cosmos after Augustine." Carol Harrison reminds us that "Time, which can distract from eternity, Ladner observes, can also, when understood as an affection or activity of the soul turned towards God, be an occasion for righting one's intention toward it; it can be a context in which man strives for reformation. He quotes *Conf.* XI.29. 'Not then according to a distention (*distentionem*) but according to an intention (*intentionem*), do I follow thee to the prize of a supernal vocation.'" Insofar as this suggests that Augustine conceives of time merely as an activity of the soul it needs further qualifications, not least by her own positive recognition of the ontological "aesthetics" of time's harmonic flow but most fundamentally by the christological determination of the time/eternity relationship. Still, against the backdrop of Augustine's "musical" ontology, where soul and matter are proportional intensifications of created *esse*, and where *magis esse* is contingent upon the soul's participation in the mind of God such that being finally is convertible with knowing and loving, it is quite possible to speak of time as an "activity of soul" after all without the subjectivistic implications it would carry for a post-Cartesian habit of mind. Harrison, *Beauty and Revelation*, p. 187; Ladner, *The Idea of Reform*, pp. 222–39, 263–83.
65 See also, Augustine, *De Trin.* IV.3.6; Studer, "History and Faith in Augustine's *De Trinitate*," pp. 35–50.
66 Though again, the relationship is not mutual. The positive ratio of time to eternity does not constitute a real relationship of eternity to time.
67 "The mutability of mutable things is itself a capacity for all the forms in which mutable things are changed" (Augustine, *Conf.* XII.6). That "a certain mutability" is not of necessity opposed to that which is immutable is evidenced by the fact that the spiritual heaven of heaven, "which is always adapted to behold your face and never turned away from it," nevertheless has a certain mutability. (Ibid. XII.15.)
68 The language characterizing *capacitas formae* as a "formless substrate" is Wayne Hankey's, following Derrida, and it is one of those features of Augustine's thought (along with the soul and the *mens*) which, he alleges, a "postmodern Augustinian" cannot countenance. While this essay has no aspirations to lay hold of the "postmodern" label, it can countenance this aspect of Augustinian thought, though for reasons that are currently emerging it would contest Hankey's characterization of it. See Hankey, "Re-Christianizing Augustine Postmodern Style: Readings by Jacques Derrida, Robert Dodaro, Jean-Luc Marion, Rowan Williams, Lewis Ayres, and John Milbank," *Animus*, 2, 1997. Online. Available: http://www.mun.ca/animus/1997/vol2hankey1.ht, para. 77.
69 Augustine, *Conf.* XII.6.
70 Augustine, *De Nat. Bon.* XVIII, *CSEL* XXV.vi.ii, 862: "nec ista ergo hyle malum dicenda est, quae non per aliquam speciem sentiri, sed per omnimodam speciei priuationem cogitari uix potest. Habet enim et ipsa capacitatem formarum; nam si capere impositam ab artifice formam non posset, nec materies utique diceretur, porro si bonum aliquod est forma, unde quia, ea praeualent, formosi appellantur, sicut a specie speciosi, procul dubio bonum aliquid est etiam capacitas formae; sicut quia bonum est sapientia, nemo dubitat, quod bonum sit capacem esse sapientiae. et quia omne bonum a deo, neminem oportet dubitare etiam istam if qua est, materiem non esse nisi a deo." Harrison, *Beauty and Revelation*, p. 100 n. 22, cites *De Vera Relig.* XI.21.

71 Augustine, *De Nat. Bon.* XVIII.
72 Harrison, *Beauty and Revelation*, p. 41.
73 This is the case not only in *De Trin.* but in *De Civ.* XI.24: goodness the end, the goodness the principle, goodness the motive and movement. *CCSL* XLCIII, 343–4. "Pater quippe intellegitur Verbi, qui dixit ut fiat; quod autem illo dicente factum est, procul dubio per Verbum factum est; in eo uero quod dicitur: Vidit Deus, quia bonum est, satis significatur Deum nulla necessitate, nulla suae cuiusquam utilitatis indigentia, sed sola bonitate fecisse quod factum est, id est, quia bonum est; quod ideo postea quam factum est dicitur, ut res, quae facta est, congruere bonitati, propter quam facta est, indicetur."
74 Ladner, *The Idea of Reform*, p. 184; Harrison, *Beauty and Revelation*, pp. 178–9.
75 Augustine, *Conf.* XIII.33. "Out of nothing they have been made by you, not out of yourself, not out of anything not your own, or which previously existed, but out of concreated matter, that is, out of matter simultaneously created by you, since without any interval of time you gave form to its formlessness."
76 Ibid. XIII.33.
77 Nor is it patient of another contrast which Hankey imposes, between the historical and the ahistorical. The intelligibility of this contrast presupposes an answer, not provided by Hankey, to a prior Augustinian question: *quid est tempus*? And as we have already discussed, his christology is definitive for the answer. Hankey, "Re-Christianizing Augustine: Postmodern Style."
78 Augustine, *De Mus.* VI.11.29.
79 Augustine, *Conf.* IV.4–10.
80 Hankey, "Stephen Menn's Cartesian Augustine: Metaphysical and Ahistorically Modern," *Animus*, 3, 1998. Online. Available: http://www.mun.ca/animus/ 1998 vol3/hankey3.ht, para. 39. Rowan Williams recognizes no ahistorical retreat from the sensible in Augustine, and Wayne Hankey excoriates him for it, contending that Williams therefore "condemns all humans to an eternal Hell by the necessity of their own nature." We may ask whether or not it is Hankey's Augustine who ironically risks such condemnation. For Hankey seems willing to sacrifice, like unruly *simulacra* which fall outside the imposition of form, that part of nature which falls outside the redeemed aspect of this dualism, forgetting that the name above all others which Christians give to intellectual union with the divine is Jesus Christ and that the final manifestation of that "self-completeness which is the whole point of Augustine's *itinerarium*" (para. 576) is the resurrection of the body. That these Christian commitments might fundamentally transfigure Augustine's neoplatonic or "proto-Cartesian" holdings seems unthinkable to either Hankey or Menn. Yet in the anti-Porphyrian polemic of *De Trin.* IV, Augustine rejects the philosophers' competence to pronounce on the resurrection, belonging as it does to the *succesio saeculorum*. Moreover, we come to discover in Book XV that it is *only* through faith in the resurrection, through the double operation of the *exemplum* and *sacramentum* of Christ, and thus only *through* the *succesio saeculorum*, that contemplation can be secured. Failure to attend well to things temporal makes us unfit to take hold of things eternal, and *sapientia* severed from *scientia* turns out not really to have been *sapientia* after all. See Augustine, *De Trin.* IV.14.18–18.24; XIII.9.12–10.13, 16.21.
    See Studer, "History and Faith in Augustine's *De Trinitate*," pp. 12–13, 44. See also, Edmund Hill's introductory essay to *De Trin.* IV. Edmund Hill, OP, (ed.), *The Trinity* (Brooklyn: New City Press, 1991), pp. 149–50. It is significant that Augustine's assault occurs from within an account of how Christ's single harmonizes our double.
81 See, for instance, *Conf.* X.6, wherein the beauty of the sensible triggers

Augustine's love and memory so as to manifest its creator iconically, yet in such a way as to point beyond itself. The problem here is not the sensible, but its use. "But men can ask questions, so that they may clearly see the invisible things of God, 'being understood by the things that are made.' However, through love of such things they become subject to them, and in subjection they cannot pass judgment on them." In this same vein, it is also worthwhile to contrast Augustine's comments on his response to the death of Nebridius ("O madness that knows not how to love men as men!" IV.7) to the death of Monica (IX.12–13). Each involves the grief that necessarily attends our attachment to sensible goods which can be lost, but he cannot counsel stoic apathy toward these goods, else "there would really be something wrong with our life" (De Civ. XIV.9). His reflections on the former prefigure his reaction to the latter, in which he arguably displays an "appropriate" attachment to his mother, though the "lot of our earthly condition," that grief must come to us, is still regrettable (Conf. IX.12). "Blessed is the man that loves Thee O God, and his friend in Thee, and his enemy for Thee. For he alone loses no one that is dear to him, if all are dear in God, who is never lost" (Conf. IV.9.).

82 Augustine, Conf. XI.29.
83 I suggest that it is within this aesthetic context that the lesser trinities of De Trin. should be situated.
84 Augustine, Conf. IV.10.
85 Ibid. X.17; X.8.
86 Augustine, De Trin. XV.27.49. See Studer, "History and Faith in Augustine's De Trinitate," p. 34.
87 Of course it is important to understand that the movement from this capacity, as a self movement, is such inasmuch as it is a divine movement. In other words, it is important not to slip back into an active/passive dualism when conceiving of the hyle's activity.
88 See Augustine, De Civ. XXII.29.
89 Hankey himself seems close to sniffing out this conclusion, "Re-Christianizing Augustine Postmodern Style," para. 77. Matter's "idealism" before form can be explicated in a manner analogous to the triune explication of good as both motive, principle, and end, or first and final cause of action. And I would even suggest that this explication could be correlated to Augustine's understanding of the modus, species, and ordo of form in trinitarian terms.
90 Augustine, De Vera Relig. XI.21 (CCSL XXXII, 201). "Habet aliquam speciem, sine qua corpus non est corpus." See also De Trin. IV.1.3. This is particularly evident at the conclusion of De Civ., as the harmony between soul and body instituted at the origin of creation comes to fruition in the resurrection. (De Civ. XXII.24 claims that these harmonies are present, but largely invisible throughout.) If resurrection, as the consummation of creation, is definitive for natures who suffer under the burden of lack in this life, resurrection conditions should be telling for an Augustinian conception of those natures. Here the notion of an ideal matter that undermines the sensible/intelligible dualism is evident. "Now the philosophers maintain that 'intelligible' things are seen by the mind's vision, and 'sensible' things are apprehended by the bodily senses, whereas the mind, they say, cannot observe intelligible things by means of the body, nor material things by its own unaided activity. If correct, this would entail the certainty that God cannot be seen at all by the eyes of the body, even a spiritual body. But in fact this reasoning is shown up as ridiculous both by reason itself and by the authority of the prophets . . . For such reason it is possible, it is indeed most probable, that we shall then see the physical bodies of the new heaven and the new earth in such a fashion as to

observe God in utter clarity and distinctness, seeing him present everywhere and governing the whole material scheme of things by means of the bodies we shall then inhabit and the bodies we shall see wherever we turn our eyes . . . God will then be seen by those eyes in virtue of their possession of something of an intellectual quality . . ." (*De Civ.* XXII.29).

91 Zum Brunn, *St. Augustine: Being and Nothingness*, pp. 55–6. For Augustine, the fate of materiality, both in its fall and decay and in its resurrection, is dependent upon the ultimate objects of one's worship. Brunn writes further, "We can ask ourselves if the extreme coherence of Augustine's thought concerning this has been sufficiently appreciated in Christian circles, if its depth and realism have been perceived—as they should be in an age which gives such importance to psychosomatic medicine. It seems that this extreme coherence has been scarcely noticed, due to the mistrust of the Platonic aspect of Augustine's doctrine, for it has been understood as a dualism of body and soul, whereas Augustine considers them deeply united, expressing this through an ontological monism. From his anagogical point of view, Augustine worried less about defining the body–soul relation on an anthropological level than about expressing the spiritual bond that connects or should connect them." See also *De Trin.* IV.3.5.

92 See Augustine, *De Trin.* III.4.9. "quid mirum si etiam in creatura coeli and terrae, maris et aeris, facit Deus quae vult sensibilia atque visibilia, ad se ipsum in eis, sicut oportere ipse novit, significandum et demonstrandum . . ."

93 Alliez, *Capital Times*, p. 80. It is obvious that Alliez is still trapped within the dualism of active and passive. Alliez is so close and yet so exactly wrong when, citing Feuerbach (*The Essence of Christianity*, p. 150), he contends that "'for them [Christians] the material posited by their subjectivity, represented subjective matter also as primary matter—much more important than real sensible matter,' which is soon reduced to the pure and simple state of material to be worked on." Rather, matter is already 'idealized' by its participation in an *esse* which is not thought prior to the transcendentals true, good, and beautiful. Only outside this conception could a "prime matter," related to the infinite merely by a + or – sign, be thought, and, consequently, reduced. It is this view, which still possesses Alliez, that foreshadows the Cartesian dualism between the *res extensa* abstracted from its formal qualities to a sheer quantum and the life of the mind devoid of extension.

94 Augustine, *Conf.* XI.31.

95 Hence causality itself becomes "simply the relation of dependence in the effect with respect to the cause." See Burrell, *Aquinas: God and Action* (Notre Dame: Notre Dame Press, 1979), pp. 132–4.

96 Though Cassian, Prosper and Cyril of Alexandria would all attack him as a Pelagian, Nestorius formally condemned Pelagianism and adhered to the anti-Pelagian consensus on original sin. Still, Nestorius provided comfort to Julian, Celestius and other Pelagian exiles, until their expulsion from Constantinople in 429. And Lionel Wickham admits a possible connection between Pelagianism and Nestorianism "at the level of ideas abstracted from the minds which speak them." He also notes its relatively small splash in the East, lending credence to the notion that it was less offensive to an "Eastern" frame of mind. See Wickham, "Pelagianism in the East," in Rowan Williams (ed.), *The Making of Orthodoxy: Essays in Honour of Henry Chadwick* (Cambridge: Cambridge University Press, 1989), pp. 200–13.

97 "ac per hoc quid habeat, et quid accipiat, Dei est: accipere autem et habere utique accipientis et habentis est." Augustine, *De Spir. et Lit.* XXXIV.60, *PL* 44, 240.

98 Augustine, *Conf.* XIII.1.
99 Aquinas, *ST* I–I, 1, 1–7.
100 Augustine, *De Grat. Christ.* XIV.15.
101 Augustine, *Conf.* XII.20.
102 Ibid. XIII.34.
103 Ibid. IV.9. "No one loses thee unless he goes from Thee; and in going from Thee where does he go or where does he flee save from Thee to Thee—from God well-pleased to God angered?"
104 Ibid. IV.7, "For my God was not yet you but the error and vain fantasy I held. When I tried to rest my burden upon that, it fell as through emptiness and was once more heavy upon me; and I remained to myself a place of unhappiness, in which I could not yet abide, yet from which I could not depart." See Brunn, *St. Augustine: Being and Nothingness*, pp. 69–77.
105 See Augustine, *Cont. Duas Ep. Pel.* II.II.3–4; *De Nat. et Grat.* 2.2, 3.3, 7.7, 9.10, 40.47, 77.
106 Dodaro, "*Sacramentum Christi*: Augustine on the Christology of Pelagius," p. 276. James Wetzel notes a certain equivocation on Augustine's part about what precisely *cognitio legis* could mean before and after grace, but it is not decisive. Wetzel, *Augustine and the Limits*, pp. 176–87.
107 It should be reiterated that I find the chief utility of these predicates to consist in the way they help think the generation and procession of the trinitarian *personae*, not the reverse.
108 In concurrence, Robert Dodaro observes that "Looked at theologically, [Augustine's] opponents' proposals about human freedom risked restricting the scope for divine freedom; in this case, the gratuity with which God acts in assuming a human being and uniting it with the Word. To presume that it was a result of his human merits that Jesus lived justly, suggests for Augustine a 'two sons' Christology. His occasional references to anti-Pelagian themes in many of his later Christological discussions signal that Augustine saw implications for the nature–grace relationship in his more mature understanding of the unity of the natures in Christ . . . It is this anticipation of a later, Chalcedonian doctrine which led Augustine to register a cautious, somewhat muted disapproval of Pelagian Christology." Dodaro, "*Sacramentum Christi*," p. 280. My only dispute with Dodaro's remark is with the suggestion that Augustine's opposition to Pelagian Christology was "somewhat muted."
109 Ayres, "The Christological Context of Augustine's *De Trinitate* XIII," p. 118.
110 Wetzel, *Augustine and the Limits*, p. 183.
111 As Wetzel notes (*Augustine and the Limits*, p. 121), whether and to what extent Augustine's reduction works as a fair representation of pagan beatitude is beside the point here; though I shall say more on this subject.
112 Pelagius isn't the first to do so, though the controversy would bear his name. Caelestius was more instrumental in igniting the original controversy, and Pelagius himself was apparently a devotee of Rufinus the Syrian. Though Rufinus' profession of faith was criticized in *De Pecc. Mer. et Rem.* and subsequently viewed with some suspicion in the West, he was never anathematized and is revered by the East. It was apparently Caelestius' refusal to recant the condemned propositions noted above which brought the controversy to a boil. This doesn't make the stoic debts of Pelagius' and Rufinus' position any less problematic, but it leads to a different characterization of that position as one which had not yet come under the discipline of Augustine's critique of pagan virtue. See Eugene TeSelle, *Augustine the Theologian* (New York: Herder and Herder, 1970), pp. 278–94.
113 See Gilson, *The Christian Philosophy of Saint Augustine*, trans. L. E. M. Lynch

(New York: Random House, 1960), pp. 135, 162; Wetzel, *Augustine and the Limits*, pp. 7–8, emphasis mine. The opposition to Menn will prove important in the final chapter. "Augustine's language is confusing here, since he uses 'voluntas' sometimes for the faculty or power of will or free will, and sometimes for particular desires or volitions. Although texts of Augustine . . . did a great deal to form the notion of the faculty of will (in which it is important that a single power can underlie contrary acts), he does not observe a consistent terminology for will" (Menn, *Descartes and Augustine*, p. 204, n. 52).

114 We will address this question with respect to predestination in Chapter 4.

115 Wetzel, *Augustine and the Limits*, pp. 138–60.

116 For instance Charles Kahn writes of Aristotelian *boulesis* that "It seems that there is no corresponding possibility for *boulesis* to deviate from whatever goal one's reason judges to be good." See Kahn, "Discovering the Will: From Aristotle to Augustine," in John Dillon and A. A. Long (eds), *The Question of Eclecticism: Studies in Later Greek Philosophy* (Berkeley: University of California Press, 1988), p. 239. MacIntyre would seem to concur for the Aristotelian tradition, recognizing *akrasia* to betray, at some point, a misstep in the sort of *phronesis* reconstructible retrospectively through the so-called practical syllogism. See MacIntyre, *Whose Justice? Which Rationality?* (Notre Dame: Notre Dame Press, 1988), pp. 124–45.

117 Albrecht Dihle, *The Theory of Will in Classical Antiquity* (Berkeley: University of California Press, 1982), p. 20. Kahn does a bit more to complicate the development from ancient to modern conceptions. Kahn, "Discovering the Will," pp. 234–8.

118 Hence I contest Charles Kahn's choice of words when he writes univocally of Chrysippus, Augustine, Aquinas, and Descartes, "Every voluntary action involves this *moment* of assent . . ." (emphasis mine). While I do not dispute the presence of such a concept in Augustine, this remark pays insufficient attention to his construal of time and his doctrine of grace. As Wetzel points out (though not against Kahn), it is just such a discrete "moment" that is missing from Augustine's recollection of his own conversion. "The means of conversion never change operation in [Augustine's] thought without also displacing the moment of human entry into grace . . . Those who come to the scene of their conversion expecting to encounter God for the first time arrive too late" (Wetzel, *Augustine and the Limits*, pp. 190–1). See also Kahn, "Discovering the Will," p. 247.

119 Studer, "History and Faith in Augustine's *De Trinitate*," p. 22. "When Augustine stresses the importance of the will for faith, he never asserts in a clear way that the assent itself is constituted by an act of will. Of course for Augustine, the will is engaged in every aspect of human activity. One must will in order to see, to remember, to think, to love and even to believe." The importance of this observation will emerge shortly.

120 "But suppose that our desires are all drawn towards a singular object of attraction. In that case choice disappears in our single-minded love for the beloved. There is no possibility of choice here, because alternative objects of attraction cannot be motivated. Nevertheless our power to will remains intact in the purity of our love" (Wetzel, *Augustine and the Limits*, p. 198).

121 That it is always God, or something idolatrously taken as God, which supremely attracts us, and is supremely attractive, I shall discuss more fully below.

122 In Book IX the argument moves rather abruptly from a critique of the stoic view of the passions, through a discussion of the relationship of pagan gods, demons, and their worshippers, to its climactic contention for Christ as mediator. Similarly, in Book XIX, the argument passes from a critique of

pagan virtue and happiness to an "ontological" critique of pagan justice and Roman politics to issue in the conclusion that the misconstrual of beatitude as virtuous *apatheia* causes the pagans to misunderstand the ontological status of happiness and, conversely, that their faulty ontology, their bad theology, has caused them finally to misunderstand even virtue itself.

123 Marcia Colish, *The Stoic Tradition from Antiquity to the Early Middle Ages II: Stoicism in Christian Latin Thought through the Sixth Century* (Leiden: E. J. Brill, 1990), pp. 223–4; Wetzel, *Augustine and the Limits*, pp. 98–111.

124 Augustine, *De Civ.* XIV.6. See also *De Trin.* IV, proem. 1. On *voluntates* as "forms of will," and similarly, on "spirit" and "flesh" as two kinds of desirous attachment, see Babcock, "Augustine on Sin and Moral Agency," *Journal of Religious Ethics,* 16, 1988, pp. 28–55.

125 Augustine, *De Civ.* IX.4

126 Ibid. XIX.4

127 Wetzel, *Augustine and the Limits*, p. 108.

128 Augustine, *De Civ.* XIX.4.

129 See Augustine, *De Civ.* IV.15; XIX.6; *Conf.* III.2. Milbank, "Can Morality Be Christian?," p. 221. Wetzel (*Augustine and the Limits*, p. 50) suggests that Augustine's knowledge of Aristotle's ethics was mediated by stoicism. And while Aristotle's definition of virtue as a mean *might* be susceptible, as Milbank contends elsewhere, to the Augustinian criticism of virtue's internal division (though one can think of ways to extricate him from this charge), I think it probable that Aristotelian friendship, as appropriated and modified by Aquinas, extricates Christian virtue from the Nietzschean charge that virtue is "reactive." Aquinas, *ST* I–II, 4, 8. See Milbank, *Theology and Social Theory: Beyond Secular Reason* (Oxford: Blackwell, 1990), pp. 326–67.

130 Wetzel, *Augustine and the Limits*, p. 106.

131 Brad Inwood, *Ethics and Human Action in Early Stoicism* (Oxford: Clarendon Press, 1985), pp. 43–101. Charlotte Stough, "Stoic Determinism and Moral Responsibility," in John Rist (ed.), *The Stoics* (Berkeley: University of California, Press, 1978), pp. 203–31; A. C. Lloyd, "Emotion and Decision in Stoic Psychology," in Rist (ed.), *The Stoics*, pp. 233–46; Justin Gosling, "The Stoics and ἀκρασία," *Apeiron*, XX.2, 1987, pp. 179–202; Kahn, "Discovering the Will: From Aristotle to Augustine," pp. 234–59; Neal W. Gilbert, "The Concept of Will in Early Latin Philosophy," *Journal of the History of Philosophy*, 1, 1963, pp. 17–35; Martha Nussbaum, "The Stoics on the Extirpation of the Passions," *Apeiron*, XXII.3, 1989, pp. 128–76.

132 Gosling, "The Stoics and ἀκρασία," pp. 180–4.

133 Ibid., pp. 184–5, 195, 199. Augustine does show a deft touch on this point at *De Civ.* XIV.8. Wetzel notes that "except in his more hyperbolic moments, Augustine does not equate the Stoic ideal of *apatheia* with insensitivity. Even should sages fail to experience disruptive emotions (*perturbationes*) that afflict those whose reason deviates from wisdom, he would suppose them nevertheless to have affections corresponding to their perfected state of reason. Augustine refers to these affections by the Greek term *eupatheiai*, and by Cicero's Latin coinage, *constantiae*. The Latin term especially suggests the stability of an emotional life under rational control, one where right reason has excluded irrational passions and brought about a state of *apatheia*, fixity and tranquility of mind. In terms of the fundamental forms of will or affection, the Stoics will preserve three in the transformation from error and ignorance to the beatitude of wisdom. Wisdom turns desire into resolve, delight into well-being, fear into reserve. There is no analogue for grief. No sage could ever experience a diminution of beatitude and still have the

credentials of a sage. Grief is not amenable to beatific transformation" (Wetzel, *Augustine and the Limits*, p. 102). See also Colish, *The Stoic Tradition II*, pp. 221–5.

134 Studer, "History and Faith in Augustine's *De Trinitate*," p. 22. For Augustine on the "intentionality of sensation," see *De Trin.* XI.2.3–5. See also Harrison, *Beauty and Revelation*, p. 155.

135 Wetzel, *Augustine and the Limits*, p. 100; Augustine, *De Civ.* IX.5.

136 Wetzel, *Augustine and the Limits*, p. 110.

137 Gosling notes this breach in a number of sources including Seneca (*de Ira* I.16.7 = SVF 1.215) and Aulus Gellius (*NA* XIX.i.14–21) reporting Epictetus. See Gosling, "The Stoics and ἀκρασία," p. 184.

138 Augustine, *De Civ.* XIX.4.

139 Gosling's reconstruction seems to repeat this gesture.

140 This will soon become clear in the case of the Pelagians, and, in Chapter 5, of Descartes.

141 See Wetzel, *Augustine and the Limits*, pp. 219–35, for a discussion on how Augustine dissociates freedom and choice and the stumbling block that has created for his modern interpreters. See especially p. 220: "[A]ugustine never identified free will with freedom from constraint. The latter he generally referred to as *liberum arbitrium*, and we have *liberum arbitrium* by virtue of being able to act on desire. Compulsory action (as in involuntary sin), blindly sinful action (as in voluntary sin), and virtuous action (as under grace) all express *liberum arbitrium*. Only the last, however, expresses free will." See also, Burnaby, *Amor Dei*, p. 227; Gilson, *The Christian Philosophy of St Augustine*, pp. 323–4 n. 85.

142 Involuntary sin, in short, is the postlapsarian condition of human agency (exemplified in *Conf.* VIII) wherein we are compelled internally, by the force of habit, to desire and to act upon what we often know to be contrary to the good; it is expressed in the oft-cited division between spirit and flesh, taken as two contrary forms of desire. Wetzel, *Augustine and the Limits*, pp. 88–98; Malcolm A. Alflatt, "The Development of the Idea of Involuntary Sin in St. Augustine," *Revue des études augustiniennes*, 2, 1974, pp. 113–34; "The Responsibility for Involuntary Sin in St Augustine," *Recherches augustiniennes*, 10, 1975, pp. 171–86.

143 Augustine, *De Spir. et Lit.* XXXI.53. The translation is from Wetzel, *Augustine and the Limits*, p. 204. Wetzel continues, "Augustine does not claim that it is impossible for someone to act unwillingly (*nolens* or *inuitus*). Forced willing (*cogi velle*), as opposed to unwilling action, is incoherent. To force willing is to eliminate it altogether . . ."

144 "Internal" and "external" here should not be read as somehow attempting to draw a circumference around the soul in such a way as to extract an unmediated and self-certain self-presence and identity. We have contended all along that the mediation by the object of desire radically exteriorizes our interiority. Rather these terms should be understood to accord with our use of them in the previous chapters, to denote "ownership" of one's actions within "the voluntary" as it is articulated here.

145 By saying that we can be hopeful of grace, I do not intend to give the impression that the question "am I saved?" and the search for signs to that effect is an Augustinian concern. This is Luther's anxiety, not Augustine's.

146 Wetzel, *Augustine and the Limits*, p. 101. One should note a measure of diversity between early stoics like Zeno and later figures such as Chrysippus. And it does appear that between the two there occurred a major shift in moral psychology, which would make the latter more akin to the position that would

be held by Augustine. Still, the shift itself highlights the aptness of the criticism. Neal Gilbert writes, "Chrysippus recognized that there was an element of intellectual judgment involved even in our passions. Our first reactions to fearful or emotionally charged sense-impressions are mere bodily changes that are caused by external events. These are not in our control, even if we happen to be wise men. But then 'we' take over, so to speak, and the resulting judgments, incorporating both intellectual and emotive elements, are 'in our control.' For example, the decision of the intellect ('*dianoia*') that 'money is worth striving for' would be regarded by Chrysippus as a kind of assent. Such assents would combine factual judgments, value judgments, and decisions to pursue or avoid certain objects. It is easy to see why a Stoic 'naturalist' like Chrysippus would be attracted to such an analysis; it made it possible for him to argue that the pursuit of objects endorsed by reason was completely 'according to nature.' But, having surrendered the sharp dichotomy established by Zeno between reason and passions, he was no longer able to explain the fool's emotions as due simply to 'weak assent' or to loss of control by reason" (Gilbert, "The Concept of Will in Early Latin Philosophy," p. 23).

147 Augustine, *De Trin.* IX.10.15. "A word . . . is knowledge together with love."
148 Ibid. XIV.12,15.
149 Importantly, as we saw in the previous chapter, these remarks occur within Augustine's account of the christological unity of *scientia* and *sapientia*. Augustine, *De Trin.* XIII.4.7–6.9.
150 This corrective will only be complete when we've returned to Augustine's Christology.
151 Wetzel, *Augustine and the Limits*, p. 216. Augustine's reflection on the pear tree incident in *Conf.* II forms the backdrop to this remark. Wetzel picks up on Augustine's insistence that there was no motive for his theft. Viewed under the aspect of a redeemed memory, former sins lose their intelligibility, and Augustine is "left with the mystery of unmotivated evil" (p. 213), which must remain a mystery precisely because there could be no true good motivating his action. Evil, for Augustine, is absurd—hence his difficulty in giving a rational account of its origin; his commitments preclude it. Wetzel explains the connection to freedom this way. "Involuntary sin is a form of unfreedom because in it our desires are at odds with one another, and the conflict prevents our motives from fully rationalizing our actions. There always remains a part of us that moves against what has moved us to act. Our actions fail, in such circumstances, to be fully attributable to us, and in that we lack free will. Voluntary sin is a form of unfreedom because in it our motives once again fail to rationalize our actions, not because our motives conflict, but because they fail to correspond to an intelligible representation of the good. We can recognize having experienced this sort of unfreedom only in retrospect, from the perspective of involuntary sin. Grace moves us from voluntary sin to involuntary sin to voluntary adherence to good. To say that it does so of necessity (the doctrine of predestination) is simply to say that knowledge of the good is fully and finally motivating" (Wetzel, *Augustine and the Limits*, p. 217).
152 See Elizabeth Anscombe, *Intention* (Ithaca: Cornell Press, 1957); Eric D'Arcy, *Human Acts* (Oxford: Oxford University Press, 1963).
153 For instance, Stanley Hauerwas writes, in distinguishing proper human actions from cause–effect events that "[I]t is impossible to describe any volition or act of will except in terms of what it is thought to have caused. For example, it is not possible for me to explain my 'will' to move a pen in order to write without the notion of my will to move my pen. My willing as such cannot

be the cause of the movement of my pen since the reference to the pen's movement is involved in my very description of my willing. My 'will' is, therefore, not contingently related to my act but a logical property of it; thus appeal to a will (or a motive or intention) as an explanation of my action cannot take the form of a cause and effect description." He later delineates motives and intentions *as forms of description* by suggesting that the former are traditionally thought of as "'in order to' or 'for the sake of'" explanations and the latter as "backward-looking or 'because of' explanations," though the point is that neither can be *explanations* in the requisite cause–effect sense at all but rather that each must be understood to be logically *entailed* in and *embodied within* our actions. Hauerwas, *Character and the Christian Life: A Study in Theological Ethics* (San Antonio: Trinity University Press, 1985), pp. 24, 106–14. Though Augustine doesn't consider the question in exactly these terms, I take Augustine's "moral psychology" to comport with this conclusion on three grounds: first, his "trinitarian psychology" causes desire to be entailed in knowledge, will to be entailed in intellect, and the formal element, the purposive "why" to inform material, indicative descriptions—and vice versa; secondly, this makes desire more the form of action than its efficient or mechanical cause; finally, his whole conception of action falls within the *aporia* of the *Meno*, and requires the mediation of infused grace to "break" the circle—or, rather, locates his action within the circular "causality" of the giving of grace.

154 On the distinction in *De Trin.* X.5.7 between knowing/being aware of oneself (*nosse*) and thinking of oneself (*cogitare*), see Rowan Williams, "The Paradoxes of Self-Knowledge in the De Trinitate," in J. Lienhard, SJ, E. Muller and R. Teske (eds), *Collectanea Augustiniana: Augustine Presbyter Factus Sum* (New York: Peter Lang, 1993), p. 129.

155 Augustine, *De Trin.* XIV.11.14.

156 It would follow from this, and from our previous discussions of language and the *De Doct.* would be necessary in order to sustain certain sorts of narratives and descriptions.

157 This is assuming that we can still speak intelligibly of "mental contents." I don't intend to elide motive and intention, and it would be intrinsic to the widened scope of Augustine's voluntary and to the account of involuntary sin that there be a distinction here. In *De Spir. et Lit.* XXI.53 Augustine distinguishes between voluntary action (*voluntate*), unwilling (*nolens*) action, and the notion of being forced to will (*cogi velle*). As the latter is incoherent for not being able to account for the subject's movement, the former must be seen to have its source in our desires. Hence "Augustine would not then be contradicting himself to claim that a saint sometimes sinned both unwillingly (*nolens*) and voluntarily (*voluntate*)" (Wetzel, *Augustine and the Limits*, p. 205). Hence, while it may be true that every intention has a motive that can be expressed in the form of "for the sake of," it would follow from Augustine's understanding of involuntary sin that while every motive still has its source in desires which embody our judgments, not every motive expresses an intention and answers the question "why?" in the sense required by Anscombe. Still, it can be argued that Anscombe's critique is purchased in part by her assimilation of "desire" to just the sort of psychological phenomenon whose ascription she refuses to "'intention," and it is precisely this, so I would maintain, that Augustinian desire does not do. I would rather contend that "desire," on Augustinian terms, is more like the "form" of action, including the action of asking the question "why" to which the answer "I intend this" has a certain application. Anscombe, *Intention*, p. 6.

158 Wetzel, *Augustine and the Limits*, p. 214.

159 MacIntyre, *After Virtue*, pp. 204–25.

160 "To have a past is not only to admit grief into wisdom but it is to face the inevitability of involuntary sin" (Wetzel, *Augustine and the Limits*, p. 109).

161 See, for instance, Michel Foucault, "The Battle for Chastity," in Philippe Ariès and André Béjin (eds), *Western Sexuality: Practice and Precepts in Past and Present Times* (Oxford: Blackwell, 1985), pp. 14–25.

162 Wetzel, *Augustine and the Limits*, pp. 138–60.

163 Augustine, *Conf.* X.17. See also X.2, 5, 16.

164 Ibid. X.2, 4.

165 "The more that the content of moral self-knowledge reveals itself to be instable on account of the ongoing nature of conversion that this self-knowledge requires, the more instable the assurance of the metaphysical 'self' in Augustine. The 'self' that he can posit, situate, is both there and is not there. It exists in what he knows of himself in the revealing love of God which he has experienced in the moment of 'self' *revelatio*, in the act of loving and being loved, in a recollection which is also a presence, a real presence, a pardoning, reconciling presence. But it cannot exist as an abstraction of that experience, for it is an experience which, if clung to, reveals itself to be illusion, to be pride" (Dodaro, "Loose Canons: Augustine and Derrida on Themselves," delivered at the Villanova Colloquium on Religion and Postmodernity, cited by Hankey, "Re-Christianizing Augustine Post Modern Style," para. 25–32).

166 See Robert Innes, "Integrating the Self through the Desire for God," *Augustinian Studies* 28.1, 1997, pp. 67–109. Innes's article contains some excellent insights, but would be much improved if he lost the concern to make Augustine relevant to modern psychology, a concern which seems to cause some category mistakes. See also Wetzel, *Augustine and the Limits*, pp. 17–37. On the nature and function of self knowledge and the inequality of self to self, see Williams, "The Paradoxes of Self-Knowledge in the *De Trinitate*," pp. 121–34; Lewis Ayres, "The Discipline of Self-knowledge in Augustine's *De Trinitate* Book X," in Ayres (ed.), *The Passionate Intellect: Essays on the Transformation of Classical Traditions Presented to Professor I. G. Kidd* (New Brunswick: Transaction Publishers, 1995), pp. 261–96.

167 Since, however, this recovery is constituted doxologically and is ecstatic, there is a positive sense in which the recovered self will still not be constituted as a strict identity of the self with itself. The beatified soul may indeed be simple, as it attains to the perfection of divine unity and recovers of itself that lost to time and memory (See Innes, "Integration through Desire," p. 83), but it will still be an ecstatic, effusive triunity. See also Coles, *Self/Power/Other*, pp. 14–53.

168 Augustine, *De Civ.* X.6. It is important to observe that the question for Augustine is not mediation or no, but rather "*whose* mediation?" Arguably the Mediator of Death in *De Trin.* IV fulfills an important function for Augustine; unfortunately it would take us too far afield to consider it in detail here.

169 Coles, *Self/Power/Other*, p. 58.

170 One could speculate, likewise, as to the different function of the specifically Christian virtue of "humility" within the two systems. David Meconi links its importance (and in contrast to the neoplatonists, a specifically Christian aspect) to one's coming to recognize the dependence implied in the "downward participation" of the incarnation. (And this could be refracted through the *exemplum/sacramentum* pair). In other words, it conforms to the account of the recovery of oneself through doxology. One can speculate that

in the tradition of Christian stoicism humility functions, as it will for Cassian in the next section, in an abnegation of the self which only serves negatively to establish its identity with itself, whereas for Augustine, it serves to remove precisely this pretense. David Vincent Meconi, SJ, "The Incarnation and the Role of Participation in St Augustine's *Confessions*," *Augustinian Studies*, 29.2, 1998, pp. 61–75.

171 Recall from our discussion of *De Trin.* and of the formal and material elements of our terms an important point intrinsic to the very idea of incorporating a *ratio* into the passions: that intelligibility and appetibility mutually entail one another. The fact that something desirable appears as an *X* already exhibits the indivisibility of this relationship: the intelligibility of X as *X* already entails a judgment; the fact that it appears already embodies a passion. Hence to say that it is "judged" desirable is not to delineate the appetible and intelligible aspects of this judgment into two moves detachable into cause and effect. Insofar as the Stoics modern interpreters are correct to insist that such an understanding was intrinsic to the stoic theory of moral action, it's a laudable discovery. However, the question that emerges from the dilemma forced on the stoics by Augustine is whether this recognition can be sustained within the context of their ontology.

172 Augustine, *De Div. Q. ad Simplic.* II.21. "Igitur non volentis, neque currentis, sed miserentis est Dei: quandoquidem nec velle nec currere, nisi eo movente atque excitante, poterimus."

173 Augustine, *De Trin.* III.3.8; XIII.5.8.

174 Augustine, *De Civ.* IX.4.

175 Aquinas, *ST* I-II, 27, 4.

176 Of course Augustine, like Aquinas, assumes that we intend the last end—successfully or not—in all our actions: "formally," as a consequence of our being created in the image and likeness of God whose name is charity, "materially", as citizens of an order of love, of either of the two cities (and sometimes both) which is both an anterior and posterior condition of possibility for the referral of end upon end. See *De Civ.* XIX.12; *De Trin.* I.8.17; XIII.4.7; *De Lib.* III.8.

177 Carol Harrison, *Beauty and Revelation*, p. 52, citing Augustine, *De Div. Q. ad Simplic*. 21: "When we are delighted by things which lead to God, therefore, this is not, Augustine observes, due to our works or reason but 'to the inspiration of God and the grace he bestows.' In this context, Augustine gives delight a central role in directing man's will, for as he writes, 'the will itself can have no motive unless something presents itself to delight and stir the mind. That this should happen,' he adds, 'is not in any man's power.'"

178 Augustine, *De Praed. Sanct.* VIII.10.

179 For more on the importance of beauty as a motive and the essentially erotic structure of action see also Harrison, "The Rhetoric of Scripture and Preaching: Classical Decadence or Christian Aesthetic?" in Robert Dodaro and George Lawless (eds), *Augustine and His Critics*, pp. 214–30.

180 Augustine, *En Psa.* 102.1.4, "The Church herself is Confession and beauty. First confession, then beauty; confession of sins, beauty of good works." Ibid. 108.6, "His Bride, His beautiful one, but by Him made beautiful; ugly before because of sin, after forgiveness and grace, beautiful." See Harrison, *Beauty and Revelation*, pp. 230–8.

181 Augustine, *De Trin.* I.8.17, *PL* 42, 831: "Haec enim nobis contemplatio promittur actionum omnium finis atque aeterna perfectio gaudiorum."

182 Such is the example of the episode of the pear tree in *Conf.* II.4.9ff, which under the description afforded by a higher desire is revealed to be a pristine

example of that "deficient causality" of *De Civ.* XII.6–8 and *De Lib.* III.17–18. For an excellent discussion of this, see Wetzel, *Augustine and the Limits*, pp. 206–18.

183 See Jose Oroz Reta, "The Role of Divine Attraction in Conversion according to St Augustine," in F. X. Martin and J. A. Richmond (eds), *From Augustine to Eruigena: Essays on Christianity and Neo-Platonism in Honor of John O'Meara* (Washington: Catholic University Press, 1991), pp. 155–67.

184 Wetzel, *Augustine and the Limits*, p. 216.

185 Of course we have discussed in the previous chapter and mentioned in this one that this referral of ends requires a historical body, a *civitas*, for its conclusion. The fact that Pelagian teaching undermines the importance of baptism should be registered as further evidence of this breach.

186 Augustine, *De Spir. et Lit.* III.5.

187 Augustine, *Cont. Duas Ep. Pel.* IV.5.11. See also Dodaro, "*Sacramentum Christi*," p. 276.

188 Augustine, *Tract. in Jo.* 26.4, cited in Harrison, "The Rhetoric of Scripture and Preaching," p. 224. Harrison assembles a number of Augustinian passages, in addition to those cited here, to illustrate the point. For further commentary on this passage, see Reta, "The Role of Divine Attraction in Conversion," pp. 158ff.

189 Wetzel, *Augustine and the Limits*, p. 191. It should be noted that it is just such a discrete moment of choice which is missing from Augustine's description of his own conversion. He writes, "Those who come to the scene of their conversion expecting to encounter God for the first time come too late."

190 This is not to say that there is, on the Augustinian view, no spontaneity or possibility. On the contrary, it is intrinsic to the conception of causality and creation elaborated previously that it is precisely in the spontaneity of action, and not in a Pelagian first–then schema, that the causality of grace is manifest. Nor does the doctrine of election or predestination minimize possibility. Augustine's assertion that Christ is, in a sense, predestination itself, should serve to contextualize the entire discussion of predestination within the ontology of the Logos. From here, *possibilitas* has to be conceived in a way perhaps better articulated by the Thomists: *possibilitas* names, from God's side, God's knowledge, in his *Logos*, of all the ways in which creatures can be related to him virtually and actually. From the side of the creature it names our coming to discover and realize this relation in its actuality. The *Conf.* can be read as an attempt at precisely this endeavor. See Augustine, *De Dono Pers.* XXIII.67; *De Praed. Sanct.* XV.31.

191 Alasdair MacIntyre, *Three Rival Versions of Moral Inquiry* (Notre Dame: Notre Dame Press, 1990), p. 187.

192 Discipleship for Pelagians consists quite precisely in imitation, and, as I argued in *Radical Orthodoxy*, a Nestorian logic, a point similarly recognized by John Cassian. For Augustine, by contrast, Christ is both our knowledge pertaining to the infinity of temporal things and the Wisdom of things eternal.

193 This is not of course to place a caesura between the act done well from grace and what law enjoins. It is to say rather, that within an Augustinian psychology, "duty," like the pagan virtues, would already testify to a division within desire that makes the act done in accordance with law already a violation if it. See Augustine, *De Spir. et Lit.* VIII.13

194 Augustine, *De Praed. Sanct.* II.3.

195 Augustine, *De Trin.* XIII.19.24.

4 THE SUBTLE TRIUMPH OF PELAGIANISM
Notes to pages 106–33

1 See Colish, *The Stoic Tradition*, p. 115.
2 Mathisen has contended, and Markus appears to concur, that there were no significant Pelagian inroads into France, that the impact of heresies generally on the theology of the monasteries was minimal, and that Augustine's teachings on grace were received against a general backdrop of affection and respect: in short, that the emphasis on "Semi-Pelagianism" is anachronistic and overstated. If this is true it strengthens my case, insofar as it primarily concerns transformations of Augustine effected through his reception. Ralph Mathisen, *Ecclesial Factionalism and Religious Controversy in Fifth Century Gaul* (Washington: Catholic University Press, 1989), pp. xi, 41, 265; R. A. Markus, *The End of Ancient Christianity* (Cambridge: Cambridge University Press, 1990), pp. 178–9; "The Legacy of Pelagius: Orthodoxy, Heresy, and Conciliation," in Rowan Williams (ed.), *The Making of Orthodoxy* (Cambridge: Cambridge University Press, 1989), pp. 214–34.
3 See Boniface Ramsey, OP, "John Cassian: Student of Augustine," *Cistercian Studies Quarterly*, 28, 1993, pp. 5–15.
4 Ralph Mathisen relegates Cassian's move to a merely polemical and rhetorical convention proper to the time. I, however, have suggested that Pelagian and Nestorian mechanics share similar logics. See Hanby, "Augustine beyond Western Subjectivity," in Milbank, Pickstock, and Ward (eds), *Radical Orthodoxy*, pp. 109–26 (120); Mathisen, *Ecclesial Factionalism and Religious Controversy*, pp. 122–40.
5 Markus, *The End of Ancient Christianity*, pp. 177–9. This thesis is bound up with issues surrounding the dating of the *Collationes* that do not immediately concern this essay except insofar as Cassian's possible anti-Pelagian bent signals his attempt to assert an economy of grace. Markus's thesis is a rejoinder to Owen Chadwick, whose later than traditional dating for the composition of *Conf.* XIII skirts a central problem in viewing Cassian's work as an attack on Augustine: that the traditional dating, *c*.426, places the composition of Cassian's *Conf.* XIII before that of Augustine's *De correptione et gratia*. See Chadwick, "Euladius of Arles," *Journal of Theological Studies*, 46, 1945, pp. 200–5. For a review of the dating controversy, see Rebecca Harden Weaver, *Divine Grace and Human Agency: A Study of the Semi-Pelagian Controversy* (Macon: Mercer University Press, 1996), pp. 93–7.
6 D. J. Macqueen, "John Cassian and Grace and Free Will, with Particular Reference to *Institutio* XII and *Collatio* XIII," *Recherches de théologie ancienne et médiévale*, 44, 1977, pp. 5–28. Peter Munz, "John Cassian," *The Journal of Ecclesiastical History*, 11, 1960, pp. 1–22.
7 Munz sees this more clearly and, though he asserts that "Cassian was as sensitive of the need for grace as any Christian writer," he is indeed less inclined than Macqueen to try to synthesize the two positions. Munz, "John Cassian," p. 15.
8 Boniface Ramsey, translator and critical commentator of Cassian's Conferences, concurs with this assessment. See his introduction in John Cassian, *John Cassian: The Conferences*, trans. Boniface Ramsey, OP (New York: Paulist Press, 1997), pp. 1–31.
9 On these influences and the dawning recognition that the Augustinian and Gallican intellectual and practical contexts were incommensurable, see Weaver, *Divine Grace and Human Agency*, pp. 71–88, 106–16; Markus, *The End of Ancient Christianity*, pp. 157–77; Munz, "John Cassian," pp. 15–22; Philip

Rousseau, "Cassian, Contemplation, and the Coenobitic Life," *Journal of Ecclesiastical History*, XXVI, 2, 1975, pp. 113–26.

10 Incommensurability theses have been prominent in philosophy of science since T. S Kuhn's *The Structure of Scientific Revolutions*. A nice summary (though a less than adequate proposal) can be found in Richard J. Bernstein, *Beyond Objectivism and Relativism: Science Hermeneutics and Praxis* (Philadelphia: University of Pennsylvania Press, 1983), pp. 51–108. As MacIntyre points out, incommensurability, while it might entail terms in a language for which there are no translational equivalents in a second language, is not prima facie an incommensurability of *meaning*. Rather incommensurability occurs when there are no common rules for adjudicating between diverse claims and thus insufficient commonality for real disagreement. Incommensurability, then, is first irreconcilability over problems and standards. In adjudicating between Cassian and Augustine, I am obviously adopting a problem and a correlative set of standards: whether the conception of human action sustains a trinitarian economy and christological mediation. Absent such a conception, one could expect Augustine to be received according to problems and standards not statable from an Augustinian viewpoint. See MacIntyre, *Whose Justice? Which Rationality?* (Notre Dame: Notre Dame Press, 1988), pp. 349–88.

11 This is in contrast to Weaver who writes "In effect, Cassian refused to make the choice that Augustine had tried to force: either grace or free will." Weaver demonstrates quite a remarkable failure to come to grips with the depths of Augustine's understanding of gift, and his consequent understanding that free-will is constituted precisely as grace. That she likewise fails to see that it is Cassian who gives the appearance of forcing this choice is a matter which we will take up in the final section. Weaver, *Divine Grace and Human Agency*, p. 112.

12 Indeed Augustine himself may not have been entirely exempt, which simply illustrates yet again the difficulty of coming to terms with one's own best insights.

13 Michael Lapidge makes clear that the logic of stoic physics makes the belief in creation *ex nihilo* impossible. Furthermore, the close association between stoic physics and stoic ethics, conceived as living in harmony with nature, is made clear by the fact that most early stoics commended the study of physics as a propaedutic to the study of virtue. See Michael Lapidge, "Stoic Cosmology," in John Rist (ed.), *The Stoics* (Berkeley: University of California, 1978), pp. 161–85.

14 For more on the recovery and reintroduction of stoic thought at the inception of modernity, see Louis Dupré, *Passage to Modernity: An Essay in the Hermeneutics of Nature and Culture* (New Haven: Yale University Press, 1993), pp. 120–44; Robert C. Evans, *Jonson, Lipsius and the Politics of Renaissance Stoicism* (Durango: Longwood Academic, 1992); and Mark Morford, *Stoics and Neostoics: Rubens and the Circle of Lipsius* (Princeton: Princeton University Press, 1991); Bouwsma, "The Two Faces of Humanism," pp. 4–60; Anthony Levi, SJ, *French Moralists: The Theory of the Passions 1585 to 1649* (Oxford: Clarendon Press, 1964).

15 See Robert B. Todd, "Monism and Immanence: The Foundations of Stoic Physics," in Rist (ed.) *The Stoics*, pp. 137–59.

16 See, Colish, *The Stoic Tradition*, pp. 144–240, for a sustained attempt to disentangle the stoic influences. See O'Connell, "*De Libero Arbitrio* I: Stoicism Revisited," *Augustinian Studies*, 1, 1970, pp. 49–68. However, O'Connell's interpretation, premised upon presumed changes in Augustine's outlook between composition of the first and third books, compromises the overall

coherence of the work in a manner which is avoidable through greater attention to neglected features of the early book. See also Wetzel, *Augustine and the Limits of Virtue*, pp. 50–5; Neal W. Gilbert, "The Concept of the Will in Early Latin Philosophy," *Journal of the History of Philosophy*, 1, 1963, pp. 30–3.

17 Though Colish (*The Stoic Tradition*, p. 149) is right to insist here that the concept of harmony is a commonplace with both Platonic and Pythagorean versions. See also Augustine, *De Lib*. III.10–18.

18 "Neither the knowledge of God's law, nor nature, nor the mere remission of sins is that grace which is given to us through our Lord Jesus Christ; but it is this very grace which accomplishes the fulfillment of the law, and the liberation of nature, and the removal of the dominion of sin" (Augustine, *De Nat. et Grat*. 27).

19 More accurately, these features help to distinguish the grammatical rules governing how Christians can speak of these "mechanics."

20 Williams, "Sapientia and the Trinity," p. 326.

21 Hanby, "Desire: Augustine beyond Western Subjectivity," pp. 109–26. See also, David Vincent Meconi, SJ, "The Incarnation and the Role of Participation in St. Augustine's Confessions," *Augustinian Studies*, 29, 2, 1998, pp. 61–75.

22 Hence again from the recognition that God is closer to me than I am to myself it follows that the increase of grace in me is the increase in my becoming myself.

23 Hankey's analysis tends in this direction. Augustine, *Conf*. VII.1.1, 20.26. See Leo J. Sweeney SJ, "Divine Attributes in De doctrina christiana: Why Does Augustine Not List 'Infinity'?," in Duane A. H. Arnold and Pamela Bright (eds), *De doctrina Christiana: A Classic of Western Culture* (Notre Dame: Notre Dame Press, 1995), pp. 195–204. Sweeney, though he emphasizes incorporeality, does not then juxtapose the sensible with the intelligible.

24 It should be noted, however, that for Augustine as for other Latins, the category of infinity is not prominent. Sweeney, "Divine Attributes in De doctrina christiana," pp. 196–201; *Divine Infinity in Greek and Medieval Thought* (New York: Peter Lang, 1992). We shall take up this issue again in Chapter 5. The stoic infinite is a matter of some controversy and necessarily a matter of reconstruction owing to the paucity of sources. Robert Todd reconstructs a Chrysippian argument for the infinitely divisible magnitude based on Diogenes Laertius VII.150. See Todd, "Chrysippus on Infinite Divisibility: Diogenes Laertius VII.150," *Apeiron*, VII, 1, 1973, pp. 21–9.

25 Among the many places where Augustine repeats this claim see *De Trin*. VI, the eucharistic allusion *Conf*. VII.10.16 and *De Lib*. II.14–16. Augustine's remarks in *De Trin*. X.4 that one knows the mind as a whole without knowing it wholly are analogous. Etienne Gilson, though referring to St. Bonaventure, contrasts the two conceptions well. "God is an absolute infinite, perfectly simple: He is therefore everywhere present in his entirety: and while a finite body could not apprehend an infinite mass (whose *infinity* is not at one instance present in any of its points) yet a finite mind can apprehend an infinite that is perfectly simple: for if it apprehends it in one point, it apprehends it in its entirety. Thus one can know the infinite in its entirety— and indeed one cannot know it otherwise, for it is perfectly simple; but one cannot comprehend it, for though it is present in its entirety at every point inasmuch as it is simple, it is not comprehended in any, inasmuch as it is infinite." Etienne Gilson, *The Philosophy of St. Bonaventure*, trans. Dom Illtyd Trethowan and Frank J. Sheed (Patterson: St. Anthony Guild Press, 1965), p. 109. Augustine's dissatisfaction here with his early "materialist" conceptions of God's infinity in the *Conf*. can be seen as both a kind of rejection and

radicalization of stoic *krasis* and *mixis*: a critique in that the conception ultimately finitized God's transcendence, or rather, converted God's absolute infinity to an infinity of mass subsequently susceptible to *mathesis*, a radicalization in that transcendence allowed him, perhaps better than the stoics themselves, to account for the presence of two agencies within the same action, the dangers of this way of speaking notwithstanding.

26 Augustine, *Conf.* VII.10, "And I said, 'Is truth then nothing at all, since it is not extended either through finite spaces or infinite?' And thou didst cry to me from afar: 'I am who am.'"

27 Recall Harrison, *Beauty and Revelation*, pp. 41, 97–139; Brunn, *St. Augustine: Being and Nothingness*, pp. 74–7.

28 Though here again it must be pointed out that transcendence, properly understood, precludes our ability to make a transcendence/immanence dichotomy intelligible.

29 Todd, "Monism and Immanence," p. 137; *Alexander of Aphrodisias on Stoic Physics* (Leiden: E. J. Brill, 1976), pp. 21–65. Lapidge, "Stoic Cosmology," pp. 161–85; Sambursky, *Physics of the Stoics*, pp. 1–49.

30 Alexander of Aphrodisias (*De Mixt.* 224.24) defines tensional motion (disparagingly) as "simultaneous motion in opposite directions." See Sambursky, *Physics of the Stoics*, pp. 29–40. The priority of force over form leads Sambursky to qualify the concept of infinite division because, strictly speaking, there is in this arrangement no static surface and no *topos* to which the process of division could correspond. Sambursky, *Physics of the Stoics*, pp. 86–106. See Todd, *Alexander of Aphrodisias*, pp. 137, 219.

31 Todd, *Alexander of Aphrodisias*, pp. 34–5; Sambursky, *Physics of the Stoics*, pp. 3–10.

32 Todd, "Monism and Immanence," p. 150, "Pneuma's motion is of a peculiar sort; it is described as 'tensional' (*tonike*, e.g., SVF 2.448) and as a form of oscillation 'from itself and into itself' (SVF 2.442, 471)." See also Todd, *Alexander of Aphrodisias*, pp. 30–7; Lapidge, "Stoic Cosmology," pp. 173–4. For the interpretation of the Nietzschean Dionysus as a reversal of Schopenhauer's reversal of Fichte, see Michael Allen Gillespie, *Nihilism before Nietzsche* (Chicago: University of Chicago Press, 1995), pp. 175–254. See Gilles Deleuze, *Nietzsche and Philosophy*, trans. Hugh Tomlinson (New York: Columbia University Press, 1983), pp. 39–72. For an interpretation of Deleuze's Nietzsche analogous to my interpretation of the *pyr teknicon*, and for a discussion on Deleuze's debt to stoicism, see Ronald Bogue, *Deleuze and Guattari* (London: Routledge, 1989), pp. 15–34, 67–72, and John Marks, *Gilles Deleuze: Vitalism and Multiplicity* (London: Pluto Press, 1988), pp. 87–90.

33 Todd, "Monism and Immanence," p. 141.

34 Ibid., pp. 138, 148.

35 Ibid., p. 154.

36 Lapidge, "Stoic Cosmology," p. 167; Todd, "Monism and Immanence," p. 154.

37 Todd, "Monism and Immanence," p. 156.

38 Fichte thought himself "more Kantian" than Kant for having the dispensed with the *Ding an sich*, or rather by showing that Kant, perhaps unwittingly, dispenses with it. See J. G. Fichte, *Introductions to the Wissenschaftslehre and Other Writings 1797–1800*, trans. Daniel Breazeale (Indianapolis: Hackett, 1994), pp. 51–76.

39 "Speculative materialism, or the materialism that develops into a metaphysics, must ultimately transfigure itself into idealism of its own accord; since apart from dualism there is only egoism, as beginning or end, for a

power of thought that will think to the end. Little was lacking for this transfiguration of materialism into idealism to have already been realized through Spinoza. His substance, which underlies extended and thinking being, equally and inseparably binds them together; it is nothing but the invisible identity of subject and object (demonstrable only through inferences) upon which the system of the new philosophy is grounded, i.e., the system of the *autonomous philosophy of intelligence.*" Jacobi, "Jacobi to Fichte," p. 502; "Concerning the Doctrine of Spinoza in Letters to Herr Moses Mendelssohn 1785 and 1789," pp. 183–251 and 350–78. See also, Frederick C. Beiser, *The Fate of Reason: German Philosophy from Kant to Fichte* (Cambridge: Harvard Press, 1987), pp. 44–91. For an account of nihilism as a tradition of this logic of nihilation which extends from Descartes, through Kant and Fichte, to Nietzsche, see Gillespie, *Nihilism before Nietzsche*. We shall draw on Gillespie more closely in the next chapter.

40 R. M. Dancy may frown on such a conclusion on grounds that *apeiron*, in context, should be translated as "unlimited" rather than "infinite," the former of which is usually quickly elided to the indeterminate and indefinite. He takes this move to be a consequence of nineteenth-century Hegelian attempts to render this conception of infinity "negative," and he terms it, rather cleverly, as "a priori lexicography." The claim merits two responses. First, Dancy does not sufficiently attend, in the manner of Sweeney, to neoplatonic uses of the word to render the claim decisive as a general claim about the ancient meaning of infinity. Second, the argument in my thesis does not rest on lexicography, a priori or otherwise, but on the implications of construing the active/passive relationship within a stoic mechanics of tensional force. See Dancy, "Thales, Anaximander, and Infinity," *Apeiron*, XXII, 3, 1989, pp. 149–90 (171).

41 See Lapidge, "Stoic Cosmology," pp. 176–7, 179–80. The stoic teaching of an infinite void (*kenon*) surrounding the universe (SVF 2.535, 539), its distinction between "'the whole' (*holon* = universe) and 'the totality' (*pan* = universe plus void) (SVF 2.522–4)," combined with its close identification of the *tonikos* and *logos* (whose *hegemonikon* most likely resided in the aither), would seem to lend credence to this view.

42 Compare these two definitions. Of the active/passive relation: "[The concept of pneuma] held that an active principle totally pervaded a passive principle as the passage of body through body; this relation was non-reciprocal, for the passive principle could not interact with the active but merely served as its medium" (Todd, *Alexander of Aphrodisias*, p. 35); of the void: "That which is capable of being occupied and vacated by body is void" (Todd, "Cleomedes and the Stoic Concept of Void," *Apeiron*, XVI, 2, 1982, pp. 129–35 (129)). It should be noted, as Todd and Sambursky indicate, that "empty place" as a definition of the infinite cannot be taken literally since *topos* is, for the stoics, consequent on body and the infinite is a receptacle for body. Indeed Sambursky contends that the stoic theory of surfaces constitutes place as a consequence of tensional motion, such that there is, strictly speaking, no such thing in an Aristotelian sense. Sambursky, *Physics of the Stoics*, p. 95.

43 Jacobi, "Concerning the Doctrine of Spinoza 1785," p. 214; "Jacobi to Fichte," pp. 500–9.

44 Lapidge, "Stoic Cosmology," pp. 182–3.

45 This in turn is a function of character as determined by a history of assent. See Gosling, "The Stoics and ἀκρασία," pp. 179–201; Margaret E. Reesor, "Necessity and Fate in Stoic Philosophy," in Rist (ed.), *The Stoics*, pp. 187–202; Todd, *Alexander of Aphrodisias*, p. 28; Suzanne Bobzien, *Determinism and*

NOTES TO PAGES 114–15

Freedom in Stoic Philosophy (Oxford: Oxford University Press, 1998), pp. 254–71.

46 Sambursky, *Physics of the Stoics*, pp. 25–6; Gould, *The Philosophy of Chrysippus* (Albany: State University Press of New York, 1970), pp. 48–66, 126–33.

47 See Cicero, *De Fato*, trans. H. Rackham (Cambridge: Harvard University Press, 1997), XVIII.40–1; Bobzien, *Determinism and Freedom in Stoic Philosophy*, pp. 255–7, 310–13.

48 Bobzien, *Determinism and Freedom in Stoic Philosophy*, p. 288. Partly for this reason, the positive capacity for assent is not itself sufficient evidence of reason, since an irrational soul can assent to some impressions which happen to be reasonable.

49 Ibid., p. 240. "However, giving and withholding assent are an asymmetrical pair of activities: to withhold assent from an impulsive impression requires some extra energy and a specific state of tension in the soul: to give assent to it is basically 'to give in,' to follow the suggestion of the impression, and does not require a comparable amount of energy."

50 For a general account of the stoic theory of apprehension and assent, see Margaret Reesor, *The Nature of Man in Early Stoic Philosophy* (New York: St. Martin's Press, 1989), pp. 49–70. See Bobzien, *Determinism and Freedom in Stoic Philosophy*, pp. 276–90. Bobzien, whose recent reconstruction of stoic moral and physical theory is arguably the most detailed, thorough and sophisticated on offer, would undoubtedly refuse this characterization. She ably dismantles the traditional objections to the coherence of stoic teachings on moral responsibility and fate, in part by changing the question. As an aspect of this program, she denies that the stoics have a stake in anything like an "indeterminist" freedom, whether understood simply as a freedom of choice between alternatives or as a "noumenal" choice of the kind I am suggesting is intrinsic to the stoic position. She likewise rejects the "decision-maker" model of mind implied by such a suggestion and insists rather that the moral character of the agent is integral to the faculty of assent and that its role "elevates rational creatures from non-rational ones." Where she falls victim to the Augustinian critique is in failing to see that the unitary conception of mind which necessitates the externalization of our sources of motivation must insinuate an indeterministic freedom in order to secure its own unity and integrity, becoming a "decision-maker" by default. See the previous chapter and Wetzel, *Augustine and the Limits*, pp. 100–1.

51 This genealogy, which has been commonplace since Jerome, has met with some dissent of late. B. R. Rees has attempted to acquit Pelagius of the association with stoicism, attributing it to an error by Jerome that made Origen a fundamental Pelagian source, rather than the *Sentences*, thought by Rufinus of Aquileia to have been authored by the bishop Xystus. (This interpretation of Origen is another question.) John Ferguson is similarly unwilling to see in Pelagius and his allies proponents of a stoic *apatheia* of the paternity that Jerome assumed. Eugene TeSelle is slightly less reluctant. As interesting as these historical questions are, they are not decisive, as the claim advanced here is more philosophical than historical. Moreover, the crux of Pelagian consonance with stoicism consists not in whether the Pelagians advocated *apatheia* (though it is undeniable that this stoic concept exercised influence over many ascetic monastic traditions), but rather on the metaphysical and christological implications for its manner of conceiving the relation of humanity to God. Establishing this consonance does not require historical reconstructions of specifically "stoic" influences on Pelagius, though it would certainly be aided by one. See Rees, *Pelagius: A Reluctant*

Heretic (Woodbridge: The Boydell Press, 1988), pp. 82–97, 132; Ferguson, *Pelagius: A Historical and Theological Study* (Cambridge: W. Heffer and Sons, 1956), pp. 72–81. See also TeSelle, "Rufinus the Syrian, Caelestius, Pelagius: Explorations in the Prehistory of the Pelagian Controversy," pp. 92–3.

52 It is perhaps worth noticing here again that Sambursky (*Physics of the Stoics*, p. 37ff.) sees, in the stoic conception of the field of force, anticipations of the physics of Descartes, Boyle, and Newton. Despite significant differences, the similarities between stoic field theory and the aether hypothesis of the seventeenth century are striking. Sambursky hypothesizes only a relationship of analogy between them, while Amos Funkenstein and Louis Dupré observe a relationship of historical dependence premised upon the Renaissance appropriation of stoic texts. Amos Funkenstein, *Theology and the Scientific Imagination from the Middle Ages to the Seventeenth Century* (Princeton: Princeton University Press, 1986), pp. 37–9, 42–7, 63–8. Dupré, *Passage to Modernity*, pp. 125–6, 182.

53 See Milbank, "The Theological Critique of Philosophy in Hamann and Jacobi," pp. 21–37, and Beiser, *The Fate of Reason*, pp. 1–126.

54 J. B. Schneewind, "Kant and Stoic Ethics," in Stephen Engstrom and Jennifer Whiting (eds), *Aristotle, Kant, and the Stoics: Rethinking Happiness and Duty* (Cambridge: Cambridge University Press, 1996), pp. 292–6, 14. The latter phrase belongs to the editors.

55 Augustine, *Cont. Jul.* I.9.42–25; V.16.59–66; VI.21.66–7, 26.83.

56 Aquinas, *ST* I–I, 5, 2, ad 1, contends that, while being may be prior to goodness in idea, they are the same in reality, and goodness is prior to being in names signifying causality. The latter two-thirds of this claim I take to be a valid inference from Augustine's claims in *De Civ.* XI.24, a text which also serves to warrant our earlier explication of the trinitarian generation and procession in terms of an explication of God's love of the good that he is, or, to use Augustine's language, love's love of love. "'God saw that it was good' makes it quite plain that God did not create under stress of any compulsion, or because he lacked something for his own needs; his only motive was goodness; he created because his creation was good. And the assertion of the goodness of the created work follows the act of creation in order to emphasize that the work corresponded with the goodness which was the reason for its creation." *CCSL* XLVIII, 343–4. "Vidit Deus, quia bonum est, satis significatur Deum nulla necessitate, nulla suae cuiusquam utilitatas indigentia, sed sola bonitate fecisse quod factum est, idquia bonum est; quod ideo postea quam factum est dicitur, ut res, quae facta est, congruere bonitati, propter quam facta est, indicetur."

57 Augustine, *Ep.* 214.1, 2; 215.1, 7, 8. Weaver, *Divine Grace and Human Agency*, p. 8.

58 Augustine, *Retr.* 2.92.

59 Augustine, *De Corr. et Grat.* VI.9; VII.13.

60 Ibid. IX.21; XI.30. The use of the phrase "by his blood" here echoes Augustine's articulation of the soteriological economy of *De Trin.* XIII.11.15. See finally, *De Corr. et Grat.* XII.33.

61 One should be careful, both on historical grounds which are complicated by the presence of rival Augustinianisms and on theological grounds, in calling the voluntaristic turn "Augustinian." (The next chapter will consider this more fully in connection with Descartes.) Ockham's *Scriptum in librum primum Sententiarum*, for instance, while containing 29 references to Augustine, invokes the authority of Aristotle 210 times. See Saak, "The Reception of Augustine in the Later Middle Ages," especially pp. 385–97. For a nice

explication of the arbitrary voluntarism of Ockham's God, its relationship to Descartes and Descartes' conception of "willing" as the projection of unqualified causal power, see Gillespie, *Nihilism before Nietzsche*, pp. 1–32. Alister McGrath, *The Intellectual Origins of the European Reformation* (Oxford: Basil Blackwell, 1987), pp. 70–121, discusses the shift from ontological to covenantal justification in Ockham and the proliferation of Augustinianisms.

62 See, for example, Faustus, *De Gratia* II.1. 60, 18–61, 3. "If God, as impiety blasphemes, arranges the human state not by equity but by power, then one who has knocked might be shut out, and one who has not sought might be drawn in. And so he will seem to have been neither merciful toward the saved . . . nor . . . just toward the lost." Thomas A. Smith, *De Gratia: Faustus of Riez's Treatise on Grace and Its Place in the History of Theology* (Notre Dame: Notre Dame Press, 1990), pp. 159–60.

63 See McGrath, *The Intellectual Origins of the European Reformation*, p. 80.

64 See Ayres, "Remember that You are Catholic."

65 This is especially true given the *Confessiones'* demonstration of the necessarily retrospective character of such adjudications, as grace appears in hindsight that was invisible prospectively. In other words, Augustine's understanding of time and memory underscores the ethical insistence upon humility—even agnosticism—in the question of citizenship between the two cities. The question is further complicated by the fact that in the course of life in time, the border between cities runs not simply between agents, but through them. That, essentially, is the meaning of involuntary sin.

66 The objections of Wetzel and Milbank (see below) hold a certain attraction. My hesitation to endorse them completely derives from the nagging concern over whether the criticisms sufficiently consider what constitutes the integrity of a creature within the Augustinian viewpoint, against which violence would be a privative notion. Augustine's "aesthetic" conception of justice in *De Lib*. III, in which defects and the damned themselves testify to the beauty of justice and of the forms which they efface, while retaining a measure of it by virtue of their continued existence, may mitigate the criticisms somewhat.

67 Wetzel, "Snares of Truth: Augustine on Free Will and Predestination," in Robert Dodaro and George Lawless (eds), *Augustine and His Critics: Essays in Honour of Gerald Bonner* (London: Routledge, 2000), pp. 121–41 (136).

68 Milbank, *Theology and Social Theory*, pp. 417–22. Milbank's remarks (pp. 419–20) about ecclesial coercion are appropriate for the question of election. "Augustine's real mistake here was in the realm of ontology. The revolutionary aspect of his social thought was to deny any ontological purchase to *dominium*, or power for its own sake: absolute *imperium*, absolute property rights, market exchange for pure profit, are all seen by him as sinful and violent, which means as privations of Being. But his account of a legitimate, non-sinful, 'pedagogic' coercion violates this ontology, because it makes punishment positive, and ascribes it to the action of divine will . . . Because punishment must, by definition, inflict some harm, however temporary, it has an inherently negative, privative relationship to Being, and cannot therefore, by Augustine's own lights, escape the taint of sin. It therefore becomes problematic to talk of God punishing . . ."

69 Wetzel first raises this question in a footnote, in response to Gerard O'Daly's insistence that Augustine's "deterministic" account of grace is incoherent, and should be replaced by an "indeterministic" one. The incoherence is correct, he contends, but O'Daly's conclusion is not. If predestination only means the redemption of some, "then from God's eternal point of view, there are some of us whose lives are by nature unintelligible." This violates

Augustine's own notion of creation, but has no bearing on free will. Wetzel states the case elsewhere with even more force. "If there is no intelligible motive in justice to move God to withhold grace, then perhaps Augustine should have gone the route of 'double' predestination, where damnation and reprobation alike are impenetrable mysteries of divine election. I do not believe that he ever really had this option. The doctrine of reprobation is not an ill-conceived rider to his doctrine of predestination; it is profoundly in contradiction with it. Predestination affirms God's priority as a lover by acknowledging the inspiration behind all human love of God; the doctrine of reprobation subverts this priority by affecting to make a hell out of desire." See Wetzel, *Augustine and the Limits*, p. 220; "Snares of Truth," p. 130. O'Daly, "Predestination and Freedom in Augustine's Ethics," in Godfrey Vesey (ed.), *The Philosophy in Christianity* (Cambridge: Cambridge University Press, 1989), pp. 85–97.

70 See Weaver, *Divine Grace and Human Agency*, pp. 37–69.

71 Prosper's *Epistula ad Rufinum*, which predates *De Correptione et Gratia*, is evidence that the controversy was already underway. Its defense of Augustine against the charges of fatalism and Manicheanism suggests how Augustine's teaching had been received.

72 The letters reported agreement between Augustine and his detractors on several fundamental points: that all had sinned in Adam, that baptism is a prerequisite to regeneration and that grace is indispensable to salvation. The crux of the disagreement, from Prosper's point of view, was the question of the origin of faith.

73 Augustine, *De Praed. Sanct.* XV.31. "Therefore in Him who is our Head let there appear to be the very fountain of grace, whence, according to the measure of every man, He diffuses himself through all his members. It is by that grace that every man from the beginning of his faith becomes a Christian, by which grace that one man from His beginning became Christ. Of the same Spirit also the former is born again of which the latter was born." *De Dono Pers.* XXIII.67. "But there is no more illustrious instance of pre-destination than Jesus Himself . . . There is no more eminent instance, I say, of predestination than the Mediator himself. If any believer wished thoroughly to understand this doctrine, let him consider Him, and in Him he will find himself also." Though the latter passage contains a lesson in miniature of trinitarian grammar, Wetzel finds the treatises unexceptional, claiming Augustine largely contents himself with validating God's antici-pation of human willing (*Augustine and the Limits of Virtue*, p. 162). Insofar as this is true, it may have been motivated by the charge of novelty which would arise more than once in the campaign and ultimately provoke Vincent's famous canon against the "predestinarians." Both letters indicate that these objections had been raised, and Prosper's later *Auctoritates* is expressly intended to rebut the charge.

74 Mathisen, *Ecclesiastical Factionalism and Religious Controversy*, pp. 41, 101. It was a common rhetorical maneuver among those later charged with Semi-Pelagianism to tar their opponents with the Pelagian brush, as Pelagianism was universally condemned and functionally illegal. Mathisen also notes that the Gauls would even unilaterally try suspected Pelagians. He concludes furthermore that the impact of heresies in this period in Gaul was relatively small, and thus is too facile in attributing the sources of theological conflict to his "factionalist" thesis.

75 Though Prosper does not mention Cassian by name in his letter to Augustine, and though there is some controversy surrounding the dating of the thirteenth

Conference, scholars generally concur, given the locale of Marseilles, that the *servi Christi* to whom Prosper refers must be the monastic circles influenced by Cassian.

76 Nevertheless, Augustine seems to have been held in high esteem and was frequently appropriated. See Mathisen, *Ecclesiastical Factionalism and Religious Controversy*, pp. 37–41, 122–40, 244–5; Ramsey, "John Cassian: Student of Augustine," pp. 5–15.

77 Ladner, *The Idea of Reform*, pp. 347–73. Ladner cites *Serm.* CCCLV and CCCLVI as important textual witnesses to this transformation of the monastic ideal.

78 Weaver, *Divine Grace and Human Agency*, pp. 37–69, 121–31.

79 Markus, *The End of Ancient Christianity*, p. 164.

80 Owen Chadwick, *John Cassian* (Cambridge: Cambridge University Press, 1950), p. 52. Chadwick's emphasis is debatable, and hinges on whether one accords coenobitism a secondary status in Cassian's thought. Rousseau, for instance, would likely take exception to this (see below). Still, it is true that Cassian links obedience to humility and a negation of self will in a manner that Augustine does not. See Cassian, *Conf.* XXIV.xxvi.13.

81 Markus, *The End of Ancient Christianity*, p. 78. See also Adolar Zumkeller, OSA, *Augustine's Ideal of the Religious Life*, trans. Edmund Colledge, OSA (New York: Fordham University Press, 1986). George Lawless recognizes that this entails a fundamentally different conception of selfhood from that of Cassian. "Two of the most introspective of men, whose deaths occurred within five years of each other, John Cassian of Marseilles and Augustine of Hippo, were contemporaries. Yet their articulations of *homo interior* and *homo exterior*, in ascetic terms, were vastly different from each other in method, doctrine, design, programme and intensity." Lawless, "Augustine's Decentering of Asceticism," in Robert Dodaro and George Lawless (eds), *Augustine and His Critics* (London: Routledge, 2000), pp. 142–63 (144).

82 Markus, *The End of Ancient Christianity*, pp. 79–80. Markus should have followed through on the implications of his own insight, that the monastic community is "a microcosm of the City of God."

83 Moreover, the emphases on charity and perfection are not mutually exclusive.

84 See, for instance, Cassian, *Conf.* III.xii, on the fallenness of free will; XXII.xxii.1, on his assent to the *tradux peccati*.

85 Munz and Macqueen, particularly, render fresh interpretations of Cassian against the backdrop of Origenist presuppositions. See also, TeSelle, "Rufinus the Syrian, Caelestius, Pelagius: Explorations in the Prehistory of the Pelagian Controversy," pp. 90–5.

86 Colish, *The Stoic Tradition*, pp. 114–15. Colish gives a full catalog of features of Cassian's thought which she attributes to Stoic origins, though not all are relevant to our thesis.

87 Chadwick, *John Cassian*, pp. 82–91.

88 Colish, *The Stoic Tradition*, pp. 118–20; Rousseau, "Cassian, Contemplation, and the Coenobitic Life," p. 117; Chadwick, *John Cassian*, p. 84; Jerome, *ep.* 133.

89 The relationship between the vices and mundane attachment is underscored by Cassian's interpretation of Col. 3.5. Cassian interprets the "members" which Paul enjoins us to put to death with vices. See Cassian, *Conf.* XII.i.1–ii.4. See *Conf.* I.iv.1, for the distinction between *skopos* and *telos*. On the interrelation of virtue and vice in stoicism, see Stobaeus, *Arius Didymus: Epitome of Stoic Ethics*, ed. Arthur J. Pomeroy (Atlanta: Society of Biblical

Literature, 1999), 5b1–13. For the Stoa, the interrelation of vices follows from the unitary and material nature of mind. Virtue and vice are dispositions (*hexeis*) or fixed dispositions (*diatheseis*), that is, qualitative modifications of the soul's pneuma. See Reesor, *The Nature of Man in Early Stoic Philosophy*, p. 94; Bobzien, *Determinism and Freedom in Stoic Philosophy*, pp. 258–71, 276–301. On *hexis*, see Sambursky, *Physics of the Stoics*, pp. 7–11,

90 See Cassian, *Conf.* V.iii. See Colish, *The Stoic Tradition*, p. 116.

91 Cassian, *Conf.* XIV.ix.2, "Maintaining the diligence in reading that I think you have, then, make every effort to get a complete grasp of practical—that is, ethical—discipline as soon as possible. For without this the theoretical purity we have spoken of cannot be acquired. The only people who attain to it, possessing it as a reward after the expenditure of much toil and labor, are those who have found perfection not in the words of other teachers but in the virtuousness of their own acts. Obtaining this understanding not from meditating on the law but as a result of their toil, they sing with the psalmist: 'From your commandments I have understood.'" See Rousseau, "Cassian, Contemplation, and the Coenoebitic Life", p. 114. If one were to cast this in Stoic terms, this state would be a combination of *eupatheia* and *apatheia*. See Colish, *The Stoic Tradition*, p. 118; she also sees Cassian's coenobitism as the monastic embodiment of Stoic friendship (pp. 120–1).

92 Cassian, *Conf.* X.vii.2.

93 Macqueen, "John Cassian on Grace and Free Will," p. 13.

94 Cassian, *Conf.* III.viii.1.

95 Ibid. VII.viii.1.

96 Ibid. XIII.iii.5.

97 The issue here is complicated by two factors: the imprecise dating of the thirteenth *Conf.* and the extent of Massilian engagement with Augustine's teachings prior to the arrival of the aforementioned treatises.

98 Cassian equates purity of heart with charity itself, which makes charity proper the conclusion to the program of *ascesis*, though one must admit that it is present in degrees throughout. See Cassian, *Conf.* I.vi.3; Rousseau, "Cassian, Contemplation and the Coenobitic Life," p. 172.

99 Cassian, *Conf.* II.iv.4; see also II.ii.3–4, ix.1.

100 For Augustine and Cassian both, the virtues themselves testify to the irascibility of our condition. For Augustine, from as early as *De Lib.*, but certainly by *De Civ.* XIX, this results in the relegation of virtue to the position of an intermediate good. It could perhaps be argued that Cassian effects the same relegation in the distinction between *scopos* and *finis*. However, Augustine's conception of charity, rooted in his explication of the Trinity, makes the performance of charity and doxology the form and precondition to the acquisition of the other virtues, including the discretion by which one knows oneself truly. Cassian, in making *discretio* the font of the virtues, appears to make self-knowledge a precondition of that purity of heart which he equates with charity, though this could perhaps be qualified by the context of the divine offices. Crudely put, in the Augustinian conception, knowledge of God precedes and coincides with knowledge of the self, in Cassian's conception, true self-knowledge is a precondition for the knowledge of God. See Chadwick, *John Cassian*, pp. 96–7.

101 Cassian, *Conf.* I.xvi–xvii.1, "GERMANUS: 'Why is it, then, that superfluous thoughts insinuate themselves into us so suddenly and hiddenly when we do not even want them, and indeed do not know of them, that it is very difficult not only to cast them out but even to understand them and to catch hold of them? Can the mind, then, sometimes be free of these, and is it ever able to

avoid being invaded by illusions of this sort?' MOSES: 'It is indeed, impossible for the mind not to be troubled by thoughts, but accepting them or rejecting them is possible for everyone who makes an effort.'"

102 Ibid. I.xix.1.
103 Ibid. I.xx.6–xxi.2.
104 Ibid. I.xxii.1, emphasis mine. "This discretion, then, will be necessary for us in the fourfold manner of which I have spoken—that is, in the first place, so that the material itself, whether good or false, *may not be concealed from us*; secondly, so that we may *reject* thoughts that lie about works of piety as being adulterated and counterfeit coins . . . then, so that with similar discernment we may be able *to turn down those*, which because of an evil and heretical interpretation portray the precious gold of Scripture in the face not of the true king but of a usurper; and finally, so that we may *refuse* . . . those coins whose weight and value have been eaten away by the rust of vanity . . ." See also Gould, *The Philosophy of Chrysippus*, pp. 48–66, 148–52.
105 "In Cassian's view this ego-building can be reduced, step by step, to the eight vices; and conversely, each of the eight vices is responsible for one feature of our make-up; from gluttony we proceed to drunkenness; from fornication to scurrility and foolish talk; [etc.]. This scheme is not exhaustive. But the trend of Cassian's thought is clear. He held that from the basis of eight positive vices there follows, step by step, the whole gamut of our activities, including all the minor sins of our daily life" (Munz, "John Cassian," p. 4).
106 Munz carries this "annihilation of the will," this "destruction of one's imaginary self-hood" to this extreme conclusion. Insofar as "the contemplation of God in any shape or form could not be compatible with 'purity of heart'" because "the contemplation of a form or a shape stamps also upon the contemplating mind a form or shape," this self-negation aims "at taking to pieces the world of sound and form we are living in." At the conclusion of this process, we are united to the love which is God. But the process of negation seems to make that unity predicated on a mutual exclusion between the two terms. "This love then is ours or God's but appropriately there is no sense in drawing a distinction because to the degree to which our self is living our loving self is no longer *our* loving self" (Munz, "John Cassian," pp. 5–7, 11–12). Rousseau balks at this characterization, on the grounds that Cassian's often misunderstood endorsement of coenobitic life reopens the door to a positive appropriation of spatio-temporal existence. The interpretation is perhaps also predicated on assimilating Cassian to a certain reading of Origen which Chadwick claims takes too negative a view of matter. Rousseau, "Cassian, Contemplation and the Coenobitic Life," p. 118 n. 3; Chadwick, *John Cassian*, 2nd edn (London: Cambridge University Press, 1968), p. 92.
107 Cassian, *Conf.* I.xxvii.1.
108 Macqueen, "John Cassian on Grace and Free Will," p. 17; Munz, "John Cassian," p. 10.
109 Macqueen, "John Cassian on Grace and Free Will," p. 13.
110 Munz, "John Cassian on Grace and Free Will," p. 17.
111 Cassian, *Conf.* IV.i.1–xi.3.
112 In speaking of a "faculty of assent" I am borrowing the terminology of Bobzien, *Determinism and Freedom in Stoic Philosophy*, pp. 239–42. My assertion of Cassian's appropriation of a Stoic conception of soul comes first, from his insistence on the autonomy of "assent," secondly, from his insistence upon an innermost citadel within the soul untouchable by demons, and, finally, from his conception of the soul's materiality. See Cassian, *Conf.* VII.xiii.1–xv.1;

Rousseau, "Cassian, Contemplation and the Coenobitic Life," p. 120; Colish, *The Stoic Tradition*, pp. 121–2.

113 Cassian, *Conf.* IV.xii.1.

114 I of course do not mean to suggest that the Stoics had a developed concept of "will" per se, but rather that the concept of will emerging here is a form of the Stoic power of assent with its emphasis on causation and control. "Chrysippus' opponents in Gellius, and Chrysippus in his arguments in Cicero, Gellius, and Plutarch, all attach moral responsibility to the fact that the agent is the main causal factor of the action—not to the idea that the agent could have done otherwise" (Bobzien, *Determinism and Freedom in Stoic Philosophy*, p. 283). I have already voiced my grounds for objection to the latter point.

115 There is a bit of equivocation or perhaps terminological confusion here as Cassian also occasionally identifies this sort of freedom with the will's weakness. Nevertheless, there is a tendency to treat the capacity for negation or refusal as a sign of freedom regardless of the origin of the idea refused. See his remarks on Ps. 81, where he treats Israel's disobedience as a sign of freedom. Cassian, *Conf.* III.xxi–xx.

116 Cassian, *Conf.* XII.i.8.

117 Weaver, *Divine Grace and Human Agency*, p. 112; Munz, "John Cassian," p. 12; Macqueen, "John Cassian on Grace and Free Will," p. 10.

118 MacQueen's understanding, noted above, could easily be assimilated to this register.

119 Cassian, *Conf.* III.xii.1.

120 On cooperating causes, see Bobzien, *Determinism and Freedom in Stoic Philosophy*, pp. 261–9; Sambursky, *Physics of the Stoics*, pp. 57–65.

121 Weaver, *Divine Grace and Human Agency*, p. 99.

122 Cassian, *Conf.* XIII.iii.5–6.

123 Chadwick, *John Cassian*, 1st edn, p. 113.

124 Weaver, *Divine Grace and Human Agency*, p. 114. Such statements of course have to be qualified theologically, in a manner analogous to predications of the divine essence. Diverse predications (love, anger, etc.) arise from our composite manner of existing, speaking and understanding, but signify what, in itself, is one, invariable, and encompassing of all predication. So too, grace, inasmuch as it names the Gift who is the Spirit, is one, though its effects in the unfolding of time and the number of predications it can bear are diverse.

125 Cassian, *Conf.* XIII.xi.1, xiv.3.

126 Ibid. XIII.xiv.4.

127 Ibid. XIII.xiii.10.

128 Ibid. X.v.1–4.

129 When Weaver writes that "Cassian refused to make the choice that Augustine had tried to make: either grace or free-will," she not only has the matter backward, but fails to see that the need to draw the careful distinctions between them that she elaborates is what necessitates the choice. This ultimately is attributable to her failure to come to grips with a genuine transcendence and to let theological categories disturb her positivist assumptions about "the human." Weaver, *Divine Grace and Human Agency*, p. 112.

130 Munz, "John Cassian," pp. 15–17. "Nor did he think that the sacrificial death of Christ on the cross was in any sense final. He was far from the protestant standpoint of regarding Christ's death as some kind of substitution sacrifice and also very far from the more catholic standpoint which has institutionalized

that sacrifice and rests content with its periodic celebration. In Cassian's view, briefly, sin cannot be wiped out or forgiven through Christ's sacrificial death." Munz has managed to provide something in this characterization for everyone to hate; however, insofar as it is a fair characterization of Cassian's views, it does speak to ecclesiological and christological deficiencies. As for the "periodic celebration" of this sacrifice, Chadwick notes that under Cassian, the Eucharist seems to lose its sense as a corporate offering and is regarded as a vehicle for the individual reception of Christ. The brief mentions it receives in the *Conf.* seem to support that view. Chadwick, *John Cassian*, 1st edn, p. 67; Cassian, *Conf.* XXII.vii.1–viii; XXIII.xxxi.

131 Cassian, *Conf.* I.xx.8, "That is to say, the devil is deceptive when he veils himself in the appearance of holiness. 'But he hates the sound of the watchman'—namely, the power of discretion that comes from the words and advice of the elders." Talal Asad, *Genealogies of Religion: Discipline and Reasons of Power in Christianity and Islam* (Baltimore: Johns Hopkins University Press, 1993), p. 113. The Foucault selections cited by Asad are from Foucault, "Le combat de la chasteté," *Communications*, 35, 1982, p. 23.

132 Rousseau, "Cassian, Contemplation and the Coenobitic Life," p. 118.

133 Asad, *Genealogies of Religion*, p. 113.

134 One suspects that the contemporary composition of the academic guilds and the genre and setting of the *Conferences* hides their philosophical relevance from view.

135 Even a good Augustinian like Bernard of Clairvaux is not wholly free of rather un-Augustinian remarks perhaps traceable to this transformation. Bernard's meditations on humility and on love contain the quite un-Augustinian insinuation that self-knowledge is more a precondition of grace than its consequence. It suggests a subjectivity somewhat alien from that of Augustine's *Conf.* See Bernard of Clairvaux, "On Humility and Pride," and "On Loving God," in *Bernard of Clairvaux: Selected Works*, trans. G. R. Evans (Mahwah, NJ: Paulist Press, 1987), pp. 101–22, 173–205.

136 See Weaver, *Divine Grace and Human Agency*, pp. 151–2, for an interpretation of how engagement with Cassian transformed Prosper's thought in Cassian's direction.

137 Markus, *The End of Ancient Christianity*, pp. 181–97.

138 See Mathisen, *Ecclesiastical Factionalism and Religious Controversy*, pp. xii–xiii, 85–97. Weaver notes a similar shift in the movement from the first generation of post-Augustinian antagonists to the second. Cassian the monk and Prosper the layman give way to the "monk-bishops" Faustus of Riez and Fugentius of Ruspe, who emblematize the breakdown of the division between the monastic and congregational settings. Weaver, *Divine Grace and Human Agency*, p. 198.

139 R. A. Markus, *Gregory the Great and His World* (Cambridge: Cambridge University Press, 1997), p. 58.

140 Gregory, *Dialogues* 4.57–62. Carole Straw, *Gregory the Great: Perfection in Imperfection* (Berkeley: University of California Press, 1988), pp. 66–106; Jacques Le Goff, *The Birth of Purgatory*, trans. Arthur Goldhammer (Aldershot: Scolar Press, 1981), pp. 88–95. The term "social miracle" is taken from John Bossy, *Christianity in the West 1400–1700* (Oxford: Oxford University Press, 1985), pp. 57–75.

141 Carole Straw, *Gregory the Great*, p. 115. Gregory, *Mor.* 4.3.8. Testimony to the moral psychology of "choice," and to a substantial shift in cosmology and theology effected by Gregory in the direction of a theodicy, is his assertion, based on his reading of Job, that the Fall was a test of man's obedience. Gregory, *Mor.* 35.14.29.

142 Straw, *Gregory the Great*, p. 85. Gregory, *Mor.* 35.14.28. For more on Gregory's conception of authority as it relates to Cassian and Augustine, see Conrad Leyser, "Expertise and Authority in Gregory the Great: The Social Function of Peritia," in John C. Cavadini (ed.), *Gregory the Great: A Symposium* (Notre Dame: Notre Dame Press, 1995), pp. 38–61.

143 Straw, *Gregory the Great*, pp. 120, 140. Gregory, *Mor.* 28.11.26–9, 2.49.76, 16.25.30.

144 Straw, *Gregory the Great*, p. 140.

145 See, for example, Canons 6, 8, 9, and Proposition 11 which, whether an accurate view of Cassian and Faustus, reflect what their error was understood to be. Hefele (p. 158) notes that from the ninth remark onwards the "numbers no longer have the form of canons, but of propositions." This distinction has been preserved in my reference to those remarks. Charles Joseph Hefele, *History of the Councils AD 451–680* (Edinburgh: T&T Clark, 1895), vol. 4, pp. 156–8. Weaver suggests, and Hefele notes this as well, that while the subsequent Church has taken Orange to be a rebuttal of Arles and Lyons, its more immediate provocation was a council held a year earlier, in 528, in Valence, whose proceedings are no longer extant. Weaver, *Divine Grace and Human Agency*, pp. 226–7; Hefele, *History of the Councils*, vol. 4, pp. 152–4, 167–9.

146 See: Thomas A. Smith, *De Gratia*, p. 60; Weaver, *Divine Grace and Human Agency*, pp. 161–5.

147 At least this is Weaver's interpretation of Proposition 13, which states that "The free will weakened in Adam is restored only by the grace of baptism," and of Canon 18 which states that "Unmerited grace goes before the most meritorious works" (Hefele, *History of the Councils*, pp. 159–60). Weaver asserts, "The priority of grace is undeniable. Nevertheless, the council also affirmed human agency. The purpose of the operation of grace is to make possible the performance of good work to which reward is owed. The critical transition occurs at baptism. Grace brings one to baptism, but the grace conferred in baptism restores the freedom of the will. One can hereafter choose either good or evil. Grace thus circumscribes its own role by conferring on human agency the capacity to choose between alternatives" (Weaver, *Divine Grace and Human Agency*, pp. 229–30). Of course the "affirmation of human agency," as Augustine understood the meaning of being human, was never in question but whether will as reified "choice," undetermined by participation in the Trinity, was intelligible. One suspects that Weaver's own presuppositions about agency affect this interpretation, and both Canons 3, 7, 9 and Propositions 11, 12, 17, 19, and 25 might militate against it. Still subsequent treatments of the will in Gregory testify to it as one possibility.

148 See Smith, *De Gratia*, pp. 126–40; Markus, "The Legacy of Pelagius," p. 220; Weaver, *Divine Grace and Human Agency*, pp. 158–65.

149 Examples of Prosper's corporate Christology can be found in *Contra Coll.* 12.4, 18.1–3; *Vinc.* 3; and *Auct.* 7. Interestingly, one of the clearest preservations in Prosper of the Augustinian connection between knowledge, love, mediation and grace, which is to say between the philosophy of action and Christology, occurs in this last passage. The passage cites the Synod of Carthage in 418 whose canons contending with the proper "Pelagian" aspects of the controversy were approved by Pope Zosimus. The relative clarity of these connections compared with Prosper's own, suggests a diminishing understanding of the fullness of Augustine's own position among his later disciples. The text is as follows: "Whosoever says that the grace of God through Jesus Christ helps us not to commit sins in this sense only, that it

shows the way to a correct understanding of the commandments, so that we may know what we ought to seek and what to avoid, but not in the sense that grace gives us the love and power to do what we know to be our duty, let him be anathema. For when the Apostle says: Knowledge inflates but charity edifies, it would be very wrong to believe that we receive grace for what puffs up but not for what edifies. Both the knowledge of our duty and the love of doing it are gifts of God. And so, when charity edifies, knowledge cannot puff up. Just as it is written of God: he that teaches men knowledge, it is also written: Charity is of God."

150 Hefele, *History of the Councils*, vol. 4, p. 20, disputes this. Of course remarks such as the following do not make Hefele very reliable. "On the other hand, the learned Cardinal Norris showed that this could not possibly be correct, that in the time of Prosper there were as yet no Predestinarians, and that only the Semipelagians had maliciously reproached the true Augustinians with predestinationism. Not until the second half of the fifth century, he argued, were genuine Predestinarians to be found, and these mostly uneducated and unimportant people, who had allowed themselves to be urged on, by the sophistical objections of the Semipelagians, from their original Augustinian point of view to an extreme predestinationism."

151 Hefele, *History of the Councils*, vol. 4, p. 20; Smith, *De Gratia*, pp. 55–9; Weaver, *Divine Grace and Human Agency*, pp. 157–65.

152 Vincent, *Comm.* 26, 6–7, cited in Smith, *De Gratia*, p. 52.

153 Prosper, *Resp. Gall.* 6. See Weaver, *Divine Grace and Human Agency*, p. 133.

154 Wetzel, "Snares of Truth," pp. 126–30; Milbank, *Theology and Social Theory*, pp. 417–22.

155 Smith, *De Gratia*, pp. 126–40, 222–9: for an overview of the history of scholarship on Faustus, see pp. 1–20. See also Mathisen, *Ecclesial Factionalism and Religious Controversy*, pp. 41, 265. On Faustus' middle way, see Smith, *De Gratia*, p. 70. Interestingly, Faustus likens this pair to the problem of regarding Christ as either solely human or divine. Faustus, *De Gratia* I.1.8, 5–7.

156 Smith, *De Gratia*, p. 215.

157 Ibid., p. 172.

158 Augustine, *De Trin* XIV.12.15.

159 Faustus, *De Gratia* II.9.77, 17–25. Smith, *De Gratia*, p. 172.

160 Faustus, *De Gratia* II.8.76, 20–25. Smith, *De Gratia*, p. 94.

161 Smith, *De Gratia*, p. 173.

162 Ibid., p. 94.

163 Ibid., pp. 88–101.

164 Faustus, *De Gratia* II.9.79, 20–9. Smith, *De Gratia*, pp. 175–6. I do not mean to imply simplistically that for Augustine the virtues are substances without which the soul cannot live. But inasmuch as virtues are virtues by virtue of their participation in charity, and insofar as charity is convertible with *esse*, one's status before virtue, before the perfection of our endowments, has nevertheless to be a participation in those perfections, just as one must in some measure participate in the goodness of being in order to exist at all.

165 Smith, *De Gratia*, p. 81. "The capacity to turn in either direction always attends human existence. One's own choice, not the *vis praedestinationis*, determines the direction of the will, and such a choice can move one either to the side of the devil or to the side of God, as Scripture frequently attests."

166 Smith, *De Gratia*, pp. 9–90. Faustus, *De Gratia* II.2.61, 7–8. See also, Smith, *De Gratia*, p. 99, and Faustus, *De Gratia* II.10.83, 29–84, 3. "I shall seem incautious not even in this matter if I profess that often in our dispositions— not in the origins of our life, but at least in the middle parts—the movement

of our will precedes the special graces which come to us from an added generosity, because God ordains it so."
167 It is also incoherent for Aquinas, who quotes Augustine. Aquinas, *ST* I–II, 6, 5. Wetzel, *Augustine and the Limits*, pp. 203–6.
168 Hence the importance of *praescientia*.
169 Smith, *De Gratia*, p. 234.
170 See John Bossy, "The Mass as a Social Institution, 1200–1700," *Past and Present*, 100, 1983, pp. 29–61.

5 AN AUGUSTINIAN PARODY: DESCARTES AND MODERN STOICISM

Notes to pages 134–77

1 Augustine, *De Trin*. XV.5.7.
2 Ibid. III.11.21–22. "Wherefore the substance, or, if it is better so to say, the essence of God, wherein we understand . . . the Father, the Son, and the Holy Spirit, since it is in no way changeable, can in no way in its proper self be visible. It is manifest, accordingly, that all those appearances to the fathers, when God was presented to them according to His own dispensation, suitable to the times, were wrought through the creature."
3 "Their diverse movements and dispositions are like so many voices crying out to us, telling us to recognize their Creator" (Augustine, *De Lib*. III.23).
4 Stephen Menn, *Descartes and Augustine* (Cambridge: Cambridge University Press, 1998), p. 133.
5 René Descartes, *Meditations on First Philosophy* III, in John Cottingham, Robert Stoothoff and Dugald Murdoch (eds), *The Philosophical Writings of Descartes Volume II* (Cambridge: Cambridge University Press, 1984), p. 24. All citation from Descartes, regardless of the work, come from the CSM English editions. If the work is subdivided or contains numbered remarks, I shall give these with the title. Otherwise the title will be followed by the designation CSM, the volume number, and the page. In addition, in keeping with standard practice, I have referenced the parallel in the standard Adam and Tannery editions, abbreviated as AT. Thus this citation would appear as Descartes, *Meditations* III, CSM II, p. 24; AT VII, p. 34.
6 Gillespie, *Nihilism before Nietzsche*, pp. 1–32. Stephen Toulmin, *Cosmopolis: The Hidden Agenda of Modernity* (Chicago: University of Chicago Press, 1990), pp. 45–87. The strength of Toulmin's reading is also its weakness. He sets the question of Cartesian skepticism against the tenor of the age (and, from the point of view of his antagonists, against the documentary evidence). The strength is that it sets Descartes more broadly against the political and social, and not merely philosophical, context. The weakness consists in its having to come to terms with Descartes' own assertions that his uses of skepticism are purely instrumental. Menn, *Descartes and Augustine*, pp. 218–44. Jorge Secada, *Cartesian Metaphysics: The Scholastic Origins of Modern Philosophy* (Cambridge: Cambridge University Press, 2000), pp. 20, 40–1.
7 In her sense of what is wrong, LaCugna is correct. See also Dupré, *Passage to Modernity*, p. 249. Michael J. Buckley, *At the Origins of Modern Atheism* (New Haven: Yale University Press, 1987), pp. 33–67.
8 Bossy, *Christianity in the West 1400–1700*, p. 121. The final qualification is important, because the introduction of the fork signals the triumph of newly emerging rites of civility that displaced the social and domestic extension of Christian sacramental rites and which reflect profound shifts in "social ontology." This displacement is visible along a number of points, in the transition from a

priority on godparenthood at baptism to biological paternity and the shift in the meaning of catechesis from exorcism to instruction (which came to include Erasmian civility). To this point, rites of domestic commensality and eucharistic rites corresponded as they revolved around common cups and dishes. The introduction of the fork divides the two and contributes as well to the transformation and decline of fasting and abstemious eating.

9 See Bossy, *Christianity in the West 1400–1700*, pp. 115–71; Eamon Duffy, *The Stripping of the Altars: Traditional Religion in England 1400–1700* (New Haven: Yale University Press, 1992), pp. 379–503; William T. Cavanaugh, "A Fire Strong Enough to Consume the House: The Wars of Religion and the Rise of the State," *Modern Theology*, 11, 4, October 1995, pp. 397–419; Milbank, *Theology and Social Theory: Beyond Secular Reason* (Oxford: Blackwell, 1990), pp. 8–26.

10 See Richard Cross, *Duns Scotus* (New York: Oxford University Press, 1999), p. 65 ff. for Scotus' vascillation on this question. See Scotus, *Ordinatio* I, d.8, q.4. I am grateful to John Milbank for this point and especially to Adrian Walker, whose prolonged discussions and comments have helped me immensely to understand Scotus' subtleties.

11 Scotus, *Ordinatio* I. d.12 q.1, n. 20; Cross, *Duns Scotus*, p. 63. "The object of God's love is his essence. This last claim places Scotus at some distance from Augustine's position. Acording to Augustine, the Holy Spirit is . . . the love the Father and the Son share *for each other*. Scotus holds that the Holy Spirit's infinity results from the infinity of the object for which the Holy Spirit is an act of love. But the personal properties of the Father and Son are not infinite, since nothing other than the divine essence itself is infinite. So it is the divine essence that is the object of divine love." Cross notes that Scotus omits consideration of *De Trin.* XV.27, where Augustine calls the Spirit "the common charity by which the Father and the Son love each other," opting instead for *De Trin.* VI.7. As Scotus follows the Franciscan tradition of distinguishing between a "natural" generation of the Word and "liberal" procession of the Spirit, one can perhaps see in this move one root of his particular version of voluntarism, in which the will has "being" and not "goodness" as its formal object, though he appears not to be of one mind about this. See n. 147 below, and David W. Clark, "Ockham on Human and Divine Freedom," *Franciscan Studies*, XVI, 38, 1978, pp. 137–8. The infinity of the essence juxtaposed to the persons is also a departure from Augustine, for whom the persons are infinite in themselves and mutually determined to each other.

12 See Scotus, *Ordinatio* I, d.8, q.4, n. 179.

13 Scotus, *Ordinatio*, I, d.2, q.2.1–4, n. 381; Cross, *Duns Scotus*, p. 68.

14 The implications of all this are potentially vast, depending upon whether one interprets Scotus' univocity of being according to the concept or the object of the term. If the latter, there is an argument to be made that a misreading of *De Trin.* necessitates the formal distinction, and inasmuch as the formal distinction of intellect and will (or the personae) from the divine essence requires them to have a common meaning with their finite counterparts, the univocity of being. The latter is a controversial notion, however, and I do not wish to make too much for the claim here.

15 This possible objection was suggested to me (not entirely sympathetically) by Adrian Walker. I am grateful for it.

16 Menn, *Descartes and Augustine*, p. 236 n. 28. While Menn traces these hypotheses to Cicero, Secada traces their vehicle, a malicious demon who proposes false presentations for intellectual assent, to Suárez (*Metaphysical Disputations* IX.2.7). See Secada, *Cartesian Metaphysics*, pp. 44–5. Secada notes that Descartes invokes Suárez in *Replies* IV.

17 See Wayne Hankey, "Between and Beyond Augustine and Descartes: More than a Source for the Self," *Augustinian Studies*, 32, 1, 2001, pp. 65–88. Zbigniew Janowski, *Index Augustino-Cartésien: Textes et Commentaire, Histoire de la philosophie* (Paris: Vrin, 2000); *Cartesian Theodicy: Descartes' Quest for Certitude* (Dordrecht: Kluwer Academic Publishers, 2000).

18 Janowski admits this more readily than Hankey, who invokes Janowski to underscore continuity. See *Cartesian Theodicy*, p. 96. To Menn's credit, he does not beg this question, noting a proliferation of Augustinianisms in Descartes' day and contending that Descartes' Augustinianism, one of many, was derived from *De Libero Arbitrio*. As we shall see, however, Menn's Augustinianism neglects crucial features of *De Lib.* Menn, *Descartes and Augustine*, p. 70.

19 See Henri de Lubac, SJ, *Augustinianism and Modern Theology*, trans. Lancelot Sheppard (New York: Crossroad, 2000), pp. 1–86, 235–77; Anthony J. Levi, SJ, *French Moralists: The Theory of the Passions 1585 to 1649* (Oxford: Clarendon Press, 1964), pp. 2–3, 51–63.

20 Janowski's thesis, though impressive, is unconvincing because it ignores both the stated goal of the *Meditations*, establishing a sure foundation for the sciences, and its relationship to Descartes' broader corpus. Descartes' may be a theodicy, but he puts it to the service of ends that are at best theologically indifferent. Janowski admits as much when he writes, "[H]aving destroyed the Scholastic conception of God, Descartes needed to put in His place a God who is 'good enough' to play the role of the Creator, and who will not 'meddle' with the physical affairs of the world" (Janowski, *Cartesian Theodicy*, p. 103).

21 Janowski, *Cartesian Theodicy*, p. 110. Descartes, *Replies* VI, CSM II, p. 292; AT VII, p. 432.

22 I have argued that Augustine's understanding of the divine will is conditioned by his trinitarian theology, by the relationship of delight between the Father and his Word. Interestingly, when questioned by Mersenne, Descartes *declined* to enter into trinitarian speculation. Janowski, *Cartesian Theodicy*, p. 92, "One cannot exclude the possibility that Mersenne was motivated to ask so many questions because he was afraid that Descartes might be tottering on the brink of heresy, even if only from ignorance of theology. In his second letter of May 6, right after making the comparison between God and a legislator, Descartes goes on to add: 'What you say about the production of the Word does not conflict, I think, with what I say; but I do not want to involve myself in theology, and I am already afraid that you will think my philosophy too free-thinking for daring to express an opinion on such lofty matters.'" *Letter to Mersenne*, 6 May 1630 (CSMK III, p. 25; AT I, p. 150). On freedom as unconditioned, see Janowski, *Cartesian Theodicy*, p. 19.

23 Descartes, *Meditations* IV; CSM II, p. 40; AT VII, p. 34.

24 Janowski, *Cartesian Theodicy*, p. 21.

25 Levi, *French Moralists*, p. 2.

26 See William J. Bouwsma, "The Two Faces of Humanism: Stoicism and Augustinianism in Renaissance Thought," in Heiko A. Oberman and Thomas A. Brady, Jr. (eds), *Itinerarium Italicum: The Profile of the Italian Renaissance in the Mirror of its European Transformations* (Leiden: E. J. Brill, 1975), pp. 3–60; Dupré, *Passage to Modernity*, pp. 128–35.

27 Levi, *French Moralists*, p. 271.

28 Ibid., pp. 11, 56–7: "It is possible that the neostoic group of moralists are to be defined precisely in terms of their alliance of an ethical vocabulary taken from the stoics with an inclination to skepticism in matters of speculation. Certainly it is the union of stoic terminology with a tendency to extol the

suspension of judgement which provides the key to the neostoic theory of passions."

29 Levi, *French Moralists*, p. 58; citing *Manuductio*, bk 3, diss. 3. "What is certain is 'reason' and compels the wise man's assent. What is not certain is assented to as 'probable' and the wise man 'uses his *epokè* and reserves his assent.' For the stoics the '*constantiae* were rational movements which constituted emotion and it was possible for the wise man to be ruled entirely by reason. But for Justus Lipsius 'reason' has become the correct judgment of the speculative faculty, opposed to 'opinion.' To avoid having to attribute omniscience to the wise man, he therefore has to have recourse to the suspension of judgment." Descartes will later reconfigure judgment as an act of will; still he will plot this distinction between the certain and the probable onto a distinction between the speculative and practical. See also, Levi, *French Moralists*, p. 288.

30 Levi, *French Moralists*, p. 264. An analogous synthesis was the goal of Descartes' rival, Gassendi, author of *Objections* V, whom Descartes upbraids as "one of those men of the flesh." His physical theory and ethics both were derived from Epicurean atomism. See Lisa T. Sarasohn, *Gassendi's Ethics: Freedom in a Mechanistic Universe* (Ithaca: Cornell University Press, 1996), pp. 32–50. For an interesting interpretation of Gassendi's project as one that tries to sustain the unity of science, philosophy and historiography, see Lynn Sumida Joy, *Gassendi the Atomist: Advocate of History in an Age of Science* (Cambridge: Cambridge University Press, 1987).

31 Hatfield, "Force (God) in Descartes' Physics," *Studies in History and Philosophy of Science*, 10, 2 (June 1979), p. 114. See also Phillip R. Sloan, "Descartes, the Sceptics, and the Rejection of Vitalism in Seventeenth-Century Physiology," *Studies in History and Philosophy of Science*, 8, 1, 1977, pp. 1–28.

32 See Descartes, *Principles* II.36; CSM I, p. 240; AT VIIIA, p. 61; Hatfield, "Force (God) in Descartes' Physics," pp. 119–40; Sambursky, *Physics of the Stoics*, pp. 33–40. See especially Hatfield, p. 129, where Descartes notes, in response to More's query about the possibility of God's extension, that God has an "extension of power" through which he constantly communicates motion to matter. Hatfield notes that the concept of force for Descartes derives not from any inherent properties of matter, which is passive, but from the constancy of God's immutable act upon it, the same constancy which is responsible for the conservation of motion. The analogy I am suggesting is between this conception and the stoic equation of God with force, with its consequent pneumatic field in which the tensions of the *plenum* are distributed. The analogy perhaps becomes clearer as the Cartesian options refract into Leibniz and Spinoza. Descartes seemed aware of the immanentist danger, commenting to More that he omitted certain features of his theory of motion because "I was afraid of seeming inclined to favour the view of those who consider God as a world-soul united to matter." Descartes to More, see Hatfield, p. 130.

33 See Stephen Gaukroger, *Descartes: An Intellectual Biography* (Oxford: Clarendon Press, 1995), pp. 38–67; Geneviève Rodis-Lewis, *Descartes: His Life and Thought*, trans. Jane Marie Todd (Ithaca: Cornell University Press), pp. 8–23.

34 Rodis-Lewis, *Descartes*, p. 16.

35 Menn, *Descartes and Augustine*, p. 393, emphasis mine.

36 Ibid., p. 110.

37 See Descartes, *Meditations* III; CSM II, p. 31; AT VII, p. 45. Jean-Luc Marion notes, "In itself, this attribute calls for no particular commentary, since it seems so evident that God must be seen to assume supreme intelligence. However, not only here, but in the full range of Cartesian texts, supreme

intelligence receives no remarkable elaboration. This discretion is all the more notable, since the superlative adverb *summe* imposes a parallel with the attribute immediately following: *summe potens*. One is thus inclined to ask why supreme intelligence does not play a role comparable to omnipotence? Undoubtedly because the latter expresses much more than simply one attribute among others." Marion, "The Essential Incoherence of Descartes' Definition of Divinity," in Amelie Oksenberg Rorty (ed.), *Essays on Descartes' Meditations* (Berkeley: University of California Press, 1986), pp. 311–12.

38 Marion, "The Essential Incoherence," pp. 323–4. Descartes, *Meditations* V; CSM II, p. 45; AT VII, p. 65. "Certainly, the idea of God, or of a supremely perfect being, is one which I find within me just as surely as the idea of any shape or number." How sure is that? As sure as one can be *after* establishing the ego as foundation through hyperbolic doubt. The determination of God as infinite transcends before and after here, thus calling into question Menn's thesis that the first name of God is *Nous*.

39 Rodis-Lewis, *Descartes*, p. 17; L. J. Beck, *The Metaphysics of Descartes: A Study of the Meditations* (Oxford: Clarendon Press, 1965), p. 31.

40 Gary Hatfield, while acknowledging an Ignatian influence in the *idea* of the *Meditations* as a kind of spiritual exercise, offers a case similar to Menn's. (He also notes the likely influence of the *Exercises Spirituels* of Eustace of St. Paul.) Hatfield then divides the tradition of spiritual exercises into Augustinian and Ignatian strains and represents Descartes as radically breaking with the latter for a "Platonic" rather than "Aristotelian" conception of cognition. There are five problems with this view. First, it overlooks the relationship between Descartes' voluntarism and his account of cognition. This doesn't derive from Augustine as much as from Scotus and Ockham, and depends just as much on their modifications of Aristotle as it does on their modifications of Augustine. Secondly, this depends upon a questionable reading of *Conf.* VII that overlooks its christological conclusion and the role of created beauty in eliciting the exercise. Thirdly, he treats the *Conf.*, or at least part of it, as a species of the genus of spiritual exercises prominent in the sixteenth and seventeenth centuries, and this is questionable. Fourthly, with the exception of the misreading of *Conf.* VII, the comparison is mostly conducted at the vague level of "stages" in spiritual exercises. Finally, however, Hatfield overlooks both the positive relationship between Augustine and Ignatius, and, more importantly, those features of the *Exercises* recapitulated in the *Meditations* that originate not with Augustine but with Cassian and the Benedictines. I call attention to those below. See Gary Hatfield, "Descartes's Meditations as Cognitive Exercises," in Vere Chappell (ed.) *Essays on Early Modern Philosophers from Descartes and Hobbes to Newton and Leibniz*, Vol. 1 Pt 2, *Rene Descartes*, (New York: Garland Publishing, 1992), pp. 41–58. L. J. Beck treats the relationship between Descartes and Ignatius more positively, but he too keeps his analysis mostly confined to the level of genre and not to concrete textual debts. See Beck, pp. 28–38. For consideration of Descartes' relationship to the Jesuits, see Roger Ariew, "Descartes and Scholasticism: The Intellectual Background to Descartes' Thought," in John Cottingham (ed.), *The Cambridge Companion to Descartes* (Cambridge: Cambridge University Press, 1992), pp. 58–90.

41 See Karl Rahner, epitomized by Harold E. Weidman, SJ, "The Ignatian Process for Discovering the Will of God in an Existential Situation," in Friedrich Wulf (ed.), *Ignatius of Loyola: His Personality and Spiritual Heritage 1556–1956* (St. Louis: The Institute of Jesuit Sources, 1977), pp. 280–9. Descartes, *Meditations* I; CSM II, p. 12; AT VII, p. 17.

42 Descartes, *Replies* II, CSM II, p. 106; AT VII, p. 149. In order to sustain his continuity thesis, Menn must follow Descartes in upholding this distinction. Whether Descartes succeeds in upholding it is another question.

43 Ignatius, *The Spiritual Exercises of St. Ignatius*, trans. Louis J. Puhl, SJ (New York: Vintage Books, 2000), [21]. The bracketed citation refers to the remark number. Ignatius appears to recapitulate Cassian's distinction between *skopos* and *telos* in the distinction between the will of God as the final goal and the elimination of inordinate attachments (i.e., purity of heart), as a proximate goal. Like Cassian, this appears to occur according to a first-then form. "so we call Spiritual Exercises every way of preparing and disposing the soul to rid itself of all inordinate attachments, and, after their removal, of seeking and finding the will of God in the disposition of our life for the salvation of our soul" (*S.E.*, [1]).

44 Descartes, *Meditations* I; CSM II, p. 12; AT VII, p. 17.

45 See Heiko A. Oberman, "Ignatius of Loyola and the Reformation: The Case of John Calvin," in Juan Plazaola (ed.), *Ignacio de Loyola y su tiempo* (Bilbao: Universidad De Deuesto, 1992), pp. 807–14.

46 Dupré, *Passage to Modernity*, p. 224. As evidence both of the "modernism" of Ignatius' exercises and their place within the transition to modernity and of the perhaps fragile balance they sustain in spite of it (fragile in the manner of Cassian), I offer Louis Dupré's account, given in *Passage to Modernity*, p. 224, and the defense of John Montag, SJ, conveyed to me in private correspondence.

Dupré: "In truly modern fashion (despite his medieval sources) Ignatius places the person at the center of the universe. No fixed place or established style constrained him or his followers. In his *Spiritual Exercises*, Ignatius assumes that persons ought to control their own lives and that they can do so only by a methodic, systematic training of their will power. The *Exercises* are arranged in an order that forces the exercitant at each stage to keep a clear eye on a self-determined goal – *id quod volo* . . . Descartes, perhaps influenced by his Jesuit masters, later adopted a comparable method for conducting the mind along paths of rigorous rationality." Montag: "In defense of Ignatius, I'd suggest the same dynamic is at work here that I see between Suárez and the Suárezians—namely, something of the master is abstracted from the context he gave it, and thus denatured entirely. More specifically, the 'method' Dupré and others make much of is, for Ignatius, precisely a method of 'discernment of spirits' which is to say, interior 'motions' of the will and desire that come from three possibilities: God, the Enemy, or ourselves. Only the first is to be attended to. ONLY. The practice of the *Spiritual Exercises* allows two things: 1) skill in discernment of desires and 2) freedom to desire only God's will. '*Id quod volo*' is never authentically anything other than '*id quod Deus volet*' for Ignatius, although Dupré doesn't emphasize this. It's really one of the most scandalously evangelical things Ignatius says: we can trust our desires because they are directly given us by God; through them we know God most intimately. This got him thrown in jail more than once by the Dominicans.

Hence, *voluntas* and *dilectio* are closely identified for Ignatius, and moreover they are only authentically so in finding God's will. You might say his method calls for a practical theology of the Will of God. Judgment is no way divorced from this process of discernment of motions, and true freedom involves the ability to judge without 'inordinate attachments' to objects of desire other than God alone. Nor do I think the Jesuits 'liberate the subject' from the context which embodies the presuppositions of an anterior gift.

251

'Anterior gift' is quite explicitly the context for the *Exercises*. However, the 'method' may indeed make it possible to do so – just as Suárez's abstracted metaphysics makes it possible (but not necessary) to do philosophy without theology."

47 Cassian, *Conf.* I.xix.1; IV.i.1–xi.3; IV.xx.1.

48 See Munz, "John Cassian," p. 5; Straw, *Gregory the Great: Perfection in Imperfection*, pp. 66–89.

49 Ignatius attests to this influence more explicitly in his epistolary writings. See Ignatius, "'*Letter 31: 'The final word on obedience,*' " in Joseph A. Munitiz and Philip Endean (eds), *St. Ignatius of Loyola: Personal Writings* (London: Penguin Books, 1996), p. 253.The book given to Ignatius by Cisneros is called *Ejercitatario de la vida espiritual*. For discussions of Ignatius's debt to Cassian and the Benedictines, see Heinrich Bacht, "Early Monastic Elements in Ignatian Spirituality: Toward Clarifying Some Fundamental Concepts of the Exercises," in Friedrich Wulf (ed.), *Ignatius of Loyola: His Personality and Spiritual Heritage 1556–1956* (St. Louis: The Institute of Jesuit Sources, 1977), pp. 200–36; Hugo Rahner, SJ, *Ignatius the Theologian*, trans. Michael Barry (New York: Herder and Herder, 1968), pp. 32–52, 175–80. Rahner suggests further that one of Ignatius's visions is prefigured in Gregory the Great's *Dialogues* and that both Cassian's metaphorical use of the "the shrewd money-changers" and his characterization of the marks of the good and bad spirit influence Ignatian consolation and desolation, though Cassian's character-izations are already prefigured in Athanasius' *Vita Antonii* and were likely available from numerous sources accessible to Ignatius.

50 Ignatius, *S.E.*, [32, 313–36].

51 Rahner, *Ignatius the Theologian*, p. 127. See Descartes, *Passions of the Soul* I, CSM I, pp. 338–9; AT XI, p. 349, "[I]t seems to me that we may define [the passions] generally as those perceptions, sensations or emotions of the soul which we refer particularly to it, and which are caused, maintained and strengthened by some movement of the spirits."

52 Ignatius, *S.E.* [179]. Balthasar contends that Ignatian "indifference" is easily misunderstood as stoic, that it is not passive or hylomorphic but rather part of an "active indifference" – perhaps analogous to Augustine's active reception – which follows in part from the Augustinian identification of love and will (and by implication, its location "within" the Trinity). Here the meditation on the life of Christ, particularly perhaps the childhood of Christ, become crucial as the exercitant's surrender participates in the Son's loving obedi-ence between to the Father. I do not wish to deny this interpretation, but I contend nevertheless that the formal structure imported from Cassian is in real tension with it and is responsible for the tendency to misinterpret. This is especially true inasmuch as indifference/election tend to be treated sequen-tially. Hans Urs von Balthasar, *The Glory of the Lord: The Realm of Metaphysics in the Modern Age* (San Francisco: Ignatius Press, 1991), vol. 5, pp. 102–14.

53 Ignatius, *S.E.* [180, 184]. If Ignatius avoids the tensions provoked by Cassian's understanding of grace, it is perhaps partly because the "grace question" can now be taken for granted in a way that it could not for Cassian. Still, subsequent interpreters would make it an issue. The *Exercises* do contain at least one explicit exception, where Ignatius sounds quite Massilian. Ignatius, *S.E.* [366–369]. However, these remarks are balanced by a very Augustinian identification of love and will. "The love that moves and causes one to choose must descend from above, that is, from the love of God, so that before one chooses he should perceive that the greater or less attachment for the object of his choice is solely because of His Creator and Lord."

54 Though he doesn't pursue the point, Heinrich Bacht notes that the notion of *spirituales motiones* which Ignatius takes over from Evagrius (through Cassian, most likely) "adheres to the terminology of Stoic psychology." Bacht, "Early Monastic Elements," p. 221.

55 Not to mention profound differences in Christology. For a treatment of the christology of the Exercises (unparalleled in Descartes), see Rahner, *Ignatius the Theologian*, pp. 53–135.

56 Cassian, *Conf.* II.ii.2.

57 Something analogous is an integral part of the judgment which makes up Cartesian *sagesse*. See Descartes, *Principles*, Preface, CSM I, pp. 181–4; AT IXB, pp. 5–11.

58 Menn, *Descartes and Augustine*, p. 313. Menn speculates that Descartes may have inherited the theory from Cicero. However, he does note one important difference between the Cartesian and stoic conceptions. "Although the Stoics say that assent is 'up to us,' they do not describe it as an act of will: they analyze volition [*horme*] as a species of assent, not assent as a species of volition." See also Descartes, *Passions* I.27; CSM I, p. 338; AT XI, p. 349.

59 Descartes, *Meditations* III, CSM II, p. 29; AT VII, p. 43.

60 Descartes, *Passions*, CSM I, pp. 335–8; AT XI, pp. 342–9. Interestingly, Descartes refers to the former kind as "spirits," though he acknowledges that they are "merely bodies" (CSM I, p. 331; AT XI, p. 335).

61 Descartes, *Meditations* I, CSM II, p. 22; AT VII, pp. 22–3.

62 Descartes, *Meditations* II, CSM II, p. 17; AT VII, p. 25.

63 Descartes, *Passions* I; CSM I, p. 345; AT XI, p. 364. The application of this conclusion to the *cogitationes* in the *Meditations* is warranted because these would qualify as passions, insofar as they are perceptions, on Descartes' definition.

64 Menn, *Descartes and Augustine*, p. 265. See Descartes, *Meditations* III; CSM II, p. 31; AT VII, pp. 45–6. It is most likely Menn's failure to attend to the Ignatian influences upon Descartes' thought that causes him to assert mistakenly that the proof of the third Meditation is "unmistakably Augustine's" (p. 263), and it is thus likely this conviction which leads him to read into *Conf.* VII.17.23 a concern which simply is not in the text: the desire to demonstrate that our idea of God is *cataleptic* (p. 268). Apart from his attempts to absolve God from responsibility for evil and praise God for justice, the concern for attributing our discrete thoughts to their respective causal origins is simply not an Augustinian preoccupation.

65 Ignatius, *S.E.* [330–6]; Bacht, "Early Monastic Influences," p. 217; Ignatius *S.E.* [336].

66 Ignatius, *S.E.* [318–21]; Descartes, *Meditations* IV; CSM II, p. 41; AT VII, pp. 58–9. I would suggest that the process of judgment in the whole of the fourth Meditation resonates with Ignatian consolation and desolation. This is especially true of the freedom of indifference, where Descartes seems to echo Ignatius. Ignatius, *S.E.* [179]; Rahner, *Ignatius the Theologian*, p. 158. See also Bacht, "Early Monastic Influences," p. 216.

67 Menn, *Descartes and Augustine*, pp. 40–2.

68 Wayne Hankey and Brian Stock contend that Augustinian certainty is the source for the Cartesian certainty. I shall address their differences below. I would only reiterate here that Augustine never makes the mind's self-certainty the "truthful basis" for subsequent speculation, and the "unbreakable reflexive unity of remembering, understanding and loving," to the extent that this description is adequate, differs from Descartes' in that the latter's includes neither remembering nor loving in the essence of the *res cogitans*. It

is precisely the inclusion of these, both of which invoke mediation, that differentiates the Augustinian *mens* from the Cartesian *cogito*. It should also be reiterated that Augustine does not link this awareness to the question of the causal origins of our ideas. Hankey, "Between and Beyond Augustine and Descartes," pp. 65–88; "Menn's Cartesian Augustine," p. 54. Brian Stock, *Augustine the Reader: Meditation, Self-knowledge, and the Ethics of Interpretation* (Cambridge: The Belknap Press of Harvard University Press, 1996), pp. 261ff.

69 Rahner, "The Ignatian Process," p. 285.

70 Rahner, *Ignatius the Theologian*, p. 155. Below I will concur with Jean-Luc Marion in calling into question the coherence of Descartes' definitions of divinity on grounds that the first set of determinations, privileging the infinite, precede the *ordo rationis* by transcending hyperbolic doubt while the second, privileging perfection, submit this idea to the principle of causality. While I do not pretend to decide on this issue, I wonder whether this might be prefigured in Ignatius's distinction between the "Second Time" and the "Third Time" of the election. In the former, which is "higher," one discerns the consolation without prior cause as something like an intuition (see Rahner, "The Ignation Process," pp. 286–7); in the latter, the election is submitted to the judgment of the director. Hugo Rahner remarks that "two things are necessary if this audacious and easily misunderstood 'Second Time' of the election is to remain on right theological lines: first, the gift of the *discretio spirituum*, and then, either during this time or afterwards, the control of the rational understanding (i.e. the 'Third Time')" (Rahner, *Ignatius the Theologian*, p. 151).

71 Menn, *Descartes and Augustine*, pp. 393, 159–67. Among these intuitions are the immediate intuition of the soul and of God as the standard of truth, the cogitarian exercises as a means to unveiling that intuition, and parallel relationships between faith and reason, natural theology and "revealed religion" and speculation and practice. Menn even understands the hypothesis of "God as the source of mathematical regularity" to have Augustinian and Plotinian origins, and he thus insinuates a clear Augustinian antecedent to Cartesian *mathesis*, though he acknowledges a clear difference between fourth and seventeenth century objectives.

72 Ibid., p. 110.

73 Hankey, "Stephen Menn's Cartesian Augustine," para. 46, 50.

74 Menn, *Descartes and Augustine*, pp. 132–3. One could suggest that Menn's decision to elide this "discipline" into a "method" (p. 106) frames it according to an a priori scheme which anticipates the Cartesian disjunction of speculation and practice. Lewis Ayres, following Pierre Hadot, problematizes the extent "neo-Platonic" interpretation of Augustine's "exercises" or rather, the extent to which either Plotinian or Augustinian exercises can be understood in the sense Menn seems to understand them, simply as "mental exercises," even if these be supplemented by "moral exercises." Hadot makes the latter intrinsic to the former, noting that "Christian spiritual exercises did indeed take on a new meaning by virtue of the specific character of Christian spirituality, inspired as it is by the death of Christ and the trinitarian life of the divine persons." But to speak, apropos of the philosophical exercises of antiquity, of simple "moral exercises" is to misunderstand their importance and significance. "[T]hese exercises have as their goal the transformation of our vision of the world, and the metamorphosis of our being. They therefore have not merely a moral, but an existential value. We are not just dealing here with a code of good moral conduct, but with *a way of being*, in the strongest

sense of the term." The *Conf.* as a whole makes this apparent, and the fact that Augustine's Christology is itself the context, not simply the *via*, but the *veritas* and *vita*, implies a stronger connection between way and goal than Menn allows, and certainly stronger than Descartes envisions. See Ayres, "The Christological Context of Augustine's *De Trinitate* XIII," pp. 111–18; Hadot, *Philosophy as a Way of Life*, trans. Michael Chase (Oxford: Blackwell, 1995), p. 127.

75 Menn does adduce numerous texts from *De Lib.* II and elsewhere to support this thesis. This thesis, and the central, organizing role which Menn gives to *Conf.* VII in painting his portrait of Augustine, locates Menn in that tradition, descending from O. du Roy, which sees a full *speculative* rapprochement between Augustine and neoplatonism. "[Augustine] grants the Platonists a full doctrine of the trinity; the Platonists know all about the Fatherland, but lack only the Way to get there." We will address this understanding shortly; as we shall see, it is central to the reconciliation Menn forges between Augustine and Descartes. See O'Donnell, *Augustine: Confessions*, Vol. 2, p. 415.

76 Menn, *Descartes and Augustine*, p. 196. Menn's claim and his treatment of the *libri platonicorum* require him to ignore Augustine's ambivalence about the neoplatonists. Augustine, *De Civ.* XII.23–4 (see also X.29). "We know what Porphyry, as a Platonist means by the 'principles'. He refers to God the Father, and God the Son, whom he calls in Greek the Intellect or Mind of the Father. About the Holy Spirit he says nothing, or at least nothing clear; although I do not understand what other being he refers to as holding the middle position between these two. If, like Plotinus in his discussion of the three 'principal substances,' he had intended it to be inferred that this third entity is the natural substance of the soul, he would certainly not have said that this held the middle place between the two others, the Father and the Son. Plotinus certainly regards the nature of the soul as inferior to the Intellect of the Father; whereas Porphyry, in speaking of an entity in the middle position, places it between, not below, the other two. Doubtless he meant what we mean when we speak of the Holy Spirit, who is not the spirit of the Father only or of the Son only, but of both . . . Thus when we speak about God we do not talk about two or three 'principles' any more than we are allowed to speak of two or three gods . . ." While Augustine's critique is clearly focused on Porphyry, it is also clear that he finds both Porphyrian and Plotinian "trinities" less than fully adequate. Menn only notes Augustine's attack on the Platonic worship of demons, failing to see any relationship between this practice and the inadequacies of their "trinitarian theology." However, without such a relationship, it seems virtually impossible to render *De Civ.* VIII–X coherent. James O'Donnell's rather more restrained enthusiasm for the *libri platonicorum* in the *Conf.* better accords with this ambivalence. See Menn, *Descartes and Augustine*, p. 77.

77 Hankey, "Stephen Menn's Cartesian Augustine," para. 15, 9. For the sake of convenience, I accept and even employ Hankey's language of a Christian and Augustinian modification to a Plotinian original. And, while I have no stake in denying the Christian debt to Platonic categories, it should be noted that such language is neither historically and philosophically innocent, nor without its theological problems. It frames, and thus subordinates, developments in Christian doctrine entirely in terms of their relationship to Platonism, thus obscuring and subordinating factors which fall outside the realm of philosophy in its current, narrow definitions. If, however, one framed these developments in terms of the need to account for the life of Jesus, in the scriptural narratives, or in terms of the liturgical practices of the

Church, then a different *ordo rationis* would emerge. Only the normative perspective of the academic seems to warrant the privileging of one set of historical and theoretical factors over the other.

78 Ibid., para. 7.

79 Ibid., para. 47.

80 Ibid., para. 48.

81 Menn is perhaps not completely oblivious to this. He does call attention to the fact "Plotinus concludes 'therefore [Nous] is the [intelligible] beings: for it will think them either in something else [*heterothi*], or in itself, as being itself. In something else is impossible: where would it be? So [it knows] itself, and in itself' (V, 9, 5, 14–15). Aristotle had used this conclusion to argue that, since Nous knows only itself, there cannot be a plurality of Platonic forms for it to know; but Plotinus says instead that 'it is itself *the things* it thinks,' identifying a singular with a plural. Plotinus thus denies the Aristotelian thesis that Nous is simple (Menn, *Descartes and Augustine*, pp. 118–19). The Cartesian doctrine of eternal truths, which are not exemplars in the mind of God, but "independent" creations, may actually be more Plotinian than Augustinian, though Descartes' notion here is the consequence of a radically voluntarist notion of God which is neither. See Menn, *Descartes and Augustine*, pp. 337–52.

82 Hankey, "Stephen Menn's Cartesian Augustine," para. 16.

83 Here I concur with Hankey that Augustine indeed advocates a kind of self-identity, a kind of self-presence, and a kind of intellectual union with the divine. The question here is *what kind?*

84 Menn, *Descartes and Augustine*, p. 203.

85 In short, no *eschaton*, no resurrection of the body, etc., the latter of which should inform the meaning of Augustine's "pre-eschatological" distinctions as the norm from which we deviate in our privations. See Augustine, *De Civ.* XXII.24–30.

86 Contrasting *De Trin.* X to *Enn* VI.4–5 on the question of self-knowledge, Lewis Ayres notes the Plotinian ambivalence toward participation between the different hypostases. The observation captures nicely both the strength and weakness of Hankey's criticisms of Menn. "Plotinus uses some common Neoplatonic themes to persuade us first to see the different implications of the dualities present in our thinking, thus encouraging us to reason to the existence of something beyond thinking, and second to persuade us to see the need for the Good to be prior to the Beautiful if we are to understand the relationships between the different hypostases. Plotinus's use of the theme of unity and duality in thinking depends upon his understanding of the structure of the universe and his understanding of how all things are characterized by their natural difference from the One. Augustine's understanding in some ways takes place in a 'flattened' intellectual universe . . . and is designed to illustrate our place in a fallen yet potentially perfectly ordered universe. It is possible for Augustine to 'think ourselves' without abandoning all knowledge of our secondary position: there is a relationship between creator and creature which permits an awareness of the presence of God to us while still being aware—while necessarily being also aware—of our created status."

   While the third *Meditation* may be analogous to Augustine's view, as Menn argues, the analogy is faint. This is for reasons derived from understanding creation christologically in the light of trinitarian love, reasons which exceed Menn's Cartesian distinction between speculation and practice. In a footnote, Ayres writes, "In some senses the key theme in Augustine's transformation of Neoplatonism is his understanding of the necessary and intended difference between God and creation which facilitates love in a way markedly different from all conception of difference in Plotinus." It is this point which eludes both Hankey and Menn. See Ayres, "The Discipline of Self-knowledge in Augustine's *De Trinitate* Book X," in Lewis Ayres (ed.), *The Passionate Intellect: Essays on the Transformation of Classical Traditions* (New Brunswick: Transaction Publishers, 1995), p. 285 n. 68.

87 I say partially correct, because I concur that Augustine does advocate a kind of union. I simply do not think Hankey has adequately specified what kind or that his criticisms of Williams on this score hit their mark. See Augustine, *De Vera Relig.*, XXXII.60; XXXVI.66. See also Harrison, *Beauty and Revelation*, p. 110; Wetzel, "Crisis Mentalities," pp. 120–9; Pickstock, "Music: Soul, City, and Cosmos after Augustine," pp. 248–9.

88 See Wetzel, *Augustine and the Limits*, pp. 33–7, for an excellent analysis of the importance of this passage.

89 The dynamic of the presence of God to the soul, which is both more intimately present to the soul than the soul to itself and yet *anticipated* as a future event, seems analogous to the Son being sent to where he already was. It deserves further investigation. Ayres notes in the prologue of *De Trin.* IX an eschatological component to Augustinian self-knowledge that is little commented upon. It gives the quest both an immediacy and an erotic character. "This latter discussion emphasizes that our desire must take shape as a desire about to be fulfilled even while we are aware that in this life it will never be. This eschatological perspective is the situation of all the analogies for the Trinity." There is no analog for this immediacy and distance in Descartes. The closest analogy is still quite remote, and derives from the proof of "continual causation" in the third *Meditation*. See Ayres, "The Discipline of Self-knowledge," p. 270.

90 Augustine, *Conf.* XI.29.

91 Ibid. XI.29.

92 Augustine, *De Trin.* X.3.5–4.6. James K. A. Smith observes this presence/absence relationship nicely in contrast to the Cartesian substantial ego. Owing to his desire to render Augustine friendly to contemporary continental philosophy, he fails to develop how this seeming "absence" is for Augustine constituted in the plenitude of a gift and instead concentrates upon (citing Thomas Carlson) "a desiring human subject that remains opaque to itself." See James K. A. Smith, "How (Not) to Tell a Secret: Interiority and the Strategy of 'Confession,'" *American Catholic Philosophical Quarterly*, LXXIV, 1, 2000, pp. 135–51. The Carlson citation is from Carlson, *Indiscretion: Finitude and the Naming of God* (Chicago: University of Chicago Press, 1999), p. 4.

93 This seems to be one of the chief points of the recollections of the *Conf.* and of denial of the possibility of willing unhappiness. See *De Trin.* XII.3.6–6.9. See also Wetzel, *Augustine and the Limits*, pp. 37–44. See also Augustine, *De Trin.* I.8.16–17; VIII.8.12; X.5.7; XIV.12.15; XV.3.5. On mediation, see Ayres, "The Discipline of Self-knowledge," pp. 268–9; Rowan Williams, "Sapientia and the Trinity," p. 323.

94 Innes, "Integrating the Self through the Desire for God," p. 93. For beauty as motive in the particular case of self-knowledge, see Augustine, *De Trin.* X.1.2. The christological claim requires a christological determination of time.

95 Augustine, *De Trin.* X.1.2.

96 This has already had important consequences for our Augustinian "philosophy of action." It will again, shortly. For further confirmation of our interpretation of "assent as an aspect of desire" and thus of the relation

between Father and Son, see Ayres, "The Discipline of Self-knowledge,"
p. 271.

97 Of course in the terms of Chapter 2, the reverse is also true. The operation
of the Trinity is intrinsic to the manifestation of Christ, with the Spirit
"interpreting" what Christ reveals.

98 As John Milbank, Graham Ward and Catherine Pickstock write of my own
earlier essay on this topic, "'will' names not, as for Pelagius or later Western
tradition, a faculty, but simply that problematic site where inner is also outer,
active is also passive, present is also past and future, and knowing is also
loving." Milbank, Ward, and Pickstock, *Radical Orthodoxy*, p. 11. See also
Ayres, "The Discipline of Self-knowledge," pp. 287–8.

99 Augustine, *De Trin.* XV.7.12; *Conf.* XIII.34.49; *De Civ.* XI.24, 28. The proper
qualifications are that Augustine denies that our mental operations provide a
clear analogy for the trinitarian *personae* or that these operations can be
allocated discretely to the respective persons. I use "mirrors" here in a very
loose sense as he does, to note a similitude by which we partially apprehend,
through a puzzling reflection. See *De Civ.* XXII.29. However, there is a
stronger sense insofar as Augustine identifies the charity with which we love
with God (*De Trin.* VIII.8.12).

100 Menn, *Descartes and Augustine*, p. 70. The first book of *De Lib.* was completed
around 387; the latter two books were almost certainly completed a good deal
later. Robert J. O'Connell contends that the second book revises the stoicism
of the first and is an inchoate anticipation of the conclusions of *Conf.*, a thesis
which is less than convincing in part for redactional reasons. The importance
here, however, is that even if one grants O'Connell's or Menn's thesis some
leeway, we already see, at this early stage of Augustine's career, some trajec-
tories which find their completion in the full-blooded trinitarianism of the
later work. See O'Connell, "*De Libero Arbitrio* I: Stoicism Revisited,"
Augustinian Studies 1, 1970, pp. 49–68.

101 Menn, *Descartes and Augustine*, pp. 110, 112. For the sake of this argument, I
am granting Menn the distinction between the sensible and the intelligible.
However, in Chapter 3, I questioned that distinction and its function with the
category of "ideal matter," and Augustine himself undermines it at *De Civ.*
XXII.29. Catherine Pickstock would concur, she writes of the *De Mus.* that
"[Augustine] regards both soul and body as numbers, and this ontology
reveals a monism more fundamental than the Augustinian dualism which
commentators have more frequently insisted upon." Pickstock, "Music: Soul,
City and Cosmos after Augustine," p. 255. As noted in Chapter, 2, Emilie
Zum Brunn appears to agree as well; Brunn, *St. Augustine: Being and
Nothingness*, pp. 55–6.

102 Menn also does not consider how the Augustinian account might differ from
the Plotinian, which would follow upon Augustine's rejection of a world-soul
and to differences derivable from the doctrine of *creatio ex nihilo*.

103 Augustine, *De Lib.* II.16.41; Menn, *Descartes and Augustine*, p. 163.

104 Augustine *De Lib.* I.15. See, for instance, Augustine, *De Doct.* I.

105 Augustine, *De Vera Relig.* XXXI.40–XXXVIII.71. It is perhaps this difference
in orientation which makes demon worship congruent with Augustine's
ambivalence toward the Plotinian and Porphyrian triads, and yet incon-
gruent for Menn.

106 Ibid. III.9ff.

107 Menn, *Descartes and Augustine*, p. 157. This truth, Menn explains is not a
property of propositions, but the standard of judgment, and so "equivalent to
Plotinus' Nous" (p. 154). I have already indicated my reservations about this

equivalence both as a philosophical and theological matter and as a matter of exegesis. Yet for this aspect of my argument it makes no difference to concede the point.

108 See Harrison, *Beauty and Revelation*, p. 114. Of course this again raises the aporia of the *Meno*, and there is evidence in all three books that Augustine is implicitly prepared to "resolve" it at this early stage by the mediation of grace and, consequently, that what "is up to us" or "in our power" carries many of the resonances of the later work. See *De Lib*. I.2, 12; II.6, 9, 16, 17, 20; III.2–3, 21–2.

109 Harrison, *Beauty and Revelation*, p. 114, emphases mine.

110 Augustine, *De Lib*. III.23.

111 We have already seen how Augustinian mediation renders the attempt to establish origins problematic, because of both the temporalizing role of memory and the anteriority of grace. Hence, as the passage cited by Menn suggests, the occasioning by the sensible is itself the consequence of grace and speaks to mediation as depicted logically and temporally in the earlier ratio/interval distinction. Therefore, the need to isolate the soul and God as the foundation of knowledge, the hypothesis that God and the soul are better known than bodies, and that we cannot know bodies without first knowing God and the soul, all conspire to break the aporias which to Augustine suggest our temporal distention and christological mediation. Menn recognizes that these are departures from Augustine, but treats them as developments of an Augustinian metaphysics and not as departures that rupture it. See Menn, *Descartes and Augustine*, pp. 219, 209. The question of priority in Descartes, or of the relationship between his fundamental principle and the God it ends up presupposing, is a question of the relationship of priority between his different determinations of the divine essence and his different proofs of God. We shall take up this question in the next section.

112 Augustine, *De Lib*. II.16.41. This accords well with the hierarchical order of the soul's judgment upon numbers in the *De Mus*. Catherine Pickstock, commenting primarily on *De Mus*. VI, describes this order thus. "[T]he numbers of sensation have priority, for Augustine, over the external sounding numbers. After the numbers of sensation come the memorial numbers, which are in turn superior, because to sense any single harmony of two things one must already have brought together a merely remembered past sound with a sensed present sound. Above the memorial numbers come the numbers which judge spontaneously a sensory stimulus, and which allow the mind to create a sensory image on the occasion of a bodily stimulation. However, above the initial number of judgment (*numeri sensuales*) comes a reflexive or recursive judgment (*numeri iudiciales*) which judges the first judgment, whether accepting, rejecting or modifying an initial enthusiasm or distaste." Importantly for our point, she notes, "[A]lthough the sounding numbers (*numeri corporeales*) eventually drop out of consideration, Augustine never takes back the affirmation that one becomes aware of one's sense of harmonic proportion only from a particular instance of hearing an actual physical harmony." See Pickstock, "Music: Soul, City and Cosmos after Augustine," pp. 255–8.

113 O'Donnell, *Augustine: Confessions*, Vol. 2, p. 446. Menn, *Descartes and Augustine*, p. 267. "The whole of the third Meditation can be understood as an extended commentary on this passage in Augustine."

114 O'Donnell, *Augustine: Confessions*, Vol. 2, p. 458. For an excellent discussion, see O'Donnell, *Augustine Confessions*, Vol. 2, pp. 413–18. "In attending as closely as we do to the *platonicorum libri* and even to the texts of scripture, we mistake Augustine's drift in a crucial way. What he is attempting to describe is

an encounter between his haughty intellect and the humbling grace of God, an encounter in which the books on the table were instruments, not in themselves indispensable." O'Donnell's comments, in discussing the theses of O. du Roy, seem particularly appropriate to Menn's position. "The substance of his criticism is that A. puts trinity ahead of incarnation, then imprudently grants the Platonists a full doctrine of the trinity; the Platonists know about the Fatherland, but lack only the Way to get there. But whether A. is depicted as coming to a full understanding of the trinity anywhere in the text of *Conf.* before Bks. 11–13 is a serious question. The sequence is not trinity, then incarnation, but rather incarnation (Bk. 8), then trinity (Bks. 11–13). The Platonists acquire knowledge that is accurate as far as it goes, but utterly insufficient. That their doctrines, described to show the alleged resemblance to Christian teachings to best advantage (Porphyry would *not* have been pleased), facilitate understanding (or even did facilitate understanding for A.), of the doctrine of the trinity is irrelevant. [T]he incarnation is the one piece of knowledge that has the greatest power to lead on to full and sufficient knowledge of God – that was, for A., the purpose of the incarnation. The Platonists stumble on to everything else, but in a way that is wholly inadequate to a real understanding, they are closer to the demons who 'believe and shudder' (Jas. 2:19) than to the humblest of baptized Christians." Menn's failure to see this point is a result of his reducing the genre of *Conf.* to autobiography and his segregation of *Conf.* VII from the broader purposes of the work.

115 Descartes, *Meditations* VI; CSM II, pp. 58–9; AT VII, pp. 84–5. See also *Principles* III.2–3; CSM I, pp. 248–9; AT VIIIA, pp. 80–1. This contention requires an elaboration on the relationship and coherency of the proofs from infinity and perfection in the third *Meditation*, but I will discuss that below. See also the remarks of Louis Dupré, *Passage to Modernity*, p. 88: "A God defined under the primary attribute of 'incomprehensible power' (*puissance incompréhensible*) excludes any motive beyond the exercise of that power. If he creates, his creative act does not bestow upon his creatures the kind of intrinsic intelligibility a theory of participative analogy between Creator and creature would grant them."

116 Menn, *Descartes and Augustine*, pp. 159, 161.

117 James O'Donnell notes that what is strictly at stake in the "ascent" of *Conf.* VII.10 is not an "ascent" but an "assumption" (*te adsumpsti me*), and there is a strong eucharistic and thus christological connection insinuated with this theme. "I am the food of grown men. Grow, and you shall feed upon me. You will not change me into yourself, as you change food into your flesh, but you will be changed into me." There is a similar echo of this theme at *De Lib*. II.7–12, and a stronger one still at *De Lib*. III.10.

118 Pickstock, "Music: Soul, City and Cosmos after Augustine," p. 255. "Grey ontology" is Marion's term used to describe the "de-qualification" that occurs as a consequence of the Cartesian geometrization of essence in the process of objectivation. As will become clear in the next section, it is a direct correlate of the Cartesian conception of will. The term appears throughout *On Descartes' Metaphysical Prism: The Constitution and Limits of Onto-Theo-Logy in Cartesian Thought*, trans. Jeffrey L. Kosky (Chicago: University of Chicago Press, 1999); however it is probably best summarized in a lecture footnoted in another article by Marion, where "'grey ontology' [is] that which 'conceals itself under an epistemological discourse' thereby 'maintaining the thing in the greyness of the object [qua mental reconstruction], and thus bears testimony to the intoxication . . . of the ego, 'master and owner' of the world

reduced to evidence." Marion, "Descartes and Onto-Theology," in Phillip Blond (ed.), *Post-Secular Philosophy: Between Philosophy and Theology* (London: Routledge, 1998), p. 97 n. 1. I would suggest that this "greyness" is redoubled, and this disjunction of quantity and quality reflected, by the indeterminacy that results from the priority that Descartes accords infinity among the divine attributes.

119 Once this disjunction is effected through doubt, perfections – even the predication of divine perfections – become a matter of "amplification" at the behest of the *ego*. Descartes, *Replies* V; CSM II, p. 252; AT VII, p. 365. See Marion, "The Essential Incoherence," p. 315.

120 Augustine, *De Mus.*, II.29. See also *De Civ.* XI.18; XXII.24; *De Vera Relig.*, XXI.41; *De Nat. Boni* VIII.

121 See Ladner, *The Idea of Reform*, p. 215. It should be noted, however, that the beauty in question is the harmonic beauty of the whole as a song of the universe. Augustine, *De Lib.* III.9.

122 Augustine, *De Vera Relig.* XXX.54; XXXVI.66. Pushed to its conclusions, this logic reconfigures criteria of truth in light of the convertibility of the transcendentals in a manner antithetical to Descartes. Truth is finally inseparable from beauty and desire.

123 This should be obvious from the fact that Wisdom is synonymous with one, and Wisdom is convertible with beauty. There is no contradiction between Augustine identifying number and form and asserting that number has to do with *harmonia*, precisely because, as we have seen, finite forms are never fully and simultaneously instantiated and are only manifest as form precisely in the harmonious time circuits. For the identity of number and form, see Harrison, *Beauty and Revelation*, pp. 40–1.

124 Ladner, pp. 217–18.

125 The *forma veritatis* of *De Trin.* VIII.

126 Augustine, *De Trin.* XV.18.32.

127 Menn, *Descartes and Augustine*, p. 267.

128 The "ascent" is also prefaced by the conclusions of *Conf.* VII.16. "From experience, I knew it is no strange thing that the bread that pleases a healthy appetite is offensive to one that is not healthy, and that light is hateful to sick eyes, but welcome to the well. Your justice offends the wicked, much more do the viper and the worm, which you have created good and in keeping with those lower parts of your creation, to which the wicked themselves are adapted. For they are in harmony with those lower things in so far as they are unlike you, but they are in harmony with higher things, in so far as they become like you." Menn will have a certain interpretation of the Christology of *Conf.* VII, but I will contend that it is inadequate.

129 Again, Menn appears to be following in the tradition of O. du Roy. See O. du Roy, *Intelligence de la foi en la Trinité selon saint Augustin* (Paris: Etudes Augustiniennes, 1966), pp. 96–106. For a synopsis of this criticism and a response which takes into account *Conf.* VII.9.15, see O'Donnell, *Augustine: Confessions*, Vol. 2, pp. 413–16, and n. 110 above. Parts of the criticisms which follow are indebted to O'Donnell's interpretation.

130 Augustine, *Conf.* VII.21.

131 O'Donnell, *Augustine: Confessions*, Vol. 2, p. 415.

132 At *De Civ.* X.29, this distinction appears again, only Augustine seems less sanguine about the clarity of the Platonists' vision of the goal. His interpretation here is more obviously in line with Rom. 1.19–23, which he cited in the prologue to the book and at *De Trin.* XIII.19.24. "You assert the Father and his Son, whom you call Intellect or Mind of the Father; you also speak of a

being who is between the two, and we imagine that you are referring to the Holy Spirit. In spite of your irregular terminology, you Platonists have here some kind of intuition of the goal to which we must strive, however dimly seen through the obscurities of a subtle imagination."

133 Studer, "History and Faith," p. 34.

134 Augustine, *De Trin*. XIII.19.24.

135 "[O]ne cannot arrive at true contemplative wisdom without faith and hope in the resurrection" (Studer, "History and Faith in Augustine's *De Trinitate*," *Augustinian Studies*, 28, 1, 1997, p. 44). Jorge Secada also observes a difference between the Cartesian and Augustinian conceptions of this relationship. "The Cartesian refutation of scepticism appeals to the innate capacity and contents of a soul which shares in the divine knowledge of essence. It belongs to the tradition of St. Bonaventure and St Augustine. There are, however, significant differences between Descartes and his Christian predecessors . . . The understanding these Christian mystics seek requires living in a certain way, having a certain character and disposition, being divinely illuminated, and in general satisfying other conditions . . . Augustine might have allowed that the impure could know many truths, but could they know God, that He exists and who He is? That one can gain philosophical and metaphysical understanding in the 'pure' Cartesian way is a supposition which separates Descartes' essentialism from its mystical predecessors. The mystic is a whole man engaged in a comprehensive transformation, corporeal and spiritual, theoretical and moral. Mystical Platonism is an enterprise that supposes the unity of these human aspects in the ascent towards truth. Assuming this Cartesian distinction between philosophy and intellectual pursuits on the one hand and practical matters on the other, we can inquire first whether, as would seem to be the case, some theoretical considerations are a condition for certain practices and second whether, as St Bonaventure and St Augustine suggest, certain non-intellectual practices are a condition for some theoretical undertakings. Descartes appears to decide the latter without argument or discussion" (Secada, *Cartesian Metaphysics*, pp. 46–9). One should note, however, that Secada can locate Cartesian essentialism in the Augustinian and Bonaventurian tradition because he deems the "relation between God's will and understanding . . . a hopeless theological matter" (p. 60) and minimizes any real differences here under the universal assent to divine simplicity.

136 Augustine, *De Trin*. XIII.24.

137 Menn, *Descartes and Augustine*, p. 132. This is a remarkable statement purely in biographical terms. It would presumably have the *Conf.* start with Book VII, whereas Augustine narrates his coming to Platonism as the result of a prior inspiration (or call), mediated by his mother and others. In the theological terms of the *Conf.*, this inspiration has no discrete origin because it sounds from all eternity, a claim Augustine confronts us with from the outset. This theological understanding and the purposes it implies raise the question of whether Menn's understanding is adequate to the literary complexity and genre of the *Conf.* This question is very different from "biographical accuracy."

138 Descartes, *Replies* II; CSM II, p. 106; AT VII, p. 149; *Meditations*, IV; CSM II, pp. 40–1; AT VII, pp. 57–60. See also Stanley Rosen, "A Central Ambiguity in Descartes," in Bernd Magnus and James B. Wilbur (eds), *Cartesian Essays* (The Hague: Martinus Nijhoff, 1969), pp. 30–2; Menn, *Descartes and Augustine*, pp. 316, 328.

139 Menn, *Descartes and Augustine*, p. 200.

140 Ibid., pp. 202–3.

141 "I was intent on the things contained in places, but among them I found no place of rest . . ." (*Conf.* VII.7.11), suggests that, before baptism and incorporation into Christ, Augustine was not simply corrupted by materiality, but was attempting such an orientation and failing. O'Donnell writes, "The 'looking' here resembles that of 9.10.25 (Ostia), with the difference that there the things of creation shrugged off A.'s gaze and passed him along to God. Here he is incapable of seeing into, through, or beyond them. In terms of Rom. 1:20ff. (see on 7.9.14), he does not yet see God in the visible things of creation, and to that end this attempt at 'nature mysticism' is a failure." In the next chapter, Augustine alludes to Christ's humility as the healing salve (*collyrio*) for the eye. "Elsewhere in A., *collyrium* is proper to the incarnate Christ (whose *dolores* were pre-eminently *salubres*) and occurs surprisingly often." O'Donnell notes here and in other texts, "a remarkable amalgam of neo-Platonic and Christian vocabulary, demanding *fides*, *spes*, *caritas* as the prerequisites for vision." O'Donnell, *Augustine: Confessions*, Vol. 2, pp. 410–11.

I alluded before to one facet of the *Conf.* that Menn ignores completely: the eucharistic overtones which are rife throughout the work, and which arguably structure Augustine's reconfiguration of creation as Church in *Conf.* XIII. (See especially XIII.6–18.) Ironically, if O'Donnell is right, there may be an overlooked partial continuity here between neoplatonism and Augustine, which would seemingly oppose Descartes. "There is no suggestion, anywhere in A. or in any of the modern commentators, that he ever took his 'Platonism' so far as to indulge in theurgy. The only possible liturgy for him now was Christianity; the ascent of the mind was non-sectarian in that important, even crucial sense. But in one significant way, the Platonic pattern may have influenced his expectations of Christianity in a way that also goes unattended. The function of theurgy is to bring about the presence of God, visibly. What does Christianity have that would have appeared to a half-Christian Plotinus/ Porphyry reader as the rough equivalent of theurgy? Eucharist: making the god to be present. The Mass as Christian theurgy? Or as Christian counterpart to theurgy?" O'Donnell, *Augustine: Confessions*, Vol. 2, p. 415.

142 Augustine, *Conf.* VII.20.
143 Menn, *Descartes and Augustine*, p. 313.
144 Ibid., p. 340 n. 3.
145 See Marilyn McCord Adams, "Universals in the Fourteenth Century," and Edward Grant, "The Effect of the Condemnation of 1277," in Norman Kretzmann, Anthony Kenny and Jan Pinborg (eds), *The Cambridge History of Later Medieval Philosophy* (Cambridge: Cambridge University Press, 1982), pp. 411–39, 537–9. On Descartes' Scotist debts, particularly in regard to the notion of the "objective being" of an idea, see Roger Ariew, *Descartes and the Last Scholastics* (Ithaca: Cornell University Press), pp. 39–57.
146 Marion notes one decisive shift away from his medieval predecessors, in how Descartes construes the relationship between God as creator and cause. "The title *Deus creator omnium* does not occur with a frequency proportional to its dogmatic importance. It concerns primarily two functions . . . [which] actually reduce to one. But at the same time it becomes clear that Descartes adds nothing to his definition of God by mentioning that he is the creator, since creation becomes intelligible only on the basis of omnipotence being exercised as cause—'*ultima causa*' (AT VII, 50). Contrary to the nominalists, who justify the (metaphysical) omnipotence of God by reference to his (theological) role as creator, Descartes renders creation intelligible by reducing it to omnipotence, rationalized as efficient cause" (Marion, "The Essential Incoherence," pp. 313–14).

147 Each, however, accords this primacy differently. Scotus does so by making will the more noble faculty; Ockham does so by making the distinction purely nominal and by following Scotus (in one application at least) in de-finalizing the will and freedom. See David W. Clark, "Ockham on Human and Divine Freedom," *Franciscan Studies* XVI.38, 1978, pp. 132–3. One should not oversimplify here; the differences between Scotus, Ockham and Descartes are significant. There seems to be an inconsistency in Scotus' various formulations. In one version, for instance, the divine will, if not necessarily the human, still has "good" as a formal object. See Duns Scotus, *Ordinatio* I. d.II q.1, I.a.2.1, II.3, in *Duns Scotus: Philosophical Writings*, trans. Alan Wolter, OFM (Indianapolis: Hackett, 1987), pp. 52–62, 70–1. Alliez's comments are instructive here. "*'Necessitas naturalis non stat cum libertate.'* Apprehended through the intellect, the end is not necessarily desired by the will. To put it otherwise: moral goodness is no longer for Duns Scotus the efficient cause of the voluntary actions that result from it. 'The *Bonitas moralis* is added to the substance of the voluntary act as beauty is added to the substance of the body.'* Being no longer that final principle in command of the voluntary moral act, the cognition of the good is only 'ostensive,' not 'directional' or 'effective,' although Duns Scotus' constructive monism at no time crosses the decisive threshold of Cartesian voluntarism, which transposes the free action of the creator into man. In Scotus, the will remains that of created being and sinner, a double weakness. (Never creative, the human will is 'receptive' at best, 'operational' at worst: such is the will of sin.) *A forteriori*, then, there is no submission of the will in God either to a good conceived by the understanding. Of course the God of Duns Scotus is not the God of Ockham and of the nominalist paradoxes, nor the Cartesian God of eternal ideas, products of an absolutely free creative will. There has quite rightly been an insurgency against such simplifications, which tend to privilege far too unilaterally the arbitrariness of the divine will when, infinite will and perfection being identical, the good is always what the divine will wants—*but in an absolutely contingent way*. It can nonetheless be asked whether the Subtle Doctor's ontological voluntarism did not clear the path from the one to the other by consecrating *de potentia absoluta* the breaking of the natural movement of the will's potential toward its good." Alliez, *Capital Times*, p. 213. The citation of Scotus (*) is from *Ordinatio*, I. d.39 q.1, n.21. See also Gilson, *History of Christian Philosophy in the Middle Ages* (London: Sheed and Ward, 1955), pp. 454–71, 489–500.

However, in a second formulation, Scotus asserts that "being" and not "goodness" is the object of volition, and it is to this that Ockham is indebted. "Ockham reserves his strongest criticism for the Scotist position of the will's nature. But take warning—Ockham expresses his objections to the Subtle Doctor more readily than his debts. For example, Ockham follows Scotus in asserting that 'being' and not 'goodness' is the object of the volitional power. Both men can claim error in the Thomistic position that the will must choose 'under the aspect of goodness.' More importantly, it is Scotus who first protests against analysing the will by means of Aristotle's four-fold 'nature' or 'appetite.' 'The more formal characteristic of the will is freedom rather than appetite; as freedom is the will's form of receptivity so the characteristic of freedom is the more constitutive feature of the will.' [Scotus, *Comm. Ox.* II, d.25, q.unica, n.6] Ockham's debt to this insight will be manifest; he is critical only of Scotus' inconsistent application" (Clark, "Ockham on Human and Divine Freedom," pp. 137–8).

148 Marion, "The Essential Incoherence," p. 318.

149 See Leo J. Sweeney, "Divine attributes in *De doctrina christiana*: Why Does Augustine Not List 'Infinity?,'" in Duane W. H. Arnold and Pamela Bright (eds.), De doctrina christiana: *A Classic of Western Culture* (Notre Dame: University of Notre Dame Press, 1995), pp. 195–204. Augustine does employ the term at *De Trin.* VI.10.12, as Sweeney says, "to express the fact that three divine persons are distinct as persons and yet are not distinct from one another in respect of the divine essence, with which each is identical," and in *Ep.* 118.24, to indicate freedom from spatial limit. Menn seems unaware of one instance where Augustine's predications do resemble the Cartesian definitions. In *Tract. in Jo.* I.1.8, Augustine characterizes God as "quamdam substantiam, vivam, perpetuam, omnipotentem, infinitam, ubique praesentem, ubique totam, nusquam inclusam." However, I suggest two cautions against assimilating this account to Descartes. First, Augustine's language is notoriously imprecise, and he frequently makes concessions to the exigencies of ordinary speech. So some allowance should be made for the homiletic context, since Augustine here uses *substantia* in a way which he cautions against in the more technical context of *De Trin.* VII.5.10. Secondly, if one understands all the terms in question as appositive, then it is impossible to accord *substantiam, omnipotentem* and *infinitem* a priority, and indeed the meaning of these terms is qualified by *vivam, ubique praesentem*, and *ubique totam*. As Augustine proceeds to contrast the temporal passing of the two syllables and four letters of *deus* with the Word of John's prologue, it becomes clear that Augustine means here the infinity of a genuine transcendence (ultimately the *totus Christus*). This transcendence is "other" to the finite and has no real relationship to it. As we shall see, this is in marked contrast to Descartes, who locks finite and infinite into mutual, negative relation. Furthermore, within the Cartesian *epoche*, infinity, which remains incomprehensible and indefinite, qualifies the other terms of the definitions, not the other way around. See Marion, "The Essential Incoherence," pp. 307–8. Finally, the respective predications must be contextualized within the purposes of texts in which we find them. Augustine's homily, its purposes and the theology toward which it is tending as he moves through John, conforms to the portrait we have sketched thus far.

150 Leo J. Sweeney, *Divine Infinity in Greek and Medieval Thought* (New York: Peter Lang, 1992), pp. 168–222. Sweeney suggests this is so for at least one sense of the term in Plotinus' usage. See Plotinus, *Enn.*VI.9. Sweeney suggests that while Augustine's God must be infinite since he is incomprehensible, immaterial, and unconstrained by local limit, Augustine nevertheless might have been uncertain about what infinity might mean when applied to God's incorporeal existence, given the neoplatonic baggage attached to the term ἄπειρον.

151 Aristotle, *Physics* III. 202b3–208a27; Sweeney, *Divine Infinity*, pp. 143–65.

152 Sweeney, *Divine Infinity*, pp. 337–63. Sweeney notes that few medieval theologians before Bonaventure discuss infinity per se at any length and when they do (such as in Lombard's *Libri IV Sententiarum*, Hugh of Saint-Victor's *De sacramentis christianae fidei*, Hugh of Saint-Cher's *In Sententiarum*, Alexander of Hales' *Gloss in Sent.*, and Albert the Great's *In Sent.*), it is made synonymous with God's eternity and incomprehensibility or applied to divine power. See Sweeney, *Divine Infinity*, p. 9

153 Marion, "The Essential Incoherence," pp. 321–2.

154 St. Bonaventure, *The Journey of the Mind to God*, trans. Philotheus Boehner, OFM (Indianapolis: Hackett, 1956), V.8. Bonaventure actually borrows the image from Alan of Lille, *Theological Rules*, n. 7. (*PL* 210, 627).

155 See n. 89, above.

156 Augustine, *De Trin.* VII.5.10.

157 Descartes, *Meditations* V.46. See Secada, *Cartesian Metaphysics*, pp. 139–47, 170–1; Menn, *Descartes and Augustine*, pp. 337–52.

158 Menn, *Descartes and Augustine*, pp. 338–9. Menn's conclusion that the Scotist conclusion is probably the best solution to the problem consists in what he takes to be the inadequacies of the Thomist position, namely, that *scientia naturalis* of a plurality of things through God's knowledge of his own perfections compromises divine simplicity. See Menn, *Descartes and Augustine*, p. 349. It is not my purpose here to dispute Menn's treatment of Aquinas, but this conclusion arguably does not take adequate account of our analogous predication (*ST* I–I, 13, 5, 6) and its relationship to how God must be understood to know particular things in his knowledge of himself. "And therefore as God contains all perfections in himself, the essence of God is compared to all other essences of things, not as the common to the proper, as unity is to numbers, or as the centre (of a circle) to the (radiating) lines; but as perfect acts to imperfect . . . As therefore the essence of God contains in itself all the perfection contained in the essence of any other being and far more, God can know in Himself all of them with proper knowledge. For the nature proper to each thing consists in some degree of participation in the divine perfection" (*ST* I–I, 14, 6). Given this, it is not clear to me why, God cannot know a plurality of truths by looking at himself, without looking to creatures for comparison. This is especially true since Aquinas says that "Inasmuch as [God] knows his own essence perfectly, he knows it according to every mode in which it can be known. Now it can be known not only as it is in itself, but as it can be participated in by creatures according to some degree of likeness" (*ST* I–I, 15, 2). The objection seems to derive from an implicit capture of God within the horizon of univocal being.

159 See Augustine, *Conf.* XIII.34.

160 Menn, *Descartes and Augustine*, p. 212.

161 Whereas Augustine had used God's nature as "good" against Julian to reconfigure *libertas* within *necessitate*, Descartes arrives at God's goodness, not from good or the nature of will; these are unavailable to him. Rather he arrives at this conclusion in the third *Meditation* by virtue of the need of an a priori perfection against which to understand his own lack. This conclusion also rests upon the principle of causality.

162 See Descartes, *Meditations* IV; CSM II, p. 40; AT VII, p. 57; *Passions* I.41; CSM I, p. 343; AT XI, pp. 359–60.

163 Menn, *Descartes and Augustine*, p. 340.

164 See Clark, "Ockham on Human and Divine Freedom," p. 147.

165 Descartes, *Meditations* IV; CSM II, p. 40; AT VII, p. 58.

166 Descartes appears to concur with Ockham on this point. Clark, "Ockham on Human and Divine Freedom," pp. 140–4.

167 Descartes, *Passions* II.137; CSM I, p. 376; AT XI, p. 430.

168 Descartes, *Meditations* IV; CSM II, pp. 40–1; AT VII, 58.

169 Ibid. CSM II, p. 41; AT VII, pp. 59–60.

170 Ibid. CSM II, p. 40; AT VII, p. 58.

171 Descartes would no doubt protest at this description. His intuition of God along with the soul is supposed to entail that God is essentially causal, i.e., essentially will. Hence, in commenting upon his argument in *Meditation* III, Descartes insists in the *Replies* II.77 that "I did not base my argument on the fact that I observed there to be an order or succession of efficient causes among the objects perceived by the senses." This would be to base the

argument on something dubitable. Rather, the force of the argument depends upon the essence/existence of God being a cataleptic idea entailed in my clear and distinct idea of myself. However, insofar as this notion requires and is subordinated (incoherently, in Marion's view) to the causal principle stipulating as much formal reality in the cause of the idea as objective reality in the idea, the innate, clear and distinct idea of God is still dependent upon me recognizing my essence as a *res cogitans*, a thing that "*doubts, affirms, denies,* understands a few things, is willing, is unwilling . . ." (*Meditations* II, CSM 19; AT VII, p. 28). Since the first three of these descriptions of the *res cogitans* are acts of *will*, one can conclude that this idea of God, taken in conjunction with this principle, is dependent upon my recognizing and having will.

172 Descartes, *Meditations* IV; CSM II, p. 40; AT VII, pp. 57–8.

173 Menn, *Descartes and Augustine*, p. 315.

174 Here again, the limited scope of the intellect (which is passive) contrasted with the active infinity of the will, signals finitude which distinguishes the *cogito* from God, whose intellect has been subordinated under and assimilated to the activity of will, similarly construed. See Descartes, *Meditations* IV, CSM II, pp. 39–41; AT VII, pp. 56–60.

175 Menn, *Descartes and Augustine*, p. 321.

176 Ibid., p. 321. Hence "the freedom that reflects the *imago dei* is not liberty of indifference: it is specifically freedom from *irrational* constraint. The right use of this freedom is negative."

177 Janowski, *Cartesian Theodicy*, p. 60. Menn affirms as much (*Descartes and Augustine*, p. 313), and we shall consider this in the next section. Interestingly, Menn appears to be searching in the things that command my assent for a Cartesian analog to Augustine's *non posse peccare* and the corresponding positive finitude. (Menn suggests that Descartes' method of avoiding error takes its roots from Augustine's "theodicy.") The things in question are undoubtedly Descartes' fundamental principle and the accompanying recognition, from the third *Meditation*, that I must think God's infinity and perfection along with myself to recognize myself as finite and imperfect. This is the root of the claim in the third *Meditation* that God and the soul are better known than bodies. Yet to treat the fundamental principle as a matter of assent, on Descartes' understanding of assent, is arguably to miss what makes the principle fundamental. While it is unnecessary to attribute to Menn an inferential sense of the ergo in *ego cogito ergo sum*, he nevertheless appears to miss the force of the fundamental principle as a performative utterance. When we consider it under in this light, as we will in the next section, Cartesian *voluntas* becomes more ominous—and even less Augustinian. On the fundamental principle as a performative utterance, see Jaako Hintikka, "Cogito, Ergo Sum: Inference or Performance?," in Alexander Sesonske and Noel Fleming (eds), *Meta-Meditations: Studies in Descartes* (Belmont: Wadsworth, 1965), pp. 50–76. See also James B. Wilbur, "The Cogito, an Ambiguous Performance", in Bernd Magnus and James B. Wilbur (eds), *Cartesian Essays: A Collection of Critical Studies* (The Hague: Marinus Nijhoff, 1969), pp. 65–76. On the ominous consequences of this conclusion, see Gillespie, *Nihilism before Nietzsche*, pp. 38–47.

178 It would not be exactly appropriate here to say that the divine will exceeds the scope of the intellect, because for Descartes there is no passive faculty in the divine essence. It is more proper to say that the divine intellect has been reconfigured as the divine will, on the Cartesian notion of will as infinite power or arbitrary choice. The effect is essentially the same, the subordination of intellect to will. See Menn, *Descartes and Augustine*, pp. 339–52; Rosen,

"A Central Ambiguity in Descartes," pp. 30–5; Secada, *Cartesian Metaphysics*, pp. 59–63; Gillespie, *Nihilism before Nietzsche*, pp. 51–63.

179 Menn, *Descartes and Augustine*, pp. 349–59; Augustine, *Conf.* XIII.38.

180 Ibid., pp. 349–50.

181 This is at least the case with "formal" truth and falsity. Descartes, *Meditations* III; CSM II, p. 30; AT VII, p. 43. On Descartes' "Scotism," see Ariew, *Descartes and the Last Scholastics*, pp. 39–76; Secada, *Cartesian Metaphysics*, pp. 77–96.

182 Menn, *Descartes and Augustine*, p. 350.

183 This is perhaps because, in spite of his insistence upon the Plotinian-Augustinian-Cartesian conception of God as *Nous*, Menn, holding in common with Descartes a very post-Suárezian concept of revelation which would have been unavailable to Augustine (in which what is revealed is a *doctrine*), consigns trinitarian considerations to the realm of faith and practice. I can have a clear and distinct idea of God in his unity (as infinite substance and will), but that this God is Trinity I can only know confusedly and obscurely as a separate article of faith. Of course for a theological viewpoint, this is backward: I do not know God "clearly and distinctly" (to the extent that this is possible in this life) until I know God as Trinity. This absolves Menn from submitting his conception of *voluntas* to trinitarian scrutiny. However, it creates all manner of problems for the legitimacy of his interpretation of Augustine. First, it is unclear how to square this rigid distinction with Augustine's emphatic insistence that there is no substantial substrate "beneath" the trinitarian *personae*. Secondly, insofar as Augustine does attribute trinitarianism to the Platonists, there could be no exercise in Augustine directed toward *de deo uno* which is not at once trinitarian. Finally, this causes Menn to neglect the trinitarian character of *exercitatio* of *De Trin*. Nevertheless, there is no question but that Menn reads this distinction back onto Augustine: "Descartes' doctrine of faith is indistinguishable from Augustine's." Menn, *Descartes and Augustine*, pp. 333, 329–30. See also, John Montag, SJ, "Revelation: The False Legacy of Suárez," in Milbank, Pickstock, and Ward (eds), *Radical Orthodoxy*, pp. 38–63.

184 Augustine, *Conf.* XIII 34, emphasis mine. Notice again the double turn.

185 He comes closer to making the requisite connections as he continues appealing to a plurality of ideas in the divine logos, "so he is not forced to conclude that the multiplicity of essences proceeds purely from the will of God." Menn, *Descartes and Augustine*, p. 350.

186 Ibid., p. 348.

187 As noted in the last chapter, that which is immutable or *actus purus* need do nothing else to become a cause. Causality is registered in the emergence of the effect.

188 Augustine, *De Trin.* XV.7.12; XI.9.16. See also *De Civ.* XI.28.24; XIV.7 "All acts of knowing or deciding involve the production in the mind of a *uerbum mentis* through assent to some trace in the memory or perceived sensory stimuli. The assent we give is an aspect of our desire and may be part of either *amor* or *cupiditas* . . . [T]o 'discover' something is to bring forth an 'appropriate' knowledge which produces a unity (of intention) in the mind, and in so doing we discover that the unifying love was there all along, prior even to the knowledge of it which also, in some sense, already exists." Ayres, "The Discipline of Self-knowledge," p. 271. Menn (*Descartes and Augustine*, p. 310 n. 7) takes Augustine's remarks in *De Praed. Sanct.* to confirm a stoic (and Cartesian) notion of judgment. In II.5 Augustine says that "'*credere* is *cogitare cum assensione*'" and in V.10 concludes that "'*credere vel non credere . . . est in arbitrio voluntatis humanae*, so that *fides . . . in voluntate est*.'" However, Menn

attends neither to Augustine's criticisms of the stoic view in *De Civ.* nor to Augustine's account of a faith that is simultaneously and voluntarily ours and a gift. This faith is already the product of a prior love, and this, we have seen, profoundly affects how Augustine conceives of the voluntary.

189 Augustine, *De Trin.* XI.9.16; XV.7.12.

190 Though it is important to remember here that this *similitudo* is grounded in, and indeed consequent upon, an even greater *dissimilitudo*.

191 Descartes, *Passions* II.79–85; CSM I, pp. 356–8; AT VIIIA, pp. 387–92. I presuppose my earlier contention that the catalectic impression of the infinite in my thinking of myself is dependent upon the principle of causality and that thus the intuition of the "I think" is logically prior to the intuition of the infinite. Menn is right to note a version of the *Meno* aporia here, and one can grant a certain similarity between Descartes and Augustine on this point. Yet the priority of will as power, the intervention of the objective reality of idea, and the principle of causality intervene to make the Cartesian version of the aporia parodic of the Augustinian version.

192 Hence it makes no sense to treat the *Conf.* as offering "proof" of their addressee, as Menn does when he treats *Conf.* VII.17 as a prototype of the Cartesian proof of God that employs the principle of causality to the objective reality of ideas. See Menn, *Descartes and Augustine*, pp. 266, 262–70.

193 See Paula Fredriksen, "Paul and Augustine: Narratives, Orthodox Traditions, and the Retrospective Self," *Journal of Theological Studies*, 37, 1, April 1986, p. 24.

194 Louis Marin, "Echographies," in Patric Ranson (ed.), *Saint Augustin* (Lausanne: L'Age d'homme, 1988), pp. 296–8; cited in Alliez, *Capital Times*, p. 117.

195 Augustine, *Conf.* XI.29.

196 Wetzel, *Augustine and the Limits*, p. 195. See Augustine, *Conf.* X.4.

197 Menn, *Descartes and Augustine*, p. 132.

198 As O'Donnell reminds us, Platonism's instrumentality in this story, not Platonism itself, is the point here. O'Donnell, *Augustine: Confessions*, Vol. 2, pp. 413–18.

199 Nicholas Paige claims, interestingly, that seventeenth-century French translations of the *Conf.* were colored by an anachronistic "autobiographical mentality" absent in the text itself, where numerous phrases such as "Inwardly I said to myself" (*dicebam enim apud me intus*, VIII.11) become "for I said within myself from the deepest part of my soul" (Car je disais en moi-même du plus profond de mon âme). The latter, from Robert Arnauld's 1649 translation, while too late to have influenced the *Meditations*, certainly comports with the emerging idea that the interior self is the ground of truth. See Nicholas D. Paige, *Being Interior: Autobiography and the Contradictions of Modernity in Seventeenth-Century France* (Philadelphia: University of Pennsylvania Press), pp. 50–61. I am indebted to Anthony Baker for calling my attention to Paige's argument.

200 This is precisely because Descartes subordinates divided passions to the unity of a free will, which is one. See Augustine, *Conf.* II.4.9–6.14; Wetzel, *Augustine and the Limits*, pp. 206–18. Contrast Augustine, *Conf.* VIII.9.21 and XI.29 with Descartes, *Passions* I.47. Augustine's and Descartes' respective accounts of will result in two different accounts of the unity and comprehensibility of the self, but I will address this more fully in the next section.

201 Augustine, *De Trin.* X.6.8. The microcosmic/macrocosmic point is buttressed by consideration of our a priori membership in either of the two cities, or the respective bodies of either of the two Adams.

202 Augustine, *De Trin.* IV.10.13, 12.15, 13.16–18.

203 See Augustine, *Conf.* I.2; I.18; II.1; II.6–9; IX.1; X.1–2; X.5; X.8; X.17; X.27; X.31; X.43; XI.29; XII.34.

204 "Augustine the convert interprets Paul's conversion through his own, and his own through what he sees as Paul's" (Fredriksen, "Paul and Augustine," p. 27). Fredriksen's essay is valuable in tracing shifts in Augustine's reading of Paul; however, it is inadequate first for failing to see how thoroughly typological the *Conf.* are at the outset, that this "mythic feed-back system which constitutes both Augustine and Paul" is already typological, and second, because her presumption of a real history, of what "actually happened" apart from the descriptions under which it is rendered imposes an alien metaphysics on the text.

205 Frances Young, "*The Confessions* of St Augustine: What Is the Genre of This Work?," *Augustinian Studies*, 30, 1, 1979, pp. 8–16.

206 Ibid., p. 16, emphasis mine.

207 Ibid., p. 13.

208 *De Civ.* X positions Platonism this way.

209 Augustine, *De Doct.* II.40.60.

210 Marion, *On Descartes' Metaphysical Prism*, trans. Jeffrey L. Kosky (Chicago: University of Chicago Press, 1999), p. 133.

211 God remains crucially important for Cartesian physics, as one whose immutable action conserves a constant quantity of motion in the universe and whose immutable act is the source of force between otherwise inert bodies. Since the essence of body for Descartes is extension, it has no intrinsic capacity to transmit motion through force by virtue of its motion. Rather, "the relation is just the reverse: 'the force of a body to act . . . is simply the tendency of everything to persist in its present state,' a tendency that does not follow from any property of matter, but from an attribute of God." The ambiguity consists in how Descartes' fundamental principle negates the traditional God only to reconstruct him as this causal hypothesis and guarantor of clear and distinct ideas. See Descartes, *Principles* II.43; CSM I, p. 243; AT VIIIA, p. 66; Gary C. Hatfield, "Force (God) in Descartes' Physics," p. 126.

212 This may be true in more than one sense. Stanley Rosen contends that the role of the imagination in Descartes' account of the faculties may belie a monism beneath Descartes' celebrated dualism which can refract either into idealism or materialism. He regards this as a failure and consequence of the incompatible Cartesian goals of identifying a rational order of nature and giving the will mastery over this order. Amelie Oksenberg Rorty detects a stoic inheritance in Descartes' distinction between passions, emotion and intellection, and suggests analogous ambiguities for his dualism. I will suggest eventually an analogy between the function of the Cartesian will in sustaining a kind of equilibrium among materially conflicting passions and the stoic *tonos*, and one might suggest a similar "materialism" in Descartes' "mechanistic account of a causal chain that starts in the sensed thing and ends in some part of the brain." Secada, *Cartesian Metaphysics*, p. 35. See *Meditations* VI; CSM II, 59–61; AT VII, pp. 84–9. *Passions* I.10–15, pp. 31–7; CSM I, pp. 335–41; AT XI, pp. 335–41. See Rosen, "A Central Ambiguity in Descartes," pp. 24, 29. Rorty, "Cartesian Passions and the Union of Mind and Body," in Rorty (ed.), *Essays on Descartes' Meditations* (Berkeley: University of California Press, 1986), pp. 529–30, 533 n. 15.

213 Menn, *Descartes and Augustine*, p. 313. See also Descartes, *Passions* I.27; CSM I, p. 338; AT XI, p. 349.

214 For thorough accounts of Descartes' scholastic debts and his departures from them, as well as his place within the history of the transformation, see Secada, *Cartesian Metaphysics*, pp. 77–114; Ariew, *Descartes and the Last Scholastics*, pp. 58–76.

215 See Menn, *Descartes and Augustine*, pp. 234–5, 269. My previous criticisms should suffice as my response to Menn's attribution of this notion to Augustine.

216 In *Principles* I.33; CSM I, p. 204; AT VIIIA p. 18, Descartes remarks, "Now when we perceive something, so long as we do not make any assertion or denial about it, we clearly avoid error. And we equally avoid error when we confine our assertions or denials to what we clearly and distinctly perceive should be asserted or denied. Error arises only when, as often happens we make a judgment about something even though we do not have an accurate perception of it." In *Meditations* VI and in *Passions* it becomes clear that what we perceive, being passive, does not depend on the soul. Compare this to Margaret Reesor's reconstruction of the stoic theory of judgment. "The apprehension (*katalepsis*) is not 'attributable to us.' Alexander of Aphrodisias writes in his *Concerning Fate*: 'For they say that "that which is attributable to us" does not apply in a situation in which we yield [*eixai*] when a presentation falls upon us, or when we yield to a presentation that is formed by us ourselves, and direct our impulse toward that which is presented' (SVF 2.981). The presentation is something that moves or puts pressure on the apprehension (*katalepsis*). Sextus Empiricus illustrates the pressure applied by the cognitive presentation graphically when he writes: 'For it [the apprehensive presentation], being clear and striking, seizes us almost by the hair, they say, dragging us into assent' (*Adv. math.* 7.257). It is precisely because of this pressure that assent to the presentation is not 'attributable to us.' The giving or withholding of assent to the presentation, however, is in the power of the individual (SVF 2.91). Because of our weakness, we give assent to false presentations. This point is made clearly in a passage in Plutarch: 'Again, Chrysippus says, "God makes false presentations, and the wise man too, requiring us not to give assent or yield to them, but only to act and direct our impulse towards the phenomena, but we, being inferior, in weakness give our assent to such presentations"' (SVF 3.177)." Margaret E. Reesor, "Necessity and Fate in Stoic Philosophy," in Rist (ed.), *The Stoics*, p. 193. See also *Principles* I.45; CSM I, p. 207; AT VIIIA, pp. 21–2.

217 Descartes, *Meditations* VI; CSM II, p. 55; AT VII, p. 79. The distinction between action and passion, and Descartes' inability to think the understanding without thinking passivity, are actually crucial to his reconstruction of an extra-mental, physical world of extension. And, of course, the theory of judgment is crucial to ensuring that only the world constructed according to clear and distinct ideas will count as true in theoretical matters.

218 Descartes, *Passions* I.17; CSM I, p. 335; AT XI, pp. 342–3.

219 See also Descartes, *Principles* I.32; CSM I, p. 204; AT VIIIA, p. 17.

220 Descartes, *Passions* I.18; CSM I, p. 335; AT XI, p. 343.

221 Rosen, "A Central Ambiguity in Descartes," p. 31.

222 Wetzel, "Crisis Mentalities: Augustine after Descartes," *American Catholic Philosophical Quarterly* LXXIV.1, 2000, p. 127.

223 Descartes, *Passions* I.47; CSM I, p. 346; AT XI, p. 364.

224 See Bobzien, *Determinism and Freedom in Stoic Philosophy*, p. 286.

225 Descartes *Passions* I.47; CSM I, p. 346; AT XI, pp. 365–6. I do not intend to imply that Cassian and Descartes concur in attributing "to the body alone everything that can be observed in us to oppose our reason," but rather that

there is a similarity in how they conceive of the will as situated between conflicting passions, whether these take their origin from the body or elsewhere in the soul.

226 Descartes, *Passions* I.46; CSM I, p. 345; AT XI, pp. 363–4. Importantly, this insistence causes Descartes to reject the distinction between concupiscible and irascible parts of the soul, which means the rejection of concupiscible and irascible passions, adding "I do not know why they [all his predecessors] have chosen to refer all [the passions] to desire or anger" (I.68; AT XI, p. 379). This reflects Descartes' "de-finalized" will. When will has good as its formal object, then "there is no other passion of the soul that does not presuppose love of some kind" (Aquinas, *ST* I–II, 27, 4).

227 Descartes, *Passions* II.79; CSM I, p. 356; AT XI; p. 387. For comment on the stoic origin of Descartes' distinction between passions, emotion and intellectual emotions, see Rorty, "Cartesian Passions and the Union of Mind and Body," p. 533 n. 16.

228 Descartes, *Passions* II.85; CSM I, p. 358; AT XI, p. 392.

229 Descartes, *Meditations* IV; CSM II, pp. 40–1; AT VII, p. 58.

230 "For undoubtedly the strong soul belongs to those in whom the will by nature can most easily conquer the passions and stop the bodily movements which accompany them." The transposition of this problem onto the theoretical plane becomes even clearer when one recognizes the Cartesian conflation of willing and thinking, as we shall later in this section. See Descartes, *Passions* I.48; CSM I, p. 347; AT XI; pp. 366–7. It is worth remembering, by contrast, that Augustine transforms the passions themselves into forms of will. *De Civ.* XIV.6. After the demolitions of hyperbolic doubt, Gillespie notes, "The chief obstacle to extending the range of human knowledge and the sphere in which the will can act to secure power lies not in nature or in God but in man's passions (Burman, AT, 5:159). We are deceived about the nature of the world because we judge and act solely on the basis of what we imagine or wish to be the case (*Replies*, AT, 7:314; CSM, 2:218)" Gillespie, *Nihilism before Nietzsche*, p. 55).

231 Descartes, *Meditations* IV; CSM II, p. 40; AT VII, p. 57.

232 Descartes, *Passions* I.41; CSM I, p. 343; AT XI, pp. 359–60.

233 See Wetzel, *Augustine and the Limits*, pp. 98–111.

234 See Augustine, *Cont. Duas Ep. Pel.* I.X.22; *De Spir. et Lit.* XIV.25. See also Wetzel, *Augustine and the Limits*, pp. 169–87. See, for instance, *Conf.* VIII.9.

235 See Gillespie, *Nihilism before Nietzsche*, pp. 51–7. The conversion of will-as-doubt into method can indeed be seen as both the exercise of and discipline for the cultivation of this autarky.

236 Descartes, *Passions* I.47; CSM I, pp. 345–6; AT XI, p. 365.

237 Descartes, *Meditations* IV; CSM II, p. 40; AT VII, p. 57; *Passions* III.152; CSM I, 384; AT XI, p. 445.

238 Augustine, *De Civ.* XII.6–7; *De Lib.* III.17.

239 Recall that we addressed this relationship already in Chapter 2.

240 Augustine, *De Civ.* XI.26. The other versions of this argument in Augustine are at *Solil.* II.I.1; *De Lib.* II.3.7; and *De Trin.* X.15.16; XV.12.21.

241 Jean-Luc Marion, *On Descartes' Metaphysical Prism*, p. 133.

242 Descartes, *To Colvius*, 14 November 1640 (AT III, p. 247), quoted in Gareth B. Matthews, *Thought's Ego in Augustine and Descartes* (Ithaca: Cornell University Press, 1992), p. 13.

243 The passage concludes, "In itself it is such a simple and natural thing to infer that one exists from the fact that one is doubting that it could have occurred to any writer. But I am very glad to find myself in agreement with St.

Augustine, if only to hush the little minds who have tried to find fault with the principle."

244 Marion, *On Descartes' Metaphysical Prism*, pp. 131–2. My only quarrel with Marion is over his calling the *si fallor, sum* the *"first* moment" of this movement. In one, prospective sense perhaps, this is true. But even this is preceded in the argument by the *eros* of a search which requires the mediation of the sought. This gets to the profounder sense of the quarrel. From the perspective of this disappropriation, retrospectively in memory, one sees that this moment itself is preceded by a gift. On Augustinian terms, no such discrete origin as is implied by this time can ever finally be isolated.

245 Descartes perhaps comes close to this by recognizing, in *Meditation* III, that his doubt constitutes an imperfection that requires the simultaneous thinking of perfection for its recognition. This recognition must be qualified, however, in light of the differing roles that the proofs for the infinite and perfection play in Descartes' argument, a topic addressed below. In short, whereas the *idea infinitii* functions as an a priori, the idea of perfection is on a par with the other innate ideas and is therefore subject to the principle of causality. This "lack" therefore does not rise to the level of a real mediation, because it is already subject to the will of the *res cogitans*.

246 Descartes' *ordo rationis* is fundamentally important here for the reasons just noted. Doubt as lack is correlative to the clear and distinct idea of perfection. But this for Descartes is one idea among others, subordinate to the infinite and not necessarily convertible with it, which is necessary for any cognition. Hence the recognition of Cartesian "lack" occurs only as a consequence of the prior certainty which is its basis.

247 Williams, "Sapientia and the Trinity", p. 323.

248 Augustine, *De Trin.* XIV.14.18. See also Augustine, *De Civ.* XI.26–8; *De Lib.* I.13; III.7–8.

249 The temporality of Descartes' *cogito*, or the lack thereof, was a subject of immediate controversy among the late scholastics at the time of the *Meditations* publication. See Ariew, *Descartes and the Last Scholastics*, pp. 188–205.

250 Augustine, *De Trin.* XIV.11.14. *Conf.* X illustrates this point.

251 In *De Trin.* XV.1.22, a passage on which Hankey places enormous weight, Augustine sets out once again to refute the skepticism of the New Academy. He distinguishes between three types of knowledge: that which the mind knows through itself, through the senses, and through the testimony of others. His defense of the former does appear proto-Cartesian, but there is no sense that the former serves as the foundation for everything else. That I will to be happy, for instance, is given the same status. More importantly, however, is that all three classes of things are known, as they are not for Descartes, as a consequence of "being laid up and retained in the storehouse of memory" from which "is begotten a word that is true." Both the relationships between the word and memory and between these three classes of things temporalize self-knowledge and commingle the classes in a way that they do not for Descartes.

252 I am heavily indebted here to Gillespie, *Nihilism before Nietzsche*, pp. 38–47.

253 Descartes, *Comments on a Certain Broadsheet*, CSM, 1, p. 307; AT VIIIB, p. 363, emphasis mine.

254 Descartes, *Principles* I.32; CSM I, p. 204; AT VIIIA, p. 17. Descartes gives a similar list in his description of the *res cogitans* at *Meditations* II; CSM II, p. 19; AT VII, p. 28. "What am I? A thing that thinks. A thing that doubts, under-

stands, affirms, denies is willing, is unwilling, and also imagines and has sensory perceptions." It is notable that Descartes describes the *res cogitans* in terms which he later uses to describe volitional activity.

255 Gillespie, *Nihilism before Nietzsche*, pp. 42–3.
256 Descartes, *Meditations* II; CSM II, p. 19; AT VII, p. 28.
257 Gillespie, *Nihilism before Nietzsche*, p. 44.
258 Descartes, *Meditations* II; CSM II, p. 16; AT VII, p. 24.
259 Menn, *Descartes and Augustine*, p. 236 n. 28.
260 Wetzel, "Crisis Mentalities," p. 123.
261 Descartes, *Discourse* IV; CSM I, p. 127; AT VI, p. 33; *Principles* I.7; CSM I, p. 195; AT VIIIA, p. 7.
262 Gillespie gives a fairly comprehensive summary of the treatment of this question, *Nihilism before Nietzsche*, p. 269, nn. 14–17.
263 See Gillespie, *Nihilism before Nietzsche*, p. 45. A problem with this interpretation, arguably, is that it fails to protect Descartes from Gassendi's objection that *ambulo, ergo sum* is equally fundamental. Descartes' counters that the premise *ambulo* is not indubitable like the *cogito* is (*Replies* V; CSM II, pp. 243–4; AT VII, p. 352). His rationale is why the inferential or syllogistic interpretation seems not to work. We will discuss this below. See Hintikka, "Cogito, Ergo Sum: Inference or Performance?," pp. 52–5, 62.
264 Descartes, *Replies* II; CSM II, p. 100; AT VII, p. 140.
265 Gillespie, *Nihilism before Nietzsche*, p. 45; Menn, *Descartes and Augustine*, pp. 209–19, 262–70.
266 Marion, "The Essential Incoherence," p. 323.
267 Descartes, *Discourse* IV; CSM I, p. 127; AT VI, pp. 31–3; *Principles* I.11; CSM I, p. 196; AT VIIIA, pp. 8–9.
268 See Gillespie, *Nihilism before Nietzsche*, pp. 45–6.
269 Hintikka, "*Cogito, Ergo Sum*: Inference or Performance?," p. 62.
270 J. L. Austin, "Performative Utterances," *Philosophical Papers*, 3rd edn (Oxford, Clarendon Press, 1979), pp. 233–52.
271 Descartes, *Meditations* II; CSM II, p. 17; AT VII, p. 25, emphasis mine.
272 If this appears to prefigure the nihilism of Fichte, that is because it does. See Gillespie, *Nihilism before Nietzsche*, pp. 64–100.
273 Wetzel, "Crisis Mentalities," pp. 126–7.
274 This incoherence is displayed in the Augustine's notion of "deficient causality" and in his motiveless sinning in the pear tree incident. See Wetzel, *Augustine and the Limits*, pp. 213–17.
275 Though I have my doubts about Descartes' aims, the success of this case for what Descartes *effects* is not dependent upon a judgment of Descartes' *intent*. He may well have believed his pious affirmations—heretics generally do. But one shouldn't mistake sincerity for either coherency or orthodoxy.
276 The following argument is heavily indebted both to Gillespie, *Nihilism before Nietzsche*, pp. 47–63, and Marion, "The Essential Incoherence," pp. 297–338.
277 It is Descartes' particular interpretation of omnipotence and infinity, not these concepts per se, which are problematic.
278 For his most concise diagnosis of Cartesian onto-theology that I am aware of, see Marion, "Descartes and Onto-Theology," pp. 67–106.
279 This circumstance is the precondition for an observation like Margaret Wilson's. "Descartes does think his power of generating conceptions of the indefinite cannot be accounted for by his own nature, but requires the existence of something outside himself. The fact that he ascribes to himself an unlimited power of willing doesn't seem to affect his judgment." Margaret

Wilson, "Can I Be the Cause of My Idea of the World? (Descartes on the Infinite and Indefinite)," in Amelie Oksenberg Rorty (ed.), *Essays on Descartes' Meditations* (Berkeley: University of California Press, 1986), p. 355.

280 Marion's characterization of "grey ontology." Marion, "Descartes and Onto-Theology," p. 97 n. 1.

281 Marion, "The Essential Incoherence," p. 308.

282 Descartes, *Replies* V; CSM II, p. 253; AT VII, p. 368. Marion, "The Essential Incoherence," p. 319.

283 Though Secada contends that Descartes is an essentialist who argues that knowledge of God's existence entails knowledge of his essence, he notes how Descartes transforms this essence, conceiving of "the Deity as pure will, a totally free and active thought which knows no bounds." Secada, *Cartesian Metaphysics*, p. 61.

284 Marion, "The Essential Incoherence," p. 300.

285 Ibid., p. 308.

286 Descartes, *Meditations* III; CSM II, pp. 28–9; AT VII, p. 417.

287 Just as earlier, Marion insists on an incompatibility between God as incomprehensible infinity and God as intrinsically causal. Marion, "The Essential Incoherence," pp. 322, 320.

288 Descartes, *Meditations* I; CSM II, p. 12; AT VII, p. 17.

289 See Gillespie, *Nihilism before Nietzsche*, pp. 57–63.

290 Descartes, *Replies* V; CSM II, p. 252; AT VII, p. 365.

291 Descartes, *Meditations* II; CSM II, p. 17; AT VII, p. 25.

292 More properly we should say the infinite will of a finite *res cogitans*.

293 See Marion, "The Essential Incoherence," p. 300.

294 See Descartes, *Principles* I.27; CSM I, p. 202; AT VIIIA, p. 15. It is because of his understanding the infinite as "limitless" that Descartes can understand the finite as the negation of the infinite. See Wilson, "Can I Be the Cause of My Idea of the World?," pp. 339–58.

295 Strictly speaking, so is the idea of the infinite. But, as I already noted, Marion contends that it is precisely in virtue of its limitlessness and incomprehensibility that the infinite should resist being encompassed by this principle.

296 Marion, "The Essential Incoherence," p. 323. The remark in question is in *Meditations* V; CSM II, p. 45; AT VII, p. 65. "Certainly the idea of God, or a supremely perfect being, is one which I find within me just as surely as the idea of any shape or number."

297 Marion, "The Essential Incoherence," p. 323; Descartes, *Meditations* V; CSM II, p. 45; AT VII, p. 64.

298 Marion, "The Essential Incoherence," p. 325.

299 Ibid., p. 325.

300 Gillespie, *Nihilism before Nietzsche*, p. 61.

301 Rosen concurs in this assessment and notes, in addition to the passage from *Med.* IV which conflates divine and human freedom, this remark from the *Passions* III.152; CSM I, p. 384; AT XI, p. 445. "[Free will] renders us in a certain way like God by making us masters of ourselves, provided we do not lose the rights it gives us through timidity." Rosen, "A Central Ambiguity in Descartes," p. 31. Of course this self-mastery consists precisely in the will's self-affirmation through its negation in doubt. See also Annette Baier, "The Idea of the True God in Descartes," in Amelie Oksenberg Rorty (ed.), *Essays on Descartes' Meditations* (Berkeley: University of California Press, 1986), p. 365.

302 Gillespie, *Nihilism before Nietzsche*, pp. 62, 61.

POSTSCRIPT: MODERNITY IN AUGUSTINIAN
HINDSIGHT

Notes to pages 178–9

1 See William T. Cavanaugh, "The City: Beyond Secular Parodies," in Milbank, Pickstock, and Ward (eds), *Radical Orthodoxy*, pp. 182–200.
2 Dupré, Passage to Modernity, p. 249.
3 Alliez, *Capital Times*, p. 136.
4 Augustine, *De Civ.* I. praef.; IV.4.
5 See Nicholas Boyle's version of the thesis that postmodern philosophy is the advocate of global capitalism: *Who Are We Now?: Christian Humanism and the Global Market from Hegel to Heaney* (Edinburgh: T&T Clark, 1998), pp. 95–120, 123–79.
6 Augustine, *Conf.* III.3. "The very limit of human blindness is to glory in being blind."
7 Ibid. X.27.
8 Marilynne Robinson, *The Death of Adam: Essays on Modern Thought* (Boston: Houghton Mifflin, 1998), p. 62.

PRIMARY SOURCES AND
TRANSLATIONS

I have consulted three Latin editions of Augustine's works each of which are indicated specifically when cited in the text. They are as follows:

Corpus Christianorum Ecclesiasticorum Latina. Vienna, 1866–.
Corpus Christianorum, Series Latina. Turnholt: Brepols, 1954–.
Migne, J. P., *Patrologia Cursus Completus, Series Latina*. Paris, 1841–5.

Stoic texts are collected in the following:
Arnim, Hans Friedrich August von. *Stoicorum Veterum Fragmenta*. 4 Volumes. Leipzig, 1903–5.

Latin texts of Scotus are to be found in:
Balíc, C., *et al.*, eds. *Opera Omnia*. Vatican, Vatican City, 1950–.

TRANSLATIONS

Citations in the text in English are from the following translations unless otherwise indicated.
Aristotle. *Nicomachean Ethics*. Translated by Terence Irwin. Indianapolis: Hackett, 1985.
——*The Physics*. Translated by Philip H. Wicksteed and Francis M. Cornford. Volume 1, The Loeb Classical Library. Cambridge: Harvard University Press, 1967.
Athanasius the Great. *On the Incarnation of the Word*. Willits, California: Eastern Orthodox Books.
Augustine. *Against Julian*. Translated by Matthew A. Schumacher, CSC Fathers of the Church. Volume 35. New York: Fathers of the Church, 1957.
——*Against Two Letters of the Pelagians. On the Gift of Perseverance. On The Grace of Christ and On Original Sin. On Grace and Free Will. On the Merits and Remission of Sins. On Nature and Grace. On the Predestination of the Saints. On the Proceedings of Pelagius. On Rebuke and Grace. On the Soul and Its Origin. On the Spirit and the Letter.* Translated by P. F. Holmes and R. E. Wallis. The Nicene and Post Nicene Fathers. Volume V, *Augustine: Anti-Pelagian Writings*. Peabody: Hendrickson, 1995.

——*Answers to Sceptics*. Denis J. Kavanaugh, OSA. Fathers of the Church. Volume 1. New York: Cima Publishers, 1948.

——*The City of God*. Translated by Henry Bettenson. New York: Penguin, 1984.

——*The Confessions of St. Augustine*. Translated by John K. Ryan. New York: Doubleday, 1960.

——*Eighty Three Different Questions*. Translated by David L. Mosher. The Fathers of the Church. Volume 70. Washington: Catholic University Press, 1982.

——*Expositions on the Book of the Psalms*. Trans. A. C. Coxe. The Nicene and Post Nicene Fathers, Volume VIII. Peabody: Hendrickson, 1995.

——*The Happy Life*. Translated by Ludwig Schopp. The Fathers of the Church. Volume 1. New York: Cima Publishing, 1948.

——*Incomplete Work Against Julian*. Quoted in Henry Bettenson, *The Later Christian Fathers: A Selection from the writings of the Fathers from St. Cyril of Jerusalem to St. Leo the Great*. Oxford: Oxford University Press, 1970, pp. 208–9.

——*Lectures or Tractates on the Gospel according to St. John*. Translated by J. Gibb and J. Innes. The Nicene and Post Nicene Fathers Series. Volume VII. Peabody, Hendrickson, 1995.

——*Letters (Volume 1, 1–82)*. Translated by Sister Wilfrid Parsons, SND. The Fathers of the Church. Volume 12. New York: Fathers of the Church, 1951.

——*Letters (Volume 2, 83–120)*. Translated by Sister Wilfrid Parsons, SND. The Fathers of the Church. Volume 18. New York: Fathers of the Church, 1953.

——*The Literal Meaning of Genesis*. Translated by John Hammond Taylor. Ancient Christian Writers. Volumes 41–2. New York: Newman Press, 1982.

——*On Christian Doctrine*. Translated by D. W. Robertson, Jr. New York: Macmillan, 1958.

——*On the Free Choice of the Will*. Translated by Thomas Williams. Indianapolis: Hackett, 1993.

——*The Nature of Good. On the Teacher. On True Religion. To Simplician—On Various Questions, Book I. On Faith and the Creed*. Translated by John H. S. Burleigh. Library of Christian Classics. Volume VI, *Augustine: Earlier Writings*. Philadelphia: Westminster Press, 1953.

——*On Music*. Translated by Robert C. Taliaferro. Fathers of the Church. Volume 4. New York: Cima Publishing, 1947.

——*On the Teacher*. Translated by Robert P. Russell, OSA. Fathers of the Church. Volume 59. Washington: Catholic University Press, 1967.

——*On the Trinity*. Translated by. A. W. Haddan. *On the Profit of Believing*. Translated by C. L. Cornish. *On the Work of Monks*. Translated by H. Browne. Nicene and Post Nicene Fathers. Volume III. Grand Rapids: Eerdmans, 1993.

——*On the Trinity*. Translated by Edmund Hill, OP. The Works of Saint Augustine. Brooklyn: New City Press, 1991.

——*On True Religion*. Translated by John H. S. Burleigh. *Augustine: Earlier Writings*. Philadelphia: The Westminster Press, 1953.

——*Ten Homilies on the First Epistle of John*. Translated by H. Browne and J. H. Meyers. The Nicene and Post Nicene Fathers Series. Volume VII. Peabody: Hendrickson, 1995.

——*Soliloquies*. Translated by Charles C. Starbuck, AM. The Nicene and Post Nicene Fathers Series. Volume VII. Peabody: Hendrickson, 1995.

Aquinas, Thomas. *Summa Theologica*. Translated by Fathers of the English Dominican Province. Westminster: Christian Classics, 1981.

Basil the Great. *On the Holy Spirit*. Crestwood NY: St. Vladimir's Seminary Press, 1980.

Benedict, St. *The Rule of St. Benedict*. Translated by Abbot Parry OSB. Leominster: Gracewing Fowler Wright Books, 1997.

Bernard of Clairvaux. *Bernard of Clairvaux: Selected Works*. Translated by G. R. Evans. The Classics of Western Spirituality. New York: Paulist Press, 1987.

Bonaventure. *The Journey of the Mind to God*. Edited by Stephen F. Brown. Translated by Philotheus Bonner, OFM. Indianapolis: Hackett, 1993.

Cassian, John. *The Conferences*. Translated by Boniface Ramsey, OP. New York: Paulist Press, 1997.

——*The Conferences. The Twelve Books on the Institutes of the Coenobia*. Translated by Edgar C. S. Gibson. The Nicene and Post Nicene Fathers. Volume XI. Peabody: Hendrickson, 1995.

Cicero. *De Fato*. Translated by H. Rackham. The Loeb Classical Library. *Cicero IV*. Cambridge: Harvard University Press, 1997.

Cyril of Alexandria. *On the Unity of Christ*. Translated by John Anthony McGuckin. Crestwood NY: St. Vladimir's Seminary Press, 1995.

Descartes, René. *The Philosophical Writings of Descartes*. Translated by John Cottingham, Robert Stoothoff, and Dugald Murdoch. Cambridge: Cambridge University Press, 1985.

Duns Scotus, John. *Philosophical Writings*. Translated by Allan Wolter, OFM. Indianapolis: Hackett, 1987.

Gregory the Great. *The Morals of the Book of Job*. 4 Volumes. Translated by J. Bliss. Library of the Fathers. Oxford: John Henry Parker, 1844–50.

——*Pastoral Care*. Translated by Henry Davis, SJ. Ancient Christian Writers. Volume 11. New York: Newman Press, 1950.

Ignatius of Loyola. *The Spiritual Exercises of St. Ignatius*. Translated by Louis J. Puhl, SJ. New York: Vintage Books, 2000.

Plotinus. *The Enneads*. 3rd edn revised. Translated by Stephen Mackenna. New York: Pantheon Books.

Prosper of Aquitaine. *Answers to the Extracts of the Genoese. Answers to the Objections of the Gauls. Answers to the Vincentian Articles. Letter to Augustine. Letter to Rufinus. On Grace and Free Will. Against Cassian the Lecturer. Official Pronouncements of the Apostolic See on Divine Grace and Free Will*. Translated. P. De Letter. *Prosper of Aquitaine: Defense of St. Augustine*. Westminster: The Newman Press, 1963.

Pseudo-Dionysius. *The Complete Works*. Translated by Colm Luibheid. New York: Paulist Press, 1987.

INDEX

action(s): (Cartesian) thoughts as 162; entailing prior desire 64, 67, 68, 91–2, 110, 125, 207 n. 196; mediated by delight 101; Pelagian 76, 79, 81; separated from motive 102–3, 126; theory of 58
active principle 111, 112, 113
Adam 67, 76, 115, 130, 212 n. 19, 214 n. 44
Adams, Marilyn McCord 263 n. 145
aesthetic soteriology 27–71; *see also* salvation
agency 103–5, 110, 114, 115
agnosticism 13
akrasia 93, 222 n. 116; *see also* involuntary sin
Alexander of Aphrodisias 233 n. 30
Alfaric, Prosper 184 n. 38
Alflatt, Malcolm A. 224 n. 142
Alliez, Eric 9, 18–26, 70, 178, 181 n. 1, 196 n. 68, 204 n. 168, 220 n. 93, 264
Alumbrados, the 143
Ambrose, Saint 76
anachronism 4; of *Confessiones* 159, 269 n. 199
angels 15, 32; *see also* theophanies
Anscombe, Elizabeth 64, 98, 204 n. 164, 225 n. 152, 226 n. 157
Anselm, Saint 43
anthropology, theological 81, 166
apatheia 92, 96, 115–16; in Cassian 120
apperception 104
apprehension 235 n. 50; of divine beauty 28, 30, 41, 46, 47, 55; and will 95
Aquinas, Thomas 16–17, 48, 51, 67, 78, 88, 90, 101, 187 n. 76, 223 n. 129, 236 n. 56, 266 n. 158

archai, stoic theory of 111, 112
Ariew, Roger 250 n. 40, 263 n. 145, 268 n. 181, 271 n. 214, 273 n. 249
Aristotle 25, 223 n. 129; cognition (Aquinas) 16
Arles, Council of 128
Asad, Talal 126, 243 n. 131
"ascent," in Augustine's works 147, 148, 260 n. 117, 261 n. 128
asceticism 107, 120, 121, 122, 127, 139, 186 n. 72, 239 n. 81
assent 95, 100, 102, 114, 123, 138, 156, 158, 235 nn. 48, 49, 50; 268 n. 188; *see also epoche*; discretion
atonement 21
attribution of motives 98
Augustine: attack on pagan/stoic moral psychology 93–4, 105, 164, 222 n. 122; "cogitarian" argument 167–9; compared with Descartes 144–61, 254 n. 71; pear tree incident 99, 225 n. 151, 228 n. 182; his philosophy as function of doctrine 2, 27; relationship to stoicism 94–5, 109–10; responses to Pelagianism 74–81, 102–5, 117; theology of language 30–41, 32, 35, 62
Augustine's works: *Ad Simplicianum* 99; Cassiciacum dialogues 7, 29; *Confessiones* 7, 10, 14, 15, 22-3, 34, 38, 65, 73, 83, 84, 86, 87, 93, 99, 111, 144, 146, 148, 150–1, 158–61, 183 n. 19; *Contra Duas Epistulas Pelagianorum* 79, 103; *De Civitate Dei* 2, 7, 10, 18, 21, 38, 42, 64, 67, 78, 92, 95, 167, 183 n. 19; *De Correptione et Gratia* 73, 117–18; *De Doctrina Christiana* 4, 30, 33, 34, 62;

Hankey, Wayne 11–12, 70, 86, 144–6,
168, 189 n. 2, 190 n. 12, 195 n. 61,
217 n. 68, 218 n. 80, 248 n. 17, 253
n. 68, 254 n. 73, 273 n. 251
happiness 95–6, 168, 169
harmony 42, 46, 60; number and
149–50, 261 n. 123
Harrison, Carol 28–9, 85, 148, 190 n.
10, 193 n. 47, 204 n. 168, 205 n.
176, 206 nn. 184, 190; 215 n. 51,
217 n. 64, 211 n. 74, 224 n. 134,
228 nn. 177, 179, 180; 229 n.188,
257 n. 87, 259 n. 108, 261 n. 123
Hart, David B. 197 n. 85
Hatfield, Gary C. 249 nn. 31, 32; 250
n. 40, 270 n. 211
Hauerwas, Stanley 10, 183 n. 25, 225
n. 153
Head and Body of Christ 55, 58, 59,
70, 134; musical analogy 37;
numerical harmonies 56; see also
Body of Christ
heavenly city 58; politics of 10, 59
Hefele, Charles Joseph 244 nn. 145,
147; 245 nn. 150, 151,
hegemonikon 73, 95, 112, 114, 163, 164
Heidegger, Martin 11
Heninger, S. K. 193 n. 44, 205 n. 168
Hilary of Arles 48, 118
Hilary of Poitiers 193 n. 41
Hill, Edmund 193 n. 47, 218 n. 80
Hintikka, Jaakko 267 n. 177, 274 n.
269
Holy Spirit 49, 185 n. 55; as *donum* 2,
12, 17, 18, 52, 67, 70, 78, 145,
185 n. 59; love defining city of
God 15
Homoians 28
human agency: and divine agency 74,
90, 110, 115, 125, 132; nature and
73, 110
humanity 55; determined by Christ
and Trinity 73; in image of God
53; and Jesus 39, 195 n. 60
humility 227 n. 170; of Christ's love
44, 110, 198 n. 88; and (divine) will
152–3, 156–7; habitual abnegation
of will 141
hyle: goodness of, in conversion to form
85–6, 87
hypostatic union 15, 27, 46, 56; cause
in effect 91; context for restoration
of creation 57, 59, 150

ideas of divine origin (Cartesian)
142–3, 161–2
idolatry 147, 148
Ignatius of Loyola, Saint 139–40; and
Cassian 140–2, 251 n. 43, 252 n.
49; Descartes's method compared
with 142–3, 251 n. 46, 254 n. 70
imago dei 68, 110, 130–1, 163, 167;
Cartesian 165; microcosm of civic
macrocosm 47, 183 n. 19, 200 n.
108; participation in trinitarian love
45
imitation: virtue and sin as (Pelagian)
76, 115, 229 n. 192
immanence, stoic 2, 3, 106, 111–14,
124, 166; and "new" immanence
178
immortality 42–3
immutability of God 32, 83, 215 nn.
53, 54; and mutability of creation in
time 84, 85, 217 nn. 64, 67
incarnation 15, 70–1, 79, 198 n. 88;
Cartesian view 157; congruity of
43; function 60, 63, 205 n. 171; as
manifestation of divine beauty 30,
152; Platonists' rejection of 152
incoherence 73; of Cartesian will
172–3; forced willing as 97, 132,
224 n. 143; from God-Man, to
Man-God 177; of Pelagian self 91;
of Pelagian/stoic account of action
100, 103; of *superbia* 104
incommensurability, of principles 231
n. 10; African and Gallican
monasticism 119–20;
Augustinianism and Pelagian
stoicism 108, 213 n. 36
indifference 137; Cartesian 155;
Ignatian 141, 252 n. 52; see also
apatheia
individualism 13
inequality: as ecstatic surplus 87;
numeric proportions of 86; of self
to self 100
infinity 110–11, 232 nn. 24, 25;
Cartesian and Augustinian
differences 153, 156, 265 n. 149;
Cartesian God as 173–5
Innes, Robert 201 n. 119, 227 nn. 166,
167, 257 n. 94
inseparability of trinitarian operations
14, 31, 48, 68–70, 83, 215 n. 50
instrumentalism 9, 33, 34

Marin, Louis 269 n. 194

Marion, Jean-Luc 153, 161, 166, 174, 176, 249 n. 37, 250 n. 38, 254 n. 70, 260 nn. 118, 119, 263 n. 146, 265 n. 149, 274 n. 276

Marks, John 233 n. 32

Markus, R. A. 107, 120, 121, 191 n. 18, 193 n. 45, 202 n. 134, 206 n. 191, 230 nn. 2, 5, 9; 239 n. 79, 243 nn. 137, 139, 244 n. 148

Marxist exchange value (in Alliez) 19, 33

Mass: crucial role of 17–18, 127

materialism 110, 233 n. 39

mathematics 157

mathesis universalis 3, 149

Mathisen, Ralph 107, 119, 230 n. 2, 238 n. 74, 239 n. 76, 243 n. 138, 245 n. 155

matter: as ideal and active 87, 219 nn. 89, 90; 220 n. 93

Matzko, David 10, 183 n. 25

measurement of time 23–4

Meconi, David 227 n. 170, 232 n. 21

mediation of Christ 14, 42, 56, 67–8; agency and 103–5; conflating *via* and *patria* 41; and cosmological time 25, 37; as solution to *distentio animi* 100

memory: and intellect, and will 9, 38, 39, 53, 134, 150, 201 n. 121; in measuring time 24; presence of mind 98–9, 168; *see also distentio animi*

Menn, Stephen 8, 11, 70, 86, 135, 137, 139, 142, 144, 147, 148, 150–8, 207 n. 204, 222 n. 113, 246 n. 4, 247 n. 16, 248 n. 18, 253 nn. 58, 64, 67, 254 n. 71, 255 nn. 75, 76; 256 n. 81, 258 n. 100, 262 n. 137, 267 n. 177, 268 n. 183, 269 nn. 188, 192; 271 nn. 213, 215

Meno aporia 49, 62, 269 n. 191; and biblical economy 54

mensura, numerus, pondus, of creatures 34, 118

mensura sine mensura, of God 29, 34

mercy 22

Mersenne, Marin 248 n. 22

Mesland 157

metaphysical tradition, Western 19

metaphysics of conversion 40–1, 88, 89; *see also* conversion

Milbank, John 186 n. 66, 187 n. 89, 199 n. 92, 216 n. 55, 223 n. 129, 236 n. 53, 237 n. 68, 245 n. 154, 247 n. 9, 258 n. 98

miracles 32

modern self 1, 6, 146; and Eastern asceticism 184 n. 40

modernity 1–2, 6–7, 26, 70, 136, 178; Pelagianism/stoicism and 73, 104, 106, 109–16, 135

modus, species, ordo, of creatures 34, 36, 118

moment of choice 222 n. 118, 229 n. 189; as spontaneity 103, 126, 154

monasticism 107, 108, 119–21, 126, 127, 133; first principles 119

Monica 219 n. 81

Monimus 128

monism 73, 111–12, 166

monk-bishops 127, 243 n. 138

Montag, John 212 n. 26, 268 n. 183

Montaigne, Michel de 135

moral life, correlated to work of Spirit 18

More, Henry 249 n. 32

Morford, Mark 231 n. 14

Moses 31

motivation: conflicting sources of 96, 97, 99, 100, 164, 165

motive(s) 98–103; attribution of, and memory 98–9, 226 n. 157

Munz, Peter 107, 125, 126, 230 nn. 7, 9, 241 nn. 105, 106, 108, 110; 242 n. 117

music 36

naturalism 72

nature: creation exchanged for 135; gratuitous creation of God 2; and human agency 73; Pelagian 115–16; question of meaning of 76–7, 110, 212 n. 24; as restoration with affection 93

Nebridius 86, 219 n. 81

negation 104, 112; Cartesian freedom of 156–7, 267 n. 177; of Cartesian infinite God 175; discretion and 122; of stoic rationality 114

neoplatonism 13, 184 n. 38; shortcomings of, for Augustine 148, 255 n. 76, 260 n. 114, 262 n. 132